# Texas

A Sesquicentennial

Celebration

*THE ALAMO — shrine of Texas liberty. The present building is the old chapel of Mission San Antonio de Valero, founded in 1718 by the Franciscan padres. In 1836, the Battle of the Alamo set the stage for Texas independence from Mexico.*

— San Antonio Convention and Visitors Bureau

# Texas

## A Sesquicentennial Celebration



*Developed and Edited by*

*Donald W. Whisenhunt*

**EAKIN PRESS**
Austin, Texas

FIRST EDITION

Second Printing



Published in the United States of America
By Eakin Press, P.O. Box 23066, Austin, Texas 78735



ISBN 0-89015-441-4

*I shall never surrender or retreat. . . I am determined to sustain myself as long as possible and die like a soldier who never forgets what is due to his own honor and that of his country.*

*VICTORY OR DEATH*
*William Barret Travis*

*(An excerpt from Col. Travis's famous letter to the People of Texas, The Alamo, 1836)*

*The Capitol of Texas in Austin, construction of pink granite from nearby Burnet County, ranks second in size only to the National Capitol in Washington. It covers eighteen acres of floor space.*

# TABLE OF CONTENTS

# INTRODUCTION

As Texas reaches its sesquicentennial, the state obviously has much to celebrate. Modern Texans owe much to their heritage of the past 150 years—not to mention the years before 1836. Today, Texas is one of the most important five or six states of the nation — depending on the criteria used to define importance.

This influence on national affairs did not come easily or early. Texas has suffered from many disadvantages — isolation, location, cultural paucity, political immaturity — but it has also benefitted from a number of factors — size, population, location, wealth, political sagacity. If these appear contradictory, the paradox merely reflects the nature and history of Texas.

Many activities will occur to celebrate the state's 150th birthday. Some of them will be superficial and transitory while others will be more serious and long-lasting. Many, of course, will fall between these two extremes. Without question, many publications will be published as a part of the sesquicentennial celebration. Some will be serious, some will be humorous, and some will be in-between. The activities — of whatever kind — will focus national attention on the state.

With these things in mind, this book was developed. Texas history has been written about as much as any state. Why then, one might ask, is another history of the state being published? The answer is quite simple. Since much new research and interpretation of the state's past has been done in the past twenty years, it seems appropriate at the time of the sesquicentennial to present this new material in a serious, but readable, fashion for Texans — and other Americans — who wish to know more about the state's past.

This book brings together a unique blend of authorities on Texas history. The twenty scholars represent the diversity of Texas itself. Some of them are seasoned Texas historians who have worked on various aspects of the state's history for a number of years. Others are newer to the professional study of history and bring new and refreshing ideas to our understanding of the state's past. They represent any number of educational backgrounds, and all but two are associated with Texas educational institutions.

The overall purpose of this book is to provide a chronological overview of Texas history and to provide special chapters that deal with the unique economic development of the state. An effort has also been made to describe and analyze the people of Texas and their origins and selected cultural traits.

In a volume designed to provide a readable book at a reasonable cost, some choices had to be made about what to include—or to exclude. Any number of additional chapters on specific topics could have been included. The selection made seems, however, to provide a balanced presentation of the state's history.

Since this is a collection of chapters written by twenty different persons, variations in emphasis and style will be readily apparent. The editor did not attempt to fit all the chapters into one mold—except for some general guidelines on length. Each person has his/her own way of presenting Texas history; for an editor to impose his own ideas or style would be to rob the book of one of its valuable unique features—not to mention the freedom of the authors.

The reader will quickly realize that there is some overlap in content between the chronological and the topical chapters. This was planned in the design of the book. It was a deliberate effort to allow specialists to deal with topics of significance that transcend time periods while still allowing those narrating the sweep of Texas development to include these special topics as they impinged on statewide events.

Many acknowledgments—many more than is possible to note—are due in a book like this. As editor, I would take the prerogative of acknowledging the assistance of many people in an anonymous block. As an exception, I think Edwin Eakin, president of Eakin Press, should be singled out. At his suggestion this book was developed. His encouragement at every step of the project was critical. Not the least, of course, was his financial commitment to merely an idea that made this volume a reality.

December 1983

Donald W. Whisenhunt
Wayne, Nebraska

# I

# The Texas Experience

## Prehistory

## To Space Travel

# 1

## The Native Texans

*Earl H. Elam*

On December 29, 1982, archeologists examining a highway construction site near Leander, Texas, in the vicinity of Austin discovered an intact skeleton of a woman who is believed to have lived about ten thousand years ago. Approximately twenty years old when she died, this "Leanderthal Lady," five feet three inches in height, was buried in soil underlying campfire charcoal with a large grinding stone resting on her knees and arrow points of Pleistocene vintage located nearby. This discovery may ultimately be of significance in answering questions about the life and culture of the original Texans: who were they, where did they originate, and how did they live? Meanwhile, in the nearly five centuries that have transpired since the dawn of history in the American Southwest, much has been learned about the natives who inhabited the land called Texas.

"Texas" as a distinct geographical entity first appears in Spanish descriptions of the country of the Hasinai Indians east of the Trinity River during the latter half of the seventeenth century. The name subsequently was given to the province when it was politically organized in the early eighteenth century, and in due course the geo-political unit of Texas came to include the territory within the present boundaries of the American state of Texas. The modern, heterogeneous population of nearly fifteen million is a mixture of people of all races and many nationalities, and the social and political institutions of the state are the result of historical developments which have occurred primarily since 1800. Prior to 1800 the population consisted of natives with diverse cultures who had been influenced significantly by European contacts during the previous century. They had clung tenaciously to patterns of life which were adaptations from earlier cultures and neighboring peoples with whom contacts had been made. They were not the "original" Texans, but they were the "native" Texans at the dawn of the European era. It is with these native people that the story of the evolution and development of the state begins.

Sometime during the late Pleistocene period about 70,000 years ago, glacial ice covered much of North America and lowered the sea level creating a land bridge across the Bering Strait which permitted the movement of *homo sapiens* from Siberia to Alaska. Just when the movement began is not known with certainty; some authorities say 50,000 years ago, others much less. It is known that these Paleo-Indians came from marginal Mongoloid populations of southeast and west-central Asia and that their descendants had scattered widely in North America by 11,000 to 12,000 B.C. Apparently moving down an ice-free corridor east of the Rocky Mountains, the first of these people entered Texas. Little is known of their lifestyle except that they were hunters whose existence depended on their ability to kill the mammoths, mastodons, and other large animals of that era. Using flint tipped spears, they killed the animals, roasted the meat in campfires, and, when all was consumed, moved on to hunt again. The high plains of the *Llano Estacado* in West Texas was their favorite hunting ground, but some people moved into the mountains west of the Pecos River and made homes in rock shelters and caves.

The presence of Paleo-Indian hunters on the high plains several thousand years before the beginning of the historical era has been ascertained by archeological studies at various sites, principal among them an ancient lake site at Lubbock and the site of the bison stampede at Plainview. The presence of Folsom points, scrapers, and charred bones at the Lubbock site leave no doubt that man hunted bison here in approximately 8,000 B.C. A few miles to the north at Plainview, implements were found in a bed of bison skeletons which were the remains of animals killed around 7,000 B.C. when hunters drove a herd over a bluff and then speared the animals with points distinctly different from the earlier Folsom points.

Human Paleo-Indian remains have rarely been found. At a site near Midland, however, human bone fragments were discovered in 1953 which consisted of a nearly complete skull, some teeth and facial parts, and two rib fragments. These were found with Folsom points and artifacts of approximately the same age as those found at Lubbock. Also, the discoveries of the skeletons of a man and a boy under a rock ledge near Waco in 1970 and only recently made public and the skeleton of the woman at the Leander site in 1982 are expected to be dated among the earliest known burials unearthed in North America.

The historical era began in Texas in the early 1500s with the arrival of Spaniards in the Gulf of Mexico. During the two to three centuries immediately preceding this event, substantial changes occurred among the native people of the Plains and the Southwest. Scholars differ concerning dates and the details of what transpired but agree that among the factors prompting the changes were severe drouths and the arrival of new people. The breakdown that had begun generations earlier in the homogeneous hunting and gathering cultures was finalized. In the Southwest, the Anasazi, Hohokam, and Mogollon communities disappeared to be replaced by Puebloans, Pimans, Hopis, and others. In the Central Plains, eastern woodland people pushed into the region of the Platte River and the upper branches of the Kansas River. And on the Southern Plains, basketmakers entered present Oklahoma from the west while people of Caddoan stock, Pawnees and perhaps Wichitas, moved into the watersheds of the Arkansas and Republican rivers. These Indians all lived in communities, were politically organized, made pottery, and raised crops of maize, beans, and squash. Another group of unidentified stock formed settlements in the Canadian River region of the Texas Panhandle, built homes of stone slabs and pueblo-style adobe, and also made pottery and raised maize. By the beginning of the historical period these Panhandle people and many others had abandoned their villages. Native Texans who had survived and inhabited the land when the Europeans came were the Caddos, Attacapans, Karankawas, Tonkawas, Coahuiltecans, and Jumanos. Native groups who were on the verge of entering Texas and did so after the arrival of the Europeans were the Lipan Apaches, the Comanches, and the Wichitas.

The first historical descriptions of Texas Indians are found in the narrative of Alvar Núñez Cabeza de Vaca, a survivor of the expedition led by Pamfilo de Narváez to colonize the country between Florida and the Rio Grande. Shipwrecked on the Texas coast in November 1528, De Vaca and three companions, two countrymen and a black slave, met and lived with numerous Indians during the next eight years. They walked across Texas from Galveston Island to the Colorado River near Austin, westerly through the Hill Country to the Pecos River, and on to the Rio Grande near its junction with the

Rio Conchos in the modern Ojinaga, Chihuahua-Presidio, Texas area. Continuing westward, they eventually reached Mexico City in 1536.

After landing on Galveston Island in 1528, the Spaniards were met and befriended by natives identified as *Capoques* and *Hans.* The former were probably Karankawas and the latter Attacapans. According to De Vaca the people were large and of fine physique. The men had pieces of cane inserted sideways through their breasts and a piece of cane through their lower lips. The women did all the work while the men hunted and fished. Fish was the basic food, supplemented by water roots and oysters. The males wore no clothing while the women dressed in deer skins and in moss pulled from trees. They generously shared their possessions and were especially tender to their children whom De Vaca said they loved more than anything in the world. The Indians had the unusual practice of weeping when they met tribesmen, finally stopping after about thirty minutes and carrying on conversations. They lived in crude houses constructed of straw mats set on oyster shells and animal skins. De Vaca noticed much sickness, possibly caused by undernourishment, a problem the shipwrecked Spaniards also faced.

De Vaca managed to stay alive, and after a little more than a year, he crossed to the mainland where he stayed for a while with a group of people he called *Quevenes.* These were possibly Karankawas later known as Hohanis. Beyond them in the vicinity of Matagorda Bay was another group, known as *Mariames,* whom he next visited. They had a very distressing custom: they killed their male children to prevent enemies from capturing and killing them, and they regularly slew their infant daughters by throwing them to their hungry dogs. They considered it better for the girls to be eaten by the dogs than to be enslaved by enemies and forced to bear children. A neighboring people, known as the *Yguazes,* also destroyed their infants. All these people avoided incest and having few friends among neighboring tribes, the opportunities for marriage were few. They were thus doomed to extinction.

The Yguazes were merry people notwithstanding the constant threat of enemies. They had many festivities, the happiest of which was associated with the eating of prickly pears. When they were harvested, the Indians ate day and night and engaged in much dancing. They also feasted on deer which the men chased down and killed with arrows or spears. Like the women in other tribes seen by De Vaca, the Yguaze women did all the work, taking only about six hours per day to rest. They dug roots, skinned animals, carried water and wood, cared for the young and elderly, kept their houses, and prepared the campsites.

After leaving the Mariames, De Vaca reached the *Avavares,* with whom he spent eight months. These Indians spoke a unique language and were ignorant of time, reckoning it by the seasons when fruits ripened and when fish died. They had neither corn nor nuts and were in great need of food. Such was true of all Indians who were within the coastal region from Galveston Island to Matagorda Bay. Everywhere they smoked a substance, probably peyote, which produced a reaction of bewilderment and lightheadedness. The same effect occurred when they drank a liquor made from tree leaves, parched in a pot over a hot fire, covered with water and boiled twice, and then swallowed while it was as warm as could be tolerated. Among the Avavares were some men who had either been emasculated or who were impotent and who lived together. De Vaca considered them deplorable, but noted that they were more muscular than the other men and served a purpose by working like women and carrying heavy loads.

De Vaca eventually traveled through the Hill Country west of Austin and met many people of diverse languages scattered in small villages who constantly stole from each other. Everywhere he was well received because in the course of his journey he had acquired the reputation of being a healer after applying basic first aid and limited medical treatment he had learned from experience to wounded and ill Indians brought to him. Finally proceeding to a river which apparently was the Pecos, De Vaca and his friends crossed over and walked more than fifty more leagues through the deserts and mountainous country of the Big Bend region to the Rio Grande near modern Presidio. There they found a dense population of Indians. Called the Cow nation because of the numerous buffalo slaughtered in their neighborhood, the Indians lived in fixed dwellings and raised crops of beans, pumpkins, and squash. These people were *Jumanos.*

Heading up the Rio Grande in 1536 the determined De Vaca walked on westward out of modern Texas. He later wrote his important narrative of his experiences. Most native Texans he encountered cannot be positively identified with historical tribes who were present when Spanish occupation began about 1690, but some of the coastal people were probably Karankawas, some of the people in the Hill Country were possibly Tonkawas, and the inhabitants of the villages on the Rio Grande were with certainty the Indians later known as Jumanos.

The Indians at La Junta de los Rios acquired the name *Jumanos* because of the Spanish practice of referring to Indians who were tattooed, striped, or painted as *indios rayados* or *Jumanos*. The use of the name in reference to people with this trait at several widely separated locations on the Southern Plains and in New Mexico and Texas has caused much confusion concerning the true identity of the Jumano in West Texas. In time, too, their disappearance through assimilation with other peoples during the eighteenth century has resulted in much speculation concerning their origins, their social and political organization, and their migrations and disappearance. It is possible, however, in the records of Spanish expeditions to trace the presence of Jumanos in western Texas from the time of De Vaca to the early 1700s.

Jumano ancestors probably migrated down the Rio Grande after A.D. 1000 to the La Junta region, which, properly defined, included the area along the Rio Grande from the present community of Redford to just below El Paso and up the Rio Conchos from Ojinaga about forty miles into the interior of Mexico. After the Indians acquired horses in the late 1500s, the Jumano hunting area was extended from the localized area of the La Junta to the plains beyond the Chisos Mountains and the Pecos River. The Jumanos brought to La Junta from upper pre-Puebloan cultures and perhaps from a branch of Mogollon culture knowledge of agriculture which they adapted to the archaic gathering and hunting culture prevalent in the region. By the 1530s when De Vaca visited them, they had a thriving agricultural and hunting economy suffering only from a drouth which had prevented corn from growing for two seasons.

In 1582 the party of Antonio de Espejo carefully described the settlements and people at La Junta, noting that the Indians called themselves *Jumanos* but that the Spaniards called them *Patarabueyes*. Espejo reported that the five villages contained numerous large flat-roofed houses arranged into pueblos, that the people had tattooed faces, and that they raised large quantities of corn, gourds, and beans. This sustenance was supplemented by game and fish of many kinds caught in the two rivers. More villages were scattered along the upward course of the Rio Grande for twelve days' journey, some with pueblo-style houses and others with grass huts. The people were dressed in tanned deer skins and buffalo hides, some of which they presented as gifts to the Spaniards. When Espejo's group returned through the area the next year after having crossed the Davis Mountains from the Pecos River near the New Mexico border the Jumanos were again cordial and hospitable, this time adding prickly pears to their presents of vegetables and fish.

Jumanos were frequently mentioned in Spanish records by the

time New Mexico was occupied permanently for the Spanish by Don Juan De Oñate in 1598. In addition to the La Junta group, other Jumanos traded or lived between the Rio Grande and the Pecos River south of Albuquerque, and others were reported east of the Pecos. Historians have generally believed that Jumanos who came to Santa Fe in 1629 seeking priests to return with them to their villages lived on the Colorado River and its tributary, the Concho, in Texas in the vicinity of San Angelo and Ballinger. Indeed, several Spanish expeditions later visited Jumanos and other Indians on the Colorado. In 1629, however, Father Juan de Salas and Father Diego López returned with the Santa Fe visitors to their villages located, according to the report made of the venture, over one hundred leagues east of Santa Fe on what seems to have been the Canadian, the Washita, or the Red River in western Oklahoma. These Jumanos were Wichitas whose homeland centered in the mountains of southwestern Oklahoma which now bears their name. Some of the Wichitas in the eighteenth century were called Jumanos.

Father Salas did make it to the Jumanos on the Colorado River of Texas. In 1632 he went two hundred leagues southeast of Santa Fe to the area and spent six months working with the Jumanos. Then, in 1650, Captains Hernando Martín and Diego del Castillo, out of Santa Fe, reached the Concho River near San Angelo where they became excited about pearls in the river. They reported that the region was inhabited by Jumanos and other tribes. In what may have been the first historical reference to the *Tejas,* Martín and Castillo also reported that fifty leagues beyond the Jumanos was the land of a people called *Tejas.* When the viceroy in Mexico City heard about the pearls, he ordered another expedition to the area. This one, in 1654, was led by Diego de Guadalajara who also reported the presence of Jumano Indians on the Concho River. The pearls, as it turned out, were worthless, but one of the soldiers with Guadalajara was a man named Juan Domínguez de Mendoza, who, some thirty years later, was destined to return to the region.

In 1683 Mendoza was stationed at El Paso del Norte when Juan Sabeata, a Christian Jumano from La Junta, appeared and requested missionaries, help in fending off hostile Apaches, and trade opportunities in his country which extended, he said, from La Junta six days eastward to the buffalo plains. Mendoza was named to head a detachment of soldiers to accompany Sabeata and investigate the situation. Beginning late in 1683 the party moved down the Rio Grande to La Junta, where a mission was established for the Indians, and as 1684 dawned, the march was continued north-eastward across the Big Bend region to the Pecos River. After crossing the Pecos, Mendoza and Sabeata headed the force eastward to the middle Concho and followed it to a point near the Colorado River at Ballinger where a camp was made from March 16 to May 1. At the encampment, named San Clemente, Mendoza built a small chapel and sent word to more than fifty bands of Indians whose names he acquired from Sabeata and from Indians who had joined the entourage to come to the Colorado for a parley and to receive the blessings of the Christian religion. He later reported that many groups, the first of whom were the Jumanos, appeared and that Christian Indians among them assisted in the celebration of mass during the Easter holy week. The Jumanos also assisted in the slaughtering of 4,030 buffalo whose hides were packed on horses when the expedition headed back to the Rio Grande and El Paso. Juan Sabeata, in the meantime, had been sent packing himself for lying to Mendoza and for encouraging Apaches who followed the expedition at a distance to kill the Spaniards. Mendoza noted in his diary of the trip that the Apaches made frequent attacks after the Pecos was crossed during the eastward march and that another group, whom he identified as *Salineros,* were bandits of an intruding tribe. These were Indians later known as Mescaleros, who have some right to claim far West Texas as part of their native habitat.

By 1686 the Jumanos on the Colorado had been forced back to the Rio Grande in the Big Bend region or to more southerly locations near the mouth of the Pecos River and into northern Mexico. That they were still traveling in and out of Texas, however, is evident from references in the journal of Henri Joutel, who accompanied the French under Robert Cavalier, Sieur de la Salle, who accidentally landed in Texas in 1685. Joutel saw a trading party of Jumanos in the region between the French encampment, called Fort Saint Louis, at the head of Lavaca Bay and the Colorado River. A few years later in 1689 a detachment of Spanish soldiers, under Captain Alonso de Leon and searching for Fort Saint Louis, came to a rancheria of Jumanos on the Guadalupe River near San Antonio. This turned out to be a band led by Juan Sabeata on another trading mission. The Jumanos gradually fell more and more under the influence of the Lipan Apaches, who were moving from the high plains to inhabit the old Jumano haunts along the upper Colorado River and who were at war with everyone around them. The tribes seem to have reached an understanding by 1731 when the Jumanos were reported to be very numerous and were seen riding with the Lipans. Thereafter, the terminology "Apaches Jumanos" was used by the Spanish to refer to the tattooed Jumanos. The name eventually disappeared in usage in southwestern Texas, but it continued to be used occasionally until the late eighteenth century to identify other *indios rayados* on the Southern Plains.

The French presence on the Gulf Coast was the primary stimulus which brought about the Spanish occupation of the area originally known as Texas. Doomed from the start because of a multitude of problems, the French venture has left to posterity valuable information about the native Texans. After landing at the head of Lavaca Bay and establishing Fort Saint Louis on Garcitias Creek, La Salle explored both up and down the coast. In the immediate vicinity of the fort were about fifty huts of Indians sitting around and curiously watching the strange white men. From the description of their huts, made of rush mats and skins, and their location, it is possible to identify these Indians as Karankawas.

During a trip across Texas in 1776, Father Juan Agustín de Morfi made notes for his "History of Texas," in which he described the Karankawas as a vile, pusillanimous, and treacherous people given to extreme cruelties. Other observers before and after Morfi have emphasized the less ingratiating characteristics of these people, prompting the view in some quarters that the coastal region of Texas was a "cultural sink" inhabited by extremely primitive and backward people in comparison with more advanced contemporary neighbors. The Karankawa culture was less developed and was based on a different economy than, say, the Caddos, but the earliest Europeans to encounter the Karankawas found them friendly, peaceful, and eager to share their limited possessions, including much needed food. Unfortunately, the demise of the tribe before serious ethnological studies of Texas Indians began leaves much unknown and has contributed to the unfavorable picture.

This portrait has also been dramatized by discussions of Karankawan cannibalism. Albert S. Gatschet, whose classic study of the extinct tribe in 1891 is still authoritative, was convinced that the Karankawas were man-eaters. Numerous stories still circulated in his day of the practice and the documentary record of it, although replete with exaggerations, was sufficient to satisfy Gatschet. Much doubt, however, has been cast in recent years about the extent and nature of Karankawan cannibalism and about the practice among other people. De Vaca provided some insight on the subject. In his narrative he stated that five men shipwrecked with him became so enfeebled from hunger that they ate their dead as, one by one, they died, until only the body of the last to die was unconsumed. These were Spaniards, not Karankawas! When the Indians with De Vaca saw what had taken place they were very upset and said that if they had known such a thing was going to happen they would have killed all five Spaniards when they landed to prevent it. The Indians' revulsion on this occasion obviously may not have extended to their relatives at a later date. In fact, accounts of Karankawas eating human flesh were more frequent after 1800 than before. Thus, for example, Jean Louis Berlandier in 1828 stated that the Karankawas were the only Indians of Texas with a reputation for cannibalism, basing his conclusion apparently on a report he heard that several shipwrecked sailors had been devoured by the Indians. A few years later one of the few surviving Karankawas reportedly told a group of Texans that the "sweetest" meat he had ever eaten was a white man's heart. Despite these references to the practice among the Karankawas, it was not unique to them. The historical record reveals that people of all races have resorted to the eating of human flesh at times in order to survive. In Texas, the Caddos, Lipans, and Tonkawas were anthropophagistic; and at least one confederated group of people who migrated into the Texas, the Wichitas, were known to eat their enemies.

The debate over Karankawan cannibalism continues, but the record is clear that these Indians were hearty eaters of fish, roots, game, and prickly pears, and they always seemed to be hungry. It was believed that the strange musky odor which emanated from their bodies was attributable to their eating habits, particularly to their fondness for alligator meat. Inhabiting the swampy coastland they naturally feasted on seafood extensively. They also wandered from the coastal islands to hunt on the mainland, using pirogues on the water with great skill and bows and arrows with such expertise to earn the guarded respect of friends and enemies alike.

The origin of the Karankawas is shrouded in the silence of prehistory, but it is believed that their progenitors either migrated to the Louisiana-Texas coast from the Carribean or were descendants of Paleo-Texans. Joutel first used the name when he reported *Koienkahe* or *Korenkahe* near Fort Saint Louis. The Indians later said that it meant "dog-lovers," or "dog-raisers," in reference to the strange-looking, fox-like, barkless dogs which they kept. Historically, Karankawan population probably never reached a thousand. Earlier groups combined and some joined neighbors. By the early eighteenth century there were four principal bands—the *Copanes, Cocos, Caujanes,* and *Guapites,* each governed loosely by civil and war chiefs.

Physically, the Karankawas were large and well-proportioned. The males wore no clothing and pierced their bodies with cane in the manner observed by De Vaca in 1528, while the women dressed in skins from the waist down. In appearance the men were distinguished by tattoos which included a small circle colored blue high on each cheekbone, horizontal lines extending from the outside corner of each eye to each ear, three parallel lines extending downward from the middle of the lower lip to the chin, and two parallel lines extending downward from each corner of the mouth. They were excellent swimmers and fast runners and were noted for their bravery. Jealous guardians of their territory, the Karankawas' reputation for dealing harshly with those whose misfortune it was to be stranded on their beaches was legendary; the Texas coast was not a place where seafarers casually went ashore.

When permanent Spanish occupation of Texas began after 1700 the Karankawas were prime candidates for missions. Mission La Bahía del Espíritu Santo was established in 1722 specifically for this purpose near the remains of Fort Saint Louis. Gifts of tobacco and clothing lured some curious Karankawas, who, in turn, brought gifts of dried fish for the Spaniards. Before long three bands were congregated around the mission under the watchful eye of a Coco chief. By 1726, however, incompetent leadership at the mission, undisciplined soldiers, and an outbreak of measles caused the Indians to disperse. Thereafter, they frequently raided the mission and stole horses and cattle.

A few Karankawas appeared from time to time at missions in the San Antonio area, but the next significant effort to attract them was in 1749 at Mission Candelaria on the San Gabriel River far removed from their usual surroundings. After a few years of coming and going, they also rejected this mission as they did a renewed attempt to bring them to Espíritu Santo in 1749. Then, in 1754 the Mission Nuestra Señora del Rosario was established for the Cujanes near present Goliad. For about fourteen years this mission flourished with several hundred Karankawas regularly visiting or living nearby. Only a few were receptive to baptism, however, a factor which convinced the Spaniards that these people were incorrigible unregenerates. Father Gaspar José de Solís, making an inspection of Rosario in 1768, found only a few Indians at the mission and reported that they were barbarians given to eating half-roasted meat dripping with blood. Most of the tribe was scattered in the woods and on the beaches, preferring, according to Solis, to be hungry and naked to the comfort of the mission where food and clothing were available. The Karankawan desire to be free of the restraints imposed on their activities at missions was common among Texas Indians, and it mattered little to them that Solís, Morfi, and others despaired for their souls or criticized their lusting, stealing, and dancing, or for that matter that the military commander of Texas,

Teodoro de Croix, was once so vexed with them that he suggested exiling them to a remote location.

The first Rosario experiment collapsed when the last of the Karankawas fled in 1779. A final effort to make mission Indians of the tribe was made a few years later when Father Manuel de Silva arrived. Determined to reach the recalcitrants, Silva reestablished Mission Rosario, and, at the request of two chiefs, built a new mission, Nuestra Señora del Refugio, near the mouth of the Guadalupe River. Endeavoring to win the Indians' friendship and trust by going to their camps and getting to know them personally, Silva was able to entice ninety to return in 1791. But it was too late for significant effects to materialize. The bands were rapidly declining because of disease, warfare with the Lipan Apaches and the Comanches, intermarriage with neighboring people, and the influx of new arrivals into their homeland. A few Indians remained associated with the missions until the end of Spanish Texas, but the tribal days of the "dog-lovers" were numbered. During the waning years of their existence, the Karankawas annoyed the Anglo-American settlers who came with Stephen F. Austin and committed occasional depredations. By the mid-nineteenth century, however, the tribe was extinct, and only a few persons with Karankawa blood were still living. The Karankawa monument to the multifaceted culture of modern Texas is to be found in the legends of these strange and interesting people and their colorful associations with other people who ventured into their coastal habitat.

Among the tribes who were associated with the Karankawas, sometimes at war and sometimes at peace, were Indians who became commonly known as Caddo and who lived northeast of the Trinity River in the region extending to the Red River in Louisiana. The name "Caddo" derives from the "Kadohadacho" tribe and means "Caddo proper" or "real Caddo." It came to represent at least four groups of people whose language and culture were similar and who lived in villages along the Red River in northeastern Texas, southwestern Arkansas, and northwestern Louisiana. These were the Kadohadacho, the Nanatsako, the upper Nasoni, and the upper Natchitoches all of whom were confederated under the head chief of the Kadohadacho. The name "Caddo" also became applied to people of the Hasinai confederacy which consisted of several groups of Indians whose language and culture were identical with the Kadohadacho and who lived in hamlets in East Texas scattered from southwest of the Neches River to the Sabine River. Various names were given the individual groups at different times in history. Within the region, however, the following Hasinai were identified at one time or another: Hainai, Nabedache, Nacogdoche, Nasoni, Nadaco, Neche, Nacono, Nechaui, Nacao, Nabiti, and Nasayaya. At the beginning of the historical era the total population of both the Kadohadacho and the Hasinai confederacies was considerable and may have been around ten thousand. Other Indians in the area who were related but independent included the Ais or Eyish and the Kichai.

By 1500 the Caddos had reached a level of cultural development unattained by other Texas people and, in fact, seemed to be in decline from a peak achieved at an earlier time. Archeological research has revealed a long Caddoan cultural tradition in East Texas and adjacent areas extending back several hundred years prior to the sixteenth century, and previous to that a pre-Caddoan archeological period extending back to around 9,500 B.C. During the pre-Caddoan period from approximately 9,500 to 500 B.C., the region was inhabited by nomadic hunters and gatherers. Around the latter date, small villages or hamlets began to appear, pottery began to be made, and the planting and harvesting of vegetable crops was initiated. The appearance of these practices represent an extension of cultural traits found to the east in the Mississippi valley to the East Texas region. By at least A.D. 800, the ancestors of the historical Caddos had developed a level of cultural sophistication involving social organization, horticultural practices, and expressions of religion never reached by other native Texans.

The first European contact with Caddos was made by Spaniards with the expedition of Hernando de Soto which reached Texas in 1542. Luis de Moscoso, who succeeded De Soto on his death, led the expedition southwestward from Arkansas across the Red River into Texas. One of the participants, a man known as the Gentleman of Elvas, recounted in 1557 how the group passed through Indian villages called Naguatex, Nissohone, Nondacao, Aays, and Soacatino before reaching a province in Texas called Guasco. All except the Guasco were Caddoan names.

The next detailed information about the Caddos is found in the journal of Henri Joutel. Following La Salle's death in 1687, Joutel made his way through the Caddo country and eventually to Canada, spending several weeks enroute in a Hasinai village in the Neche River area. In his descriptions of the people, Joutel noted that they were considerably darker in complexion than surrounding Indians. The men's dress consisted of goatskins painted several colors and worn around the shoulders, buckskin leggins, and, in some instances, breechclouts over the leggins. They wore plumes of feathers of several colors in their hair which was cut short except for a lock on top and sideburns. Their faces were colored black and red

*Early explorer, Enrico de Tonti with Indian guide in East Texas.*

— Institute of Texan Cultures
Painting by Bruce Marshall

when Joutel saw them. Some carried swords of Spanish origin with feathers and hawk-bells attached to the hilts. Some had clubs and some only bows and arrows. Joutel observed that the men tattooed themselves, making streaks on their faces from the tops of their foreheads down their noses to the tips of their chins. This was accomplished by pricking the skin with needles and mixing powdered charcoal with the blood until it sank into the wound. They also made designs of animals and plants on their shoulders, thighs, and other parts of their bodies. The women, who generally had good figures, streaked their faces, adding more designs than the men, including marks at the corners of their eyes. They tattooed their bodies with particular attention to their breasts; those with the most elaborate designs in that area were considered the prettiest. Joutel observed that the pricking in that part of the body was extremely painful to them. Their dress consisted of skins, mats, and clouts hanging around them like petticoats reaching down half their legs. Their hair was unadorned, plaited and tied in a knot in the back.

The houses of the Hasinai were round, bee-hive shaped structures made of trees and grass. Joutel saw them scattered about for quite a distance interspersed with fields where the principal crop was corn. Some lodges housed fifteen to twenty persons who slept on beds made of canes, raised two or three feet above the ground, and fitted with mats and hides. In the center of each house was a fire which never was permitted to go out. Other, larger structures were public places used for meetings and ceremonies. The main meal of the Hasinai was sagamite, a porridge of corn, beans, and bread.

When Joutel was with the Hasinai, a war party made a raid on enemies they called *Cannokantino,* probably Apaches, and returned after killing or taking prisoner forty-eight men and women. One woman prisoner was sent home with a charge of powder and a ball signifying that the next time the Hasinai would wage war with firearms. Another less fortunate woman became the symbolic enemy upon whom the Hasinai women who had lost husbands and relatives could vent their wrath. Armed with sharply pointed stakes, they danced around the poor woman, jabbing her with the points, pulling her hair, and tormenting her in various ways all the while attempting to outdo one another with various forms of torture. Finally, one of the Hasinai women struck the miserable creature on the head with a club and another ran a stake through her body several times until she was dead. Then, according to Joutel, they cut the corpse into bits and pieces and made some of the other prisoners, including two little boys of her nation, eat them.

The men then rejoiced in their victory in a ceremony lasting three days and performed in the cottages of all the head men. In each instance, following a speech by an elder, a procession of warriors, carrying bows and arrows and followed by their wives, entered the house and presented scalps taken in the recent engagement to the elder. He took each scalp and, turning to each direction, offered it to the four quarters of the world and then laid it on the ground. He next ate a portion of sagamite as an offering to the heads of hair and lighted a pipe of tobacco and blew smoke on them. All the people then ate meat, including the dried tongues of the enemies they had killed, and concluded each ceremony with dancing and singing. Then they went to other cottages to repeat it.

The Hasinai visited by Joutel are believed to be the *Tejas* who Martín and Castillo had heard about years before on the Colorado River. No Spanish contacts, however, were made with people identified as Tejas until soldiers and priests led by Captain Alonso de León, searching for La Salle's French colony were met on April 16, 1689, at a point east of the Guadalupe River not far from the French location by Indians who greeted them with the words "techas," "techas." Father Damian Massanet, who reported the incident, interpreted the words to mean "friends." It is now believed that long before the coming of the Spaniards the word "Tejas" or a variation was widely used by the Hasinai and others east of the Colorado to refer to groups of people, some speaking different languages, who were allied against the Apaches. From 1689 onward, however, the name "Tejas" was commonly used by Spaniards to identify Indians living in the vicinity of the upper Neches and Angelina rivers and the country they inhabited.

In May of the next year Massanet and De Leon reached a valley near San Pedro Creek northwest of the present community of Weches which was thickly settled with houses in the midst of extensive fields of maize, beans, pumpkins, and watermelons. A chapel was constructed near the Indian village and three priests and three soldiers were left to serve the Indians. One of these was Father Francisco Casanas de Jesús María who closely observed the people during the next year and wrote a lengthy report to the Viceroy in August 1691 describing the geography, the flora and fauna, and the Indians. He also reported the presence of nine tribes, occupying about thirty-five leagues of land, in the region, each ruled by a leader called a *caddi* and all subject to a grand priest or *Xinesi* whose position was hereditary and the most exalted in the confederacy.

The discovery of these Indians and the continued fear of French encroachment on Spanish territory prompted the creation of the province of Texas and Coahuila in 1691. The new Governor, Domingo Terán de los Ríos, accompanied by Father Massanet, entered the region that year to plan for missions and permanent Spanish occupation. Massanet, of course, was anxious to convert the Indians to Christianity. In his zealousness, he contributed to the perpetuation of a myth which involved a nun in a convent in Agreda, Spain, Mother María de Jesús. Mother María first came to the attention of authorities in New Mexico about 1630 when she was identified by the head of missions, Father Alonso de Benavides, as the mysterious lady who in the 1620s reportedly had miraculously appeared on numerous occasions to the Jumanos and other Indians on the plains. Stories of her activities had spurred Father Juan de Salas and other priests to make trips, supposedly resulting in the conversion of thousands of Indians. Benavides was so intrigued by the reports that he visited Mother María, who had been reported to make flights to administer to the needs of natives in remote lands, in Agreda and was convinced from his discussions with her that she, indeed, was the lady who had appeared on the plains of North America. Some sixty years later, therefore, it is interesting to find Father Massanet in the land of the Tejas having a conversation with a chief concerning the devout Mother.

Massanet reported that while he was at the village, near present Weches, the chief asked him for a piece of blue cloth for a shroud in which to bury his mother when she died. Massanet told him that any cloth would be suitable, but the chief insisted on blue because long ago his people had been visited frequently by a beautiful woman who came down from the clouds dressed in blue and the chief wanted his mother to be dressed like her. Interrogated about the "lady in blue," the chief said that his mother and other old people had seen her. Thus, Massanet, having knowledge of the legend of Mother María was convinced that she had appeared to the Hasinai, a circumstance that impelled the Spaniards to name one of the first missions established among the Hasinai Santisimo Nombre de María and one of the many arroyos in the province La Venerable Madre de Jesús de Agreda.

Unfortunately, Mother María's powers apparently did not extend any further in time. After Governor Terán left the area in 1691 an outbreak of smallpox soon left three hundred Indians and one priest dead. By 1693 the disease and ruthless tactics by the priests to force the Indians to refrain from their own religious practices were the principal factors contributing to the abandonment of the region by the Spanish. They did not return until 1716 when, responding to a renewed threat from the French who now occupied Louisiana, an expedition of missionaries, soldiers, and settlers marched from Mexico to the Neches River where a band of curious Caddos was encountered. An atmosphere of joviality and friendliness prevailed during which the calumet was smoked and gifts of Indian agricultural products were exchanged for Spanish blankets, tobacco, and clothing.

The mission effort among the Caddos was adversely affected from the start by the vicissitudes of Spanish-French politics and the competition that ensued for control of the Indian trade. In 1718 Bernard de la Harpe established a French trading post at the Nasoni village on the Red River for the Kadohadacho confederacy, the Indians of which were never brought under Spanish influence. Then, the threat of war between France and Spain in 1719 prompted the retreat of the Spaniards from the Caddo country. They returned in 1721, reoccupied the missions, and established the capital of Spanish Texas at the Adaes village where it remained for more than half a century, but the Caddos were unreceptive to efforts to Christianize them.

The very reasons why the Caddos seemed to be good candidates for missions turned out to be reasons for the failure of the system among them. While they recognized a supreme being, they were not monotheists, and the highly developed system of priests, rituals, and beliefs which encompassed the Caddo world was dominant over the alien Christian faith propagated by a few men strangely garbed in robes and performing rituals which were interesting to watch but did nothing for the Caddo psyche. Factors of lifestyle also were involved. Athanase de Mézières in 1779 remarked that the efforts of priests among the Eyeish had been in vain because the Indians were so materialistic they would not accept the spiritual food proffered by the zealous priests. Finally, the nature of Caddo society with the people dispersed in scattered agricultural hamlets with a well-established system of work, leisure, and trade worked against mission requirements of residence in or near the missions to receive instruction in Christianity, the Spanish language, and vocational training emphasizing agricultural pursuits. Already religious, already farmers, already well organized, and preferring French traders to Spanish priests, the Caddos rejected the system which was pressed on them and which, in time, contributed to their decline.

The decline was attributable to a number of things, including continued warfare with Apaches, Osages, and Choctaws, a growing dependence on white men's trading goods, the introduction of Spanish settlers, and disease. The smallpox which first struck in 1690 became a plague in the 1700s and periodically devastated the bands of both Caddo confederacies. By 1800 several bands had disap-

*Tonkawa Indian woman.*

— Smithsonian Institution

*Engraving of a Kiowa Indian camp of grass huts, around 1850.*

— Photo by Institute of Texan Cultures
From *Le Tour du Monde, Hachette et C'e,* Paris, 1860.

peared, and the total population had been reduced to a few hundred families. As the old century ended and new one began, the proud Kadohadacho and Hasinai confederacies were but shadows of their former selves and other Indians had long since assumed a more significant role in influencing the course of Texas history.

Another group of native Texans who declined rapidly during the last century of Spanish Texas was the Attacapans. The Attacapan tribe consisted of several bands of Indians whose historical habitat was the region of southeast Texas and southwestern Louisiana extending from east of the Sabine River to west of Galveston Bay and inland for a hundred miles or more. The southernmost bands shared many cultural traits with the Karankawas whose coast they partially occupied, and the northernmost bands were sometimes mistaken for Caddos, but the Attacapans apparently descended from a separate linguistic family of ancient people who inhabited the lower Mississippi valley. The name "Attacapa" was derived from a Choctaw word meaning "cannibal" and applied by the Choctaws to the Indians of the region inhabited by the Attacapans. Although numerous Attacapan bands existed earlier, little is known about them prior to the eighteenth century when four bands became distinct—the Bidai, Arkokisa or Orcoquisa, Deadose, and Attacapa. The name of the latter is used to refer to the collective body, but this band was basically indigeneous to southwestern Louisiana. The Bidai, Arkokisa, and Deadose may more properly be described as native Texans. They were wandering hunters whose economy was adapted to the humid forests, river bottoms, and marshes where they lived.

The *Hans,* whom De Vaca met in 1528, may have been Arkokisas, and some of the Indians mentioned by Joutel in 1687 were probably Attacapans, but the first definite historical information about these people was acquired by a young French officer who spent more than a year with the Arkokisa in the vicinity of Galveston Bay during 1719-21. Stranded in the bay area with four other Frenchmen after having debarked a ship to search for fresh water, Simars de Bellisle managed to survive after the others died and was eventually taken in by a band of Arkokisa. Although they treated him badly and made him a slave, the Indians provided food and restored Bellisle to full strength. After several months of wandering in the region, the Arkokisa were visited one day by a band of Hasinai who took papers belonging to Bellisle and, upon returning to their village, decided to take them to Louis Juchereau de Saint Denis, the French commandant at Natchitoches. St. Denis immediately sent two Hasinais to rescue Bellisle.

In the meantime, the Arkokisa had continued to wander and

had gone to hunt buffalo in an area beyond the forests where they lived. They possessed horses and, according to Bellisle, who later related his experiences, they were exceptionally skilled in killing buffalo using bows and arrows while astride horses. But they were unwilling to permit Bellisle to ride a horse, not, as might be suspected, for fear that he would escape, but for fear that because he was a man of different color some evil might befall them if he was given a horse.

When Hasinai messengers arrived at the Arkokisa camp, they took Bellisle and returned to the village of Hainai on the Angelina River, where he spent over two months living with an Indian woman named Angelica. Thus blossomed a short-lived romance with all the ingredients of selfless love on the woman's part. When the Hasinai men went on a war party, they told Bellisle to stay in camp until they returned. However, he was anxious to see his countrymen in Natchitoches but not desirous of leaving Angelica. One day, nevertheless, he told her he was leaving. She sadly but lovingly presented two of her young children whose father apparently was dead to guide the Frenchman to Natchitoches, saying that she understood. Bellisle was not without remorse. His account of the departure and final embracing poignantly depicted the strings tugging at his own heart. In any case, the decision made, he took the children in tow and reached Natchitoches on February 10, 1721, where he was welcomed by St. Denis. Later in the year, Bellisle served as a guide and interpreter for Bernard de la Harpe in a voyage from Biloxi to Galveston Bay. Going ashore the voyageurs met the Arkokisa, who had enslaved Bellisle and took nine of them back to New Orleans.

News of continued French activities in the region of the Attacapans prompted the Spanish in 1746 to send Captain Joaquin de Orobio from Los Adaes to investigate. Orobio visited the Bidai at a camp between the Trinity and Neches rivers south of Nacogdoches and Arkokisa camps near the San Jacinto River north of present Houston. Both bands told him this was the first time they had seen Spaniards. Orobio reported that the Arkokisa lived on fish, game, and wild fruits and that they traded pelts and bear fat to the French. This trade was soon taken over by Spaniards operating out of Los Adaes. Ironically, the Bidai and Arkokisa then stole horses from Spaniards farther west and traded them along with corn to the Spaniards in East Texas for French goods illegally purchased from the French at Natchitoches.

The Arkokisa, reported by Orobio to have five rancherias and three hundred families, requested missions in their country, one of the factors which prompted the establishment of the missions on the San Gabriel River for the Karankawas, Attacapans, Tonkawas, and other wandering "rancheria grande" bands. With the help of an Arkokisa chief, the Spanish located the Attacapans, including Bidai, Deadose, and Arkokisa, at Mission San Ildefonso established in 1749 near present Rockdale. The effort was short-lived due to raids by Apaches and internal dissension, and by 1755 the Indians had returned to their old ways. The next year another attempt to maintain Spanish control of the lower Trinity River region resulted in the building of a presidio, San Agustín de Ahumada, and a mission, Nuestra Señora de la Luz, near the mouth of the river. The Arkokisa were receptive to the venture at first, but it also failed because of management problems, isolation from the mainstream of Spanish activity, and Indian apathy.

During the 1770s and 1780s the Attacapans were allied with the Karankawas in depredations, and the Bidai, in particular, carried on a traffic in guns and ammunition with the Lipan Apaches who had moved into the region west of San Antonio. The Lipans exchanged horses, mules, and captives of other tribes for the weapons secured in Louisiana by the Bidai. Then, the smallpox epidemic which struck the Texas Indians in 1777 severely reduced the Attacapans. Morfi, with characteristically negative views, in 1781 said that the Attacapans were cowardly and lazy and still wandered without fixed abodes near the mouth of the Neches and Trinity rivers while the Bidai, hard hit by smallpox, included only about one hundred men. The survivors lived in great poverty after 1800. In time a few joined the Caddos and Wichitas on the Brazos River and a few others joined the Alabamas and Coushattas, who moved into southeast Texas after 1815, but Attacapan bands as distinct entities became extinct. Their legacy to Texas is primarily in the fact that they existed. The value and potential of the Attacapans as subjects worthy of comparative and contrastive ethnohistorical studies has yet to be realized.

Much also remains to be revealed about western neighbors of the Attacapans and Caddos known as Tonkawas. Consisting of several bands loosely confederated and speaking a language distinct from all surrounding tribes, the Tonkawas ranged central Texas from the Red River to below San Antonio, usually staying west of the Trinity and Brazos rivers. The Wacos, who lived on the Brazos early in the nineteenth century, called the various bands "Tonkaweya," meaning "they all stay together." A century earlier the principal bands were the *Yojuane*, the *Mayeye*, and the *Ervipiame*. Possibly early inhabitants of the Edwards Plateau, the bands were descendants of Paleo-Indians whose presence is gradually being revealed in archeological studies of central Texas sites. Whether there are links with the recently discovered "Leanderthal Lady" and Brazos remains has not yet been determined.

De Vaca probably encountered Tonkawas during his trek across Texas in the 1530s, and some of the people met by the Spanish expeditions to the Concho and Colorado rivers in the 1600s were Tonkawas. Joutel's account of French activities in the 1680s, however, was the first to mention groups who were unmistakenly Tonkawan. He placed the Mayeye in the area between Fort Saint Louis and the Colorado River and other bands of the same language to the northwest of the Colorado. A few years later, both Father Massanet and Father Jesús María noted Tonkawa groups west of the Caddos and Bidais. Jesús María specifically identified the *Tancaquaay* as enemies of the Hasinai.

Culturally, Tonkawas were little more advanced than the Karankawas. They shared many characteristics of plains tribes because of their border location; they did not farm, relying instead on trade with other Indians for agricultural products, and they made use of dog and horse travois, skin teepees, and the buffalo.

Physically, Tonkawas were lighter complexioned than Caddos and Wichitas, but otherwise were not unusually distinctive. The men wore breechclouts, adorned their hair with ornaments, and wore earrings and necklaces. On the warpath they placed feathers in their hair and painted their faces as did other tribes with a plains orientation. The women wore short skirts tied in a point at each side and tattooed their faces and bodies. Black lines extended down the face from the forehead across the nose to the chin, and numerous concentric circles were painted on each breast around the nipple.

Cannibalism among the Tonkawas was observed on numerous occasions, presumably as a ritual to give them the strengths of the individuals consumed who, incidentally, were invariably captives taken in war or slain warriors of enemy tribes. As with the practice among other tribes, eating human flesh seems to have occurred in some instances for other than ritualistic reasons. On one occasion, an eyewitness reported seeing a group of Tonkawas strip the flesh off a Comanche they had killed and cook it in a kettle with corn and potatoes. When the stew was done, the band gathered around, dipped their hands into the pot, and ravenously consumed the mixture. Afterwards, they fell asleep. When they awoke, they danced the scalp dance until well into the night.

The mission efforts among the Tonkawas were no more successful than with other native Texans. The Tonkawas were among the "rancheria grande" Indians in the Austin-San Antonio area who in the 1730s began asking for missions. In 1748 Mission San Francisco

Xavier was established on the San Gabriel River and reserved for the Tonkawas. It soon failed because of fickleness of the Indians, poor management, and quarrels between soldiers and priests. Thereafter, the Tonkawas wandered, joined other Indians who were referred to as *Nortenos* (Comanches, Caddos, and Wichitas) by the Spanish, and in 1758 raided Mission San Saba de la Santa Cruz, which had been established for the Apaches at present Menard. Never numbering more than a few hundred people, the Tonkawas became estranged from the Nortenos later and were friendly with the Lipans by the end of the eighteenth century.

Tonkawas suffered from smallpox in 1777 and in 1801. Living in abject poverty, they were disliked by the semisedentary Tawakonis of the Wichita confederacy, who moved to the Brazos River in the latter 1700s, and they were tormented by powerful Comanches on the plains to the west. Yet, the tribe did survive in spite of hardships, massacres, and removals, and remnants eventually found homes on reservations in present Oklahoma. The Tonkawa experience in Texas has not been thoroughly investigated, but as native Texans, the historical significance of these people may just be that they were true to the meaning of their name: they all stayed together.

Coahuiltecans were other native Texans at the beginning of the historical era about which little is known. Coahuiltecan is a generic name based on the geographical location of about seventy bands, some in Texas, others in Coahuila and other Mexican states on both sides of the Rio Grande from its mouth to its junction with the Pecos River. In Texas the principal groups included Payaya east of San Antonio, Orejons near Matagorda Bay, Carrizos near Eagle Pass, Malaguites near the coast below Corpus Christi, and Aranamas who roamed below San Antonio.

A primitive people struggling to live in one of the harshest environments in Texas, the Coahuiltecans scoured the cactus and brush infested countryside for food, devouring any type of living creature—bugs, rodents, lizards, snakes, deer, rabbits—to be found as well as seeds and plants. They spoke a language closely related to Indians found in other parts of North America but nowhere else in Texas, prompting the suspicion that they were remnants of a once-united body which at some distant prehistoric time had split. Moving about in clans with little formal social organization, they were among the first native Texans to be considered for missions after the Spanish reentered Texas in 1716, and the members of a few bands went to the San Antonio missions. Lipan Apache encroachment into their territory later gave the rest of the scattered bands little choice but to move beyond the Rio Grande, to submit and be assimilated, or to be annihilated. Well before the end of the eighteenth century these processes had run their course. Extinct long before the end of Spanish Texas in 1821, the Coahuiltecan heritage remains in place names and references in Spanish documents to a people whose society was unable to withstand the changes brought by the introduction of European institutions and the inroads of other Indians.

Ironically, Indians who assumed dominance among the Texas tribes during the last century of Spanish rule were not native Texans. These were the Lipan Apaches, Comanches, and Wichitas who swept into western and northern Texas, alternately waging war, concluding alliances, and engaging the native tribes in schemes which contributed to their instability and ultimate decline. Numerous in comparison to the native Texans, these immigrants overwhelmed the smaller bands. By the end of the eighteenth century Spanish Indian policy was directed almost entirely to the control of the Lipans, Comanches, and Wichitas.

Before the coming of Europeans to Texas, people of the Athapascan linguistic family migrated southward from the northern plains into New Mexico and the Texas Panhandle. When the Coronado expedition entered the region in 1541, people called *Apaches,* a name believed to be derived from the Zuni Indian word for "enemy," were seen at widely scattered locations. On the high plains, or Llano Estacado, in West Texas, Coronado encountered nomadic buffalo hunting Apaches called *Querechos* and *Teyas.* Later, in 1601 Don Juan de Oñate, the founder of New Mexico, came into contact with *Vaqueros, Apachi,* and *Escansaques* on the plains. The latter, located in present Oklahoma on the Cimarron River, were the *Kantsi* or *Cancey,* who were at war with the Wichita and Caddo bands to the east and who were known later as the *Lipan.*

The name *Lipan* is derived from "Ipa," a personal name, and "n'de," a word meaning "people," thus *Ipan'de* and *Lipan.* Physically taller than neighboring Indians, Lipan men wore breechclouts, leggins, and moccasins and sometimes carried buckskin cloaks. A typical warrior's hair was cropped short above the ear on the left side and permitted to grow to shoulder length on the right side. The men plucked their beards, wore copper ear trinkets, and painted their faces and bodies. The women wore buckskin skirts and blouses and long stocking-like shoes of deerskin. Their hair hung loose or was plaited in back, and they wore copper earrings and bracelets on their wrists and ankles. Possessing a culture adapted to the plains environment, the historical Lipans were teepee dwelling, nomadic buffalo hunters and warriors with no permanent campsites and no agriculture, although they were descendants of semisedentary Indians who had raised crops of melons and vegetables along the banks of high plains streams.

In company with other plains Apaches, including Faraones, Jicarillas, Natages, and Mescaleros, the Lipans gradually migrated southward from central plains locations until, in the 1600s, they controlled the vast expanse of West Texas between the upper Nueces and Medina rivers and the headwaters of the Colorado and Red rivers. After acquiring Spanish horses and firearms, they raided as far as Kansas, Mexico, and New Mexico, incurring the enmity of all neighboring tribes. Lipans were skilled horsemen and experts in the manufacture and use of bows and arrows, which they preferred over firearms in combat. Until pressured by Comanches who moved into West Texas from the north about 1700, Lipans had no equals in warfare.

Comanches soon forced the Lipans to more southern locations. About 1720 a major battle, lasting nine days, was fought between the tribes on a river in West Texas called the Rio del Fierro. It ended in disaster for the Lipans. Thereafter, the Comanches emerged as the "lords of the plains." By the 1740s the Lipans were living within fifty miles of San Antonio, and Spanish authorities were considering missions to pacify them. Finally, in 1757 Mission San Saba de la Santa Cruz was established, but before many Lipans could be enticed to it, the mission was laid waste by Nortenos led by Comanches and Wichitas. Soon Spaniards were seeking the friendship of the Nortenos in a deliberate effort to pit the tribes against the Lipans in a war of extermination.

The Lipans moved to the region between the Nueces River and the Rio Grande, old Coahuiltecan country, secured weapons and munitions from the Bidai, and raided widely. Although seriously crippled in a battle involving several hundred Spaniards, Comanches, and Wichitas united under Juan de Ugalde in 1790, Lipans continued to plague Spanish settlements. Generally decimated and pacified after 1821, they maintained their tribal identity until well into the nineteenth century. A few Lipans eventually joined other Apaches in New Mexico and Oklahoma.

The Comanche advance into Texas was facilitated by an alliance concluded in 1746 with Wichita bands, including the Tawehash, Tawakoni, and Yscani, who established villages about the same time on the Red River. Comanche warriors visited the villages and traded Apache slaves and Spanish horses and mules for Wichita agricultural products and French goods packed to the villages by traders from Louisiana. Following the destruction of the San Saba mission in 1758 and the routing of a Spanish retaliatory expedition to the Red River villages the next year, the Comanches controlled western Texas above the Edwards Plateau and west of the Cross Timbers to the Llano Estacado and raided southward beyond San Antonio to the Texas coast.

The Comanches were of Shoshonean stock and originally lived in the northern Rocky Mountains. After migrating to the plains, at least twelve separate bands developed, numbering perhaps as many as 20,000 people; and the name *Comanche,* from the Ute *Komantcia,* meaning "enemy," became commonly used by the Spanish to identify the tribe. The largest of the bands, the *Penateka,* or Honey-Eaters, led the migration southward into Texas.

Comanche people were of medium height with round heads and broad faces. Shorter in stature than some neighboring people, Comanche warriors, nevertheless, became feared raiders astride the mustangs they originally acquired from Spanish sources. Particularly in the summers by the light of the August moon, they raided deep into South Texas and Mexico, ravaging and plundering and creating a wave of terror among people unfortunate enough to be in their path. Ranging across the landscape in typical plainsmen style, Comanches struck their teepees in temporary camps, made no effort to farm, and thoroughly utilized the buffalo that they hunted with an intensity unequaled by most other tribes. They were astute and manipulative in their relations with other tribes, not hesitating to trick and plunder friend and foe alike or to use force as they deemed necessary to secure their wishes. In time Spaniards, Mexicans, and Anglo-Americans came to realize that peaceful relations with the native Texans could be maintained only with the cooperation and acquiescence of the powerful Comanches.

The semisedentary Wichita people were closely associated with Comanches. Historically occupying a broad area between the big bend of the Arkansas River in Kansas to central Texas west of the Caddo country and east of the high plains, the Wichita confederacy was composed of several autonomous bands who spoke a common Caddoan dialect, lived in permanent villages of bee-hive shaped grass houses, and raised extensive crops of corn, tobacco, pumpkins, and squash in the flood plains and bottoms along the streams where they made their villages. Because of their strategic location after migrating to locations near the Red, Sabine, and Brazos rivers during the middle of the eighteenth century and their previous involvement with French traders on the Arkansas and Canadian rivers, Wichitas became important middlemen in trading activities involving the Indians and the Spanish in Texas and the French and

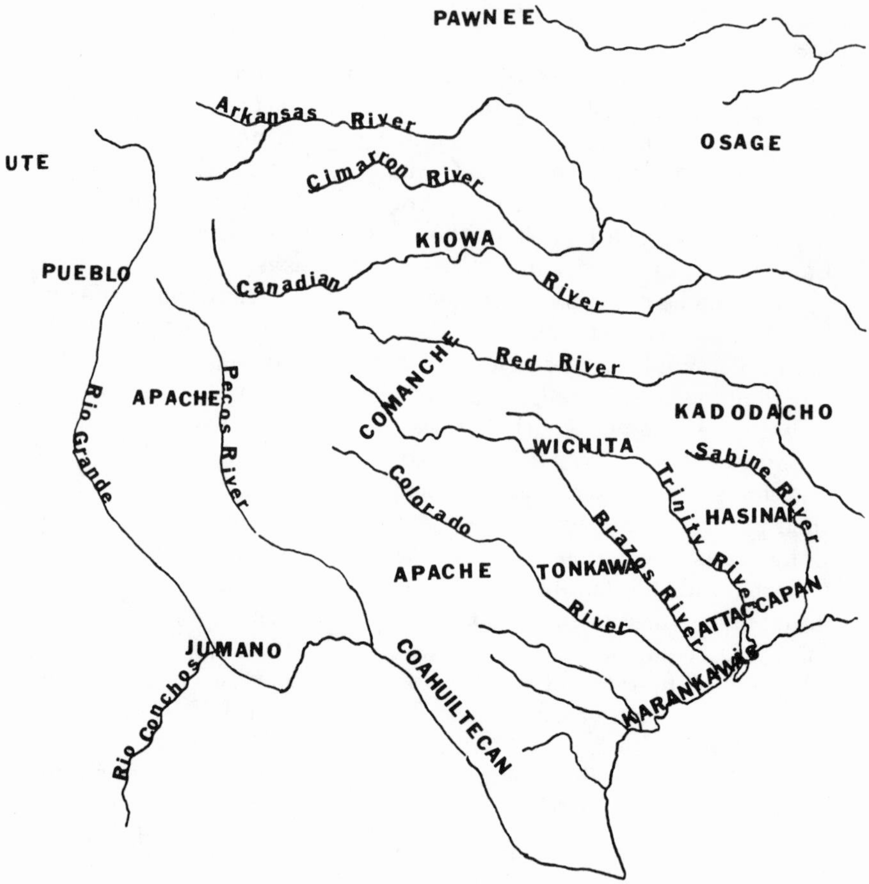


*General locations of Texas Indians in the eighteenth century*

later the Anglo-Americans in Louisiana. Their villages in the vicinity of present Waco and north of present Nocona became emporiums where French and Spanish goods, Wichita agricultural products, and the plunder of the numerous tribes were regularly bartered.

The origin of the Wichitas is shrouded in the silence of pre-history, but their ancestors possibly were aboriginals of North Texas and Southern Oklahoma who also were ancestors of the Pawnees, Arikaras, Caddos, and Kichais. The principal Wichita bands who appeared in Texas following the southern migration were the Tawehash or Taovayas, Tawakoni, and Yscanis. A group known as *Ouisitas* to the French and as *Ouedsita,* or a variant thereof, to the Spanish was probably the Wichita proper. The darkly complexioned people called themselves *Kitikiti'sh,* a word in their language referring to unique tattoos around their eyes which gave them the appearance of being raccoon-eyed. The Wichita proper assimilated with the other bands prior to 1800, leaving its name, Wichita, to be applied regularly thereafter to the combined bands of the confederacy to which was also added the Kichai who increasingly made their villages alongside the Wichitas. Each village was governed by a civil chief, who was advised by a council where both men and women could speak.

Wichita men were warriors and hunters and, like Comanches, were especially fond of horses, which they regularly bartered and stole. They dressed similar to the Comanches and, like their Pawnee cousins, wore the scalp lock. Women wore buckskin skirts, remaining nude above the waist and tattooed their breasts elaborately believing that by doing so the organs would not become pendulous in old age. All work in the villages was performed by the women, and when the men went on the annual hunt, the women went along to butcher the buffalo and tan the skins. While on the hunt, lasting several months, the people lived in teepees. They cached their village belongings, particularly the harvests of their fields in holes in the ground or in caves along the banks of streams in the vicinity of the villages. These caches provided sustenance for more than one weary and hungry traveler who came across them.

In the early 1760s the Tawakonis and Yscanis sought a mission for their town on the upper Sabine River, and Father Jose de Calahorra, who went from Nacogdoches to investigate, recommended that one be established, but the project never materialized. Beyond the pale of mission activity during the latter years of the century on the Brazos and Red rivers, the bands, with a population of about six thousand in five or six villages, reached the zenith of their importance as traders, diplomats, and participants in Spanish frontier relations.

A decline in their power and prestige began about 1810 and village sites changed, but they remained in the same general localities until well into the nineteenth century and were influential in developments affecting the advance of the Anglo-American frontier.

In any age existence and survival depend on a large number of factors, including access to the bare necessities of food, shelter, and clothing, the absence of disease, adequate protection from hostile forces, familial or community associations to strengthen individual needs for love and companionship, and social and cultural institutions which promote the lifestyle of a people, provide hope and insight about life and its problems, and link past, present, and future in traditions and customs deemed worthy of passing down generation to generation. These factors were as necessary for the native Texans in the 1500s as they are for Texans today, even though circumstances of existence differ. Primitive, superstitious, and barbaric by certain standards of contemporary society, Indians were in many respects more civilized than the people who have inherited their land. Their appreciation for the natural habitat prevented the wanton destruction of its resources, and their understanding that somehow all of creation, animate and inanimate, had meaning and was linked in a great circle of being is a concept anathema to the modern exploitative, materialistic, technological society which measures progress in terms of dollars, goods produced, and material possessions. And, the picture which is partially revealed in the historical record of warring, cannibalistic, inhuman, greedy natives is ethnocentric and does not, because of the paucity of the record and the absence of Indian sources, do justice to the native Texans or really tell the modern generation much about them.

What then can be said? In summary, the modern literate Texan must appreciate the struggle for existence on an hour-to-hour, day-to-day basis, which native Texans faced. The Karankawas, Attacapans, Tonkawas, and Coahuiltecans most clearly exemplified this bottom line, basic level of existence, but even the agricultural Jumanos, Caddos, and Wichitas had to be on guard constantly in a world of enemies, particularly Apaches and Osages, whose attacks and atrocities were recounted night after night around scores of campfires from the Rio Grande to the Red River. Also, in the preceding pages, little has been said about the individuals who comprised the various Indian societies. The problem again is the scarcity of Indian sources and a dependence on white records which, unfortunately, results in a distorted, homogenized view of Indian life. Indians were individuals just as modern Texans are, and the inevitable stereotyped surveys of tribal activities and cultures usually do not result in making that fact evident. There were great Indian leaders like Juan Sabeata of the Jumanos, Quiscat of the Tawakonis, and Tinhiouen of the Kadohadacho whose stories beg to be known. And there was the brave Wichita chief, name unknown, who, mounted on a magnificent horse and with colorful plumes of feathers in his hair, led his warriors on sally after sally against the Spaniards on the Red River in 1759 until he also fell, fatally struck by a white man's bullet. Or what about the intrepid Comanche leaders who crossed the plains to conclude a treaty on the enemy's home ground in Santa Fe in 1785, an act with important consequences for Spanish-Indian relations in Texas.

Finally, there were undoubtedly many staunch, responsible native men and women whose unsung contributions to their own people kindled the values and principles of their societies. Many years later, a descendant of one of those natives, Acaquash, Chief of the Waco, accompanied a group of Indians and government agents to Washington, D.C., after a treaty was concluded at the Tehuacana Creek council grounds in central Texas. Washington officials took the Indians on tours of factories and buildings; they rode trains and steamboats; they were given white men's clothing; and they dined in hotels and even visited President James K. Polk in the White House. Returning to Texas, Acaquash, who had worked for many years to maintain peaceful relations between whites and Indians, was asked by a reporter if he had been impressed by what he had seen. The sagacious chief replied that what was remarkable to him was not that all the things existed which he had been shown, but that the white people should think that the Indians stood in need of those things. As for him, he would be impressed when he once again saw his village and could rejoin his people and live in peace. Speaking of bottom lines! These are noble goals worthy of being sought by any people in any time.

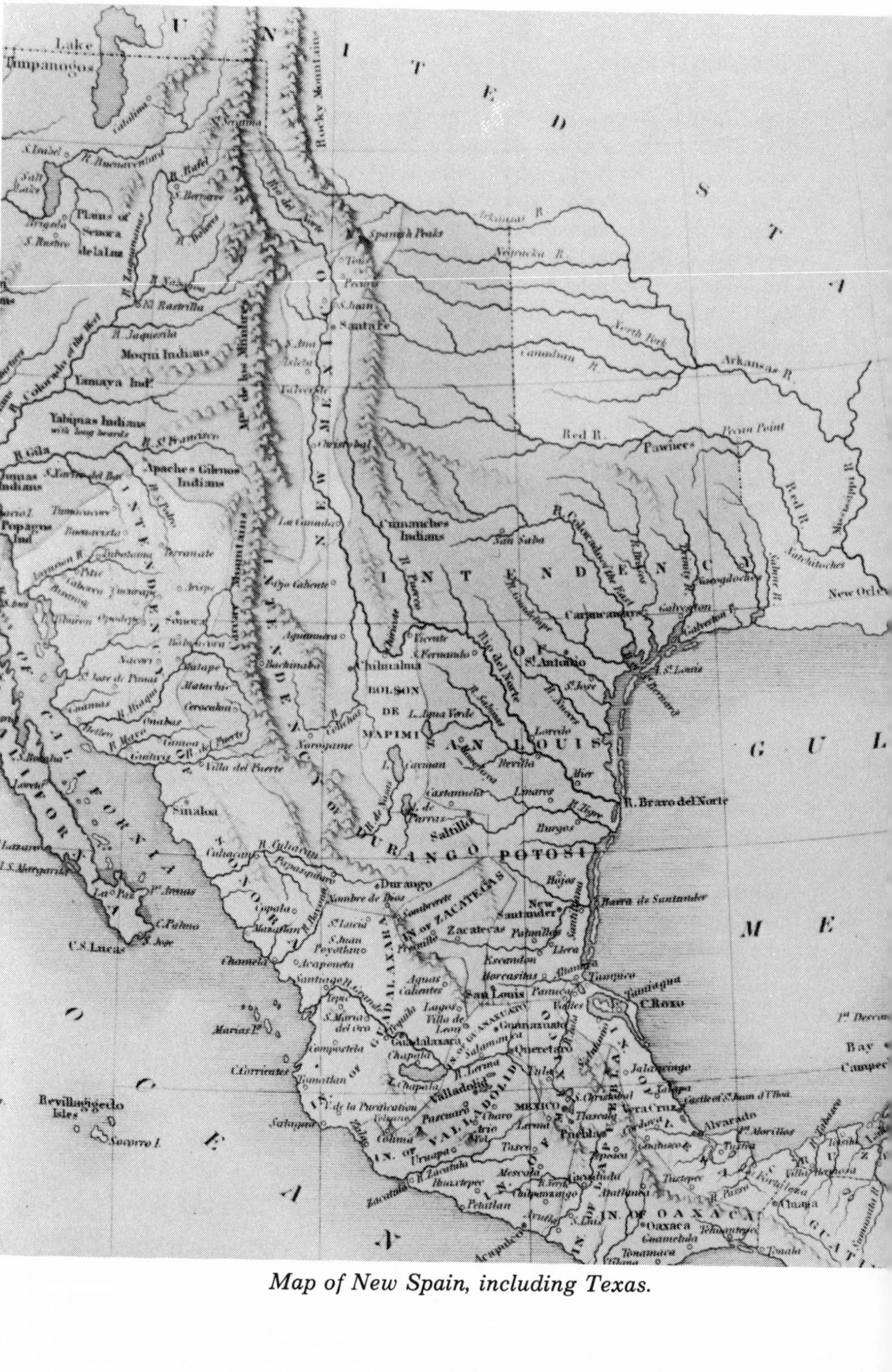


*Map of New Spain, including Texas.*

# 2

## Hispanic Texas, 1519-1836

*Margaret Swett Henson*

Spain claimed Texas for almost three hundred years from the desultory coastal observations of Alonso Alvarez de Piñeda in 1519 until 1821 when Mexico won its independence. Between 1821 and 1836, Texas was a state in the new Mexican republic, and it was during this period that the great influx of Anglo-Americans occurred. Three centuries of Hispanic influence left its mark on the Lone Star State in place names and some terminology, such as in ranching activities, but beyond those obvious contributions, there are others less well known. Anglo-Texans adopted certain advantageous legal traditions from Spain, including the homestead law that protects a person's home and tools from seizure for debt, the concept of community property, and the extension of offshore rights from the standard three miles to ten, a regulation that affects both fishing and petroleum interests. Unfortunately, with the coming of the Anglos, most Texans of Spanish descent suffered repressive discrimination, an injustice only recently recognized deserving a remedy.

The history of Spanish Texas parallels that of the English colonies in that a few sturdy pioneers had to cope with rugged frontier conditions far from their homes. Unlike the English colonies, however, Texas experienced three stages of development: first, cursory overland explorations that resulted in almost total neglect because of the apparent lack of valuable minerals; second, a missionary period intended to change the Indians into Christian serfs; and third, a belated and generally futile effort to establish permanent colonies in order to hold the remote frontier province from external aggression.

Hispanic leaders valiantly struggled to overcome a sometimes hostile environment, usually suspicious and unfriendly natives, and ambitious foreign adventurers. Moreover, they had to cope with these problems poorly supplied, undermanned, and insufficiently financed because Spain had overextended herself trying to colonize both North and South America. In the end, brash American frontiersmen who appreciated the agricultural potential of the rich river bottoms of eastern Texas outnumbered native Hispanics and they soon imposed their own culture, traditions, and values. Taking advantage of a continuing civil war between opposing political factions in the new Mexican republic, Anglo-Texans and a few native republicans declared independence in 1836 and successfully severed ties with Mexico.

During the sixteenth century, Spain became a world power because of the riches discovered in her colonies, but European rivalries and ultimately the movement for colonial independence led to her decline. Spain bankrupted herself by allowing the minerals extracted in the Americas to trickle into the hands of her European neighbors in exchange for needed goods and by costly wars. Following the traditional mercantile theory of the times, Spain viewed her colonies solely as a source for exploitation while limiting trade to a favored few Spanish merchants and banning all foreign commerce. To control the collection of duties, goods could enter only at Vera Cruz, a policy that led to exorbitant prices as necessities traveled inland and north to the frontier.

Spanish leaders also were interested in spreading Christianity by the close of the sixteenth century. The colorful and poorly supervised conquistadores at first enslaved Indians at will to work in the mines or on plantations, but pressure from concerned churchmen resulted in laws requiring Spaniards to recognize that Indians had souls like their conquerors and deserved religious instruction. Between 1600 and 1800, missionaries led or accompanied expeditions to the frontier to Christianize the heathen. In addition to instructing their charges in religious matters, the versatile friars introduced Spanish techniques of herding, agriculture, weaving, and local government in order to change the Indians into productive docile settlers. In theory each mission would succeed in establishing a viable secular community within ten or twenty years, a goal seldom achieved in Texas, where the native population was migratory and often reluctant to accede to Spanish orders.

The Spanish introduced a patriarchal, orderly bureaucracy to administer colonial affairs. Commands from the king passed to his viceroy in Mexico, and from there the dicta systematically traveled to provincial capitals and on to frontier outposts. Likewise, standardized, regular reports returned along the same chains of command in parallel civil and military branches of government with a similar format active in church matters. Special inspectors investigated complaints and also reviewed the paperwork of officials at the conclusion of their appointments. Nothing was left to chance and almost nobody acted without orders from a superior.

Organized exploration reached Texas in the 1540s, and in spite of an inviting seacoast, the two entradas approached over land and then barely touched the eastern and western boundaries of modern Texas. Both expeditions were searching for rumored cities of gold. The journey of Francisco Vásquez de Coronado crossed the Texas Panhandle in 1541 and stemmed from an account of a supposed treasure city by Alvar Núñez Cabeza de Vaca. He was a member of a large expedition launched from Cuba in 1528 to explore and conquer western Florida. Instead of gold, all that they found was heat, humidity, mosquitoes, and hostile natives. Reduced to eating their horses, the gentlemen adventurers built clumsy rafts in order to drift along the coast to Vera Cruz. A hurricane reduced their number and fifteen survivors landing on Galveston Island were enslaved by the wandering Karankawa bands visiting the sand spit. After six years of captivity, De Vaca and three associates eluded their masters and slowly worked their way southwest by trading and performing faith cures among the tribes that they encountered. From them, the Spaniards heard tales of golden cities, stories that inspired avarice among Spaniards in the Mexican capital when the hardy four reached the city in 1536. The viceroy dispatched a small scouting expedition under the leadership of Esteban, a black former slave who had been with De Vaca, but hostile Indians near the Zuni villages in Arizona killed him. Father Marcos de Niza, however, returned with glowing tales of actually seeing a golden city from the distance, presumably one of the cliff dwellings bathed in sunlight.

Coronado set off for the north with 1,000 men and a suitable complement of horses, mules, cattle, sheep, camp followers, and a few priests, all financed by private investors including Coronado and the viceroy. And while they noted bison and the canyons of Arizona and Texas, the party failed to discover the legendary Quivira of the Indians, which the Spaniards supposed was one of the seven cities of Cibola. The natives, exhausted by the Spanish horde, continued to assure the Europeans that Quivira lay just beyond the next range or across the next mesa. Finally disillusioned and with no treasure to justify the huge expenditure, the conquistador returned to the capital in 1542.

About the same time that Coronado struggled across the high plains in Texas, his counterpart, Hernando de Soto, reached eastern Arkansas. He had landed in Florida with 600 men in 1536 and for two years had explored the lower south. De Soto died on the western bank of the Mississippi River, and leadership of the greatly reduced force devolved upon Luís de Moscoso. Discouraged by the events and the lack of treasure, the party traveled southwest hoping to reach Mexico City, but after visiting the Caddo Indians in northeastern Texas and noting oil seeps, the survivors returned to the Mississippi, where they built boats and successfully navigated to Vera Cruz. Their dismal report coupled with that of Coronado ended interest in the northern frontier for almost fifty years. Moreover, the era of the conquistador ended in 1543 when the crown forbade further personal expeditions that tended to exterminate the natives while searching for treasure. Henceforth, the extension of the frontier would be by miners, ranchers, missionaries, and settlers all protected by the king's troops.

The next 125 years witnessed missionary activity in western Texas and the upper Rio Grande combined with some exploration and the establishment of settlements. In 1598, Juan de Oñate planted missions and settlements in the vicinity of Santa Fe, and then like Coronado, he wandered around on the high plains without discovering anything of value. Missionaries and a few adventurers went as far as the upper Nueces and the Edwards Plateau in the 1600s while ministering to the Indians. These efforts resulted in the establishment of the oldest permanent settlement in modern Texas at Ysleta in 1681, but a similar undertaking on the San Saba River in 1683 for Apaches convinced the Spaniards that some of the wandering tribesmen were too fierce to convert. Mission activity in western Texas halted at this time because rumors that the French had invaded the coast absorbed the time and money of frontier commanders.

Missions in eastern Texas between the 1690s and the 1750s resulted from perceived threats of French occupation. The first of three separate intrusions occurred in 1685 when René Robert Cavelier, the Sieur de La Salle landed a party of French colonists on Garcitas Creek, a well-concealed tributary of the Lavaca River in upper Matagorda Bay. He had been seeking the mouth of the Mississippi for his colony, but somehow, perhaps intentionally, he had missed the great muddy delta and landed instead far to the west and clearly within Spanish territory. At this time, Spain claimed the entire gulf coast from Vera Cruz to Florida, but in 1682, La Salle had descended the Mississippi almost to its mouth thereby making that river and all of the lands drained by it and its tributaries French by the right of discovery. This expansive unilateral pronouncement claiming all of the land between the Rockies and the Appalachians was the basis for French Louisiana, and La Salle's brief occupation of Matagorda Bay added Texas to the claim according to some at the time of the Louisiana Purchase. The tiny French fortification in Texas suffered the usual frontier hardships and in 1687, La Salle started towards Canada with a handful of stout men to seek aid. He was murdered by one of his associates and the remainder continued the journey while Indians wiped out the little settlement.

Rumors about the presence of the French sparked ten unsuccessful Spanish expeditions by land and sea, and finally in 1689, Alonso de León, the governor of Coahuila, discovered the ruined French fort. De León had come with settlers intending to establish a colony along the coast as an indication of Spanish sovereignty, but adverse weather forced the party to return home. The expedition met a wandering band of Tejas Indians from eastern Texas who asked that a mission be established for them, and the following year, 1690, De León returned bringing with him Father Damian Massanet. The pair dedicated San Francisco de los Tejas on the Neches River in present Houston County, which with an additional mission, they hoped would form the nucleus for a permanent Spanish settlement. But disaster struck in the form of a flood and an epidemic and the superstitious Indians attributed the trouble to the new religion and became hostile. Discouraged and disheartened, the missionaries and soldiers abandoned eastern Texas in 1693. The authorities saw no purpose in trying to keep open missions so far away amidst unfriendly natives when there seemed to be no threat from foreign invasion. Such prudent thinking left eastern Texas without Spanish influence for twenty-three years until the appearance of a second French incursion.

In July 1714 a party of French traders arrived at the presidio and mission of San Juan Bautista on the Rio Grande asking to open trade as long as France and Spain were now at peace. The surprised commandant arrested Louis Juchereau de St. Denis and his associates and awaited instructions from his superiors. St. Denis, a French Canadian who had arrived in Louisiana in 1699 with Pierre Lemoyne d'Iberville, had become an important trader on the lower Red River; in 1713 the French governor asked him to undertake a double mission to the Spanish to request reopening the Spanish missions for the Tejas, and more importantly from the French point of view, open new markets. The French governor had received a letter from Father Francisco Hidalgo, one of the Franciscans who had been with Massanet in eastern Texas, expressing concern over the neglect of religious instruction for his former charges. What an opportune excuse for expanding French commercial activities!

While under house arrest on the Rio Grande waiting for the Spanish authorities to decide his fate, St. Denis won the heart of the commandant's granddaughter. Subsequent orders for him to be questioned in the capital resulted in St. Denis charming the viceroy who authorized an expedition to eastern Texas to reestablish the missions and made the Frenchman the official guide with equal rank and pay as the commander. Returning to San Juan Bautista, St. Denis married young Manuela Sánchez and early in 1716 led the Spanish expedition to the Tejas in company with his bride's uncle, Domingo Ramón, Father Hidalgo and eight priests, twenty-five soldiers, and thirty settlers plus their livestock. St. Denis marked the trail which became known as the Old Spanish Road between San Antonio and Nacogdoches, today's State Highway 21. The party reached the Neches in June and reconstructed San Francisco with a presidio nearby. St. Denis and Father Hidalgo continued eastward and established four more missions in the vicinity of modern Nacogdoches and San Augustine. Crossing the Sabine into territory considered part of Texas, the pair placed another mission at the Adaes village about fifteen miles southwest of St. Denis's trading post at Natchitoches. In this manner St. Denis and the Franciscan friar complied with the wishes of the French governor by creating a Spanish market for French goods in eastern Texas. While Spanish authorities never gave official approval for trade with the French, geography was on the side of French traders because of the great distance from the Rio Grande, the closest Spanish outpost.

To alleviate the problems of supplying the eastern missions, the Spanish decided to establish a depot on the San Antonio River. In May 1718, Martín de Alarcón, the governor of Coahuila, and Father Antonio de San Buenaventura Olivares dedicated the mission San Antonio de Valero, later called the Alamo, and the nearby presidio of San Antonio de Bexar. Alarcón visited eastern Texas in the fall with a supply train but learned that the Indians seemed more interested in receiving presents than religious instruction. In general, the Tejas and their cousins in the Hasinai confederacy rejected efforts to reduce them to mission life. The final blow came in 1719 when a small party of French attacked Los Adaes, having learned that the war between France and Spain had resumed. The Spaniards fled west to another mission where hysteria mounted causing all to rush to the tiny presidio on the Neches. Fearful of another French attack, the entire Spanish contingent retreated in panic to Bexar. The French failed to move into eastern Texas except to trade, and smoldering Spanish anger demanded a quick return to occupy the frontier.

The Marqués de San Miguel de Aguayo led the third and most successful attempt to occupy eastern Texas in 1721. Prominent and wealthy, Aguayo financed the entire expedition and in return the viceroy made him governor and captain-general of a combined Coahuila and Texas. He recruited five hundred men, acquired perhaps five thousand head of livestock, and secured other necessary supplies for a permanent establishment on the frontier. His was a grand plan and the first step was to place a presidio and a mission, both called La Bahia, near the site of La Salle's old fort to defend the middle coast. In Bexar, he discovered that the former East Texas missionaries had already completed a new mission that he had authorized below the village and had named it San José y San Miguel de Aguayo in his honor. The new governor continued his eastward journey to the Neches, where the Indians seemed genuinely glad to see the Spaniards again. Finding no French in the area, Aguayo reestablished the former presidio and the six missions and then turned his attention to fortifying Los Adaes, which had been chosen for the provincial capital. There within a day's march of the French outpost at Natchitoches, Aguayo built a strong fort guarded by six cannon and one hundred men.

A visit to St. Denis revealed that France and Spain were friends again and the determined Marqués extracted a promise from the French trader that he would not conduct business in Spanish territory. Leaving eastern Texas secure, Aguayo returned to Bexar, where he remodeled the presidio making it of adobe and stone instead of wood. At La Bahia he began a permanent octagon-shaped fort with bastions, a tower, a moat and garrisoned it with ninety men. Aguayo's accomplishments were laudatory: four presidios at strategic entries to Texas and nine missions. Now he asked the crown to provide colonists from Cuba or the Canary Islands and to underwrite the initial expenses. Unfortunately this able man was forced by ill health to resign in 1722.

The authorities responded slowly to the request for Spanish colonists, but finally in 1730 they provided funds for one hundred families from the Canary Islands. Only one-fourth of that number were sent when the order was canceled, and of those twenty-five, only ten families reached Vera Cruz, the starting point for the long overland journey to Bexar. Some of the young people married along the way increasing the families to fifteen and included fifty-six persons when they reached Bexar in 1731. One of their first steps was to form a village named San Fernando de Bexar and to divide the land into town lots and farming tracts in the horseshoe bend in the river. Unwilling to mingle with the Indians at the nearby Alamo, the Canary Islanders erected their own parish church and eventually welcomed soldiers from the presidio as husbands for their daughters.

Even as the first civilian colony was being established at Bexar, economic difficulties forced closing three of the east Texas missions. Reorganizing below Bexar near San José, the former eastern missions became San Juan Capistrano, San Francisco de la Espada, and Nuestra Señora de la Purísima Concepción de Acuna. Although weakening the frontier, the transfer made the San Antonio neighborhood the most successful mission field in Texas. About this same time, the unfavorable climate along the coast forced the La Bahia complex to move up the Guadalupe River, and finally in 1749, the mission and presidio both moved to the lower San Antonio River.

The middle of the eighteenth century witnessed a revival of interest in missions and colonies on the southern and western fringe of modern Texas. The most successful were those established by José de Escandón along the Rio Grande and south along the coast of Tamaulipas. Within a seven-year period, between 1748 and 1755, about 2,500 people settled in twenty-three towns and fifteen missions. The former army officer became the first governor of the new province of Nuevo Santander, which touched Texas' southern border along the Nueces River. While only Laredo and Dolores were established on land now part of Texas, the northern bank of the Rio Grande was lined with ranches.

A second effort organized presidios and missions for the Tonkawas and Lipan Apaches on the San Gabriel River in Milam County and on the San Saba, near Menard, plus the upper Nueces. But attacks from the fierce Comanches, traditional enemies of the other tribe, forced the effort to be abandoned in 1771. Christianization among the nomadic plains Indians was a dismal failure.

A third missionary effort at mid-century resulted from the appearance of French traders for a third time in Texas. This incursion took place on the lower Trinity River among the Orcoquisas, a subtribe of the coastal Attakapas. Joseph de Blancpain, a well-established Louisiana trader, organized a trading post near the mouth of the Trinity in 1754. Almost immediately a Spanish patrol arrested him and his associates and distributed their goods to the loyal Indians who had betrayed their presence to the Spanish. Following the traditional practice, the authorities organized a mission on the site of the trading post and placed a presidio nearby to guard against

*Priest, soldiers and Indians arriving at El Paso del Norte to establish the first towns of Texas and New Mexico.*

— Institute of Texan Cultures
Drawing by Jose Cisneros from
Cleofas Calleros Estate

French intruders entering Texas by Galveston Bay or along the road from Opelousas that skirted present-day Beaumont and Liberty. Like their counterparts on the plains and eastern Texas, the Orcoquisas refused to enter mission life and plans to establish a civilian colony fared no better. A hurricane in 1767 hastened the end of El Orcoquisac, but the transfer of Louisiana from France to Spain in 1763 at the close of the French and Indian Wars ended efforts to occupy eastern Texas. Although not immediately implemented, the treaty moved Spain's eastern boundary from the Red River to the wide Mississippi. Texas was no longer a frontier province.

The 1760s introduced a period of reform initiated by the Spanish Bourbon king, Carlos III, designed to make his failing empire more efficient. A special investigator, the Marqués de Rubí, traveled across Texas in 1767 to evaluate the usefulness of the missions and presidios. He found no Indian converts at any of the missions except those at Bexar and La Bahia, and because most local Indians appeared docile although uninterested in mission life, he recommended closing the missions and presidios east of San Antonio as an economy measure. In 1772 the missionaries, soldiers, and civilians between Los Adaes and the San Antonio River were ordered to move to Bexar, and the following year, the evacuation of the provincial capital from Los Adaes to San Antonio was accomplished.

Many of the settlers objected to the transfer and immediately made plans for their return to eastern Texas. They finally received permission to return as far east as the Trinity in 1774, but the little town of Bucarelli lasted only until 1779, when under the leadership of Antonio Gil Ybarbo, they moved to the old mission site at Nacogdoches. The Texas governor in San Antonio reluctantly accepted the de facto establishment at Nacogdoches, well understanding that these people, many of them former Indian traders, would engage in illicit trade with Louisiana. Although both Texas and Louisiana were Spanish, trade between the two was forbidden because each was governed separately—one from Mexico City and the other from Havana.

Other reforms included a change in the Indian policy and the creation of Provincias Internas, an interim bureaucracy between the viceroy and the provincial governors with both civil and military powers. Based on Rubí's observations and those of other reformers, Spain would henceforth court the Comanches as a means to diminish the power of their traditional enemies, the southwestern Apaches, who were menacing Spanish settlements. Instead of the old mission-presidio system, the Spanish intended to adopt a modified version of the Louisiana French licensed traders who lived in certain villages and monitored the Indians as well as supplying their needs. Understanding that the sudden change from French to Spanish allegiance for the tribes along the upper Red River posed difficulties, the Spanish employed influential French traders such as the son and son-in-law of St. Denis to implement the new plan to seek alliances with the norteños, the name given to the plains Indians living along the upper Red. Not all Spanish officials in Texas approved of the innovation, and it required the influence of the new commandant general of the interior provinces to secure an uneasy truce between the Comanches and Apaches in 1780. But with a few exceptions, the peace lasted for the next decades in the San Antonio neighborhood.

Twenty years after the administrative and economic reforms began, the missions were secularized in San Antonio and the churches turned over to diocesan priests who took charge of the parishes. Some of the lands were distributed for the former mission Indians' use, but much of the cultivated land eventually found its way into private hands of prominent families. Three missions remained near La Bahia, including the one opened in 1793 at Refugio, where Franciscan efforts to educate the primitive coastal tribes continued. There were a few widely scattered missions and presidios along the Rio Grande, but these were not a part of Texas until after 1848. Overall, missions had proved expensive to maintain and had accomplished little in Texas towards Christianizing the native population. At best, one hundred years of effort had produced a few converts and a couple of small communities.

Tightening control over the frontier and abolishing ineffective missions did little to solve the main problem in Spanish Texas—underpopulation. At the close of the eighteenth century there were three settlements: San Antonio de Bexar, the provincial capital; La Bahia, about 100 miles to the southeast; and Nacogdoches, over 300 miles to the northeast. One well-traveled trace connected the three villages, but the road was devoid of any habitations. A network of lesser trails provided alternative routes for smugglers and others who wanted to avoid official scrutiny, and the still illegal trade with Louisiana continued to provide commodities for many in exchange for horses and cattle. Except for a small detachment from the presidio at La Bahia, there was no defense for the long Texas coastline with its many inviting bays and rivers. Efforts to recruit Spanish colonists to settle in Texas proved futile, while the unpredictable plains Indians threatened the settlements at will. Including Indians, there were about 5,000 people scattered over Texas in 1800.

International events introduced new dangers to Spanish hegemony in Louisiana and Texas. Anglo-American tories fled the eastern seaboard and settled near Natchez early in the war, and after 1778, when Spain joined France in supporting the colonial rebellion, a number of Anglo frontiersmen joined the ranks of the Spanish army at New Orleans and Pensacola. The treaty ending the war in 1783 awarded Florida to Spain, but the northern boundary remained unclear and adventuresome Anglo-Americans wanted to pass through Spanish territory to deliver their produce in New Orleans by way of the Mississippi River. By the 1790s there were a number of Anglo-Americans living in Louisiana, and while some applied for citizenship and became ranchers, others engaged in the Indian trade in Texas.

The sudden secret retrocession of Louisiana to France and the subsequent sale of the territory to the United States in 1803 surprised Spanish officials in Texas. Once again, Texas was an international frontier and the aggressive, often unruly Anglos appeared a threat to Spanish control. While the traditional western boundary had been the Red River, some Anglo-Americans now insisted that the Louisiana Purchase included eastern Texas perhaps as far west as the Guadalupe or Colorado rivers because of La Salle's early occupation. The matter remained a diplomatic game of chess until 1819, when a compromise set the Sabine and awarded Spanish Florida to the United States.

During the long period of negotiation, Spanish Texas suffered a series of invasions by foreigners. Upon learning about the transfer at the close of 1803, Spanish authorities sent a detachment of troops to Nacogdoches and Los Adaes (only fifteen miles west of a United States army post at Natchitoches) to defend the border. A flurry of confrontations soon convinced local military leaders in Texas and Louisiana that unnecessary bloodshed could be avoided only by declaring a neutral strip between the two contenders. Thus the Spanish withdrew from Los Adaes and both sides agreed that their respective troops would not enter an area between the Sabine on the west and the Arroyo Hondo, a dry creek bed west of Los Adaes on the east. South of the Arroyo Hondo, the neutral ground line followed the west bank of the Calcasieu River to the Gulf of Mexico. The Neutral Ground Agreement, signed in 1806 by the frontier commanders, was a surprise to their superiors, but the sensible pact remained in force though unofficial until replaced by the Treaty of 1819. The only difficulty with the de facto arrangement was that it created a haven for renegades, and respectable travelers between Natchitoches and Nacogdoches had to organize caravans in order to pass through safely.

Between 1804 and 1810, Spain tried to solicit settlers for southeastern Texas, but few native-born Mexicans wanted to live on the remote frontier. A number of offers to colonize the lower Trinity came from former Spanish subjects in Louisiana who claimed that they were not content under United States rule. But a brief experiment of allowing such settlers into Texas convinced the authorities that those who requested the privilege were more interested in smuggling than in colonizing. Thus Sabine Lake and the Sabine and Neches rivers remained unguarded and unsettled as did Galveston Bay with its convenient waterways — the Trinity, San Jacinto, and Buffalo Bayou.

The *Grito de Dolores* on September 16, 1810, signaling the commencement of the Mexican independence movement, ended Spain's ability to defend its eastern frontier even as inadequately as had been done since 1804. Concentrating money, men, and equipment in central Mexico to repel republican revolutionaries, Spain neglected frustrated frontier commanders, who continually pleaded for shoes, horses, arms, and ammunition in order to mount forays against both hostile Indians and foreign invaders.

Cautious and essentially conservative, Texas settlements avoided making any commitments regarding independence until 1811, when San Antonio was held by revolutionaries for three months. In January, Juan Bautista de Las Casas, an officer of the garrison, staged a rebellion and seized royalists headquarters by arresting both the military commandant and the governor. He proclaimed himself the supreme executive in the state and successfully captured both La Bahia and Nacogdoches. A counter-revolution organized by loyal residents of Bexar, including Juan Manuel Zambrano, Juan Martín de Veramendi, Erasmo Sequin, and Francisco Ruíz, seized Las Casas and restored the royal governor; Zambrano, noted for his aggressive behavior, was given a commission in the army and soon cleared Texas of revolutionaries, even extending his activities into the Neutral Ground. Within two years, Veramendi, Seguin, and Ruíz changed sides and supported the revolutionary expedition under Bernardo Gutiérrez de Lara.

Texas remained quiet for almost a year until the first filibustering expedition captured Nacogdoches in August 1812. Led by Gutiérrez de Lara, a resident of the Rio Grande and an ardent republican, and his American associate, Lieutenant Augustus W. Magee, a graduate of West Point stationed at Natchitoches, the party consisted of 130 men but gradually increased to 700 by September. The army, composed of both native Mexican and Anglos, was divided between idealists who wanted to expel the Spaniards from Texas in order to help the Mexican republicans and adventurers who hoped to sever Texas in order to annex it to the United States. Easily securing eastern Texas, the party marched to La Bahia, which they took on November 7, but a royalist siege prevented the army from reaching Bexar until March. Magee died and leadership of the Anglo contingent passed to Samuel Kemper; the American members of the expedition were horrified by a massacre of royalist prisoners committed by their Mexican colleagues in the name of revenge, and many departed for home. Gutiérrez formed a junta and declared Texas independent of Spain, but a royalist attack in August sent survivors of the engagement in flight to Natchitoches, including Veramendi, Seguin, and Ruíz.

Refugee republicans in Louisiana regrouped for another attack on Spanish Texas, but were delayed when most of them joined General Andrew Jackson to help the Americans defeat the British at New Orleans in January 1815. By fall, Henry Perry, one of the American leaders who had fled in 1813, led volunteers to Galveston Bay, which he intended to use for a staging area for an attack against La Bahia. The party wintered near the mouth of the Trinity, where they received supplies and recruits from Louisiana. Early in 1816 Perry and his men joined a larger expedition that had arrived on Galveston Island.

Luís de Aury, a French privateer and a former associate of Simón Bolívar in Venezuela, arrived on the island carrying a dual commission issued by the Mexican republican government in exile in New Orleans as governor of Texas and commodore of an invasion fleet to attack La Bahia. He immediately organized a government, including a court to adjudicate prizes brought in by his corsairs. Aury also named the peninsula northeast of the island for his friend, Bolívar, the liberator of Venezuela. His proposed expedition faltered within a few months because of insufficient supplies and a mutiny among disgruntled crew members displeased with routine salvage duties.

The timely arrival of a new charismatic leader, Francisco Xavier Mina, saved the expedition although the former Spanish guerrilla had slightly different goals. A veteran opponent of the French occupation of his homeland, Mina had been disappointed by the return of the conservative Spanish monarch and had to flee because of his republican ideas. In the spirit of revenge, Mina intended to strip Spain of its new world colonies, and he had recruited an outstanding army of international soldiers of fortune. Outnumbered, Aury agreed to ferry Mina to Sota la Marina midway between the Rio Grande and Tampico, where the Spaniard expected to join rebel guerrillas. The expedition left Galveston in April 1817, and Mina quickly captured the royalist fort at Sota la Marina but soon suffered defeat when the royalists killed Mina and scattered the survivors.

Galveston Island, however, did not remain vacant. Even as the Mina expedition left, Jean Laffite and his followers moved in to make the island headquarters for privateering against Spanish ships. He, too, held a commission from the republican government in exile, and like Aury, Laffite organized a local government on the island although he did not assume the governorship of Texas. While his corsairs captured some specie and commodities, the main contraband was blacks taken from Spanish slavers. Laffite sold slaves from the island, and he also delivered them to Louisiana agents by way of the Sabine and Calcasieu rivers.

While Laffite occupied the island, a quixotic band of Napoleonic refugees arrived in 1818 with a bizarre plan to release Napoleon from St. Helena in the south Atlantic and to place his brother, Joseph, then in New York, on a Mexican throne. Posing as simple agriculturists, General Charles Lallemand and some 120 men and women made their way up the bay to the Trinity River with the help of Laffite. They were unaware that he was a Spanish informer in addition to his privateering interests. The French officers constructed a remarkable fortress on a bluff a few miles up the river while the Spanish governor in Bexar struggled to equip a retaliatory force. In July 1818 even before the Spanish could mount an attack, the heat, mosquitoes, and the lack of supplies defeated the former Napoleonic officers, and with the aid of the ever-genial Laffite, most returned to New Orleans.

The Spanish expeditionary force arrived on the Trinity in October to order all intruders—the French, any Anglos, and the illegal islanders—out of Texas. The French, of course, had already left, and the few illegal Anglo squatters agreed to move, but the pirate community remained out of reach of the poorly equipped Spanish army. The scouting party had scarcely returned to San Antonio when another filibustering expedition entered Nacogdoches.

Dr. James Long, a veteran of the Battle of New Orleans, led a movement to liberate Texas financed by Natchez merchants who believed that the recent treaty setting the Sabine as the boundary had "given Texas away" in order to secure Florida. Long and about 120 men occupied Nacogdoches in June 1819, and soon their number more than doubled. The party made no pretense to be aiding the Mexican revolutionaries, but instead, declared Texas independent and organized a provisional government with Long as president. Long journeyed to Galveston to invite Laffite to join the movement and serve as admiral, but the wily privateer remained noncommittal while at the same time informing his Spanish contacts. The Texas governor in Bexar massed 500 troops in September to drive the Anglos back across the Sabine, and Long and his wife, Jane, who had joined him, barely escaped capture. Having previously declared Galveston a port of entry, the refugees agreed to reassemble on Bolivar Peninsula in April 1820. The project discovered new difficulties in securing financial support because the United States government frowned on such an obvious violation of the 1794 Neutrality Law at a time when the diplomats were seeking Spain's ratification of the boundary treaty.

A few merchants, however, remained interested in aiding the Mexican revolutionaries who promised to open trade with the United States whenever they gained control of Mexico. Bowing to such consideration, Long resigned his presidency and leadership of the undertaking passed to José Félix Trespalacios, a Cuban-born insurgent, and Gutiérrez de Lara. The volunteers on Bolivar erected a fort from driftwood and named it Fort Las Casas for the 1811 martyr in Bexar. The Longs arrived just in time for a last dinner with Laffite who was leaving the island at the request of the United States government. By May 1820 the privateer village was destroyed, and the embarrassing presence of Spain's enemy so close to the United States was removed.

The last filibustering expedition into Texas remained on the peninsula restless and inactive while the rival leaders struggled to find money and supplies. Events in the south moved to a successful conclusion in early 1821, when Agustin Iturbide, a native-born royal officer, defected and forged an alliance with the insurgents against whom he had been fighting. The resulting Plan de Iguala united native Mexicans of all classes and political beliefs against the Spaniards in a drive to expel the Europeans from Mexico. The final struggle continued through the summer and conflicting rumors reached New Orleans and Bolivar Peninsula. In August Trespalacios left for Mexico City to aid the movement and assure himself of a place in the new regime, and in September Long and fifty-two men sailed for La Bahia to determine if the garrison there had declared for independence. If it had not, he intended to capture it and Bexar. He left Jane seven-months pregnant on the peninsula guarded by a detachment and some friends. All soon departed begging Jane to accompany them, but she remained steadfast in her promise to wait for her husband's return. In late December, aided only by a teenage servant girl, Jane delivered herself of her third child. Passing ships paused to ask her to leave with them, but Jane stoically remained on Bolivar until the summer of 1822.

Long, unfortunately, misjudged the Spanish authorities at La

Bahia and Bexar who had adopted the Plan of Iguala and viewed his arrival with armed men as a party of foreign filibusters bent on severing Texas from the new Mexican republic. Long and his followers were arrested and sent overland to Mexico City; there, on parole, a guard accidentally shot and killed Long although his friends believed it was an assassination arranged by Trespalacios, recently named governor of Texas under the new regime.

The coalition of liberal republicans and conservative monarchists struggled to create a suitable government for Mexico. Despite an interruption by a year-long empire under Iturbide, Mexican leaders hammered out a constitution for a republic in 1824. Outwardly it resembled the government of the United States with an elected president and a bicameral congress, but the fundamental law lacked a Bill of Rights or the checks and balances that allowed a government responsive to the will of the people. The leadership divided between conservative Centralists, who wanted a strong central government and weak states, not unlike a monarchy, and liberal Federalists, who believed that states' rights should prevail with a limited central government. Churchmen, large planters, and the army (which had more generals and colonels than enlisted men) preferred the Centralist party, while middle-class reformers and small landholders, particularly those in the northern states, aligned themselves with the republican Federalist faction. Under such a volatile arrangement, it is not surprising that only the first elected president served his allotted four-year term, and that for the next fifty years, a series of military coups and revolutions kept Mexican politics in turmoil.

At the state level similar conditions existed, and it was 1827 before a constitution for the combined states of Coahuila and Texas was adopted. Both lacked sufficient population to stand alone, so the national government joined the two dissimilar states and made Saltillo the capital. The state legislature composed of ten members from arid, ranching Coahuila and the lone Texas representative could agree on little, especially when Texas' population became increasingly Anglo-American. The immigrants naively believed that all republics must resemble that of the United States and thus had difficulty in understanding the unfamiliar judicial system that lacked trial by jury, indictments, or bail, as well as the absence of the right to assemble or express opinions. Of major concern for many Anglo-Texans was Mexican antipathy toward slavery; reflecting the idealism of the Rights of Man, Mexican leaders, both at the national and state levels, wanted to forbid slavery although they condoned a system of debt peonage that differed but little. Nevertheless, the pressing need for slave labor to develop cotton culture in Texas, and thereby improve the overall Mexican economy, temporarily overcame idealism and slaveholders were allowed to bring their blacks into Texas under a variety of strategems, including lifetime indenture contracts.

This basic misunderstanding of each other's culture led to disrespect on the part of the Anglos and suspicion on the side of the Mexican hosts. Inheriting the values and culture of their Spanish predecessors, the Mexicans became increasingly paranoid about the intent of the Americans in regard to Texas. United States efforts to buy the eastern portion of the state in the 1820s increased Mexican anxiety over Anglo immigration. At the same time, the continuing lack of land titles for Anglos living outside of Stephen F. Austin's colonies revived and increased sentiment to reject Mexican hospitality and seek annexation to the United States.

The empresario system, intended to hasten the development of Texas, was both a boon and a detriment. The state contracted with an individual who promised to introduce a stated number of sober, industrious, Roman Catholic families into an assigned area within a six-year period, and in return, the empresario would receive 23,000 acres of land for every 100 families. Each family could receive a minimum of one league (4,428 acres) and one *labor* (177 acres) of grazing and farming land upon the payment of about $60 in fees to the state and its officials or about a penny an acre. Austin, Green DeWitt, and Fernando DeLeon (a descendant of the founder of the eastern missions) all complied immediately with the terms of their contracts, but other empresarios regarded their grants as speculations or encountered overwhelming difficulties in securing suitable settlers. This default left certain promised tracts vacant, and a few contracts were reissued to other empresarios. Several of the original grants were only partially filled such as the Irish settlements of John McMullen, James McGloin, James Power, and James Hewetson. In 1830, Sterling Clack Robertson endeavored to rescue a portion of the Nashville investors' contract by bringing in settlers at a time when the government decided to abrogate incomplete contracts.

The great bargain in land attracted many residents of the United States impoverished by the Panic of 1819. Even Protestant families willingly agreed to become Roman Catholic citizens of Mexico in order to acquire such a vast estate at such low prices. The United States land offices sold vacant tracts for $1.25 per acre, but the minimum parcel was 80 acres which cost $100 in specie, a sum well above what most small farmers could pay. In 1822, Austin began advertising land in his colony at 12½ cents per acre, one-tenth the cost of vacant land in the United States, and many started overland after chalking "GTT" (Gone to Texas) on their doors before disappearing with their movable property. Sheriffs who missed arresting these fleeing debtors were out of luck because the United States had no agreement for extradition or for collecting debts in Mexico. Austin's first terms, arranged before the colonization laws were even written, had to be changed to the lower state figure, a severe blow to his goal to recover his family's fortune through the empresario system. Austin ultimately received over 108,000 acres in premium land, but finding buyers at 50 cents per acre proved difficult during the colonial period when each family could receive 4,605 acres for a penny an acre.

The first real trouble between the Anglo immigrants and the Mexican authorities occurred in 1826-27 in the Nacogdoches area and was known as the Fredonia Rebellion. Haden Edwards, a former resident of Mississippi, had received an empresario contract to settle eight hundred families in an area from north of Nacogdoches almost to the coast except for the border reserves — the fifty-two miles west of the Sabine and twenty-six miles inland from the coast — which was forbidden to former residents from the United States. Already the Mexican government feared encroachment by aggressive Anglos, who settled, complained of injustice and revolted, and then sought annexation to the United States as had happened in Baton Rouge and the Mobile neighborhoods earlier. Edwards demanded proof of ownership from residents within his grant, but most of the earliest settlers lacked titles and the Nacogdoches archives had been scattered and destroyed during the various attacks on the village. Edwards also became involved in local politics by forcing his son-in-law upon the residents as alcalde in a contested election with an old resident. Not all of the Anglo residents agreed with Edwards and his brother when the pair declared the Republic of Fredonia in December 1826 and occupied an old stone trading post in the center of town. Their red and white flag symbolized union with local Cherokees who were unhappy that they had failed to receive title to lands west of Nacogdoches, but the Indians soon quit the tenuous agreement, becoming disgusted with the unruly and often drunken behavior of the Edwards supporters.

The jefe político, a sort of subgovernor for Texas, in San Antonio called out the militia from Austin's colony and that of the Atascosito community on the lower Trinity to accompany the regular troops from Bexar who marched toward Nacogdoches in January. By the time they arrived, however, loyal Anglo citizens had recruited supportive local Indians and had routed the Edwards and their followers, who precipitously fled toward the Sabine. The au-

*Spanish soldiers in East Texas, around 1780.*
— U.T. Institute of Texan Cultures

*Antonio Gil Ybarvo (left) and settlers from Bucareli arriving at the abandoned mission of Nacogdoches, 1779.*
— Institute of Texan Cultures
Watercolor by Lynn McConnell

thorities had already abrogated Edwards' contract, and in early 1827 they ordered a permanent military garrison for Nacogdoches to oversee local politics and to suppress smuggling and guard the main road from the United States. The Fredonia incident served to increase Mexican suspicion concerning the intent of Anglo Americans, and at the same time, caused concern among the Anglo community over the ease with which the government withdrew Edwards' contract.

A second event that added to the Anglo's uneasiness about the security of contract, a basic American doctrine, occurred in 1829 when the second president emancipated all slaves in the republic. Persuaded by those who wanted to discourage Anglo-American immigration, the president issued an executive proclamation as a commemorative gesture on September 16, Independence Day. Austin's friends in government moved quickly to have the order amended to except the colonies in Texas from the order which would have doomed the nascent cotton cultures. As slavery existed only in Texas, eliminating the Anglo-American settlements from the order made it moot, but Texas residents and potential immigrants worried that their expensive investment in black labor was subject to the whim of politicians.

Immigrants from the United States continued to arrive and by 1830 the Mexican government took steps to limit the number of Anglo-Americans in Texas fearing that control of the area was in danger. An inspection tour the previous year indicated that Anglos greatly outnumbered native Mexicans, and furthermore, the Anglos were not being assimilated as the government had hoped. Instead, the Anglo residents continued to speak English, observe their native customs and traditions, and even improvise on the Mexican legal system by incorporating Americanisms. The Law of April 6, 1830, forbidding further Anglo immigration into "incomplete" colonies and barring the introduction of slaves under the pretext of indenture contracts shocked the Anglo-Texans. This abrogation of empresario contracts was what they had feared, but Austin secured an exemption for his and DeWitt's colonies on the grounds that they were not "incomplete," as both men had been awarded premium land for introducing families, and therefore, more immigrants could enter until the maximum stated in their contracts was reached. Fortunately for the Anglos, the government allowed this interpretation to stand although it contradicted the intent of the law.

The promulgation of the Law of April 6 coincided with the termination of exemption from Mexican duties enjoyed by the colonists under a special order. The Mexican federal and state governments both depended entirely upon revenue from the collection of customs and tonnage duties and various licensing fees because there was no tax on income or land. Thus, the support for bureaucrats and the army came from collection of tariffs and fees, and it was only natural that both groups assiduously aided in the enforcement of those laws. Americans, on the other hand, traditionally opposed levying customs duties and they viewed most fees a form of graft that supported undemocratic monopolies and special privileges. And so the stage was set for confrontation between Anglo-Texans imbued with traditions of democracy and the protections of the American system of justice and the Mexican Republic which derived its governmental patterns from the Roman Empire.

The first clash came at Anahuac, a new town and garrison established by the national government to enforce the federal Law of April 6, 1830. The cause was complex but rested on a familiar concept: which took precedence, federal or state law? The issues involved granting titles to those squatters in eastern Texas outside of Austin's colony, the ability of the military to interfere in perceived individual and state rights, and the collection of customs duties.

The national government sent Colonel Juan Davis Bradburn to build and command the garrison at Anahuac in 1830. As a native of Virginia and former resident of Kentucky who knew many of the Texans, he seemed the perfect commandant for the Anglo portion of Texas. Moreover, he was respected by many highranking officials in both the civil and military branches of the nation. Once a liberal republican revolutionary who had accompanied the Mina expedition, Bradburn had moved towards the conservative Centralist faction during the 1820s as had many native Mexicans. Thus he was a strong supporter of the repressive centralist administration of Anastasio Bustamante which had gained supremacy in 1830. Although the national government was temporarily in the hands of the Centralist faction, that of the state of Coahuila-Texas tended to favor the Federalists.

The first encounter at Anahuac was between Bradburn, the enforcer of national laws and a Centralist, and the state-appointed land commissioner, José Francisco Madero, a strong Federalist. Madero arrived on the Trinity in January 1831 to issue the long-awaited titles to residents. Both the national and state governments had approved a petition for titles from the settlers in 1828. But according to Bradburn's interpretation, the Law of April 6, 1830, abrogated the right of the state to allow Anglos to settle, a narrow view that failed to recognize that many squatters had been there since before 1824. Bradburn arrested Madero, and the superiors of both men had to wrestle with the basic issue of whether the state or nation was supreme. Finally a compromise was reached that freed Madero to complete his immediate task before his removal. Madero quickly issued sixty-two titles, and before he left in May, he established an ayuntamiento (town council) at the Atascosito crossing of the Trinity and called it Liberty. Located about thirty miles up river from Anahuac, this new civil government was an affront to Bradburn's federal authority.

Commandant General Manuel Mier y Terán, Bradburn's superior, arrived in November 1831 and ordered the removal of the ayuntamiento from Liberty to Anahuac, where the military could supervise its activities. Mier y Terán also was disturbed by the number of Anglo-American lawyers practicing at Liberty without Mexican licenses and with little understanding of Mexican law. Henceforth Bradburn would inspect their credentials. One of the offenders was William Barret Travis, a hot-tempered twenty-five-year-old who had recently arrived from Alabama. Travis represented a Louisiana slaveholder who was trying to recover several runaway slaves to whom Bradburn had granted asylum and had incorporated into his garrison. Mier y Terán ruled that neither he nor Bradburn had jurisdiction in the matter which could only be settled through Washington and Mexico City. Travis, however, decided to secure the blacks' release by ruse. To add to the tension, local residents had organized a vigilante group, clearly illegal under Mexican law, to intimidate certain members of the garrison who allegedly had committed crimes in the village but went unpunished. Bradburn arrested Travis and ten to fifteen others on charges of sedition committed on federal property (the fort and town), an act within his powers and entirely legal under law. The Anglo community, however, accustomed to limitations on the powers of the military and the traditional rights of trial by jury, bail, and warrants, refused to accept Bradburn's actions and labeled him an arbitrary despot who arrested civilians without cause.

While this was taking place, the federal customs collector, George Fisher, a former Hungarian soldier of fortune and a citizen of both the United States and Mexico, added to the turmoil. Acting on Mier y Terán's instructions, Fisher ordered all ship captains trading in the Brazos River to clear their papers at Anahuac, a distance of seventy miles by land and an inconvenient similar journey by water. He neglected to explain that this was a temporary order until the arrival of a deputy collector destined for the Brazos. Already angry over the collection of the tariff which many believed illegal, erroneously supposing that the temporary six-year exemption was permanent, Fisher's order caused violent objections. Not only did the populace hold protest meetings (illegal because there was no right to assemble), but exiting vessels fired on troops stationed at the mouth of the Brazos causing bloodshed.

Finally in June 1832 irate Anglo-Texans marched against Anahuac. While Fisher fled, Bradburn and perhaps one hundred troops faced over 130 insurgents. After some skirmishing that resulted in a few killed on both sides, the matter was settled when the ranking commander arrived from Nacogdoches. Because he feared a general Anglo uprising and knowing that government troops were badly outnumbered, he agreed to the demands of the rebels: Bradburn's removal and the release of Travis and the others. In the interim, the insurgents had learned that the Federalist faction had regained control of the national government, and they sensibly aligned themselves with the Federalist cause. In the Turtle Bayou Resolutions adopted on June 13, 1832, they explained that they were not opposing the Mexican government—only the despotic centralist commander, and that the encounter at Anahuac (and a subsequent battle at Velasco at the mouth of the Brazos) was an effort to aid the Federalists in their struggle against Centralism. The new regime accepted this somewhat ingenuous explanation and shortly afterwards, ordered the withdrawal of all Centralist troops from Texas.

Hispanic influence in Texas ended in 1832. The effort to Mexicanize the frontier state by the Law of April 6, 1830, failed dismally: too little too late. Without the presence of troops in Texas and under the erroneous assumption that the Federalist administration would react favorably, the Texans met in conventions (illegal, of course, under Mexican law) in 1832 and 1833 to discuss grievances against the national government. One of the main issues was separate statehood for Texas, a request never granted by the federal authorities. The more moderate administration, however, responded favorably to some of the requests such as revoking the ban on foreign immigration, granting a short-term exemption from tariff collection, and allowing the use of English in conducting some official business.

But the internal struggle between Centralism and Federalism continued in the capital casting a pall over the Texans. While the Federalist faction flourished on the northern frontier, the national government again moved toward Centralism when President Antonio López de Santa Anna reversed his earlier course and began concentrating power in the hands of the executive. Beginning in 1835, he systematically reduced state power and even abolished state governments, making them mere departments of the national government with appointed officials. When the President started north at the head of his army to squash Federalist resistance in Zacatecas and Coahuila, Texans realized that they were next. A Federalist rally failed in December 1835 and the Anglos in Texas joined a few native republicans in declaring Texas independent of the oppressive regime the following spring.

So after 317 years since its discovery, Texas was no longer under the control of Spaniards or their descendants. While the Spanish heritage has always been recognized, Texans have been somewhat slow in appreciating the importance of Hispanic contributions, dwelling instead on the more exciting events of the Texas Revolution.

*Stephen F. Austin and Felipe Enrique Neri issuing deeds at San Felipe de Austin.*

— Mural formerly in Southern Pacific Railroad Station, Houston, Texas

# 3

## Lone Star on the Rise

*Archie P. McDonald*

The successful movement for the independence of Texas from Mexico began long before the first public meeting of protest or the first shot was fired in anger. It came along as a part of the cultural baggage of Anglo-American immigrants, and was rooted as far back in their history as the Magna Carta, the first tangible recognition that there were limits to the prerogatives of government. It blossomed during the European development of nationalism and Protestantism, crossed the Atlantic in the hearts of those who yearned for opportunity and escape from the still restrictive societies of the old world, and came to full development in the decade of the American Revolution.

This had not come suddenly, of course; the American movement was more evolutionary than revolutionary, at least during the seventeenth and eighteenth centuries. These early Americans earned their independence by doing for themselves in the day of government and society while their parent country was either too busy or unconcerned. As early as 1619 they experimented with self-government in Virginia, and by the following year different methods of worship than the Established Church were practiced in New England.

After doing things their own way for a century and a half, the later Americans were not prepared to return to now forgotten ways at the demands of a newly assertive parliament or king. And so they rebelled; and, succeeding, launched a new government to mark finally what had really happened to them over a long period of time.

They argued with a mother country after decades of neglect, they argued across a great distance, and they argued over money. All these issues found expression in the dispute between the Americans in Texas and the Mexican government in the 1830s, but these events happened much quicker. And there were a few new arguments. Not all of the American cultural baggage was positive. Along the way they had picked up the institution of African slavery, they had disregarded the territorial or natural or property rights of Native Americans, and they had learned a certain disregard for the political rights of other empires on the North American continent. Even without a name, the concept of Manifest Destiny already existed in American minds.

These Americans spread out across their continent gobbling up territory claimed by the Dutch and the French, and of course that occupied by the Indians. States joined the American Union, and by purchase or treaty additional masses of land accrued to the United States. But even the additional lands did not satisfy them. Prices, particularly of land, and the westering spirit drove them on to other places beyond the nation's borders, including Texas. The principal difficulty in Texas lay not with the Indians, although they could and did prove formidable obstacles to Anglo migration sometimes. Their real problem was the Spanish empire still ruled in Texas, despite internal weakness few could yet appreciate. The Spanish tried to keep the Americans out; they sent military expeditions to capture the filibusters Philip Nolan and Augustus Magee and James Long, only three of many who tried to take some or all of Texas from them. Then, defying their recent stand, the Spanish reversed their policy and admitted some Americans to their northern provinces. They might as well have done so — the Americans came anyway.

Crossing the border, now defined by the Adams-Oñis Treaty as the Sabine River to its confluence with the 32nd parallel, then north to the Red River, thence westward, these silent and single invaders chose their new homes and farms and were ready to defend them from the government or Indians or even the environment. So the Spanish let them in lawfully for the price of a change of citizenship, and for some, a change of religion. Those willing to become Spanish, and later, Mexican, citizens, and to convert to Roman Catholicism, were awarded generous land grants. The Spanish and the Mexicans thus dealt with a law enforcement problem by decriminalizing the act of migration, and in the bargain hoped for an economically profitable development.

The arrangement worked about as long as it could have, although this time the Americans moved to a position of revolt in only fifteen years, rather than the 150 years it had taken their ancestors to find their identity and to proclaim it. This resulted so quickly in Texas because *these* Americans inherited their identity as a birthright from their Revolutionary parents. Their traditions of limited government, religious diversity, taxation with representation, indeed, their conscious concept that government should result from participatory democracy and be noninterferring and not overly regulatory, was exactly the kind of government they had wanted for the United States and hoped they would find under the liberal Mexican Constitution of 1824. But by 1830 they saw the beginnings of changes in that government. The law of April 6, 1830, stifled future immigration, redirected their cultural and economic connections southward, and began, for the first time, a system of tax collection.

The Texan-Americans balked. And, for their part, the Mexican government's officials who moved to enact and enforce these provisions could not understand the American reaction. Their whole frame of reference, routed to them through the centralist government of imperial Spain, was not one of citizenship but of subjectship. Residents of Hispanic lands received their directions from above; government officials transmitted these orders on to the subjects, and they were unaccustomed to the process working the other way. And so the clash came.

Trouble first surfaced in eastern Texas in the empresarial grant awarded to Haden Edwards. This Kentuckian had partnered with Stephen F. Austin in Mexico to establish the Colonization Law of 1825 in the province of *Coahuila y Texas,* which permitted American settlement. Like all *empresarios,* Edwards operated under the restriction that previous land grants from either the Spanish or Mexican governments should be honored. Of all the *empresarios,* only Edwards had a significant number of such grants within his area.

Edwards arrived in Nacogdoches in 1825 to proclaim his authority. Since he had no way of knowing what part of his territory had been previously granted, he determined that the claimants themselves must prove ownership or all lands would revert to him for regranting to new arrivals. Naturally, the residents took exception to this and after nearly a year of arguing the matter, by which time Edwards actually had resold only one grant, the situation turned for the worse following an election dispute. Edwards had supported his son-in-law, Chicester Chaplin, in an election for *alcalde* against Samuel Norris, the representative of the older settlers. When Edwards, as *empresario,* ruled in favor of Chaplin, the Norris faction protested to the Mexican political chief in San Antonio who reversed the results and moved closer to his ultimate solution to the problem, which was to declare the Edwards grant forfeited.

Despairing of ever untangling the complicated situation, Edwards sought an alliance with the Indians of the region, proclaimed his grant area as the Fredonia Republic, and declared it free of any political connection with Mexico. His republic's flag, a red and white banner which symbolized the white-red alliance, bore an inscription which read "Independence, Freedom, Justice," but it promised more than it could deliver. Edwards rallied a few friends, both red and white, but these disappeared with the arrival of the news that a military force moving towards them would soon arrive in Nacogdoches.

The Indians put their leaders to death for involving them in the matter, and Edwards fled to the safety of the Louisiana border. The only positive result of the affair was that Austin, who had sided with the Mexican authorities, bought more time for his own colonists to live in peace. Otherwise, the Fredonia Rebellion only served to alarm some Mexican leaders that perhaps other Americans nurtured the desire to take Texas from them.

This malaise received encouragement from the intervention of Joel R. Poinsett, the first American minister to Mexico, into the politics of his host nation. Poinsett's mission from President John Quincy Adams was to offer to purchase eastern portions of Texas from Mexico, thus moving the boundary westward from the Sabine River. Probably Adams only wanted to court western American expansionist votes with his offer, but Poinsett took his mission seriously. He also blundered greatly. Soon involved in internal Mexican political affairs which he did not understand, he sided with the liberals who seemed to be in power only to lose the friendship of the rising centralist-conservatives not only for himself but for Americans in Texas.

When he founded a York Rite masonic lodge in Mexico in direct competition and in opposition to the established Scottish Rite version of freemasonry already dominated by the conservative element, and attempted to use this connection to further his government's offer to the Mexican government, he offended still more Mexicans. Ultimately declared *personna non grata,* Poinsett left Mexico with only the beautiful flower which now shares his name, and he left in his wake a Mexican leadership greatly troubled by American interference.

The Mexican government now demanded that the United States renounce all interests west of the Sabine River, and some of the Mexican officials wanted closer control of the Americans who had already crossed the river. General José María Tornel, General Manuel Mier y Terán, and Foreign Affairs Minister Lucas Alamán persuaded President Vincente Guerrero to abolish slavery in Mexico by proclamation in 1829. Since only the Americans held chattel slaves in Mexico, obviously this was aimed only at them. Then these officials and others in the government moved the Mexican Congress to enact the Law of April 6, 1830. This important measure restored power over colonial affairs to the central government. It also closed down further immigration of Americans, provided for the settlement of more Mexicans—even convicts—in Texas, called for the introduction of European colonists to dilute the influence of Americans, redirected all trade from the Mississippi River towns to Mexican ports, called for the introduction of customs collections—which were due anyway since a seven-year exception from taxes for Texas had nearly expired—and provided for the sending of investigators to Texas to gather information.

Clearly, the leadership of Mexico believed that a crisis of sorts existed. None did. Most Americans followed Stephen F. Austin's example of becoming as loyal and contented under the Mexican government as their backgrounds would allow.

They reacted as if struck in the face. Most Americans believed that only continued immigration, including the further introduction of slaves, could ever make their colonial efforts successful. They began to look for ways to evade the burdensome law, and found Mexican states' righters on their side. The government of Coahuila, citing the Constitution of 1824, continued in its efforts to grant lands to Americans who had arrived in Texas before the law's enactment. This produced a clash at Anahuac, where an American in the military service of the central government, Colonel Juan (John) Davis Bradburn, commanded a small garrison. Nearby at Galveston, a Serbian, John Fisher, who had become an American citizen, then had moved on to Mexico, also established a customs house. When these two government officials began to enforce the law, trouble resulted immediately.

American ship captains merely evaded Fisher's agents until Bradburn issued an order that all clearance from Texas rivers under his jurisdiction must be issued from his headquarters at Anahuac, thus requiring a lengthy trip to the eastern end of Galveston Bay. And he quarreled with the state's agent, Francisco Madero, who continued to issue land grants and found new communities, notably the settlement of Liberty, not far from Anahuac. Bradburn arrested Madero and dispersed the settlers.

Protests from the resident Americans and from a growing number of new arrivals who had come to Texas in the expectation of receiving lands now denied led to further arrests. Twice Bradburn arrested several citizens, only to back down in the face of greater protests. Then, in May of 1832, the first of the disturbances of that year which began the Texas revolution occurred.

A Louisianian named William T. Logan arrived in Anahuac in pursuit of runaway slaves whom he found living and working under Bradburn's protection. Bradburn refused to surrender the slaves without proof of ownership, which was only a ruse — he never intended to allow Logan to reclaim them. Before departing to obtain the required evidence of ownership, Logan employed William B. Travis as his attorney and threatened Bradburn and made him easy prey for a harrassing prank played on him by Travis. Late one night Travis slipped a note to a sentry which claimed that Logan had returned with a large force. Bradburn called out his entire garrison and sent them off into the night in search of Logan's force. Finding no one, his embarrassment and anger brought about the arrest of Travis and his law partner, Patrick Jack, who protested the arrest of his friend. Jack's brother William hastened to San Felipe for help, and since Stephen F. Austin was absent, he had little difficulty in rallying a force. More joined them on the way to Anahuac.

These men gathered at Turtle Bayou near the upper end of Galveston Bay and adopted the Turtle Bayou Resolutions, a kind of pledge of loyalty to their concept of the Mexican republic but also a denunciation of its representative in Anahuac. Some of them then followed John Austin to Velasco to obtain a cannon that they thought might be needed; the others remained in the vicinity, menacing Bradburn. Travis and Jack were moved to a brick kiln and kept constantly under guard, with orders that they should be killed if a rescue attempt developed. The Americans captured a Mexican patrol, but a proposed exchange of prisoners went awry when Bradburn convinced them to release their hostages first. Then he refused to release Travis and Jack.

Meanwhile, Colonel José de las Piedras, a senior officer stationed at Nacogdoches, learned of the trouble. He hurried to Anahuac to assist Bradburn, but upon arriving there he quickly saw that the Americans had the small garrison outnumbered. He resolved the situation by firing Bradburn, who temporarily fled to the United States for safety, and turned the prisoners over to civil authorities, who soon released them.

Upon returning to Nacogdoches, Piedras determined to prevent this kind of trouble in his own district. He ordered everyone in his area to turn in their firearms. The men of the Ayish Bayou area brought them to town in late July, but they used them to attack Piedras' troops and drive them from the town. Piedras was later captured near the Angelina River and escorted to San Antonio. And the small force under Austin had to fight its way past the command of Colonel Domingo Ugartechea, with both sides suffering several casualties.

These three actions, known collectively as the Disturbances of 1832, mark the real beginning of the Texas Revolution, but few in either camp recognized them as such. The Americans did, however, realize that something needed to be resolved about their relationship to the government. An opportunity to explain themselves came quickly. Mexican states' righters under Colonel José Antonio Mexía, loyal to Antonio López de Santa Anna, who was then in revolt against the centralists, arranged a truce with their opponents to investigate the troubles in Texas.

Stephen F. Austin met Mexía and quickly convinced him that the events in Texas amounted to nothing more than support for his own and Santa Anna's position in the states' rights cause. Following a feast at Brazoria in his honor, Mexía returned to Mexico convinced that the Americans in Texas were on his side. And they were. But the Americans had misjudged Santa Anna, a crafty, sly centralist who only temporarily espoused federalism to advance his own cause. He even won the presidency in general elections in 1833 as a federalist, with Vice President Valentín Gómez Farías, who soon led a movement within the government for reforms within the army, the power of landowners, and the church.

Santa Anna retired to Vera Cruz to allow Gómez Farías to institute these reforms, waiting for the propitious moment to return to lead what amounted to a revolution against his own administration, a revolution that would replace all constitutional government with his own brand of absolutism.

To the Americans, it seemed a likely time to consolidate their position in Texas. The *ayuntamiento,* or council, of San Felipe, called for a convention of delegates from all settlements to gather at that place on October 1. They elected Austin as their presiding officer and drafted petitions to the government calling for the issuance of more land titles, exemption from taxation for three more years, the approval of a militia for Indian defense, the repeal of the Law of April 6, 1830, and a return to the admittance of immigrants, and, most significantly, for separate status as a state of the Mexican union. Their petition got no further than the political chief at San Antonio, who sent it back with an angry reminder that the meeting itself had been held illegally. To the Americans it had represented an orderly petition to their government; to the Mexican official, and others like him, it looked like the familiar pattern of a revolution.

Misunderstanding the rebuff, a second convention gathered in January 1833 to clarify their request. This time the more militant William H. Wharton presided, although Austin drew the assignment to carry their petition directly to the central government. And this time they added a proposed constitution should their request for separate statehood receive approval.

Austin left for Mexico City on April 22, and he arrived while Gómez Farías still exercised authority in Santa Anna's absence. Gómez Farías devoted all of his energy to his own programs and had little time for the concerns of the Americans in Texas, but he did agree to submit their requests to the House of Deputies. Lobbying this group brought Austin into contact with Lorenzo de Zavala, who became active, although unsuccessfully, in the Texan's behalf. After several months passed with no favorable results, Austin again approached Gómez Farías. In a heated session, Austin candidly told the president that his government might as well go on and give the Texans what they desired regarding statehood because they lived thus anyway. Austin's candor sounded like a threat to Gómez Farías, and the *empresario's* next action confirmed this view. Austin wrote to the *ayuntamiento* at San Antonio to urge them to take the lead in making peaceful preparations for a separate state government.

This letter was returned to government officials in Mexico City before Austin left for Texas. Before leaving he had an audience with Santa Anna, who had returned to the capital from Vera Cruz. The meeting was cordial, and Santa Anna seemed to agree to work for all of Austin's requests except separate statehood. He demurred on this because Texas lacked sufficient population. This was an argument Austin could accept since the United States had always had such requirements. And, as a final statement, Santa Anna also told Austin that he intended to send more military personnel to Texas to help with Indian defense. This should have warned Austin because the government rarely showed such concern.

Austin quit the capital in early December, intending to return to Texas. He paid a duty call on the state officials in Saltillo on the way home, but that was as far as he got. He was arrested, returned to Mexico City, and incarcerated in the Prison of the Inquisition and even held in solitary confinement for the first few weeks. Austin's arrest quieted political activity in Texas; the Texans feared that any protest might provoke reprisal against him. Things became so calm, in fact, that Austin despaired that he had been forgotten. Learning this, Peter Grayson and Spencer Jack raised money and traveled to Mexico to secure his release from prison. Austin emerged from prison walls in December 1834, but he remained under a kind of house arrest and could not leave the city.

Meanwhile, the Gómez Farías reforms had some impact on Texas. Immigration was reopened, Texas received three deputies in the Coahuilian legislature, and local government in the form of departments, with headquarters at Nacogdoches, San Felipe, and San Antonio, was created. English was recognized as an official language, and modifications in religious requirements were allowed, as was trial by jury.

Then all was repudiated. Santa Anna ousted Gómez Farías, repudiated liberalism, and abolished the Congress and all local government as well. A new, subservient Congress received office by his proclamation and, in one session, voided the Constitution of 1824 and placed all power in the hands of the central government—meaning Santa Anna.

Texas experienced the first assertions of the new regime when Santa Anna sent General Martín Perfecto de Cós, his brother-in-law, to Coahuila with troops to settle a jurisdictional dispute between Saltillo and Monclova over which would be the state capital. The losers fled to Texas with news of the military take-over.

Then the customs agents returned. The most troublesome, Captain Antonio Tenorio, arrived at Anahuac and reinstated the collection of taxes. He also angered the Americans by arresting several of them on a charge that they sought to deceive him by smuggling untaxed goods in casks marked "ballast."

In San Felipe a secret meeting chaired by J. B. Miller elected William B. Travis to lead men to run Tenorio out of Anahuac. Travis did so successfully in early July 1835, but when he started back toward San Felipe with his prisoners he was shocked to learn that the majority of the Texans resented this action, and particularly his leadership of it, as a harbinger of more trouble with the government. In fact, when they reached Brazoria Travis's men were ridiculed and Tenorio and his men became the honored guests at a Fourth of July barbeque. Then those advocating a strong stand against the government, called the War Party, became unpopular, while the Peace Party temporarily grew in assertiveness. Cós reversed this trend by a demand that the "criminals" who had attacked his men at Anahuac be surrendered to him by their fellow Americans for military trial. He threatened to take harsh reprisals if this was not done immediately. This proved too much for the Texans. Many of them disliked Travis, but they would not surrender him to a Mexican military trial.

Committees of Correspondence sprang up, and in mid-August

William Wharton presided over a meeting at Columbia which sent out a call for a Consultation of all citizens to convene on November 1. Into this tinder box Austin finally returned from imprisonment in Mexico City. Holding the issue of war or peace in his hands, he boldly advocated resistance. "War," he said, "is our only resource. . . ."

Already there was general agreement that Cós' troops must be resisted if they entered Texas and that the Consultation should be held to determine the Texans' ultimate position; but opinion over such matters as independence was sharply divided. Then the first real shots of the revolution were fired at Gonzales, and things were never the same again. The incident began when Cós ordered Ugartechea to confiscate a cannon held at Gonzales for Indian defense. *Alcalde* Andrew Ponton refused the military patrol's request on grounds that they lacked written orders while others buried the cannon to hide it. The Mexican patrol returned to obtain the order, and as supporters arrived from the countryside, they elected John Moore as their colonel, dug up the cannon, and prepared it to defend itself. A second patrol under Captain Francisco Castañeda arrived with 200 men to demand the cannon, but now they found an armed camp, a flag emblazoned with "COME AND TAKE IT," and a loaded cannon staring at them.

The Americans fired first in the incident which has been called the Lexington of the Texas Revolution. Castañeda retired because he lacked orders to assault the town. More Americans gathered until they numbered about 300 men, then they determined to move on to San Antonio when they learned that Cós had arrived there with 800 men, reportedly bringing iron hobbles for his prisoners.

Ugartechea wrote to Austin asking him to prevent a confrontation, but instead Austin joined the men at Gonzales and became their "general." His "Army of People" arrived at San Antonio on October 24, a week before the Consultation was to begin, and laid siege to the town after a brief skirmish at Mission Concepción. More and more men arrived to help out, but soon many also drifted away to return to chores on their farms. When it became time for the Consultation to begin, the army voted that those who had been elected to represent their communities should leave to do so; otherwise, none would leave and be called cowardly. On November 26 the Americans attacked a suspected supply train, only to learn that it was but fifty foragers out gathering hay for Cós' horses. The quixotic "Grass Fight" characterized the siege until Austin left to answer the Consultation's call that he travel with Branch T. Archer and William Wharton to the United States to solicit aid. Edward Burleson succeeded Austin, and by early December he decided to withdraw to winter quarters. Then the Texans learned from a captured Mexican that Cós' men were disconsolate and ready to surrender. Ben Milam issued a challenge: "Who will go into San Antonio with old Ben Milam?" Over 300 eagerly volunteered, and on December 5 these men began an attack with Burleson commanding a reserve. The prisoner had exaggerated. The assault required five days to succeed, and cost many casualties, including Milam himself. Francis Johnson then succeeded Milam and carried the attack to completion. Burleson, resuming command, paroled Cós and his men on their pledge to leave Texas and never return.

Meanwhile, the Consultation continued to function. In addition to sending its solicitors to the United States, this body also created a governing agency to replace one with the unlikely name of the Permanent Council which lasted less than a month. The first group had been organized at San Felipe with Richard Royall as president. His "government," not yet even declared independent from Mexico, and certainly not representing the majority of Texans, nevertheless commissioned privateers, set up a postal system, and attempted to borrow money from the United States. Then, with the convening of the Consultation on November 3, the Permanent Council ceased to exist.

The Consultation debated the issue of independence, but decided to defer a decision, mostly because the majority of the delegates were bona fide settlers who were uncertain that such a course was in their best interests. But the frontier element arriving daily in Texas clamored for independence, so the Consultation was pushed to a compromise: they organized to fight and to function as if independent, but they stopped short of an actual declaration. They endorsed the Constitution of 1824 and implied that they would support a *Mexican* revolution which would restore it. They decided to adjourn on November 14 but agreed to reconvene on March 1, 1836, and to allow Henry Smith to run their administrative affairs as a "governor," with James Robinson of Nacogdoches as lieutenant-governor. Sam Houston was appointed to command their "army," which did not then actually exist outside of the assault troops who had remained at San Antonio. A few others, mainly recruits from the United States, had gathered at Goliad under the command of James Fannin.

Then a new element entered the affair. Dr. James Grant arrived in San Antonio and persuaded the Texans to accompany him to Matamoros. He forthrightly admitted to them that he wanted to use their fighting skills to regain lands confiscated from him by the government, but he offered the men the booty of the town as their

*Stephen F. Austin, "Father of Texas" from engraving in* Harper's Weekly, *May 12, 1888.*

— U.T. Institute of Texan Cultures

*Drawing of Antonio Lopez de Santa Anna, Mexican president of Texas from April 24, 1834 to January 28, 1835. Drawing by Gene Bustamante in the collection of the Presidential Museum, Odessa, Texas.*

— U.T. Institute of Texan Cultures

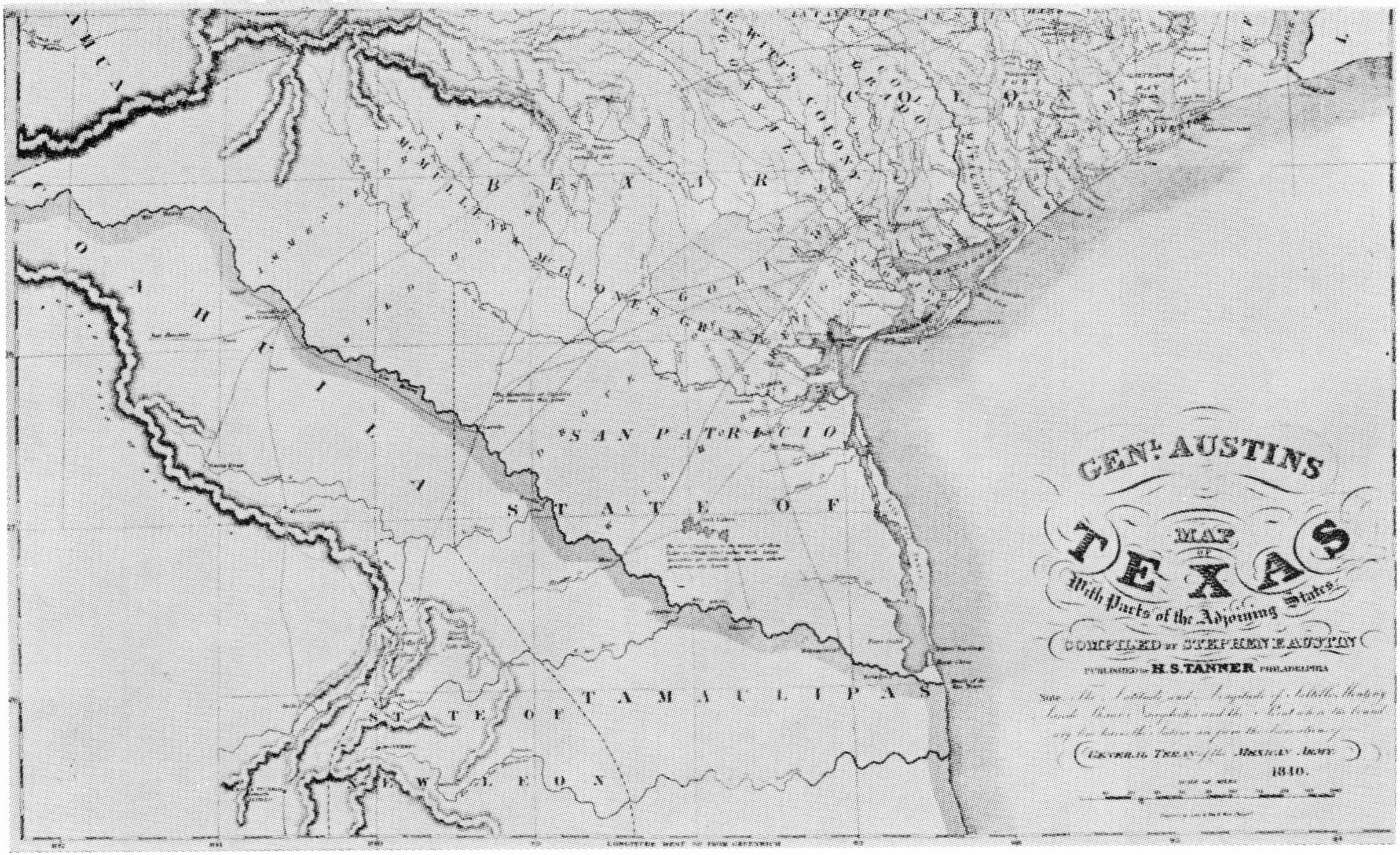

GENL. AUSTINS
MAP
OF
TEXAS
With Parts of the Adjoining States.
COMPILED BY STEPHEN F. AUSTIN
PUBLISHED BY H. S. TANNER PHILADELPHIA
1840.
BEXAR
SAN PATRICIO
STATE OF
STATE OF TAMAULIPAS
COLONY
LONGITUDE WEST OF GREENWICH

# TEXAS

## FOREVER!!

The usurper of the South has failed in his efforts to enslave the freemen of Texas.

The wives and daughters of Texas will be saved from the brutality of Mexican soldiers.

Now is the time to emigrate to the **Garden of America.**

A free passage, and all found, is offered at **New Orleans** to all applicants. Every settler receives a location of

**EIGHT HUNDRED ACRES OF LAND.**

On the 23d of February, a force of 1000 Mexicans came in sight of San Antonio, and on the 25th Gen. St. Anna arrived at that place with 2500 more men, and demanded a surrender of the fort held by 150 Texians, and on the refusal, he attempted to storm the fort, twice, with his whole force, but was repelled with the loss of 500 men, and the Americans lost none. Many of his troops, the liberals of Zacatecas, are brought on to Texas in irons and are urged forward with the promise of the women and plunder of Texas.

The Texian forces were marching to relieve St. Antonio, March the 2d. The Government of Texas is supplied with plenty of arms, ammunition, provisions, &c. &c.

*"Texas Forever," an advertisement for land in Texas, 1836.*

— Institute of Texan Cultures
From Broadside folder from Barker Texas History Center

*Painting of the delegates voting on the 1836 Texas constitution on the evening of March 16, 1836 at Washington-on-the-Brazos. This was the start of the "runaway scrape."*

— Institute of Texan Cultures
from painting by Bruce Marshall

*Reading of the Texas Declaration of Independence. Painting by Fanny and Charles Normann.*

— Institute of Texan Cultures

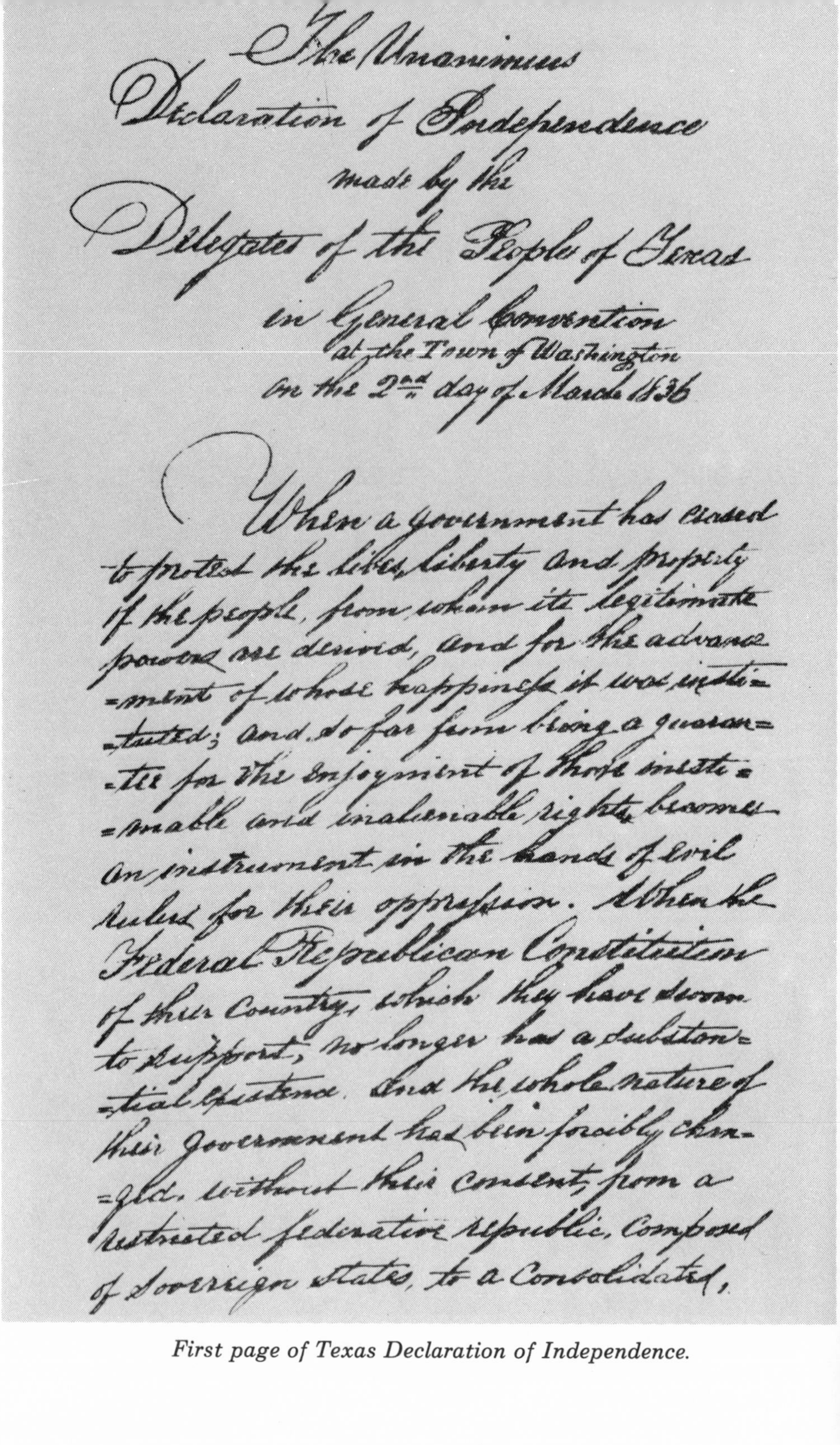
The Unanimous
Declaration of Independence
made by the
Delegates of the People of Texas
in General Convention
at the Town of Washington
on the 2nd day of March 1836

When a government has ceased to protect the lives, liberty and property of the people, from whom its legitimate powers are derived, and for the advancement of whose happiness it was instituted; and so far from being a guarantee for the enjoyment of those inestimable and inalienable rights, becomes an instrument in the hands of evil rulers for their oppression. When the Federal Republican Constitution of their country, which they have sworn to support, no longer has a substantial existence, and the whole nature of their government has been forcibly changed, without their consent, from a restricted federative republic, composed of sovereign states, to a consolidated,

*First page of Texas Declaration of Independence.*

*Heroes of the Battle of the Alamo*

*David Crockett*

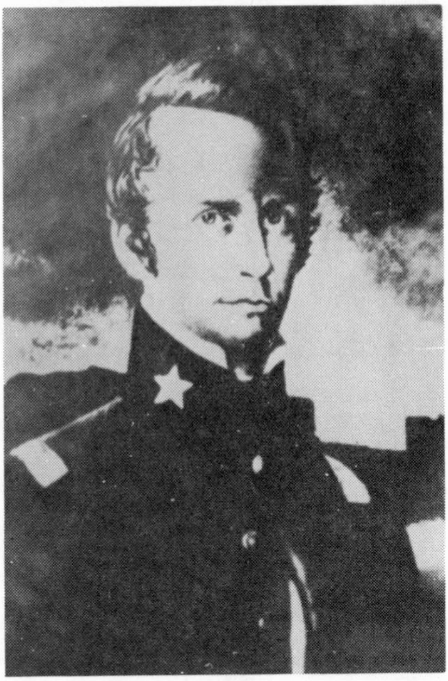

*William B. Travis*

*James A. Bowie*

Commandancy of the Alamo—.
Bejar, Feby. 24th 1836—

To the People of Texas & all Americans in the world—

Fellow citizens & compatriots—

I am besieged, by a thousand or more of the Mexicans under Santa Anna—I have sustained a continual Bombardment & cannonade for 24 hours & have not lost a man—The enemy has demanded a surrender at discretion otherwise the garrison are to be put to the sword, if the fort is taken—I have answered the demand with a cannon shot, & our flag still waves proudly from the walls—I *shall never surrender or retreat*. *Then*, I call on you in the name of Liberty, of patriotism & every thing dear to the American character, to come to our aid,

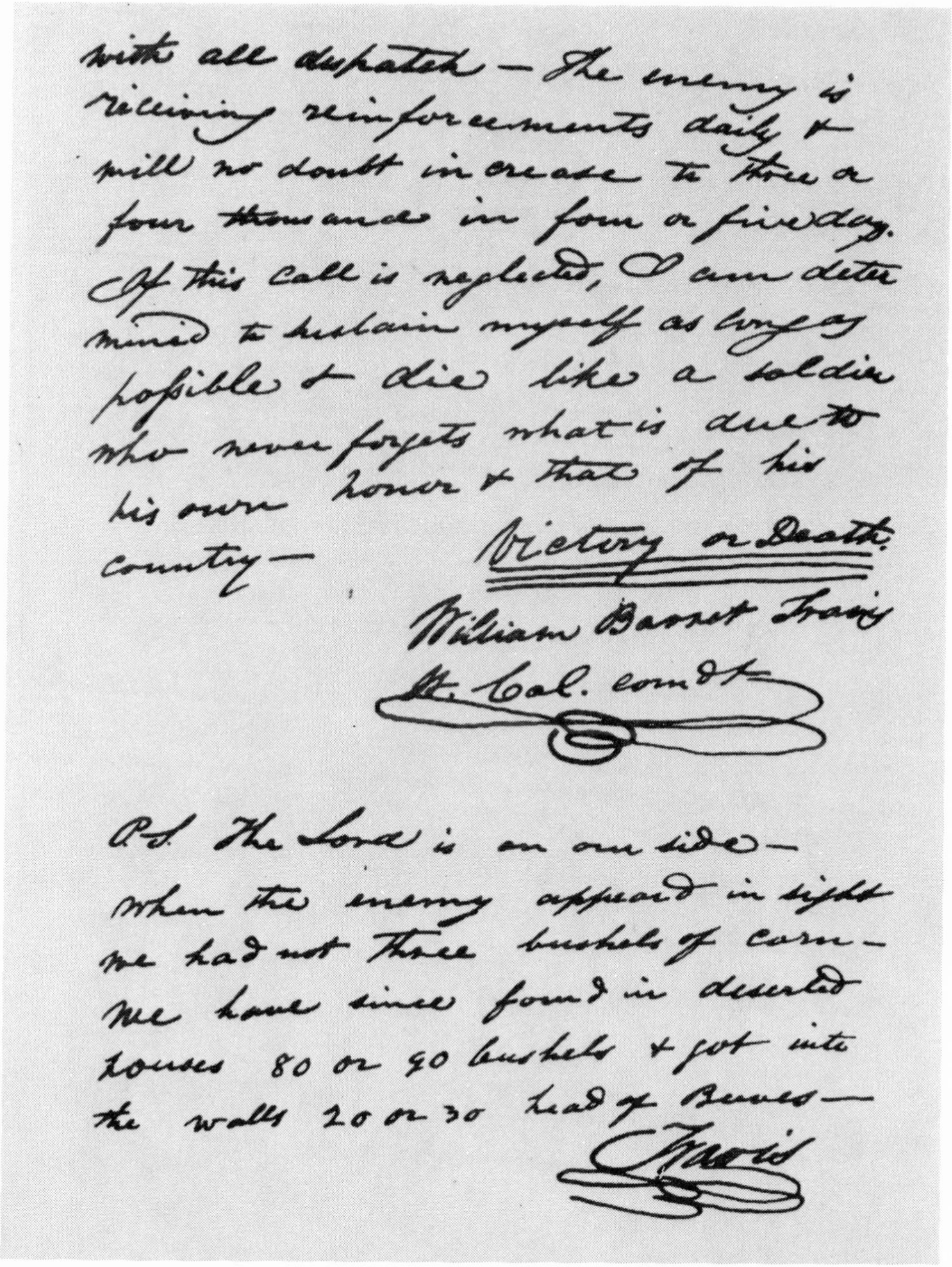
with all dispatch — The enemy is
receiving reinforcements daily &
will no doubt increase to three or
four thousand in four or five days.
If this call is neglected, I am deter
mined to sustain myself as long as
possible & die like a soldier
who never forgets what is due to
his own honor & that of his
country —

Victory or Death.

William Barret Travis

Lt. Col. comdt.

P.S. The Lord is on our side —
When the enemy appeared in sight
we had not three bushels of corn —
We have since found in deserted
houses 80 or 90 bushels & got into
the walls 20 or 30 head of Beeves —

Travis

*Col. Travis' famous letter "to the people of Texas."*

*Battle of the Alamo from painting by Harry A. McArdle hanging in the Senate chamber, Texas State Capitol, Austin.*

— Institute of Texan Cultures

*An engraving of the storming of the Alamo, by Mexican soldiers.*

— Institute of Texan Cultures
from Barker's *A Texas Scrapbook.*

*Painting of the battle of San Jacinto, 1836 by Harry Arthur McArdle. Copied from the original in the Senate chamber, Texas State Capitol, Austin.*

— Institute of Texan Cultures

reward. Johnson's men, especially the new arrivals who had not yet established homes, were anxious to strike another blow at the Mexicans and reap the rewards of their venture. Houston opposed this move but he agreed to withdraw his opposition if the expedition were commanded by James Bowie, a man he trusted. The scheme divided the government, but finally Smith authorized the expedition over Houston's objections and appointed Johnson to command it. Johnson unexpectedly declined now, but changed his mind again when Fannin was offered the command. At this point there were at least four men pretending to lead the armies of Texas: Houston, Fannin, Johnson, and Bowie.

Houston departed and furloughed himself until the full Consultation met again in March to unravel the situation. He also wanted to absolve himself from responsibility for the Matamoros scheme, which he was certain would fail. He did, however, travel to East Texas to negotiate a treaty of peace with the Cherokee Indians, thus removing a threat to the Texans from this potential second front.

Johnson and Grant left San Antonio with most of the army and nearly all the available provisions, leaving James C. Neill in command of about thirty men and few supplies. They never made it to Matamoros, stopping instead near San Patricio. Fannin did not move with his force from Goliad, although he still had authorization to do so. Even the government stopped functioning; Smith quarreled with his council, which then impeached him and named Robinson to replace him. All seemed in chaos. Smith tried to continue to act as governor. He ordered his cavalry commander, William B. Travis, to recruit 100 men and go to Neill's relief in San Antonio.

Travis could muster only twenty-nine men, but he arrived in San Antonio in January with these few reinforcements, and shortly afterward Bowie arrived with nearly 100 volunteers. Their orders conflicted: Smith wanted Neill and Travis to hold the place, while Bowie had been ordered by Houston to destroy it. Events rather than orders dictated their course of action, however. Neill soon left to deal with personal business, and after Bowie and Travis quarreled over who should command, they finally worked out a joint command agreement which called upon each to co-sign all orders. Bowie was soon incapacitated by injury and illness, and Travis assumed full command. But of what? An isolated garrison with no reason to exist. Santa Anna provided them with that. Fresh from crushing a revolt in Zacatecas, he now determined to lead an *entrata* into Texas to personally remove all its American residents. He pledged as much to his nation before starting the march.

While Santa Anna moved northward, a few more Americans

drifted into San Antonio. The most notable party was led by David Crockett, late of Tennessee and the United States Congress, off for adventure and perhaps a renewed political career. His group brought the Alamo garrison to nearly 150, while Santa Anna moved toward them with some 7,000 troops. He rested his men at the Rio Grande, then pushed on toward San Antonio, arriving on February 22. By then Travis had moved all his men into the compound of the Mission San Antonio de Valero, now commonly called the Alamo, and with the labor of the men and the skill of engineer Green Jamison, he had turned it into a fairly defendable fortress. All he lacked was a few thousand men.

Santa Anna laid siege to the Alamo on February 23. Travis wrote furiously to Smith, to Fannin, to anyone, seeking aid. All he received was the entire male population of Gonzales, thirty-two men, who arrived on March 1, the same day the Consultation reconvened at Washington-on-the-Brazos. So with 187 men Travis defended his fortress against the main body of Santa Anna's command. Some of the Mexican troops under General José Urrea had moved northeastward to intercept Johnson and Grant at San Patricio, then moved on toward Fannin and Goliad. But Santa Anna personally commanded General Ramirez y Sesma's troops at San Antonio. He bombarded the fortress; he serenaded the Alamo's defenders with the *Deguello,* and finally, on the morning of March 6, he assaulted the Alamo. Travis died early in the battle, Bowie was slain on his sick bed, and Crockett perished after the battle proper at the hands of Santa Anna's staff. All Americans there, save Mrs. Susanna Dickinson, her daughter, and a slave, were also slain. These survivors were dispatched down the Gonzales road to carry the news of the Mexican victory.

While these events occurred, Urrea captured and killed Johnson's and Grant's men, then captured Fannin's 500 troops at Goliad. They were all executed by Santa Anna's direct order, even after Urrea had accepted their conditional surrender.

Meanwhile, although the men in the Alamo and at Goliad never knew it, the Consultation met and on March 2 declared Texas independent of Mexico. They quickly accepted George Childress' draft of the declaration, closely patterned in form and language after the document written for an earlier generation of revolutionaries by Thomas Jefferson. The fifty-nine delegates then moved on to write a constitution for their new republic, and they appointed an *ad interim* government headed by David G. Burnet as president and Lorenzo de Zavala as vice president to conduct their affairs until elections designated permanent officers. Houston was again named commander-in-chief with Thomas J. Rusk as secretary of war.

The Consultation closed on March 17 and the government moved to Galveston while Houston, who had left on March 11, hastened toward San Antonio. At Gonzales he found nearly 400 men awaiting direction, as usual coming to a crisis after it was too late. With them he learned from Mrs. Dickinson of the fate of the men in the Alamo. The memory of the town's weeping widows fixed their battle cry: "Remember the Alamo!" Later, when they learned of the second atrocity at Goliad, they resolved to avenge it as well.

Houston ordered his men to burn Gonzales and march toward the Colorado River. There he briefly rested and drilled his men, then headed on to the Brazos River. They stayed there ten days and drilled even more. As the army swelled to nearly 1,400 men, many grew anxious for a fight. But Houston, learning now of Goliad, moved on. When the civilian population learned of these losses and of Houston's retreat, they fled in the frightful Runaway Scrape. Abandoning homes and farms, they struggled against muddy roads and swollen rivers to save themselves.

Burnet wrote Houston frequently, urging, even daring, him to fight. Still Houston moved east. Santa Anna pursued the Americans relentlessly, sometimes with Sesma's main command, sometimes with an advance of only a few men, and sometimes he trailed them in his fancy coach until river crossings became impossible in the vehicle.

When Santa Anna decided that Houston would flee all the way to the Sabine River, and also learned that the government had moved to Harrisburg, he moved ahead with only 500 men to capture Burnet. He thus moved south and slightly ahead of Houston, who continued to move his army but at an angle parallel to that of Santa Anna's smaller force. Their lines converged just south of the Buffalo Bayou on the field known as San Jacinto.

Houston had already determined on a fight there, but he did not take anyone into his counsel, and the officers and the men began to grumble. Several refused to retreat anymore; these were dispatched on various duties. There is still a dispute over Houston's conduct on the day of action, April 21, but most historians now agree he had come to fight.

The forces first clashed indecisively on the afternoon of April 20, but during the night Santa Anna received reinforcements under Cós. With their forces now nearly equal, with perhaps a slight edge among effectives going to the Mexicans, Santa Anna's troops were allowed to rest on the 21st. In late afternoon Houston led a line in an advance across the San Jacinto plain for a nearly complete surprise of the Mexican camp. Marching to the strains of "Will you come to the bower I have shaded for you?" played on fife and drum, and flying a flag with the phrase, "Where Liberty Lives, There is our Homeland," in Latin upon it, his men overran the Mexican camp. In less than eighteen minutes the battle was over, but the carnage continued for several hours. Houston received a severe leg wound, and his men suffered two deaths and thirty wounded from the ranks; seven of the latter subsequently died of their wounds. The Mexicans suffered more: nearly 630 were killed and over 700 were captured.

Santa Anna escaped, only to be captured the next day and brought before Houston. Positive identification of the Mexican president was confirmed by his own men. Despite the clamor of the camp that he should be executed immediately, Houston guarded Santa Anna's life. Dead, he would be of no value; alive, he represented the Mexican government.

Houston negotiated with Santa Anna for a while, securing his order to General Vicente Filisola, who commanded the Mexican troops remaining elsewhere in Texas, to withdraw. Miraculously, Filisola complied. He had more than enough men to finish off the Texans, yet he obeyed his president and stayed where he was encamped, then slowly withdrew to Mexico.

Houston had to leave for better medical treatment in New Orleans, so the negotiations with Santa Anna fell to Governor David G. Burnet. Burnet, who still did not feel charitable toward Houston for nearly allowing him to be captured by Santa Anna, nonetheless negotiated well. The resulting Treaty of Velasco received their signatures on May 14, 1836. Of course, Santa Anna gave Burnet anything demanded of him to save his life, realizing that it would be repudiated by the Mexican nation. They did so, and on lawful grounds; treaties thus negotiated are not binding under international law. But the Texans liked their treaty, and were willing to pursue its provisions as if they were scriptural.

The treaty had public and private provisions. In the public portion, Santa Anna agreed to cease all hostilities toward the Texans and never again to take up arms against them; he agreed to keep all Mexican soldiers south of the Rio Grande and to release all prisoners. These things he would do to gain his release and transportation to Vera Cruz. In a private portion, he also agreed to work within Mexico to achieve recognition of Texas' independence from the entire Mexican government and to secure a treaty of commerce between the nations. Most surprisingly, he also agreed to the Rio Grande as the political boundary between Mexico and Texas. It had never been so regarded in either Spanish or Mexican times. The traditional boundary between Coahuila and Texas had been the Nueces River; now Texas claimed this additional territory, a strip nearly

200 miles in breadth and as long as the course of the river itself. Mexico repudiated all these concessions, and the Texans did not immediately live up to their part of the bargain, although Burnet tried. He put Santa Anna and his aide, Juan Almonte, aboard the *Invincible* to sail for Vera Cruz, but angry soldiers under General Thomas Green prevented the vessel from sailing and Burnet had to retain Santa Anna for his own safety.

Meanwhile, Texas agents in America produced results. Thomas McKinney and Adolphus Sterne recruited men and money in New Orleans, and Archer, Wharton, and Austin raised more further north. The United States officially remained aloof from the affair, but President Andrew Jackson did allow General Edmund Gaines to call out the militia in several southern states to defend the Sabine River border in case Santa Anna tried to cross it. They did not really expect this would happen, but Gaines was able to reassure the Runaway Scrape refugees when they arrived in Louisiana. Private citizens in the United States pledged money and crops; the city of Cincinnati sent two cannons which arrived in time for use at San Jacinto, and even after that event, hundreds continued to arrive to enlist in the army.

Soon the army itself became a problem. These men had come to fight and they clamored for action. Burnet knew that the Texans had better leave well enough alone, so when Secretary Rusk, who had assumed field command after Houston's wound forced his withdrawal to New Orleans, could not control the army, Burnet attempted to replace him with Mirabeau Lamar. Lamar had arrived in time to earn laurels commanding the cavalry at San Jacinto, but he could not control the army, which now began to think again of the Matamoros scheme and possible plunder. Additional clashes did occur, particularly on the coast, where Isaac Burton's troops captured a Mexican ship at Copano Bay in early June, but the war had ended if the recruits did not renew it with a rash act.

In July, Burnet called for a general election for the first Monday in September to elect the permanent officers and to bring the Republic of Texas into existence. This was in advance of the Consultation's timetable, but Burnet feared, with justification, that if he did not go on and do so now that the rapid changes in the wind would prevent it from happening later.

Henry Smith declared his candidacy immediately, and soon Stephen F. Austin joined him as a candidate. Then, just eleven days before the election, Houston agreed to be a candidate. On election day the voters had two primary decisions: on the one hand they elected officers for their new government, and on the other hand they voted in a plebiscite to determine if Texas should seek admission to the United States. Out of 6,640 votes cast, Houston received 5,119 and was elected president with Lamar as his vice president. The constitution of the Republic was overwhelmingly ratified. And with only about half as many casting ballots on the second issue, Texans voted 3,277 to 91 to seek admission to the American union.

Sam Houston assumed the presidency of the infant Texas Republic with adequate preparation. Not only had he led the Texan armies to miraculous success against Santa Anna's troops at San Jacinto, thereby redeeming his reputation from its ebb during the Runaway Scrape, he also had served in the legislative and executive branches of the Tennessee government prior to coming to Texas. But the government he headed in Texas experienced problems quite different from that of an established state. Since the decade of the 1780s no one in the United States had known such difficulties as how to disband a revolutionary army after its usefulness had passed, how to deal with a former government which yearned to control once more, or how to establish a viable currency and commercial system, among other things.

Houston's hope for the solution to these and other problems lay in immediate annexation of Texas to the United States. If "immediate" proved impossible, then he hoped to effect such a union eventually, and he worked hard to dampen Texas' difficulties until that day came. But his pressing problems demanded attention. The army enlarged daily as new recruits hustled to Texas to get into a fight already over and to claim the generous land rewards for participating in the revolution and its aftermath. The Texas Congress promised a headright of 640 acres to each family plus a bounty grant of 320 additional acres for each three months military service to the Republic. Subsequent acts of the Congress continued this largess for several years, preventing the sale of public land as a revenue source because the government simply gave so much land away. All these new men grew restless without anything to do before they drew their lands. Many dreamed and schemed of renewing the conflict with Mexico, which Houston feared would prove disastrous for the weak, new government in both military and financial ways.

Houston tried to control his army by appointing Albert Sydney Johnston as its leader. But the army refused Johnston's leadership, preferring Felix Huston instead. Then Huston severely wounded Johnston in a duel in which the latter had hoped that victory would secure his command. Now the triumph of Huston made the president feel that he would lose control of his army entirely. To prevent Huston from leading the men off on some ill-advised assault, or perhaps even a military takeover of the government itself, Houston furloughed all but 600 of the men. This had the added advantage of not requiring mustering-out pay since the troops were only furloughed, and it also left them available in case Mexico renewed the war.

Houston's secretary of the treasury, Henry Smith, kept him informed about the poverty of the new government. Not only did they lack revenue, Smith informed Houston that he even lacked money for correspondence paper. To provide funds for government operations and to prime the economy of the Republic with a medium of exchange, the Congress authorized the issuance of paper currency called "Star Money" because of the imprint of a star on each bill. This issue maintained its value fairly well because it was for only a limited amount. Subsequent issues depreciated rapidly, however, and by the end of Houston's term, paper currency circulated for as little as twelve cents to the dollar.

President Houston also tried to prevent Indian wars, partly because of their expense and partly because he favored a place for the Indians of Texas. Soon after his inauguration Houston recommended that the Texas government honor the Cherokee treaty he had negotiated with Philip Bowles during the Revolutionary War. This treaty called for the Cherokees to hold title to vast acreages in East Texas. Now that the exigency of war had passed, the Congress refused to honor the treaty. Instead they prepared for the removal of these Indians. Many whites coveted their lands, and besides, a revolt in 1838 led by Vincente Cordova attempted to use Indians and half-breeds in East Texas to reaffiliate Texas with Mexico. This was all the Congress needed as an excuse to reject the treaty and to take the land from the Cherokees. Thomas J. Rusk led the forces which dispersed Cordova's supporters, and the following year Kelsey H. Douglass led the militia in further action against the Cherokees. At the Battle of the Neches in July 1839 Chief Philip Bowles was killed and his followers were driven northward to Indian Territory, or Oklahoma.

Houston pushed the efforts of his government to gain admission to the American Union as a solution to these problems. Memucan Hunt, and later Isaac Van Zandt, tried to persuade the United States to approve annexation, but President Martin Van Buren did not want Texas in the Union for a variety of reasons, including the fact that Texas would enter as a slave state and, besides, as Secretary of State John Forsyth explained, a solemn treaty with Mexico renouncing lands west of the Sabine River prevented such action. Violation of the treaty, Forsyth claimed, would have justified Mexico's declaring war on the United States. Obviously, the United

States just did not want Texas at that time, so Houston instructed Anson Jones, then representing Texas in Washington, to withdraw Texas' offer because to continue it would have been an embarrassment.

The rejection of the proposed treaty of annexation advanced the political cause of Vice President Mirabeau Lamar, who did not want annexation anyway. As Houston's two-year administration drew to a close, Lamar prepared to seek the office since under the Constitution the Texas president could not succeed himself. Houston favored first Peter Grayson and then James Collingsworth in the race, but both took their own lives before the election. Robert Wilson entered the race at the last minute, but it mattered little; Lamar could have won the election against any of them. He and his vice president, David Burnet, then took Texas on a very different course.

The physical contrast between the first two presidents contradicted their policies. Houston's tall frame fits the image of modern Texans as a bold, daring individual, while Lamar's more average size and chronic ill-health and his reputation as a poet would seem to indicate a cautious, contemplative executive. Actually, their roles were played just the opposite. Whereas Houston sought to solve the Republic's military and financial problems with admission to the American Union and in the interim attempted to keep them from worsening, Lamar adopted a bold stand on all fronts. In the absence of revenue, or real taxable sources, he launched expensive Indian campaigns and expeditions against Mexican territory in New Mexico; he attempted to borrow money from European nations and when he could not obtain such loans he operated with deficit spending; and he did not particularly desire annexation to the United States at all.

Lamar is noted for his interest in education. During his administration "universities" were chartered and lands were set aside for future development in this field, earning him the title of Father of Education in Texas. He applauded the campaign against Cordova and the Cherokees, and during his administration he authorized "ranging" companies to again police the Indian frontier, especially against the Comanches and Apaches. When he failed to receive outside money to finance these activities, his administration issued "redback" dollars, so-called because of the color of the ink on the reverse side of the bills. They depreciated even further in value than even Houston's later issues.

Lamar's activities in international affairs proved even bolder. He dispatched James Hamilton to seek capital and recognition in Europe. Hamilton failed on the first of these duties, but he did secure recognition and a working arrangement for trade and commerce from England, France, The Netherlands, and Belgium. And the commander of the Texas navy, Commodore Edwin Moore, affiliated with rebels from the Yucatan region to harrass Mexico. Despite these activities against the Mexicans, Lamar nonetheless boldly offered that nation $5 million for a renewal of their recognition of the independence of Texas and the acceptance of the Rio Grande as the border. Just where he expected to obtain the money, had they accepted the offer, is unknown.

Lamar's boldest scheme, and perhaps his greatest failure, occurred when he sent a military expedition to claim the lands east of the Rio Grande in New Mexico. Lamar believed that the residents of the territory would accept Texas sovereignty if they had the opportunity to do so. In 1841 he dispatched a body of military men, merchants, and adventurers, including New Orleans newspaper editor George Watkins Kendall, to the ancient city of Santa Fe to claim it for Texas. Lamar did so without a clear authorization from his Congress. The New Mexicans refused to join the Texans and instead supported Mexican troops who captured the Texans and marched most of them to imprisonment in Mexico. Later, Lamar sent a group under Jacob Snively to capture a wagon train on the Santa Fe trail. They succeeded in routing a band of Mexicans intent on the same duty, but were themselves captured by United States troops guarding the wagon train. Thus both of Lamar's schemes to expand Texas' borders westward failed completely.

Lamar's greatest success lay in his relocation of the Republic's, and now the state's, capital city. Burnet began the interim government at Columbia, then moved it to San Jacinto, Harrisburg, and Galveston; mostly Houston's administration resided in a new city founded by the Allen brothers which they shrewdly named for Old Sam. The government even promised to remain there until 1840 to aid the Allens in the development of their city. Lamar disliked serving in a capital city named for his opponent, so he persuaded the Congress to authorize a new capital to be named for Stephen F. Austin and located somewhere east of the Colorado River and south of the old San Antonio road. While on a buffalo hunt, he selected a hilly site near the community of Waterloo, reportedly dubbing it fit for the headquarters of an empire. Many, including Houston, who claimed that this placed the capital at the mercy of raiding Indians and Mexicans because it lay beyond the frontier line of American settlement, objected to this move.

In the election of 1841 Lamar could not succeed himself as president, but Houston, who had served in the Congress as a delegate from San Augustine, was again eligible. He defeated Vice President Burnet, with Edward Burleson winning the vice presidency as an independent. Now it was Houston's turn to relocate the capital. He refused to go to Austin and instead summoned the Congress to Washington, although it also met back in Houston during this three-year term. However, the archives remained in Austin despite Houston's efforts to have them removed. In the quixotic "Archives War," the citizens of Austin used force to prohibit the removal of their one tangible claim to being the Republic's capital. And even though Houston did not serve there, his successor and all subsequent governors did.

Lamar's belligerent and expensive policies aided the return of the Old Peace Party to power in Texas. Under Houston's leadership Congress cut off expenditures as quickly and as completely as possible. And Houston ordered Moore to bring all Texas naval vessels home. When the commodore refused, Houston invited the navies of the world to take Moore's ships as prizes and he ordered their commander discharged from the service.

In this second term Houston inherited over $5 million in debts, most of them accrued during Lamar's administration. So for the next three years he spent only about $600,000. His curtailment of the ranging activities against the Indians renewed charges that he was an "Indian lover." Houston did take firm stands when necessary. For example, he temporarily settled trouble in East Texas known as the "Regulator-Moderator" War, a feud among several families which grew out of an election dispute. Branding it a danger to law and order, Houston persuaded the opposing sides to stop fighting for a while. And he had to respond with strength, although reluctantly, to two raids from Mexico.

The first invasion of Mexican troops came during the spring of 1842, when troops penetrated as far as San Antonio before withdrawing. They were mostly just signaling the Texans that the war had not ended, but it caused another Runaway Scrape. Then, in September 1842, nearly 1,000 Mexican forces under General Adrian Woll again captured San Antonio, and when they left the city they took sixty-seven hostages with them. This time Houston called out the militia under General Alexander Somervell to pursue Woll's men. The Mexicans succeeded in crossing the Rio Grande before the Texans caught them, however, and Somervell refused to cross the border because he lacked orders to do so. But the Texans would not be denied. Rejecting Somervell, they elected W. S. Fisher as their leader when he agreed to lead them across the river to assault the Mexican town of Mier. They demanded tribute from the Mexicans, and while they waited for an answer, General Pedro Ampudia quietly reinforced Mier. When the Texans attacked they found themselves overwhelmed by superior numbers and they were taken prisoner, then marched overland to Mexico City and held in Perote Prison until their disposition was decided. They escaped for a time, but most were recaptured. This, plus the death of others, reduced their number to only 176. The first order was that all were to be executed, but when the prison commander refused to follow orders to do so, the sentence was reduced to decemation—one in ten would die. They determined who should be sacrificed by drawing black and white beans; seventeen were shot immediately while the remainder languished in prison until freed as a gesture to European and United States requests.

Houston prevented other action against Mexico, knowing that Texas lacked the resources for renewed war. Meanwhile, interest in annexation to the United States revived. Many Texans had continued to nurture the hope that some day Texas would be a part of the American Union, and with the advent of President John Tyler's pro-southern administration, more Americans added their voice in asking for the admission of additional slave territory. This provoked just as many protests from abolitionists, of course, but now the Southerners seemed to have the strong voices. But it was not to be, at least not yet. After extended negotiation, Isaac Van Zandt and J. Pinckney Henderson signed a treaty of annexation with Secretary of State John C. Calhoun on April 12, 1844, which called for Texas to join the Union as a territory. It was not as good a deal as the Texans had hoped, and it might have been rejected in Texas had not the United States Senate done so first on June 8.

Many Texans felt insulted again, but actually the action soon provided them with a better deal. The Senate's rejection of the annexation treaty forced the issue into the forefront of the United States presidential campaign of 1844. Whig candidate Henry Clay tried to sidestep the issue, as did Free Soil candidate James Birney and Democratic ex-president Martin Van Buren. But the victorious Democrat James Knox Polk seized the nomination and the presidency by boldly campaigning for the "re-annexation of Texas and the re-occupation of Oregon," and Manifest Destiny won the day. Tyler raised the issue even before Polk could take office, and the Congress accepted Texas as a equal state of the Union by joint resolution on February 16, 1845.

The Texas response to the United States fell to the new president, Dr. Anson Jones, who defeated Edward Burleson in the Texas campaign in 1844. Jones favored annexation, but he moved cautiously. When the British and French agents asked him for a ninety-day delay to persuade the Mexican government to acknowledge Texas' independence in return for the Republic's agreement not to join the United States, he agreed. Then, when he officially received the Mexican offer, he submitted it and the United States offer of annexation to the Congress. Congress and the people favored the American Union overwhelmingly. They approved annexation and drafted a constitution for statehood which was accepted on October 13, 1845. Jones signed the final bill of acceptance on December 29, 1845, and in a valedictory statement, he proclaimed ". . . the Republic of Texas is no more." As the Lone Star flag descended its staff for the last official time, Sam Houston received it into his arms and clutched it to his breast. James Pinckney Henderson won election as the first governor of the state of Texas, and the legislature selected Houston and Thomas J. Rusk as the first United States senators.

The tenure of the Lone Star Republic was brief, but the memory of that unique time in the state's history remained vivid for those who lived then, and a special feeling about that time continues for many Texans. Unlike the Camelot of myth, the Texas Republic was, and is, reality. Troubled with money problems, a continuing war, Indian difficulties, a harsh environment, and with only the beginnings of settlement and civilization, the Lone Star Republic became romanticized as the memory of hardship dimmed. But for most contemporary Texans, especially those with roots deeply bedded in Texas history, the Lone Star burns brightly.

# *Republic of Texas*

*SAM HOUSTON First and Third President*

— Library of Congress

*MIRABEAU B. LAMAR Second President*

— Library of Congress

*DAVID G. BURNET*
*President, Ad-Interim Government*

— Institute of Texan Cultures

*ANSON JONES*
*Last President*

— University of Texas Library

# 4

## Statehood, War, and Reconstruction

*Ralph A. Wooster*

Admission of Texas into the American union in 1845 ushered in an era of prosperity and economic growth. In the next fifteen years the population of the new state increased more than four-fold as thousands of settlers from other states and foreign nations, attracted by the fertile soil and generous land policies, migrated to Texas. The cultivation of cotton, corn, and sugar cane expanded and opportunities for merchants, craftsmen, and professionals grew as new towns and cities were established. The value of assessed property in 1860 was eight times greater than at the time of annexation.

Not all the problems of the Republic disappeared with statehood. The public debt incurred by the Republic was inherited by the state, Mexico refused to recognize annexation by the United States, the dispute over the southern and western boundaries of Texas was unresolved, nomadic Indian tribes continued to attack outlying frontier settlements, and much of the western part of the state was unexplored and unsettled.

The controversy with Mexico over annexation and boundary questions demanded immediate attention. James K. Polk, who took office as president of the United States four days after congressional approval of annexation, sent John Slidell of Louisiana as American representative to Mexico with instructions to resolve all differences between the two nations. At the same time, General Zachary Taylor was ordered to move 1,500 American troops from Louisiana to the mouth of the Nueces River in south Texas. When Polk learned that the Mexican government refused to receive Slidell, Taylor was ordered to proceed to the Rio Grande.

The Mexican government, now headed by General Mariano Parades, proclaimed a "defensive" war against the United States and ordered Mexican troops to cross the Rio Grande into south Texas. On April 24, 1846, a small skirmish occurred north of the Rio Grande between American and Mexican cavalry. On May 8 and 9 larger battles, with casualties on both sides, took place at Palo Alto and Resaca de la Palma. On May 11, President Polk, stating that Mexico had "shed American blood on American soil," asked Congress for a declaration of war. Two days later Congress approved the declaration by a vote of 40 to 2 in the Senate and 174 to 14 in the House.

Most Texans were enthusiastic in their support for the war. Governor J. Pinckney Henderson was granted a leave of absence by the state legislature in order to command Texas troops mustered into American service. Slightly over eight thousand Texans enlisted during the war, but only five thousand actually saw service in Mexico. The most famous Texas unit in the war was a regiment commanded by John C. (Jack) Hays and included among its officers Ben McCulloch, Sam Walker, Mike Chevaille, "Big Foot" Wallace, and John S. ("Rip") Ford, all well-known Texas Rangers. George T. Wood, Peter H. Bell, and Edward Clark, all future governors; Albert Sidney Johnston, a former cabinet officer in the Republic and later a full general in the Southern Confederacy; and former President Mirabeau B. Lamar were other prominent Texans who participated in the war.

American military forces were successful on all fronts in the war. General Zachary Taylor captured Monterrey in September 1846 and defeated a large Mexican army commanded by Santa Anna at Buena Vista in February 1847. Another American army commanded by General Winfield Scott landed at Vera Cruz on the southeastern coast of Mexico and moved inland to capture Mexico City in September 1847. Texans served with distinction in both Taylor's and Scott's armies, although there were charges that the Texans made little distinction between civilians and military personnel, taking the opportunity to gain revenge for past Mexican atrocities, real and imagined.

In the treaty signed at Guadalupe Hidalgo ending the war, Mexico recognized Texas independence and accepted the Rio Grande as the southern boundary of Texas. Mexico agreed to cede the provinces of New Mexico and upper California to the United States. The United States agreed to pay Mexico fifteen million dollars and assume claims of over three million dollars held by American citizens against Mexico.

With the Mexican War ended, most Texans assumed they could now assert their rights to the area around Santa Fe. By an act of December 19, 1836, the Congress of the Republic had claimed all the area north and east of the Rio Grande from the north to its source and then to a line running northward to the 42nd parallel. During the Lamar administration unsuccessful efforts had been made to assure Texas rights to this area. When U.S. troops occupied Santa Fe during the Mexican War, Governor Henderson reminded Federal authorities of the Texas claims.

In March 1848, the Texas legislature created Santa Fe County with boundaries including the eastern half of New Mexico. George T. Wood, who succeeded Henderson as governor in 1847, notified President Polk that Spruce M. Baird had been appointed judge of the Santa Fe district. Wood asked that Federal officials cooperate with Baird, who was charged with organizing county government in Santa Fe.

When Baird arrived in Santa Fe in November 1848 he found that Colonel John M. Washington, military commander at Santa Fe, refused to recognize Texas' jurisdiction in the region. Washington supported local business leaders and politicians who wished to form a separate territory. Baird remained in New Mexico for seven months, but failing to gain support from either federal or local authorities, he departed in disgust in July 1849.

Excitement over the New Mexico question was growing. The next president of the United States, Zachary Taylor, was even less sympathetic to Texas' position than was his predecessor and favored creation of a new territory or separate state. Taylor's attitude was denounced by Texas newspaper editors and political orators. Governor Wood was defeated in his bid for reelection in the fall of 1849 by Peter H. Bell, Virginia-born fireater who advocated a more aggressive stand on the issue. Bell sent Robert S. Neighbors, a noted Indian agent and frontier explorer, to New Mexico with instructions to organize county government at Santa Fe. Neighbors had no more success in Santa Fe than Judge Baird. In June 1850 he returned to Texas and reported his failure to Governor Bell.

Neighbors' report created much excitement in Texas. The editor of the *Texas State Gazette* summarized the views of many Texans when he wrote "never since the foundation of the Union was there so highhanded and shameless an outrage committed against a sovereign state." Public meetings were held in various localities to denounce the federal government and assert Texas' claims. At a special session of the legislature Governor Bell reaffirmed Texas' determination to hold the area.

The death of President Taylor in July 1850 did not at first appear to change the situation. His successor, Millard Fillmore, reinforced the army in New Mexico and stated that he would use military means to resist Texas efforts to occupy Santa Fe. Even so, Fillmore was more amenable to compromise than was his predecessor. The new president supported efforts of congressional leaders to include the New Mexico question as a part of a general settlement of sectional difference. This settlement, known as the Compromise of 1850, was completed after months of debate in Congress. Under its provisions Texas surrendered her claims to the Santa Fe region and in return received ten million dollars from the federal treasury.

The boundary bill, proposed by Senator James A. Pearce of Maryland and supported by the Texas congressional delegation, fixed the northern and western boundary of Texas as a line beginning at the intersection of the 100th meridian and the 36°30′ parallel, west along that parallel to the 103rd meridian, south to the 32nd parallel, and then west to the Rio Grande.

Reaction in Texas to the boundary settlement was mixed. Charles DeMorse, editor of the Clarksville *Standard,* praised the work of Congress and in particular the efforts of Texas Senators Sam Houston and Thomas J. Rusk: "three cheers for the ten millions, three cheers for Texas and the Union and three times three for Sam Houston and Tom Rusk, the noblest Romans of them all." R. W. Laughery, editor of the Marshall *Texas Republican,* took the opposite view, urging readers to "reject the infamous Texas bribery bill." The influential *Texas State Gazette* published in Austin also opposed the settlement.

The lure of the monetary compensation was strong. At a special election held in the fall of 1850 Texas voters endorsed the settlement by a two-to-one majority. The legislature gave its approval, and Governor Bell signed the acceptance act on November 25, 1850.

Part of the money received from the boundary settlement was used to pay the public debt. This debt was of two types: revenue (consisting of principal and interest on Republic of Texas securities) and non-revenue (consisting of claims of participants in the Revolution and suppliers of military goods). Under the terms of the boundary settlement, the federal government held five million dollars to cover all revenue claims. The other five million went to Texas at once; 1.25 million of this was used to settle non-revenue claims. The remaining part of this money was used by the state for education, public buildings, and internal improvements.

The revenue debt was not settled until 1858. By that time interest on the five million and additional money given to Texas by the federal government for damages caused by Indians made available $7,750,000 for the settlement of claims totaling $10,078,703. As a result bondholders were paid at about 77 cents on the dollar. Although some bondholders protested this scaling, state authorities argued that the settlement was equitable as the Republic had not received par value for the bonds at the time of issue. Too, the bonds had passed from their original holders into the hands of speculators.

Elisha M. Pease was serving as governor when the debt question was finally resolved. Pease, a Connecticut-born lawyer, was elected in 1853. Like his predecessors Henderson, Wood, and Bell, Pease had been active in the movement for Texas independence and had a long record of public service. Pease was keenly interested in public education. While he was governor the legislature passed an education bill in 1854 whereby two million dollars of the money acquired from the United States in boundary settlement was set aside as a permanent endowment for public schools.

Pease's administrations are noteworthy for the acceleration of political activity and the formulation of political party organizations. Prior to Pease's candidacy state politics had been conducted mainly on a personal basis with much attention focusing upon the hero of San Jacinto, first president of the Republic and now United States Senator, Sam Houston. In many ways Houston was the dominant figure in Texas politics during the period of the Republic and early statehood. For over a decade Texans were "pro-Houston" or "anti-Houston." Because the Democratic party supported annexation, most Texans considered themselves Democrats, but party organization was virtually non-existent. The early contests for governor had been between Democrats of various political persuasions. In 1851 Ben H. Epperson ran as a Whig candidate in the race for governor but came in fourth in a five-man contest won by Peter H. Bell.

In 1853 Texas Whigs, supported primarily by planters and merchants, made a serious effort to capture the governorship with the candidacy of William B. Ochiltree. When it became apparent that Ochiltree might profit from Democratic division, two of the stronger Democratic candidates withdrew from the race and threw their support to Elisha M. Pease. Pease was victorious, receiving 13,091 votes, but Ochiltree with 9,178 votes was a strong second in a four-man contest.

Pease's victory momentarily unified Texas Democrats, but with the decline of the Whig party nationally interest in political organization again lapsed. The Democratic state convention that endorsed Pease's bid for reelection in 1855 attracted delegates from only twelve counties. But soon thereafter a new force emerged which caused Texas Democrats to abandon their lethargy and give more attention to party organization.

This new element was the American, or Know Nothing, party, which originated on the East Coast but made deep inroads in the South. In Texas the Know Nothing party, which included both anti-foreign and pro-Union elements, won local elections in San Antonio and Galveston in 1854 and 1855. Party leaders held a closed convention at Washington-on-the-Brazos in June 1855 and selected a slate of officers for the coming state elections. David C. Dickson, who previously had been endorsed by the Democrats in his bid for reelection as lieutenant governor, headed the Know Nothing ticket as candidate for governor.

The Democrats hastily called another meeting in Austin, where they reaffirmed their support for Pease, denounced Dickson and secret political factions, and nominated Hardin R. Runnels, Bowie County planter and legislator, for lieutenant governor. So effective was the Democratic counter-attack, some Know Nothings, including commissioner of the General Land Office Stephen F. Crosby, returned to the Democratic party. Although the Know Nothings managed to elect twenty state legislators, their ticket as a whole, including gubernatorial candidate Dickson, was soundly defeated.

Though defeated, many believed the Know Nothing Party would grow in Texas. A statement of support for party principles by Sam Houston late in 1855 seemed a good omen. The 1856 party convention, open to the public and held in Austin, attracted a good crowd. Even so, the party disintegrated on both state and national levels in the late 1850s, in part due to growing sectional conflict which led to increased polarization of factions (Republicans in the North and Democrats in the South) and in part due to the undemocratic and secretive nature of the movement. By 1857 the Know Nothing Party had virtually disappeared in Texas. In that year remnants of the party supported Houston, who was running for governor as an independent opposed to the Democratic nominee, Hardin R. Runnels.

The contest between Houston, whose nationalistic policies in the United States Senate were increasingly unpopular in Texas, and Runnels was a fierce one. Although Houston campaigned on his record as a Jackson Democrat, the regular party organization now dominated by southern extremists supported Runnels. Much criticism was leveled against Houston's opposition in the Senate to the Kansas-Nebraska bill, action which opponents charged was a betrayal of Texas' interests. Although Houston fought gallantly to overcome these criticisms the odds were too great. Runnels defeated Houston by a margin of nine thousand votes.

Two years later, in an equally bitter contest fought on much the same issues, Houston reversed the verdict, defeating Runnels by almost the same margin by which he had lost in 1857. In this election Houston campaigned on the theme that Runnels and state party leaders were too radical on the sectional question. Houston was aided also by dissatisfaction with Runnels' frontier policies in some western counties.

Increasing attention was focused upon frontier development throughout the period of early statehood. The discovery of gold in California and the general acceleration of the westward movement led to various efforts to improve communication and transportation in the western parts of the state. In 1849 veteran frontiersmen Robert Neighbors and John "Rip" Ford explored the area between San Antonio and El Paso trying to find a practical wagon route between the two cities. On their return from El Paso they went through Guadalupe Pass, crossed the Pecos River at Horsehead Crossing, traveled eastward to the site of present-day San Angelo, and then southward to San Antonio by way of the San Saba River and Fredericksburg. This trail, known later as the "Upper California Road," became a major route for wagon trains going to California.

Even more widely traveled was a trail explored by army Captain Wilt C. Whiting. This route, later known as the "Lower California Road," went westward from San Antonio to Fort Clark (present-day Brackettville), then northwest to cross the Pecos near present-day Ozona, and from there westward to El Paso.

Farther north, Captain Randolph B. Marcy led a wagon train along the Canadian River across Texas into New Mexico in 1849. On his return he traveled from El Paso eastward through Guadalupe Pass, crossed the Pecos River near the present-day town of Pecos, then moved northward past present-day Big Spring, Snyder, Stamford, and Henrietta, and crossed the Red River at Preston north of Sherman. This route, known later as the Marcy Trail, was widely used by pioneers and was the general route followed by the Butterfield Mail Line in the late 1850s.

The desire to improve transportation in the American West led to an experiment using camels as beasts of burden. At the request of Secretary of War Jefferson Davis, the U.S. Congress appropriated $30,000 for this project. Seventy-three camels were purchased in North Africa and Asia by the naval department, transported to the United States, landed at Indianola and Galveston, and driven to

Camp Verde, south of present-day Kerrville. From here various expeditions were conducted testing the animals' usefulness in the western environment. On several occasions the camels showed they could carry heavier loads and travel greater distance than mules. Even so, the military and most civilians remained skeptical and the experiments were halted. Some of the animals were auctioned to California freighters; others were simply turned loose to roam in the desert. For years to come western travelers reported sightings of "Jeff Davis's camels."

As more settlers moved into and through the state, Indian problems became more acute. In early 1849 the War Department established a line of eight military posts running from Fort Duncan at Eagle Pass on the Rio Grande to Fort Worth in north central Texas. Because of the expansion of settlements, these forts were soon abandoned, and another string of posts, about 100 miles to the west, was completed in 1852. A third string of forts, running east to west, was later constructed between the Concho River and the Rio Grande.

The presence of federal troops helped to stabilize the frontier but did not completely solve the Indian problem. In 1855 two Indian reservations were established in the hope of improving Indian relations. One reservation, near the present-day town of Graham on the Brazos River, was established for sedentary tribes such as the Caddo, Tonkawa, and Waco. The other reservation, located on the Clear Fork of the Brazos in present-day Throckmorton County, was established for the southern Comanches. By 1857 over 1,000 Indians were at the Brazos agency. The number of Comanches at the Clear Fork agency always varied considerably, but was usually between 350 and 400.

Frontier conditions improved during 1855-56, in part due to the reservation system and in part due to the presence in Texas of the Second U.S. Cavalry Regiment commanded by Colonel Albert Sidney Johnston. In the summer of 1857 conditions worsened. After Johnston and part of his regiment were ordered to Utah, the northern Comanches began a series of raids into Texas. Several battles were fought in North Texas and Indian Territory (Oklahoma) in 1858 between Indians and the U.S. Cavalry and Texas Rangers.

Many settlers were convinced that reservation Indians took part in the raids and demanded that these Indians be removed from the state. As a result, the reservation Indians were moved to the Washita River valley in present-day Oklahoma. Their departure did not mean an end to the raids, however. In the latter part of 1859 and early 1860 major raids were carried out by Comanches and Kiowas.

While some Texans were exploring the West or defending the

frontiers against Indians, the majority of Texans were clearing the land, planting cotton and corn, and tilling the soil. The rich native soils and the long, warm growing season provided almost ideal conditions for farming. The number of improved acres devoted to farming increased from nearly eleven million in 1850 to nearly twenty-three million in 1860. The cash value of farms increased during this same period from slightly over sixteen million dollars to over eighty-eight million dollars.

Cotton was the major cash crop in early Texas. In the days of the Republic, cotton was grown along the lower Brazos and Colorado rivers and in northeast Texas. During the years of early statehood cotton cultivation spread into central Texas. By 1860 Washington County was the largest cotton-producing county in the state. Total production of cotton increased from 57,596 bales in 1849 to 431,463 bales in 1859.

Corn was the principal food crop in early Texas. Here, too, an enormous increase occurred in the decade, from under six million bushels in 1849 to over sixteen million bushels in 1859. Sweet potatoes ranked second as a food crop, 1¼ million bushels grown in 1849 and 1¾ million bushels grown in 1859. The production of wheat, mainly confined to north Texas, increased more rapidly than either corn or sweet potatoes in the pre-Civil War decades, rising from approximately 41,000 bushels in 1849 to nearly 1½ million bushels in 1859.

Sugar cane was an important money crop on plantations along the middle Texas coast. In 1849 over seven thousand hogsheads of sugar cane were produced in Texas; nearly five thousand in one county alone, Brazoria. Many predicted that Texas would soon rival Louisiana as a major sugar producer, but poor weather in the late 1850s resulted in lower production. In 1859 only 5,099 hogsheads of sugar cane were produced in the state.

The expansion of agriculture in early Texas was accompanied by an increase in the number of black slaves. Although the Mexican government had discouraged slavery during the colonial era, there were approximately five thousand slaves in Texas at the time of the Revolution. This number increased rapidly during the period of the Republic and early statehood: 58,161 by 1850 and 182,566 in 1860.

Texas whites defended the institution of slavery on historical, scriptural, social, and economic grounds. Most newspaper editors and political leaders argued that the treatment of slaves was more humane in Texas than elsewhere. Many visitors to the state agreed. Young Rutherford B. Hayes, who visited the plantation of his college classmate, Guy Bryan in Brazoria County, reported to his family, "we have seen none of 'the horrors' so often described." William Bollaert, an English visitor in the 1840s, wrote that he could bear witness that slaves "are not over-worked, or ill-used." Not all visitors were so convinced. Frederick L. Olmsted, a prominent New Yorker who toured the state in the early 1850s, reported that Texas slaves were poorly housed and inadequately clothed. He noted that slave families were frequently separated by the sale of plantations. Olmsted felt that slavery and the plantation system was an inefficient and wasteful system of agricultural production.

The majority of Texas slaveholders were farmers who held fewer than ten slaves, in many cases a Negro man and woman and their children. Of the 21,878 Texans who owned slaves in 1860, less than 10 percent held twenty slaves or more, the number usually taken to indicate planter status. Only fifty-four of these held one hundred slaves or more in 1860. David G. Mills of Brazoria County, who was listed in the 1860 census as the holder of 313 slaves, was the largest slaveholder in antebellum Texas.

Saw milling and grain milling were the two most important industries in early Texas. These two industries produced over half of the manufactured goods (in terms of cash value) and employed over two-fifths of all factory workers in the state. Blacksmithing, leather tanning, iron and machine manufacturing, alcoholic beverage brewing and distilling, wagon and carriage manufacturing, and newspaper publishing and printing were other significant industries.

Transportation was a matter of much concern to early Texans. Although river boats plied the waters of major Texas rivers, there were many frustrations involved in river traffic as many of the state's streams were narrow and shallow with sand bars and tangled brush at the mouths. Buffalo Bayou, a narrow stream that connected Houston with Galveston on the coast, was the most heavily traveled waterway in the state.

Most Texans depended upon the roads for transportation. The most important of these were the old military road, from the Red River through Dallas, Waco, and Austin; the old San Antonio Road, passing through Nacogdoches, Crockett and Bastrop; a road from Dallas southward to Houston; and the old Spanish Trail from Louisiana through Beaumont and Houston on to San Antonio. Ox-carts and wagons carried heavy freight along Texas roads, while stagecoaches transported mail, men, and freight. By 1860 thirty-one stage lines operated within the state. In addition, the San Antonio-San Diego Mail Route, opened in the summer of 1857, offered semimonthly service to the west coast. The Southern Overland or Butterfield Mail Line, which crossed northern Texas, inaugurated service from St. Louis and Memphis to San Francisco in 1858.

Rail construction in Texas began in Harrisburg, near Houston, in 1852. By 1860 this road, the Buffalo Bayou, Brazos, and Colorado, extended southwestward to Alleyton, a distance of eighty miles. In 1856 a seven-mile line, the Houston Tap, was built connecting Houston with this line. Soon thereafter another railroad was built connecting these two with the town of Columbia on the Brazos.

Meanwhile, work had begun on a railroad linking Houston with the rich cotton belt of central Texas. The road, the Houston and Texas Central, was financed by Houston merchants headed by Paul Bremond. Another road, the Galveston, Houston, and Henderson, linked Houston with Galveston in 1859. The Texas and New Orleans Railroad was begun in 1857 and by 1861 connected Houston with Beaumont.

Although there was much talk and discussion of railroad building little actual construction was completed elsewhere before the Civil War. A small line connected Indianola with Victoria and another railroad in East Texas connected Marshall with Shreveport, Louisiana.

Texans became increasingly concerned in the late 1850s over the growing tensions between the North and South. Although the majority of Texans did not own slaves, their sympathies lay with the slaveholding states from where many of them had come. John Brown's raid on the federal arsenal at Harpers Ferry in the autumn of 1859 alarmed Texans and played into the hands of southern extremists. A states' rights delegation represented Texas in the National Democratic convention held in Charleston, South Carolina, in the spring of 1860. At this convention delegates from Texas and seven other states withdrew when it became apparent that the platform to be adopted would not guarantee protection of slavery in all the national territories. The Texas delegates later participated in a meeting of southern delegates who nominated John C. Breckinridge of Kentucky for president on a platform promising protection of slavery in the territories. The National Democratic party chose Stephen A. Douglas of Illinois as its candidate. John Bell of Tennessee was nominated by the newly formed Constitutional Union party, a group which favored a moderate course on the slave question. The Republican party, which was purely a sectional group, selected Abraham Lincoln on a platform opposed to any expansion of slavery.

The presidential campaign of 1860 in Texas was conducted in an atmosphere of tension and hysteria. A series of mysterious fires occurred in northeast Texas during the summer months. Many Texas

*THOMAS JEFFERSON RUSK Texas statesman and hero of the battle of San Jacinto*

— Martha Anne Turner

*EDMUND J. DAVIS Republican governor of Texas during Reconstruction*

— Institute of Texan Cultures
Texas State Capitol, Rotunda, Austin

*JUDGE ROBERT A. WILLIAMSON Texas patriot, newspaperman and attorney, known as "Three-Legged Willie."*

— Texas State Historical Association

*GENERAL EDWARD BURLESON Commander-in-chief of the Federal Volunteer Army of Texas*

— Sam Houston State University

*Painting of early Texas Legislative meeting inside the Republic of Texas capitol in Austin in 1839.*

— Institute of Texan Cultures
Painting by Mike Waters

*San Antonio de Bexar around 1850, drawn by Hermann Lungkwitz, lithographed and drawn in stone.*

— Photo by Institute of Texan Cultures
Original owned by Mrs. William Ochse

*GENERAL ALBERT SIDNEY JOHNSTON, Secretary of War for the Republic of Texas and later a General in the Army of the Confederacy.*

— Texas State Capitol, Austin

*Members of Wigfall's Texas Brigade at Seven Pines, Virginia during the fall and winter of 1861. This unit later became Hood's Texas Brigade.*

— Institute of Texan Cultures
From Confederate Research Center, Hill Junior College

*Battle of Corpus Christi, August 18, 1862 in which the Union soldiers were defeated and driven back to their gunboats after an attempt to take Confederate shore batteries.*

— Institute of Texan Cultures, Original by T. J. Noakes in La Retama Library, Corpus Christi, Texas newspaper editors attributed the fires to the work of abolitionists. Rumors spread concerning slave uprisings, attempted assassinations, and suspected poisonings. Vigilance committees were formed and suspects, black and white, were arrested. Several hangings occurred and rumors circulated that others would follow. The Knights of the Golden Circle, a secret order determined to preserve slavery and to secure additional slave territory in Latin America, was active in many communities.

Although Breckinridge carried Texas and the deep South in the election, Lincoln was victorious nationally, receiving 180 electoral votes compared to 123 for his three opponents combined. Lincoln's victory convinced many Southerners that their rights would no longer be respected within the Union. Several states called conventions to consider withdrawal from the Union. Letters, resolutions, and petitions were sent to Governor Houston urging that he call a convention to consider secession in Texas. Houston paid little heed to these demands, but an address to the people issued by a group of prominent state leaders urged elections to such a convention anyway. This address was widely publicized and on January 8 elections for delegates were held. Houston called a special session of the legislature and recommended that the legislature refuse to recognize the convention. However, the legislature gave its approval to the convention, requiring only that its actions be submitted to the people for final ratification.

The Texas convention began its deliberations in the state capitol on January 28. Numbered among its ranks were ex-Governor Runnels, Congressman John H. Reagan, Texas Supreme Court Judge O. M. Roberts, four future governors, and one signer of the Declaration of Independence from Mexico. Two-thirds of the delegates were slaveholders but the majority of them held fewer than ten slaves.

The convention lost little time in acting. An ordinance of secession was presented on the second day. After two days of debate members passed the ordinance by 166-8. On the following day the delegates adopted a declaration of causes which impelled the state to leave the Union. This declaration, addressed to the people of Texas to whom the secession ordinance was referred for ratification, recounted the abuses the state had suffered, including the lack of protection of slave property, failure to offer protection of slave property, failure to offer protection from Indian raids, and the election of a president not sympathetic to southern institutions. Before adjournment the convention chose seven delegates to represent Texas at a convention of southern states in Montgomery, Alabama, and named a Committee on Public Safety.

During the next two and one-half weeks the campaign for ratification of the secession ordinance was waged throughout the state. Meanwhile, the Committee on Public Safety negotiated an agreement with Major General David E. Twiggs for the surrender of federal property and evacuation of federal troops from Texas.

Five days after Twiggs agreed to evacuate all troops, Texans gave overwhelming endorsement to the secession ordinance by a vote of 46,129 to 14,697. The vote for secession was particularly strong in East Texas and along the Gulf Coast. Only in Angelina County did voters in these regions reject secession. Voters in all twelve Texas counties with a slave population in excess of 50 percent of the total population endorsed secession. Travis was the only one of twenty-nine Texas counties with over 35 percent slave population in which a majority of voters did not support secession.

Opposition to secession was greatest in two clusters of frontier counties in central and north Texas. In part, the resistance in central Texas was due to the German population, but Germans did not vote as a single bloc on this issue. In Gillespie, a frontier county with Fredericksburg as its seat, citizens voted overwhelmingly, 398-16 against secession, but in Comal, another German county less exposed to the frontier, voters endorsed secession 239-86.

The other center of opposition was in the frontier counties of north Texas where opponents of secession carried seven counties and nearly carried three others. Several factors, including origins of the people, economic status of the settlers, and fear of less adequate protection against Indian depredations, contributed to the opposition to secession in the area.

The state convention reassembled in March to canvass the vote. It then adopted an ordinance uniting Texas with the newly formed Confederate States of America. Governor Houston refused to recognize this action as binding and declined to take the oath of allegiance to the new government. The convention declared the office of governor vacant and elevated Lieutenant Governor Edward Clark to the position. President Lincoln offered to send troops to assist Houston if he would resist the convention, but Houston rejected the offer rather than bring on civil conflict within the state. Houston retired to his home at Huntsville, where he lived until his death in July 1863.

Fighting between the Union and Confederacy broke out in April 1861 when federal authorities refused to evacuate Fort Sumter in Charleston harbor. Shortly thereafter, President Lincoln called up the governors of the various states to provide 75,000 troops to help suppress the rebellion in the lower South. Within the next four weeks four additional slave states of the upper South seceded from the Union and joined Texas and the other six states of the lower South in the Confederacy.

Most Texans greeted the outbreak of war with enthusiasm. There is disagreement as to the number of Texans who saw military service; estimates range from sixty to ninety thousand. Practically all accounts agree that the mustering of men into military service was poorly coordinated. For one thing most Texans wanted to serve in the cavalry and took exception to be assigned to infantry and artillery units. In addition, weapons, clothing, blankets and mess equipment were not always readily available.

The majority of Texans enrolled in military service spent the war in the Southwest, either defending the states from Union invasion or participating in expansionist movements to the West. The month after the firing upon Sumter, Colonel W. C. Young and a regiment of Texas cavalry crossed the Red River and captured Forts Arbuckle, Cobb, and Washita. A second unit, the Frontier Regiment, commanded first by Colonel James N. Norris and later by Colonel J. E. McCord, fought several major engagements with the Comanches. Another state regiment, commanded by Colonel "Rip" Ford, guarded the Rio Grande from Fort Brown on the coast to Fort Bliss at El Paso.

As the most western state of the Confederacy, Texas was interested in expansion into New Mexico and Arizona. In the summer of 1861, Lt. Colonel John R. Baylor led a small Confederate force of 300 men into southern New Mexico and set up the territorial government of Arizona. Several months later Brigadier General Henry H. Sibley, commanding three regiments of Texans, moved into New Mexico. Sibley defeated a large Union force at Valverde on February 2, 1862, and moved on to capture Santa Fe and Albuquerque. In March Union forces halted Sibley at Glorietta Pass east of Santa Fe and captured his supply train. Sibley retreated back into Texas in late spring. The territorial government set up by Baylor withdrew to Texas at the same time. Sibley himself was in disgrace and the Confederate dream of western expansion was shattered.

The defense of the long Texas coastline was vital to the state and Confederacy. From the beginning of the war Union naval vessels patrolled Texas coastal waters, attempting to maintain a naval blockade, and occasionally shelling coastal communities. Paul O. Hebert, Confederate commander of Texas, was convinced that outlying areas could not be held and urged people to move from Galveston and other coastal towns. In October 1862 Union naval units sailed into Galveston Bay and demanded surrender of the island. At first the citizens of Galveston refused, but, after reconsidering, determined resistance was futile and decided to surrender.

Soon after the fall of Galveston, John Bankhead Magruder replaced Hebert as Confederate commander of Texas. Magruder began preparations for recapture of the Isle City almost immediately. In late December he put together an assortment of infantry, cavalry, artillery, and two battered river steamers that had been converted into warships. An hour after midnight on New Year's morning while Union forces slept, Magruder led his troops into the city while the Confederate gunboats steamed into the harbor. After several hours of determined fighting Union forces surrendered to Magruder.

Even more spectacular was the Confederate defense of Sabine Pass on the upper coast in September 1863. A large Union force consisting of four gunboats, twenty-two troop transport vessels, and 4,000 troops commanded by Major General William B. Franklin was repulsed by a Confederate artillery battery of forty-seven men commanded by Lieutenant Richard Dowling.

Later in the year a combined Union naval-army force captured Brownsville, cutting off Confederate trade through Matamoras. The invading force then divided, one column moving up the river to Rio Grande City, the other moving up the coast to Corpus Christi and Aransas Pass. Magruder feared that all of the Texas interior was in danger but suddenly the Federals halted their advance as troops were shifted to reinforce General Nathaniel P. Banks in his efforts to come into Texas by way of the Red River of Louisiana. This gave Texas a breathing spell and time to recruit additional troops. In July 1864 "Rip" Ford recaptured Brownsville after heavy fighting.

Banks's Red River campaign meanwhile had been halted at Mansfield, Louisiana, by Confederates commanded by Richard Taylor. On April 8, Taylor completely outgeneraled Banks and forced the Union army to retreat. The defeat of Banks's Red River expedition marked the last serious threat to Texas.

The larger battles of the war were fought beyond the Mississippi far from the boundaries of Texas. Thousands of Texans took part in the great battles in Tennessee, Georgia, the Carolinas, and Virginia that determined the outcome of the war. A Texan, Albert Sidney Johnston, commanded Confederates in the bloody battle at Shiloh. Many believe that had Johnston not been killed at Shiloh, the outcome of the war would have been different. Others, pointing to Johnston's earlier failures, argue that Union strength was so great no one person could have stemmed the tide.

John Bell Hood, who served in Virginia under Lee and later commanded the Confederate Army of Tennessee, was another prominent Confederate general from Texas. Hood's Texas Brigade was one of the finest in the war and highly regarded by General Lee. Another Texas unit, Terry's Texas Rangers, fought in as many battles and campaigns as any regiment in the war. Ross's Brigade, commanded by Lawrence Sullivan Ross, was yet another outstanding Texas unit that saw extensive service in Mississippi and Tennessee.

Francis R. Lubbock, who succeeded Edward Clark as governor in the fall of 1861, worked diligently to provide troops and equipment needed by the Confederacy. Under his leadership the legislature created the Texas State Military Board, which struggled to sustain foreign trade by supporting blockade running and established factories and munitions plants for the manufacture of military supplies. A cotton trade overland to Brownsville and across to Matamoras, Mexico, was developed and a cannon factory, several powder mills, and small-arms factory were established by the Board.

In 1863 Lubbock entered Confederate military service and was not a candidate for reelection. In the election Pendleton Murrah, a Harrison County lawyer, defeated Thomas Jefferson Chambers. Although Murrah promised to support the Confederacy and work in harmony with Edmund Kirby Smith, commander of the Trans-Mississippi Department, he soon found himself in controversy with Confederate authorities over conscription laws, transfer of Texas troops outside the state, and supply matters. After the Confederate losses at Vicksburg and Port Hudson in July 1863, the Trans-Mississippi Department, which included Texas, Arkansas, Louisiana, and Missouri, was thrown more and more upon its own resources as contacts with the Confederate government at Richmond were reduced.

Although the majority of white Texans supported the Confederacy, Unionist sentiment was strong in some areas, especially the German counties of the Hill Country and in a group of counties north of Dallas. Some of the early Texas unionists, such as James W. Throckmorton, who cast one of the eight negative votes in the Texas secession convention, accepted the Confederacy after Fort Sumter and actively supported the Southern cause. Others, such as Sam Houston, David G. Burnet, and Elisha M. Pease, withdrew from public life and attempted to remain neutral. A third group left the state or attempted to do so. Included in the group that left were S. M. Swenson, the father of Swedish migration to Texas, and William Marsh Rice, wealthy native of New York who later established an endowment for Rice University. Some 2,132 whites and 47 blacks from Texas served in the Union army. Best known of these was Edmund Jackson Davis, who was serving as a state judge when the conflict began. He escaped the state by boarding a federal blockader at the mouth of the Rio Grande. He organized and commanded the First Texas Cavalry Regiment (Union), which served in Louisiana and in the Rio Grande valley areas. After the war he was a member of the 1866 and 1868 conventions and governor of the state, 1869-1873.

Andrew Jackson Hamilton was another prominent Texan who left the state. Hamilton had served three terms in the state legislature and was representing Texas in Congress when secession occurred. He moved to New Orleans in 1862, and from there he went to Washington, where President Lincoln appointed him military governor for Texas. He was unable to return to the state, however, and spent the remainder of the war in New Orleans.

Not all those who attempted to leave the state were successful. A group of sixty-five German unionists attempting to flee to Mexico was overtaken by state troops near the Nueces River and thirty-five of the unionists were killed. Another fifty unionist sympathizers were hanged in the Hill Country several weeks later. The greatest roundup of suspected unionists occurred in Cooke and Grayson counties, north of Dallas. A citizens court at Gainesville tried 150 individuals for unionist activities. Some confessed, some were convicted, and thirty-nine were executed in what contemporaries called "the great Gainesville hanging."

Economically, Texas suffered less than any of the other Confederate states. Although many items such as coffee, medicine, clothing, and farm implements were difficult or impossible to obtain, the lively trade across the Rio Grande with Mexico made more materials available to Texas than to other states. Even so, the war forced many readjustments in life style. Farmers were urged to plant more corn because of difficulties in moving cotton out of the state, railroad building was halted, and new factories were established for manufacturing wagons, shoes, tents, and blankets. In many communities there was a shortage of houses; this was especially true of areas along the coast and near Arkansas and Louisiana as thousands of refugees poured into the interior. One such refugee from Louisiana, Kate Stone, declared that East Texas was headquarters for "ticks, redbugs, fleas by the millions, and snakes gliding through the grass by the hundreds." She concluded that in Texas she had "found the dark corner of the Confederacy."

The lengthening shadow of military reversals on fields of distant battle had its effect upon Texas. The crushing defeat suffered by Hood in the battle for Nashville in December 1864 convinced many Texans that the end of the war was near. Efforts were made through the press and the pulpit to keep up morale but the news of Lee's surrender to Grant at Appomattox in April 1865 made further resistance appear futile. Colonel John Ford defeated Union troops at Palmito Ranch near Brownsville on May 13, 1865, in what proved to be the last battle of the war, but from captured prisoners learned that Confederate forces were surrendering all over the South. Kirby Smith attempted to keep his command intact, but found his soldiers deserting and heading for their homes. Some Texans fled to Mexico rather than surrender. Governor Murrah, former governor Clark, and the governors of Louisiana and Missouri crossed the Rio Grande in late May. On June 2, 1865, Kirby Smith, with General Magruder at his side, boarded a Union ship at Galveston and signed the formal terms of surrender for forces in the Trans-Mississippi Department.

On June 19, 1865, the first Union occupation troops commanded by General Gordon Granger landed at Galveston. On that day Granger declared that Lincoln's Emancipation Proclamation was in effect in Texas. Thereafter black Texans celebrated "June Teenth" as the initial day of freedom from slavery.

Andrew Johnson, President of the United States following Lincoln's assassination in April, had announced a plan for reconstructing the South. Johnson's plan, similar to one previously developed by Lincoln, provided that a provisional government would be established in each state. The provisional government would function until the voters of the state who had taken an oath of allegiance to the United States could draft a new state constitution and elect their own officers. High ranking civil and military officers of the Confederacy and individuals with taxable property over $20,000 were excluded from voting. Under Johnson's plan each state would be required to abolish slavery, repudiate secession, and cancel debts incurred during the war.

Johnson appointed Andrew Jackson Hamilton as provisional governor of Texas to serve until the reconstruction process was completed. Hamilton arrived in Texas in late July and began appointing state and local officials. In keeping with Johnson's plan for reconstruction, Hamilton called for elections in early January 1866 for delegates to a constitutional convention which would meet in February.

The convention met in Austin as scheduled. The majority of the delegates were former secessionists, but the convention did include a handful of unionists. The delegates worked on a new constitution for two months. They accepted the requirements that secession be declared illegal, that slavery be abolished, and that state war debts be repudiated. While the convention delegates provided some minor legal rights for blacks, they did not extend voting rights to blacks.

The convention submitted its work in the form of amendments to the Constitution of 1845 under which Texas entered the Union. Those changes were approved by the voters in June 1866. At the same time voters elected state officers, including James W. Throckmorton, who was chosen as governor.

Governor Throckmorton and members of the new state legislature took office in August. Later in the month President Johnson announced that the insurrection in Texas was at end. Most Texas whites believed that Reconstruction was over but they were soon disappointed. The U.S. Congress, increasingly under the control of Radical Republicans, was displeased that Texas and other southern states failed to provide adequate safeguards and voting rights for newly freed blacks. They were also unhappy that former Confederate officers and sympathizers were elected to positions of leadership in state government. As a result, Congress in March 1867 declared that the governments set up under the Johnson plan were inadequate or illegal. At the same time Congress imposed its own plan of Reconstruction.

The Congressional plan divided the South into five military districts, each under a major general of the Army, declared existing southern governments provisional and subject to military authority, and demanded that new state constitutions be drafted. The new constitutions were to give black males the right to vote and hold office. The states were required to ratify the Fourteenth Amendment to the U.S. Constitution. Congress also imposed an "Iron-clad Oath" upon prospective voters, requiring them to declare that they had not voluntarily served in the Confederate army or given aid to the Confederacy.

Governor Throckmorton was removed from office by federal military authorities who declared he was an impediment to Reconstruction. Former governor Elisha Pease was appointed provisional governor in his place. Pease was an able man, respected by most Texans, but he had little power. Army officials controlled the state and during the summer and fall of 1867 removed dozens of state and local officials, replacing them with individuals more acceptable to Congress.

In February 1868 those Texans qualified to vote elected delegates to a new convention. This convention met in June. Only six of the ninety members had served in the convention of 1866. The majority of delegates were former unionists who had opposed secession. Nine delegates were black Texans. Six or seven delegates were so-called "carpetbaggers," i.e., northerners who had come South after the war.

The delegates worked on a new constitution for three months, adjourned until December, and then returned to work two more months. The constitution as finally adopted permitted male black suffrage by providing that suffrage should not be affected by "race, color, or former condition." The new document provided for much greater centralization than before. The governor would serve four years and would appoint most executive and judicial officers. The convention provided more support for public education than any previous Texas constitution.

Ratification of the new constitution and election of new state officers took place in late November. Edmund J. Davis, former commander of the First Texas Cavalry (Union) and a Radical Republican, was chosen governor over A. J. Hamilton in a bitterly contested election.

The newly elected state legislature moved quickly to ratify both the Fourteenth and Fifteenth amendments to the United States Constitution as required. Morgan Hamilton and J. W. Flanagan, both Republicans, were chosen to serve in the United States Senate. On March 30, 1870, President Grant signed a proclamation declaring that Reconstruction in Texas was ended.

Many Texas conservatives did not consider that Reconstruction was over as long as Edmund J. Davis served as governor. Davis was a controversial figure who exercised great power while serving as chief executive. The twelfth legislature, controlled by Davis supporters, created a new state police force directly under the governor's control. While the state police did help to curb the lawlessness prevalent during the period, opponents claimed the police were used to threaten and intimidate those opposed to the governor. In addition, the use of black policemen, who constituted about 40 percent of the force, was unpopular with conservative whites. Governor Davis also antagonized conservatives by his use of martial law in Limestone, Freestone, Hill, and Walker counties. Davis' supporters argued that this action was necessary to quell an armed insurrection, but his opponents contended his use of martial law was unnecessary.

Davis was also criticized for his generosity toward railroads. The Constitution of 1869 prohibited land grants to railroads, so the legislature issued state bonds to encourage construction in the state. The restriction relating to land grants was removed by constitutional amendment in 1873 and in later years Democratic controlled legislatures substituted land grants for bond subsidies.

Davis and the legislature enacted much constructive legislation. A public road system was planned and a number of new roads were built. Frontier defense was strengthened and a new homestead law was enacted. Strong support was given to the public school system; attendance was made mandatory and adequate taxes to provide necessary funds were levied. The system was highly centralized under a state board of education and a state superintendent.

The cost of the Davis programs offended many Texans. By 1872 state and local taxes were over two dollars per $100 evaluation, an increase of ten times the rate of 1866. Even so, the public debt under Davis increased by more than two million dollars.

Unfavorable public reaction to the Davis programs led to a Democratic victory in the 1872 legislative elections. The new legislature immediately moved to reduce the governor's powers, abolishing the state police, limiting his authority to declare martial law, and reducing his appointive power. Modifications of the public school system were also made.

In general elections held in December 1873 the Democratic candidate for governor, Richard Coke, defeated Davis in his bid for reelection. Davis and the Radical Republicans protested that the election was invalid and appealed to President Grant to send military aid. When Grant refused to intervene, Davis retired under protest. On January 15, 1874, Richard Coke was inaugurated governor.

Governor Coke and the Democratic-controlled legislature acted quickly to remove any vestiges of radical rule in Texas. Republican appointees to public office were replaced as soon as possible and retrenchment in governmental expenditures was undertaken. Steps were also made to replace the Constitution adopted during the period of Congressional Reconstruction. An effort to remodel the document through a legislative commission failed, and the legislature submitted the question of a constitutional convention to the people. In August 1875 voters approved the convention and elected ninety delegates to meet in Austin the following month.

The membership of the 1875 convention was quite different from the one in 1868. Seventy-five delegates were Democrats, and fifteen were Republicans, including six black delegates. Over forty members belonged to the Patrons of Husbandry, or Grange, an agrarian organization determined to reduce taxes and restrict corporate and railroad practices. From the opening of the convention delegates seemed determined to cut governmental expenditures and reduce the scope of government.

The constitution drafted by the 1875 convention was long and complex and contained many provisions normally left for statutory enactment. The governor's term was reduced to two years as it had been prior to 1869. His appointive powers were limited and he was given no control over the lieutenant governor, comptroller, treasurer, commissioner of the land office, and attorney general, all of whom would be elected by the voters. The powers of the legislature were also restricted. It was prohibited from incurring indebtedness in excess of $200,000 and the maximum tax rate was set at a low level. Laws for the regulation of railroads were authorized and grants of money for railroad construction were prohibited. The office of the state superintendent of education was abolished as was compulsory attendance. The legislature was authorized to give only limited tax support to public school maintenance but did set aside a large portion of public lands for a permanent school fund.

The 1875 convention, like the one in 1869, stipulated that the right to vote could not be restricted because of race. A petition for the right of women to vote was referred to a committee and did not reach the floor of the convention.

Although there was opposition in some quarters because of the reductions in support for public education, the new constitution was approved by the voters on February 15, 1876, by the margin of 136,606 to 56,652.

Most white Texans considered the adoption of the 1876 constitution to be the final step in the restoration of governmental control to the people of the state and the final end to Reconstruction. Black Texans could not help but wonder if the limited gains they had made in political, social, and economic areas would be safe in the future.

# 5

## The Texas Frontier

*Paul H. Carlson*

The story of the frontier in Texas is a remarkable saga that has become the stuff of a hundred novelists' and script writers' plots. Its essentially free but tough and danger-filled conditions of an often barbaric grandeur have captured popular imagination to burn their image deep into the American consciousness. Indeed, the story of the Texas frontier claims a vivid place in the collective memory of people not only in North America but also over much of the world. And in Texas today many people by their dress and life style seek perhaps a romantic identification with the more dramatic features of the Texas frontier.

The Spanish established a Texas frontier of sorts in 1690 when Alonso de Leon, governor of Coahuila, and Fray Damian Massanet, a Franciscan priest, with a party of 110 soldiers and three missionaries crossed Texas to the fertile Neches River Valley. Here they erected among Tejas natives a mission station, San Francisco de los Tejas. The tiny outpost served to convert Indians to Christianity and to guard Texas against French intrusion from Louisiana. The frontier proved more imaginary than real, however, and when no Frenchmen were found in the area, Spaniards in 1693 abandoned the place.

For nearly a quarter-century afterward, Texas remained unoccupied, but in 1716 Captain Domingo Ramon, in command of twenty-five soldiers, thirty civilians, nine missionaries, an amazing French trader named Louis Juchereau de St. Denis, and two other

*Mission San José y San Miguel de Aguayo in San Antonio, established in 1720.*

— San Antonio Missions National Historical Park
Photo by Zintgraph

Frenchmen, reestablished Spanish East Texas. Ramon's group immediately set about constructing homes, planting crops, and grazing livestock. By the end of the year, it had built six missions in the Nacogdoches region, each well-equipped and guarded by a small presidio.

Quickly others followed Ramon. One of these, Martin de Alarcon, governor of Coahuila and Texas, established in 1718 both the presidio and the village of San Antonio de Bexar near the mission San Antonio de Valero, later known as the Alamo, which had been founded a few days earlier by Fray Antonio de Buenaventura Olivares. The fort guarded the mission and village as well as the long road, called Camino Real, over which soldiers and settlers carried goods and livestock between Mexico and the Nacogdoches frontier.

During the next two decades Spain quietly consolidated her position. She created in the San Antonio area several new missions whose inhabitants raised fruits and vegetables in such abundance the surpluses were sold to presidio soldiers. She built a presidio near modern Victoria, known as Nuestra Senora de Loreto, or La Bahia, with an accompanying mission called Espiritu Santo de Zuniga. She strengthened her Texas capital at the Nacogdoches missions. Sometimes she encouraged enterprising colonists, such as a group of Canary Islanders who in 1732 settled near missions at San Antonio, to take up residence nearby.

Thus, the Texas frontier grew, pushed along by Spain's three symbiotic frontier institutions: the presidio, the mission, and the civil settlement. Presidios, often unpretentious fortifications, stood generally a few miles from the missions. Presidio soldiers, or *presidiales,* subdued the Indians and protected the missions. While it was almost always undermanned, a presidial company at full strength included one captain, one lieutenant, one first degree ensign, one second degree ensign, a chaplain, an armorer, two sergeants, one drummer, four corporals, four riflemen, and fifty-six soldiers. The soldiers provided their own uniforms, horses, arms, and food. If they had families settled in the area, they had to provide for their welfare on their own responsibility. But presidio families helped to bring an agricultural civilization to the frontier.

The missions were unique frontier institutions. They not only provided an outlet for the crusading zeal of the padres, but also helped to secure the frontier. At each station the missionaries taught the Indians Christianity and Western ways while the natives provided a labor force for the agricultural and pastoral pursuits associated with each complex. Most of the missions remained small, but a few, such as San Jose y San Miguel de Aguayo near San Antonio, were elaborate with a granery, a carpenter shop, a furnace for burning lime, a tailor shop, a flour mill, and irrigated, fenced-in fields of hundreds of acres, where in season the priests and their Indian laborers grew corn, beans, melons, potatoes, and other items.

Spanish civilians who settled in the vicinity or on neighboring ranches, following in the footsteps of the *conquistadores,* often hoped to acquire vast holdings in Texas and use Indian labor to develop their *haciendas.* That had been the practice elsewhere in the Spanish world. They quickly learned, however, that the situation was quite different in Texas, for most Indians in the province, in spite of the presidio soldiers, could be neither conquered nor converted. The lordly Comanches, the truculent Apaches, and the fierce tribes of the coast refused to submit tamely to a life of farming or ranching for someone else. But, since crops grew well in the bountiful soil and climate of Texas, and cattle and horses ran wild in the province, most early Spanish Texans made out. Corn was the staple crop, but inhabitants also produced beans, chilies, and a little sugar cane. Cattle became the dominant livestock, although there were plenty of sheep, goats, and pigs in Texas too.

Then, beginning about 1740, Spain's frontiers in Texas and elsewhere were threatened. Britain had founded Georgia and threatened Spanish supremacy in Florida. The French from Canada and Louisiana were edging into Texas and across the Great Plains toward New Mexico. A number of Indian tribes menaced positions across the north. In response, from about 1740 to 1765, Spain pressed additional missions, settlements, and presidios, planning to tame and hold Texas as a defensive province. She founded a mission along the lower Trinity and some on the San Marcos, Llano, San Gabriel, and San Saba rivers, and a few in other scattered and isolated places.

A vigorous frontier policy notwithstanding, by 1765 colonization of Texas had begun to slip, population to decline, and political authority to weaken. As a result Visitor-General Jose de Galvez, an agent of the Spanish king, sent the Marques de Rubi on a tour of inspection to reexamine Spanish policies in Texas and across the northern frontier. After visiting San Saba, San Antonio, Nacogdoches, La Bahia, and other outposts in Texas, the keenly observant Rubi recommended that Spain quit most of the region and use the southern fringe as a defensive border. A royal decree in 1772 followed his ideas. It called for the abandonment of all missions and presidios except San Antonio de Bexar and La Bahia, the strengthening of San Antonio, and a new Indian policy.

Teodore de Croix, as commander of the Spanish Internal Provinces, accepted the task of putting the Rubi recommendations into force. While most of the recommendations were followed, settlers in the Nacogdoches district eventually returned to the East Texas woodlands, and missionaries delayed the closing of their stations when they could. Nonetheless, from 1780 until Mexican independence in 1821, Texas became less and less stable. Despite all of Spain's efforts to people the area, the population dwindled until Spain had only the settlements at San Antonio, La Bahia (which had been moved to present Goliad), and Nacogdoches. Between these scattered outposts there were vast stretches of land occupied only by wild game and roving bands of Indians. From the mouth of the Rio Grande north and east along the entire Gulf shoreline to Matagorda Bay, there was not a single Spanish community, and no towns existed on the Texas side of the Rio Grande above Laredo. The population of the huge Texas area, consequently, was small in 1800 — perhaps four thousand persons.

The period between the decline of Spanish influence in the 1790s and the retreat of Mexico from the region in the 1840s witnessed the birth of Anglo-American interest in the region. The first Anglo-Americans who reached the area from the east and northeast were traders, such as Philip Nolan, who with a handful of men searched for wild horses and cattle, or filibusters, such as Augustus Magee, who with a small military force invaded the country unsuccessfully. The intruders looked upon the region as a land of easy opportunity, whose rich river bottoms beckoned farmers and whose large Indian populations attracted traders. In the three decades after 1790 more than a dozen men led hundreds of others on trading, hunting, exploring, and military forays into the area.

In the meantime, Spain adopted a new plan to control and develop Texas. She hoped to hold the region by admitting Anglo-Americans as permanent settlers. But before she could carry through her plans, the Mexicans secured their independence. The new regime in Mexico thereupon concluded arrangements in 1823 for granting a huge tract of land to Stephen F. Austin, with the understanding that he would bring to Texas three hundred families.

When other grants followed, aggressive, pioneer Americans poured into the Mexican state. As they moved to settle their grants, the *empresarios,* or land agents, such as Austin, wrote favorably of their country. In 1829 Austin penned a note to Commodore David Porter, an American merchant who planned to establish a colony south of the Rio Grande, urging him to consider Texas. The climate, Austin admitted, did not allow cultivation of coffee or cacao or tropical productions, but there were other advantages. The pasturage, he said, "or 'range' as we term it, is certainly superior to any thing I have seen in any country, and the facilities for raising cattle, horses, mules, sheep, and hogs, etc. almost exceeds credibility." Within a year Porter had applied for a grant in Texas. Others agreed with Austin, prompting nearly every *empresario* to encourage his settlers to mix sheep, goats, and pigs with the horses and cattle. While the Anglo-American population increased, Texas remained largely a Mexican frontier province whose citizens were farmers and planters living in rural and often isolated communities.

Then, suddenly, Texas' brief but successful struggle for independence from Mexico in the 1830s brought changes. As more people immigrated to it, the Republic of Texas turned from a frontier province to a rural commonwealth. Nearly all of the settlers came from states of the Old South, but there were northerners, too, and Europeans, especially Germans, migrated from Old World countries. The new citizens tended to settle in colonies east of the Trinity River before moving to western frontier portions of Texas, where they struggled to cultivate their crops and protect their homes from the Indians, whose land they had abruptly invaded.

The assault was massive. It included penniless immigrants, well-to-do planters and their slaves, opportunistic merchants, sturdy yeoman farmers, and others. The population, which was estimated in 1836 by Henry M. Morfit, a special representative from the United States to Texas, at almost 40,000, including Mexicans and blacks but not Indians, had reached 142,000 by 1847. Three years later the population reached to over 212,000, and by 1860 it had jumped to 604,000. Land hungry immigrants from the United States, perhaps driven by an elusive sense of achieving their manifest destiny, were largely responsible for the phenomenal migration. Virile and prolific, they poured across the border to take advantage of Texas' liberal land policy. When space became crowded in the rich and well-watered eastern portions of Texas, they rushed to the frontier. By the end of the War with Mexico in 1848, the frontier line of settlement in Texas, now a state, extended roughly from the Red River near present Denison southward near the long curve of the Balcones Escarpment to San Antonio, thence to Corpus Christi. Twelve years later the western edge of settlement, reaching a line in places one hundred miles farther west, ran irregularly from Henrietta southward through Belknap, Palo Pinto, Brownwood, Llano, Kerrville, and Uvalde to the coast a few miles south of Corpus Christi. Here, on the eve of the Civil War the advance halted for a time.

As the surge of population westward halted, Texans in the face of the Mexican War and Indian attacks could look back at fifteen years of rapid growth. The state east of the frontier line was filled in

*One mode of conveyence during the frontier days of Texas was this Mexican-style ox cart photographed in the village of Fredericksburg.*

— UT Institute of Texan Cultures

with a rural farming and livestock population dominated by customs and values of the Old South. None of the towns were large; the biggest one, San Antonio, through trade with Mexico and growth as an army center, showed a total population of only 8,236 persons. Most people in the state made a living as self-sufficient, yeoman farmers who raised cotton as a money crop, but produced corn, wheat in the north, sweet potatoes, and other vegetable fare as well as livestock — mostly cattle, horses, sheep, and hogs. These rural Texans lived in simple homes. Occasionally one could find a well designed and carefully built frame or brick dwelling or a pretentious Grecian styled, white pillared mansion, but the prevailing residence was a log cabin. The double log cabin, or dog-run house, which consisted of two rooms under a continuous roof, separated by an open space, or dog run, was the most popular. Settlers in the Hill Country, however, especially Germans, frequently used stone in their construction. Most Texans on the frontier subsisted almost wholly on salt pork, corn bread, syrup, and sweet potatoes.

The state west of the 1860 line, roughly corresponding to the 98th meridian, belonged to the Indians. This great expanse included the High Plains, a shimmering sea of grass reaching farther than the human eye could follow; the Edwards Plateau, a broken tableland of shallow soil and in its eastern portions covered with cedar brakes; the South Texas Plains, a territory of eroded brushlands and chaparral-lined savannahs; the Rolling Plains, an area of highly eroded terrain interspersed with spacious prairies; and the Trans-Pecos, a colorful basin and mountain country of yucca, catclaw, and cresote bush. Representing about half the state, it was a beautiful, but incredibly harsh, land of few trees and little rainfall. A southern extension of the Great Plains, the region was utterly unintelligible to Anglo-Texans, coming out of the piney woods, rich soil, and humid counties of East Texas, who probed its eastern fringe. But it was here that the West began.

Texans began to penetrate this strange but beckoning kingdom after the War with Mexico. Between 1848 and 1853 several exploring parties crossed the region either to open trade lines between San Antonio and El Paso or to provide overland routes for argonauts heading for the recently discovered gold fields in California. John C. Hays, the famed Texas Ranger, in 1848 unsuccessfully tried to open a wagon road by way of the Llano and Devils rivers. The next year Robert S. Neighbors, an Indian agent, and John S. (Rip) Ford, a famous Texas Ranger, reached El Paso by way of the Middle Concho River, Horsehead Crossing on the Pecos, and the Davis Mountains. Captain W. H. C. Whiting of the United States Army made a reconnaissance to El Paso a little below the Neighbors-Hays route. When leaders of both expeditions reported favorably on their routes, army officers surveyed the roads. In a more famous undertaking, Captain Randolph B. Marcy in 1849 escorted a party of immigrants to Santa Fe. His return route, known as the Marcy Trail, ran through Guadalupe Pass, across the Pecos near the present town of that name, to the vicinity of present Colorado City, and then northeastward to the Red River at Preston. It became a major highway for immigrants heading west. In 1853 Captain John Pope, to survey possible railroad lines, traversed much of the Marcy Trail.

Others closely followed the explorers. In an unusual and ill-fated experiment, Jefferson Davis, then United States Secretary of War, imported camels. The army took the strange smelling beasts in 1856 through San Antonio to Camp Verde near Kerrville where they were to help solve difficult transportation problems in the arid Southwest. While they could carry more than horses or mules, the camels could not be shod, and their soft feet could not withstand the rocky Texas terrain. Within a short time the animals were sold; many of them were taken by freighting contractors who used them for a few years in Arizona and Nevada.

Before the camels were withdrawn, stagecoach lines cut across the West Texas frontier. In August 1857 entrepreneurs began a semimonthly mail and passenger service between San Antonio and San Diego, California. Although relatively fast and dependable, a trip was expensive, costing two hundred dollars. The next year John Butterfield opened his famous Southern Overland Mail. Its route, which skirted settlements in North Texas before cutting southwestward to wind its dusty way over much of the Marcy Trail, through Horsehead Crossing of the Pecos, and passed the Davis Mountains, connected Saint Louis, Missouri, and San Francisco, California, with twice weekly service in twenty-five days or less.

Because western Indians, resenting these unwelcomed intrusions, struck to prevent them, the United States War Department, beginning in 1849, built a series of defensive posts. It established eight garrisons between the Rio Grande and the Red River. Two years later it replaced the posts by seven new forts, generally along an irregular line about one hundred miles to the west. And it located several other posts at strategic points along the Rio Grande and in the Trans-Pecos. When the posts were well-manned, as they were in 1853 when 3,256 soldiers patrolled Texas, the frontier was comparatively tranquil. At other times a fiery Indian war swept the West.

During the Civil War, when troops were withdrawn to eastern campaigns, the Texas frontier broke down. Indians from both Texas

*Engraving of Indians attacking a wagon train at Beaver Creek, around 1864.*

— Institute of Texan Cultures
From Frank Leslie's *Illustrated Newspaper*

and Mexico struck isolated ranches over a wide area, burning and pillaging to such an extent that they drove many settlers eastward up to one hundred miles in some places. To combat the marauding natives, the Frontier Regiment, a state organization, was created in 1862. Reorganized the next year and again in 1864, it proved ineffective and was transferred to Confederate service. To offset the loss, men in the western counties enrolled in militia companies, but these, too, failed to provide protection. People along the frontier found safety only by moving into stockades; "forting up" it was called. Many ranchers as far east as Waco fled from their land, and at Denton in 1866 a large group of citizens resolved to abandon their homes unless help arrived before the year was out. Farther west in Wise and Young counties, whose combined population of 3,752 in 1860 declined to 1,585 in 1870, people left everything behind. All totaled, Indians killed perhaps 163 whites, carried away 43 others, and wounded 24. Confusion reigned.

To end the chaos, as well as oversee Civil War reconstruction efforts and defend the country, the United States War Department created a system of geographic commands: the Divisions of the Atlantic, Pacific, and Missouri. The latter division, which included the Great Plains, was subdivided into the Departments of the Dakota, Platte, Missouri, and Arkansas. Reorganization shortly afterward added the Department of Texas, which from time to time the army subdivided into two or more districts. The whole system provided a highly centralized but loose chain of command.

But in Texas protection afforded by the military was inadequate. The army adopted a defensive policy designed to keep Indians out of the settlements through a system of scouting expeditions rather than one of attacking villages. Besides the troops in Texas, often a collection of ill-trained misfits, were too few, too scattered, and too conditioned to fighting a foe who stood his ground. The Indians they faced, particularly Lipan and Mescalero Apaches, Kickapoos, Comanches, and Kiowas, used guerrilla methods—tactics the soldiers, under inept leadership, learned only slowly.

The Comanche and Kiowa were typical Plains Indians whose armed and mounted warriors were highly mobile fighters. Each could carry a hundred arrows, and, as the late Walter Prescott Webb pointed out, he could fire them from his running horse rapidly enough to keep one in the air continually. These Indians, Webb concluded, were better equipped for successful warfare on the Plains than the American soldiers who came against them.

Although the Mescalero and Lipan Apaches show some Plains influence, they were people of the mountains but equally at home in the desert. The Mescaleros roamed the Sierra Blanca and the Guadalupe and Davis mountains of Texas and Mexico, but they moved about freely, wintering on the Rio Grande or farther south, ranging to the buffalo plains in the summer, and always following the sun and food supply. The Lipans ranged over northern Mexico below the Rio Grande, where they had raided ranches and villages for generations. The elusive Apache warriors depended on success in raiding for wealth and honor in their tribes.

The Kickapoos provide a dramatic tale. Originally living south of the Great Lakes, these Indians under Anglo-American pressure moved southwestward. One group settled on the Missouri River near Fort Leavenworth, but most moved into Indian Territory and Texas. In 1839 one band of eighty, which had confederated with the Cherokees in East Texas, fled to Mexico. During the Civil War at least two other discontented groups joined the refugees below Piedras Negras, where Mexican officials gave them land. The Kickapoos came to rely for their livelihood on Texas plunder.

Although Indian depredations had always been a problem for westward moving pioneers, the difficulty in Texas became desperate about 1870. The reasons were many. By then the Plains Indians had been crowded from their land; Comanches and Kiowas as early as 1867 had been forced to accept a small reservation in present southwest Oklahoma. While they had hunting privileges off the reservation, the buffalo, their main source of sustenance, was slaughtered by white hide hunters in numbers so shocking they seemed to increase exponentially each year. In addition, pressure from eastern humanitarian groups had forced the government to adopt more peaceful practices in its relations with Indians.

In response to the latter, President Ulysses S. Grant in 1869 inaugurated the Quaker Peace Policy. The policy, a supplement to the general concentration policy of 1851 that confined Plains Indians to areas away from main-traveled roads, was designed to divorce the War Department from official Indian relations. It provided that churchmen would serve as Indian agents, that military personnel must stay away from reservations, and that a general humanitarian approach to Indian problems would be followed. From the very first, however, without the presence of troops many reservations became sanctuaries for Indians who disliked their new, idle, and monotonous life.

Comanches and Kiowas proved particularly troublesome for settlers in West Texas. They raided from Indian Territory (present Oklahoma) with increasing fury in the months after the adoption of the Quaker Peace Policy. After a raid they rode back with their plunder to the sanctuary of the reservation.

Texans complained often and loud, but to little avail — until 1871. In that year William T. Sherman, General of the Army, who never believed that Indian depredations were as bad as Texans portrayed them, visited the state. On May 18 with a small escort enroute to Fort Richardson he crossed Salt Creek Prairie, watched by a party of about one hundred Indians including such noted war leaders as Satanta, Satank, Big Tree, Eagle Heart, and Big Bow. Only a medicine man's prediction of richer prey saved Sherman. That night a wounded teamster staggered into Fort Richardson to tell Sherman that a train of ten wagons manned by twelve teamsters had been attacked. Only four had escaped, the wagons had been burned, and the mules stolen. Finally convinced of the validity of the Texas appeals, Sherman turned loose the troops.

During the next several years soldiers in Texas struck back. Now well-trained, seasoned, and led by an aristocracy of talent that included the masterful Ranald S. Mackenzie — "the most promising young man in the army," said President Grant — of the fourth Cavalry, mild-mannered Benjamin H. Grierson of the all-black Tenth Cavalry, unrelenting William R. Shafter and tough, desertwise John L. Bullis of the black Twenty-fourth Infantry, they punished Indians everywhere off the reservations. They crossed the Rio Grande to attack Kickapoo and Apache bands in Mexico, scoured the mysterious Llano Estacado to strike Comanche and Kiowa camps in deep canyons of the ranging tableland, penetrated the Trans-Pecos to pursue Apache warriors through its deserts and blue-topped mountains, and invaded the once-safe reservations to surprise and arrest renegades. Occasionally, they attacked Indians peacefully hunting buffalo. The troops burned villages, slaughtered Indian ponies, and destroyed camp equipage to disrupt raiding activities and return Indians to reservations.

The most telling of the many engagements was the Red River War. Following a large scale attack by Plains Indians on June 27, 1874, on a small party of buffalo hunters presumptuously encamped at Adobe Walls on the Canadian River in the Texas Panhandle, the army dispatched forty-six companies, about three thousand men, marching in five columns from as many directions, into the region. In the difficult and hazardous campaign that followed, the federal troops routed the Indians from their traditional hunting grounds and favorite winter camps in protective canyons and colorful breaks at the eastern edge of the Llano Estacado. Ranald Mackenzie delivered the critical blow in September when his Fourth Cavalry flushed

*CHARLES GOODNIGHT, pioneer Texas cattleman.*
— Panhandle-Plains Historical Museum, Canyon, Texas

*Cattle roundup on the Palo Duro Ranch at Paloduro, Texas, around 1905.*

— Institute of Texan Cultures
Published by Keystone View Company

Indians from Palo Duro Canyon, burning tipis, destroying winter supplies, and capturing over 1,400 horses and mules. He snared very few people, but his attack broke Indian resistance. After the surrender of the great Comanche chief Quanah Parker and his small band in June 1875, the Texas High Plains was clear. The fighting in West Texas, together with that which occurred elsewhere on the Great Plains, did not last long and engaged only a handful of regular army troops, but it has captured the American imagination to create legends and images of heroic proportions.

As the army, aided by the extermination of buffalo, destroyed the Southern Plains Indians' nomadic way of life, but not before then, the Texas range cattle industry expanded across western grasslands and onto the verdant High Plains. The industry began in the diamond-shaped brush country below San Antonio, where mission fathers and a few *haciendados* had grazed during the Spanish era herds that sometimes numbered up to fifteen thousand head. It declined in the late eighteenth century but reestablished itself when Anglo-Americans, such as H. L. Kinney, Richard King, and Mifflin Kenedy, built empires in the region; although, it should be noted, James Taylor White, who had a sprawling ranch in present Liberty and Chambers counties, was Texas' first cattle baron. Nevertheless, the origins of the range cattle industry were Spanish. Its methods, terms, and paraphernalia were Spanish. The cattle, which over the years grew taller and lankier as their horns spread into the fabled longhorns, were Spanish; but, happily, during the Republic of Texas years and afterwards Anglos crossbred them with fat, round-barreled stock from the East. Immigrants from the Old South also brought to Texas their own time-honored systems for raising cattle.

Under Anglo-American leadership, the Texas range cattle industry prevailed along the frontier as a sort of advance guard of civilization. During the 1840s, as Spanish cattle left to themselves ran wild in South Texas and multiplied, the industry spread elsewhere into the wide prairie region of North Texas near present Dallas. In the 1850s it pushed into the Hill Country northwest of San Antonio and Austin, and farther north it advanced westward to the Cross Timbers and beyond.

The cattle were cheap and plentiful. Consequently, thousands were slain for their hides and tallow. Rockport on the Gulf coast near Corpus Christi contained a dozen plants to render out tallow and ship the product to eastern buyers. There were other such plants along the coast, too. Beef markets were more difficult to reach. Some men rounded up wild cattle to sell to farmers in East Texas. A few, such as James Taylor White, drove them to markets in Louisiana. In 1846 Edward Piper moved a herd to Ohio. After the discovery of gold in California, a few drovers pushed cattle through Indian lands and deserts to the Pacific coast, and there were various drives to Missouri and in 1856 one to Chicago. These were minimally organized cattle drives, however, and had only limited effect on the Texas industry.

Of far greater impact was the Civil War. Not only did it halt the western advance, but it also caused the neglect of many herds. George Wilkins Kendall, founder of the New Orleans *Picayune* and famed Hill Country sheepman, complained during the war that untended cattle trampled through his fields and overran his sheep range. He shot them. Cattle markets dried up, especially after Yankee soldiers closed off the Mississippi to Confederate sales in 1863, and the herds increased until there may have been some four to five million cattle in Texas in 1865. Charles Schreiner, father of the Texas Hill Country and founder of a large cattle-trailing firm, noted that cattle were so plentiful near Kerrville that nobody bothered to brand the mavericks.

The close of the Civil War opened new, lucrative markets. Most of them were in the North, where burgeoning cities contained a discriminating population that demanded fresh meat. In response large slaughter houses, especially those in Chicago, sought beef at almost any price. Texas ranchers, whose cattle were worth about three dollars a head, soon learned of thirty or forty dollar prices for a grown animal offered by northern buyers. During the winter of 1865-1866, consequently, they gathered a number of herds in preparation for a northern drive as soon as the grass turned green.

Thus, in the spring and summer of 1866 the era of the great cattle drives began. The first year some 260,000 head were started on the trail to Sedalia, Missouri, on the Missouri Pacific Railroad and to other points in the state from where they could be shipped to northern markets. But when Missouri farmers, claiming that Texas livestock destroyed their crops and transmitted to their animals the dreaded Texas fever, turned back drovers and scattered the cattle, there was trouble. In addition, border bandits demanded protection money for safe passage, and Indians ran off sizable numbers of steers. Another railhead was needed, preferably one beyond the timberlands of Central Texas and eastern Oklahoma and away from the irate farmers who imposed "shotgun quarantine" against the longhorns.

Joseph G. McCoy, an Illinois cattle buyer, provided the answer. He went to the railroad companies, asking them to promise favorable rates for shipping cattle to Chicago. Two agreed. The Kansas

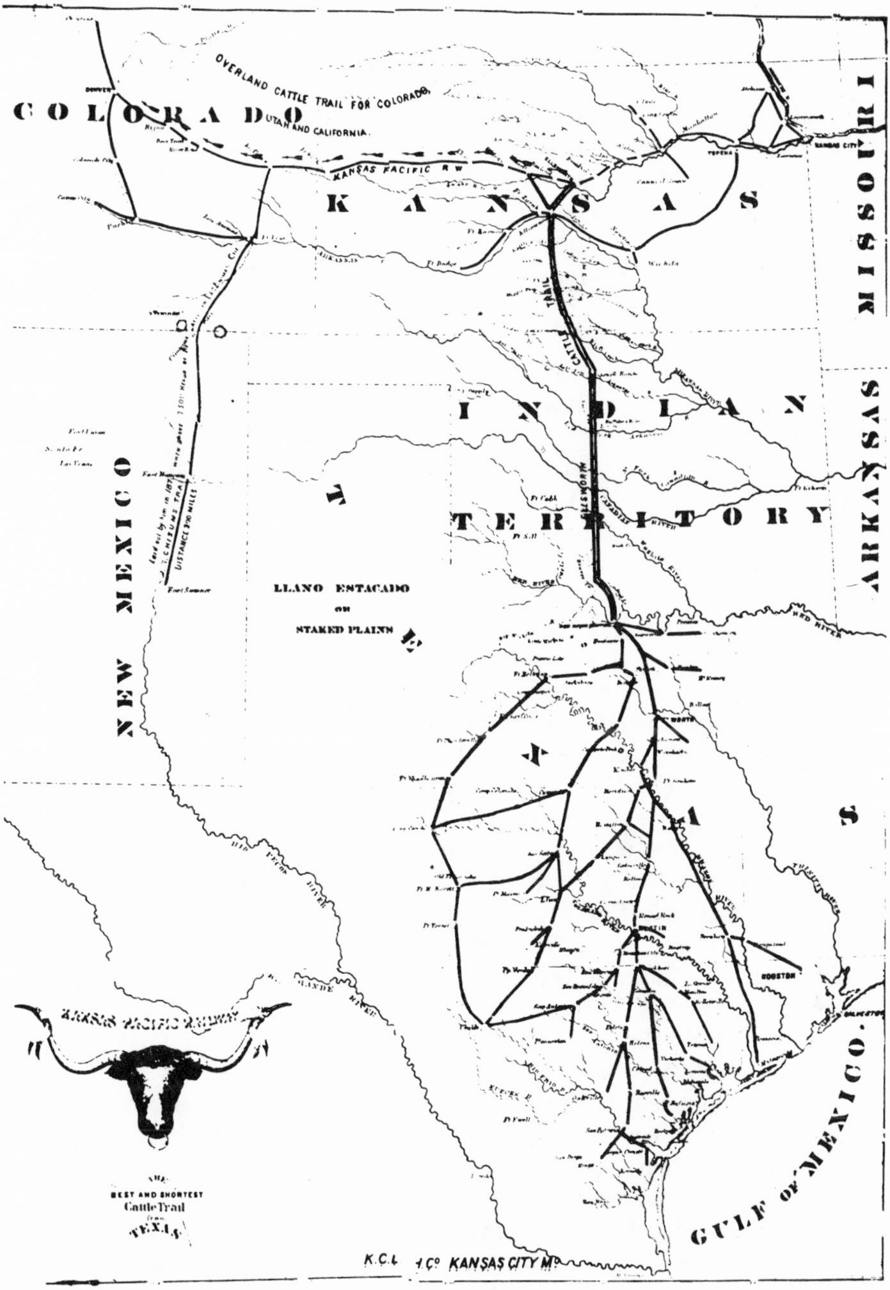


*The best and shortest cattle trails from Texas to the Kansas-Pacific Railroad, 1875.*

— Institute of Texan Cultures
From University of Texas Archives

Pacific guaranteed low rates to the Missouri River, while the Hannibal & St. Joseph made a similar commitment for the remainder of the route. Abilene, Kansas, the loading point, was only "a small dead place . . . of about one dozen log huts," McCoy wrote. But he soon had the place swarming with activity. His men built shipping pens, barns, livery stables, and a hotel called Drover's Cottage. He sent riders south to invite Texans to bring their herds to Abilene, and he even marked a trail, first used by the Scot-Cherokee trader Jesse Chisholm, through Oklahoma and Kansas. Only 35,000 longhorns reached Abilene in 1867, but each year thereafter for more than two decades drovers "pointed them north" to Kansas railroad stations. Although accounts of the number of cattle driven over the trails vary, the 1880 census estimates the drives to Abilene, 1867-1871, totaled 1,460,000; to Wichita and nearby points, 1872-1875, 1,072,000; to Dodge City—"the Gomorrah of the Plains"—and Ellsworth, 1876-1879, 1,046,732; to Dodge City and Caldwell, 1880, 382,000.

Longhorns that were driven north did not all go to Kansas. Indeed, drovers led 60 percent of them farther north. They sold them to military posts or to Indian reservations. The longhorns also stocked ranges in Nebraska, Colorado, Wyoming, Montana, and Dakota. When the prices were down, as after the panic of 1873, cattlemen pastured the herds until the market improved. Colorado received the first large herds from Texas, and by 1869 there were one million cattle in the territory. Most of these animals went north along the Goodnight-Loving Trail, named for Charles Goodnight, one of America's finest plainsmen, and Oliver Loving, who pioneered it in 1866. It ran west from Fort Concho to New Mexico and then north to Colorado through the western heart of Comanche and Kiowa country. Of all the many cattle trails leading "north of 36," it was in its early days the most dangerous.

The trail drive was a basic institution of the Texas frontier. While some ranchers themselves delivered the cattle to northern railheads, most contracted with firms operated by others, such as Charles Schreiner and John Lytle, to move the cattle. Fees ranged from about $1.00 to $1.25 per head for the service. The trailing contractors agreed to supply the manpower and equipment as well as to sell the livestock. This practice saved ranchers from the time-consuming deliveries and allowed them to keep their "hands" — their men were rarely called cowboys — on the ranch where they were needed.

Cowboys — more correctly "cow boys" in the mid-nineteenth century — composed the cattle-trailing crew. They tended to be young men whose average age was about twenty-four, and they remained cowboys only a short time. They were often black or Hispanic. They had to endure extreme physical punishment. Risking life and limb in stampedes, blizzards, and Indian attacks, it was not unusual for them to remain in the saddle for thirty-six hours at a stretch. For all this, they received wages of $15 to $20 a month plus board. The trail boss, or ramrod, usually a man of some experience in cattle-trailing, picked the route, assigned guard watches, and was wholly responsible for delivering the cattle. The cook was obviously important, for he could make the trip a pleasure or a nightmare. He supervised the chuck wagon, which was loaded with beans, corn meal, molasses, and coffee to supplement the basic fare of beef and wild game. A crew of a dozen men or so could trail two thousand or more animals.

The long drives and the concomitant removal of the Indians allowed the Texas range cattle industry to spread across the state with what some have called marvelous rapidity. Beyond the 98th meridian ranchers staked out a piece of land along a good stream, and his "range right" ran back to the nearest divide. Free rangers they were called, for they had no legal title to the land. Among the earliest cattlemen to claim the public domain were John Chisum, Charles Goodnight, John Hittson, C. C. Slaughter, George Littlefield, A. H. (Shanghai) Pierce, and Oliver Loving. If need be, they kept competitors out at gun point. When the state offered land in the public domain for sale, they acquired title to as much good pasture as possible, buying it up as quickly as it became available and leasing grazing rights to neighboring land the state retained. With longhorns cheap and land plentiful, cattlemen covered West Texas.

By 1880 cattle raising had become the hottest investment in Texas. Eastern and British capitalists formed huge "land and cattle" companies that came to control well over half the land and cattle in West Texas. These included such well-known spreads, commonly referred to by their brands, as the JA, the Spur, the Pitchfork, the Four Sixes, the Spade, the XIT, and the Matador. The Matador Land and Cattle Company of Dundee, Scotland, perhaps the most successful ranching venture in American history, in 1882 purchased 300,000 acres of land and 60,000 head of cattle. Its Scottish manager, Murdo Mackenzie, who made significant contributions to the American cattle industry, built the Matador Ranch until at its height it owned or leased some 1.6 million acres from Texas to Saskatchewan.

But for every Murdo Mackenzie or Richard King or C. C. Slaughter who became a cattle king, there were five others who lost their shirts, and most of the big trail operators died broke. The chief danger was overstocking of the ranges, which wrecked the grass and destroyed cattle prices. Then, the increased use of barbed wire after its introduction about 1874 reduced the amount of grazing land: the XIT, for instance, had an estimated six thousands miles of fence. By 1885 cattle raising was ceasing to be a frontier enterprise. The Chisholm Trail was virtually closed, and traffic on the others was tapering off. Finally, catastrophic winters in 1885-1886 and 1886-1887 brought the Texas range cattle period to a sudden end. Cattlemen who survived transformed ranching from an adventure to a carefully managed business. Although it was ephemeral, the cattle frontier by its sheer majestic grandeur continues to capture the imagination of people everywhere.

Sheep raising had none of the majestic qualities of cattle raising, but an old Texas adage had it that "you raise cattle for prestige, sheep for money." In South Texas Richard King was not unaware of the financial possibilities in sheep raising, and his herders tended some 30,000 head as early as 1860. Milton Favor, after he established in 1858 his veritable fiefdom in the Big Bend, grazed thousands of sheep with his cattle. C. C. Slaughter, called by a Dallas newspaper the "Cattle King of Texas," maintained sheep. Of course, there were others, too, such as John Scharbauer, Charles Schreiner, and William L. Black, who accepted sheep.

The Texas sheep industry paralleled that of cattle. It entered Texas in the Spanish period, changed in the days of the Republic of Texas when Anglo-Americans streamlined the herding system to meet their needs and imported blooded stock, and moved westward with the advancing population. The first animals were *chaurros,* an inferior race of sheep in Spain. They were lean and gaunt but able to walk great distances. Under Anglo-American leadership they were bred to the magnificent Spanish Merino, the foundation breed of all modern fine-wool sheep. Merino-*chaurro* crossbreeds proved to be excellent range sheep in the Southwest.

Most sheepherders were Mexicans, *pastores* they were called, who often lived in a serf-like existence. But there were plenty of Britishers who found no social stigma in "foolin' with sheep," Germans especially in the Hill Country, and Yankees who brought eastern methods with them. Texans and immigrants from the Old South, preferring cattle, rarely became wool growers—as sheepmen liked to call themselves.

The earliest promoters of wool growing in Texas were George Wilkins Kendall and Charles Schreiner. Kendall from his ranch near Boerne imported purebred rams from Europe and developed range sheep that produced a profitable wool clip. His grade rams were distributed throughout Texas and helped to improve the breed of many flocks. He perfected the dipping vat to combat disease and vermin, and more than any other person he shifted the Texas industry's emphasis from mutton to wool production.

At Kerrville, Charles Schreiner through his unique banking and marketing operations spread sheep husbandry through much of the Edwards Plateau. Whenever a cattleman of his area entered Schreiner's bank to borrow money, the rancher found it necessary to use at least half the loan for sheep raising. Many borrowers agreed to the unusual terms. He also bought and sold wool, acting as a warehouseman and a commission salesman. For several years he freighted wool by wagon through San Antonio to the Gulf coast. When the railroad reached Kerrville in 1887, Schreiner erected on the main track a warehouse that handled wool from several western counties. In 1890 he doubled his warehouse capacity to become the largest wool warehouseman in the state.

These men and others helped to create a Texas sheep boom. Having started after the War with Mexico, the boom spread in the 1850s, hovered weakly or even retreated during the Civil War, and after the war started afresh. Rapid expansion came after the mid-1870s when the entire area of the state west of the 98th meridian opened to sheepmen, who with cattlemen and others soon occupied state-owned land from San Antonio westward to the Pecos River and beyond. The boom peaked in 1885 when, according to *Texas Historic Livestock Statistics,* there were 6,620,000 sheep in the state. Afterward the number declined for twenty years before starting up again to reach a peak during World War II. Today Texas, the leading sheep and wool producing state in the country, accounts for over 20 percent of the nation's output.

On the Texas frontier large sheep operations used a modified Spanish organizational system for dividing work among four types of employees: the lowest in rank was the *pastor* who kept watch over a flock of about 1,500 to 2,000 sheep. Over two or three *pastores* was a rustler, who selected the watering places and the area to be grazed for the day. A *caporal* had charge of several rustlers, and the *mayordomo,* or foreman, supervised the *caporales* and accepted responsibility for the entire operation. Wages for Mexican herders were about $12 to $15 per month plus board. The *pastor's* camp was always plain and unobtrusive, consisting of a bed roll, cooking outfit, and an old bleached cow skull or two for chairs. He slept in a tent, kept his personal belongings in a bag or box, and prepared simple meals from his supplies of bacon, flour, beans, and coffee. He came to the home ranch only at shearing and lambing time.

Closely associated with the advancing sheep industry was the raising of Angora goats. First brought to Texas about 1857, Angoras, which produce a silky white fleece used in plush upholstery, knitted garments, rugs, and blends of other material, became an attractive proposition in the late 1880s when William L. Black, an enterprising Fort McKavett rancher, who was also a charter member of the New York Cotton Exchange, vigorously promoted their adoption. By 1900 Texas Angora raisers, chiefly concentrated on the Edwards Plateau, led the nation in production, and today they provide over 90 percent of the country's total.

Occasionally sheepmen and cattlemen fought one another. They argued over grazing rights, water supplies, fences, and other matters, particularly between the early 1870s and late 1880s. Contrasts in life styles, background, and equipment helped to produce the hostility. Fundamental differences between sheep and cattle meant that the animals required different amounts of water, different types of food, and different manners of herding. The longhorn was a wild creature, requiring long grass and plenty of water. His very nature required men on horses to cope with his feral constitution. Sheep on the other hand were thoroughly domesticated, subsisting on short grass and weeds. Except in hot weather or when being trailed, they needed little water, but got by on the morning dew. They needed a constant attendant, preferably one who went on foot.

These differences, which promoted hostility and in some instances death, were accentuated by a group of sheepherders called drifters who moved their sheep from range to range. Without title to western lands the drifters grazed their sheep leisurely on another's property, searching for the best grass and reliable water supplies. When they located a favorable range, they sometimes camped out for weeks. If cowboys or rustlers rode into camp to hurry the intruder on his way, the drifter, who in preparation for such a contingency had removed one of his wagon's good wheels, hidden it, and put a broken one in plain sight, said he would move on as soon as he repaired the wagon. When his animals had depleted the range, he retrieved the good wheel, placed it on the wagon, stashed the broken one inside to use again, and hastened on his way to another verdant range.

Barbed-wire fencing also produced frontier disturbances. Brought to Texas on a grand scale after 1880, the fences closed the range restricting the movement of all livestock. Sheepmen, coming late to the land, often could not obtain leases for adjoining pastures. It became necessary for them to acquire land separated by property belonging to others. When moving from one leasehold to another, the sheepmen grazed their animals on pastures owned by cattlemen, who objected to the practice. To solve the quandary livestockmen worked out a code that required the herder to drive his flock at least three miles per day. Yet the fences caused a problem, for cowmen found that the sheepmen fenced their ranges, too, restricting the movement of cattle. Cattlemen also fenced their pastures, but unless the fences were of more than three strands, the sheep could walk through them without great difficulty. Furthermore, farmers, pushing into the western livestock regions, sometimes found themselves entirely surrounded by a fence without adequate outlet. Or, building their own fences, the farmers cut off sheep and cattle from needed water supplies and grazing land.

Fence-cutting followed. Farmers, cattlemen, and herders all cut fences, but most accounts support the idea that cattlemen were more aggressive in the practice. Among sheepmen the notorious drifters were the most flagrant fence cutters. The drifters in moving their sheep from range to range cut fences to get their animals and wagons through. In the early 1880s in Scurry County a cowboy shot and seriously wounded a drifter who had entered his range. While another drifter in the vicinity hauled the wounded man to a local doctor, the cowboy recruited some of his friends who then burned the drifter's camp and equipment, killed some of his sheep, and scattered the rest.

In 1883 the trouble reached epidemic proportions. That year fence cutting, precipitated by a severe drought, occurred in more than half the 171 organized counties as cattlemen moved to get their animals to water. Farmers and sheepmen fought back to protect their range. News of the "range war" was headlined in a Chicago newspaper as "Hell Breaks Loose in Texas." Local officials and Texas Rangers seemed helpless. The problem got bad enough to cause many sheepmen to collect packs of dogs and ride their fence lines with them each day. To deal with the critical situation Governor John Ireland called a special session of the legislature. After that body in 1884 made it a felony, fence-cutting slowly disappeared. That many cattlemen had begun raising sheep also helped to establish peace.

The sheep and cattle culture spread slowly until the late 1870s, after which it swept across the big ranch country of the High Plains and Trans-Pecos, reaching in six years the very limits of Texas. Not far behind came farmers, pushing beyond the 98th meridian into semiarid and desert land where no nineteenth-century farmer should have gone. The eternal optimism of Anglo-Americans, a sense of individual and national progress, and the moral and personal courage of western settlers who planned to tame the country and adapt it to their use all encouraged settlement. Railroads, needing people to use their western lines, likewise promoted farming ventures in West Texas.

The first railroads connected cities. C. P. Huntington, Jay Gould, General Grenville Dodge, and others who built rails across Texas watched their lines join El Paso and San Antonio, Fort Worth and Denver, and El Paso and Fort Worth. The Corpus Christi, San Diego, and Rio Grande reached Laredo in 1881. Early in 1882 the Texas and Pacific joined the Southern Pacific at Sierra Blanca in far West Texas. The San Antonio and Aransas Pass Railroad expanded as far as Kerrville in 1887, and the Fort Worth and Denver built across the Panhandle the same year. The Gulf, Colorado, and Santa Fe reached San Angelo in 1888. Soon feeder lines extended to many other areas. Farmers followed quickly.

The farming frontier of West Texas in some respects was a triumph of imagination over reality. The area was deficient in rainfall for ordinary agriculture, the state granted over thirty million acres to railroads, and when government officials in the 1870s began again to sell parts of the public domain, cattlemen, using their cowboys to claim alternate sections, quickly usurped land along the best streams. Nevertheless, as the state disposed of its land through grants, headrights, bounties, donations, and homesteads, farmers secured title to some of it. The state also sold millions of acres to farmers at prices, it should be noted, well below their true value. With land cheap and markets for the wheat they would raise reachable via railroads thousands of farmers — including liberal numbers of Germans, Scandinavians, and other Europeans as well as native Texans — seeking their own El Dorado on a Texas homestead went west.

For the farmers, dream and reality were miles apart. West Texas was not only deficient in water but also in other resources, most notably timber. The "hoeman," or "nester," as the farmer was variously called, found mostly a tough, dirt-filled life in the strange western environment. In the absence of trees he sometimes carved as his first home a dugout in the side of a hill, or taking a spade to cut three-foot blocks of earth, he built a sod house that was cool in summer, warm in winter, fireproof, and lasted about six years. But it also attracted vermin, mice, lizards, and rattlesnakes. Rain water filtering through the sod roof could create a muddy mess on the tables, chairs, and beds. The shortage of wood also forced the farmer to burn cow or buffalo chips for fuel; he burned cornstalks and twisted prairie grass, too. Until the adoption of barbed wire, he could not fence off his vegetable patch from hogs or wheat fields from cattle.

The West Texas frontier farmer faced other problems. The soils were thin in most places. Drought was a constant attendant. Grasshoppers were more than a nuisance. In 1874 a veritable plague of grasshoppers devoured everything as they cut a wide swath from Texas to Dakota. They consumed wheat, chewed on harnesses and hoe and pitchfork handles, munched curtains, and got into water buckets, tea kettles, and coffee pots. They were numerous but less destructive in 1875 and 1877. Prairie fires, as in 1882 and 1884, raced uncontrolled across the Texas range, burning grass, fields, stacked hay, and recently cut cedar posts being prepared for fencing. Winter blizzards, as in 1886 and 1887, occasionally brought crushing hardship and death. Farmers heavily in debt or living on narrow financial margins were forced out.

It was a bleak picture, one made worse by the isolation, loneliness, and general despair of trying to carve out a living in a country where one's energy, courage, and hard work were less important than the sometimes brutally harsh climate. Conditioned to more humid regions, farmers watched helplessly and with disbelief when for lack of rain their crops under a hot Texas sun withered and died. Missing the companionship of friends and relatives in the East, frontier women suffered particularly hard, for in addition to endless heavy chores they were forced to endure drab, cheerless surroundings made worse by the often flat, treeless terrain over which the winds blew with relentless pressure. In a psychologically provocative novel, *The Wind,* set on the West Texas frontier, Dorothy Scarborough studied the tragedy that oppressive winds and frontier isolation could bring to the soul of a sensitive woman.

The difficulties were real, though it is possible to exaggerate the sufferings. The nesters survived and even prospered in a difficult land. They celebrated holidays, organized dances, attended parades, and enjoyed barbecues that continue to be a popular Texas tradition. The churches they established fairly quickly after settlement became the centers for much community activity. Marriages were followed by a shivaree, at which friends gathered at the house of the newlyweds to bang on tin pans or cow bells until treats were offered. Spelling bees, quilting bees, taffy pulls, and other customs brought people happily together, as did traditional public speeches to commemorate the Fourth of July, perhaps the most popular frontier celebration.

Nor did farmers idly accept the harsh, natural conditions. They built surface tanks to supply water, drilled wells, and erected windmills. The adoption of windmills was of particular importance. Their use on the Texas frontier began in the 1870s, but mass-produced factory-made windmills had been used elsewhere in the state for perhaps two decades. The U.S. Solid Wheel mill produced by an Illinois firm was one of the first windmills used successfully in West Texas. The most common windmill on the western plains, however, was the Eclipse. The regular-pattern Eclipse windmills were made in sizes ranging from 8½ feet to 14 feet in diameter, but larger ones were also built. Another popular windmill on the Texas frontier was the Star, made by an Indiana company. Unable to afford patented windmills, many farmers built homemade contraptions from crates, timber, and spare machine parts. Whatever their source, windmills brought water to the farm home, kept the garden blooming, and solved one of the most difficult problems of frontier living.

In addition to erecting windmills, the farmers planted trees, hedges, and fruit orchards. They built frame houses as soon as they could afford them, and added outbuildings, stables, and pens. By the mid-1890s they were bringing larger areas under cultivation, adding machines for both planting and harvesting, adopting dryland farming techniques, and, in short, changing a forbidding frontier into a pleasant agricultural commonwealth of productive farms, busy towns, and progressive citizens.

In the process the farmers with cattlemen and others established county governments, extending in the decade of the 1870s the line of counties westward by two tiers. Over the next ten years the line of organized counties moved into the Panhandle, neared the South Plains, and reached the Big Bend. In the 1890s more counties were created, leaving by 1900 only twenty-four of Texas' 254 counties unorganized. The advance of agriculture onto the High Plains around Lubbock, along the lower Rio Grande, and through the Trans-Pecos occurred in the twentieth century—long after the close of the Texas frontier.

# 6

## The Era of Agrarian Protest

*Robert A. Calvert*

In 1870, 818,579 Texans lived and worked in a frontier setting. Ninety-three percent of them resided in rural areas, defined as communities of under 2,500 inhabitants, and toiled in subsistence, that is, a self-contained agricultural environment. They occupied the eastern half of the state.

A farmer hoped that his farm, averaging thirty acres of harvested land in 1870, would be blessed with some rain and no insects so that he could produce enough to feed his family. A market for his crops was appreciated but not essential. Rather, he thought of a farm that produced almost all that he needed, with a few surplus crops, such as tobacco or cotton, being exchanged for food stuffs, like coffee or salt, or for necessities, like bolts of cloth or plowshares. He looked to the land for succulence and stability.

But the years from 1870 to 1901 changed all that. As did the rest of the United States, Texas underwent an economic revolution in the late-nineteenth century. Farms became commercialized and dependent upon markets over which rural Texans had no control. Population more than tripled from 1870 to 1900, and cities and industries increased in size and value until they competed with rural Texas for control of the fate and economy of the state. Rural and frontier Texas did not adjust to the beginnings of an urban environment without social anxieties, political and economic instability, and an attempt to cling to older ways. When Spindletop erupted in 1901 and oiled the transition of the economy into the twentieth cen-

*Engraving of a session in the Texas House of Representatives in Austin from sketch by H. A. Ogden, 1880.*

— Institute of Texan Cultures
From Frank Leslie's Illustrated Newspaper

*The capitol at Austin in 1870, an engraving.*

— U.T. Institute of Texan Cultures
From *Pictorial History of Texas*

tury, agricultural leadership of the state was doomed. The idea of a frontier economy, however, had passed away in the preceding three decades.

Without railroads commercial agriculture could not develop. In 1870 Texas had 583 miles of track, existing in the southern and eastern parts of the state. Furthermore the state lacked navigable rivers and good natural harbors. Jefferson, located on Cypress Bayou and with entry to the Red River, served as a center of northern Texas trade as boats carried cotton and other agricultural commodities from there to New Orleans. The Gulf ports, principally Galveston, had contact with the interior through wagons and stagecoaches. Such transportation was slow and expensive. Pleading widespread poverty county commissioners avoided building or maintaining all-weather roads or dependable bridges. Indeed a comprehensive system of all-weather roads would not emerge until well into the twentieth century. Thus Texans who wanted cheaper, more efficient and dependable transportation had to rely upon railroad companies in the nineteenth century.

By 1872 the Missouri, Kansas and Texas (Katy) Railroad reached Denison in North Texas. Although the building of track was slowed by the depression of 1873, the Houston and Texas connected with the Katy that year, and now farmers could trade from Houston to the north and to the east. By 1875 the state boasted of 1,650 miles of track, which included the Texas and Pacific. The T&P also carried goods through Texarkana to the East Coast. These two roads made St. Louis the marketing center for North Texas, hurt Galveston's economy, and, since they bypassed Jefferson, destroyed that Bayou City's commerce.

The destruction of the buffalo, ending the threat of the Plains Indian, allowed railroads to move West in 1876-77. By 1881 the T&P had connected El Paso with the rest of the state. That year, too, saw Galveston united to Fort Worth by the Gulf, Colorado and Santa Fe. Galveston, however, would not necessarily compete with the rapidly growing city of Houston once railroads joined it to the interior.

In 1880 there were 3,244 track miles operating in the state; by 1890, 8,700; and by 1900, 10,000. These roads tied Texas together commercially, allowing farmers to sell their produce to cities and to emerge as commercial rather than subsistence units and caused industries to develop to sell products to rural markets. The railroads spurred the growth of some urban areas — Dallas, Fort Worth, and Houston for example — and helped to depress or destroy the economic viability of others, such as Jefferson and Galveston. To both farmers and cities the railroads were economic panaceas, promising growth and profits, and when they did not bring instant prosperity disillusionment followed.

Complaints against railroads reached a crescendo from 1882 to 1890. As a railroad penetrated each new frontier area and good times did not follow, complaints soon did, mixing together voices of protest from South and West and North and East Texas. The railroads' conduct raised these complaints to higher decibels. In 1882 Collis P. Huntington of the Southern Pacific and Jay Gould of the T&P divided the state between their systems. This "treaty of alliance" growing out of a threatened court suit on the part of Gould, who argued that the Southern Pacific built on the T&P right-of-way and deprived his railroad of land grants, stifled competition between their railroads. Consequently this pooling arrangement created a decline in rail construction after 1882, and fixed interstate rates. Three years later trunk lines, which were largely intrastate, formed the Texas Traffic Association. The association or its successor, formed after the courts ruled the original one violated the antitrust laws, fixed local rates for the next forty years.

Because of efforts of farmers, particularly members of the Patrons of Husbandry—or Grange—the Constitutional Convention of 1876 included Article X in the new Constitution defining railroads as public carriers. Thus the state had a mandate to regulate railroads. As complaints grew so did demands for regulation. It was 1891, however, before a commission could be created. The credit for the commission went to James S. Hogg, who in 1888 as attorney general, led the fight against the Texas Traffic Association, and then won the governor's race in 1890 on the slogan of "Hogg and a Commission." In April 1891 Governor Hogg established a three-man Texas Railroad Commission and asked John H. Reagan to resign from the Senate and head the new body.

By 1892 the political left, led by the Populists, and the right, led by the railroads who sued in the courts to stop regulation, attacked the new governor. The left wanted an elective commission and more reforms and nominated Thomas L. Nugent for governor. The right — big cattlemen, corporations and railroads — wanted no commission and less reform. Hogg won in 1892, and with Populist support wrote the Perpetuities and Corporations Land Law of 1893 that allowed the commission to oversee the way railroad companies sold stocks and bonds. In 1894 the members of the commission became elective rather than appointive.

The opponents of the commission backed a suit by the International and Great Northern that challenged the constitutionality of the Texas Railroad Commission. In *Reagan* v. *Farmers' Loan and Trust Company* (1894) the court upheld the right of the state to regulate. By 1898 the commission had prosecuted 135 violations, collecting for the state $67,500 in fines. In 1899 the legislature passed a law that defined as a felony the paying of rebates or practicing a rate discrimination. After the turn of the century, the legislature also outlawed the abuse of granting free passes. Indeed, Reagan, replying to farmer criticism of the commission, said that the agency had forced a lowering of the rates on the transport of cotton alone that saved farmers $800,000 by 1897.

Thus by the dawn of the twentieth century, farmers had their regulatory agency. They also had their railroads. In 1904 Texas had more track miles than any other state. The building of these railroads had stimulated other industries.

The growth of the lumber industry, which furnished crossties, corresponded exactly to railroad expansion. According to John S. Spratt, the T&P alone ordered 500,000 crossties in 1880. That year, too, it purchased 2,000 tons of rails and spikes. Its payroll included 8,000 laborers, who, along with thousands of draft animals, consumed hundreds of tons of agricultural products, turning subsistence farmers into commercial ones. The T&P experience was repeated with each road each year. All these new businesses, developing in a symbiotic relationship with railroads, served as pools of capital to finance more industrial expansion. Each mile of track joined the frontier farmer and his market and eliminated his subsistence farm. The very unregulated and unsystematic development of the railroad, which exploited customers, insured the unsystematic but rapid development of the tracks that criss-crossed haphazardly, but quickly, across the state and ended the family farm as they helped create new businesses.

Railroads needed to survey and to sell land grants if they were to profit from them. Counties and cities wanted new settlers to increase land values. Farmers wanted neighbors for protection and for markets. All Texans wanted population growth, and they assumed this increase would be immigrant-farmers coming to what one emigrant handbook described as "pre-eminently an agricultural country."

States besides Texas solicited population growth. All other southern states published guides, founded private and public emigrant societies, and recruited immigrants from each other and from Europe. The middle western states did the same. But Texas was more successful than all other southern states and competed favorably with middle western ones in the race for population.

Texas had encouraged immigration in the Mexican and Repub-

*German immigrants preparing to embark for Texas.*
— Gilbert Jordan, *Faces of Texas.* Painting by Johannes Gehrts.
Photo courtesy the Focke-Museum, Bremen

lic period. In 1871 the state formalized this policy, establishing the Texas Bureau of Immigration. The superintendent of the agency, always short of funds, relied upon railroad guides to extol the beauties and agricultural glories of the state. He collected statistics of rainfall and land prices, solicited volunteer agents to travel in other states and in Europe, arranged for reduced fares on transportation lines into the state and tried to find immigrants gainful employment. Always under-financed, the bureau was not overly successful, and the Redemption government of 1876 identified it with Radical Reconstruction and prohibited the use of state funds to finance immigration companies.

The state had not carried the burden of emigrant companies alone. Private business wanted immigrants in their areas, and railroads offered reduced rates to immigrants, sent promotional literature, sold off their land grants at bargain prices to settlers, and sent agents to convince prospective customers to locate on their line. Cities and counties conducted rival colonization programs of their own. They told outlandish tales about the beauties and fertility of their areas. Anxious to increase population, they paid agents bonuses to recruit in Europe and the South. For example, John Hill, a plantation owner near New Waverly, Texas, looking for prospective immigrants, wrote to old friends in South Carolina. When that failed, he and others near Huntsville, Texas, hired an agent to recruit Polish laborers, with a promise to allow emigrants to work out their fares and acquire farms. They found around eighty Polish families willing to move into the area.

The lure of land was what caused emigration to Texas. Unlike other states Texas kept its public lands when it joined the Union. Some of this land, some 30,000,000 acres, went to railroad companies and then much of it was sold cheaply to settlers. The state in 1874 began the sale of the alternate sections along the railroad lines for $1.50 an acre. In 1879 the state lowered the price to $1.00 an acre for school lands, and fifty cents, with unlimited amounts for any purchaser, for the other sections. In 1883, after a political controversy over the disposal of lands, the legislature created a State Land Board to regulate the sale of public lands and to reclassify them according to agricultural, timbered, or pastoral values. The former two sold for three dollars an acre, the latter for two dollars, with actual settlers given priority over speculators.

Thus from time to time settlers could purchase tracts from 40 to 640 acres, and until 1899 a married man could claim a 160-acre homestead, if he established proof of a three-year residence. A single man could claim one-half that amount. Payment periods varied from ten to forty years; interest rates on unpaid balances were low (usually around 5 to 10 percent). Equally generous land policies were extended to the grazing lands of West Texas.

Hence the land attracted settlers to Texas. Newspapers after the Civil War told of line after line of wagons from the upper South carrying migrants to Tennessee and to Arkansas and on to Texas. Immigrants from overseas joined others of their nationalities in established areas or created towns such as New Sweden, near Austin, or Norse in Bosque County. New settlers, 400,000 in 1876 alone, moved the frontier from Northwest Texas into the Cross Timbers by 1877 (Clay, Archer, Young, Stephens, Erath, Brown and Mill counties), and by 1880 on across the 100th meridian. Then following railroad lines, settlers spoke of Abilene or Sweetwater or Big Spring. But the drought of the mid-eighties drove many settlers back to the East. The tide of settlers began again in 1887, but they moved more slowly. Nevertheless, by 1890 settlers were farming in the Panhandle; and by 1900, 230 of Texas' 254 counties had been organized. The Texas frontier was gone by the turn of the century. In 1900 the state, half-occupied in 1870, could boast of over three million people, a comprehensive railroad system and widespread settlement. The new settlement had changed the nature of frontier Texas farming.

The 1850s had been prosperous years for the American farmer. Most settlers going to Texas in 1870 expected agricultural prosperity to continue for decades too. Such was not to be the case. The decades from 1870 to 1900 were bleak years for the American farmer. No single reason adequately explains why. The central issue, however, was steadily decreasing agricultural prices. In the same period tenant farming increased from 37.6 percent of the farms in 1880 to 49.7 percent in 1900. The deadly depression years of the seventies were followed by a drought from 1885 to 1887 and then the depression of the 1890s. The Texas farmer seemingly joined an industry that was permanently depressed.

Immigration and farming did not abate, however. The everhopeful immigrant spilled into the state, pushing from fertile, well-watered lands of East Texas to the marginal land of the Cross Timbers and on to the Panhandle that never seemed to receive enough rain. Farmers harvested more land: 48 million acres in 1870 to 691.7 million in 1900. The value of farms rose from $80.7 million in 1870 to $962 million in 1900. But the individual farmer did not seem to prosper, particularly in relationship to his city cousin. The wholesale price index of farm goods did not rise correspondingly to the wholesale price index of manufactured goods. Thus the explosion of the American dream: he worked hard, bought new implements, moved to the West, produced more crops — and became a tenant farmer, not a successful, self-made man. The result was the farmer protests of the 1890s: Populism.

It would take thirty years of pain, anguish, and despair to produce Texas Populism. It would also take a commercial farm economy because the subsistence farmer was not dictated totally by the whims of a stable crop market. His expectations, to survive and not to earn sizable profits, came from a farm that would hopefully produce all that he and his family needed in the 1870s. But with the railroads, the increased population, and the new markets, he made a logical choice—sell a staple crop and buy a better standard of life for himself and his family. He wanted to move from homemade items to commercially produced ones. The increase in the kinds and type of crops tell his story.

Corn was the leading grain crop in nineteenth-century Texas, serving as food for animals and a staple of the farmer's diet. In 1870 farmers planted one million acres of corn, in 1900, five million; production increased from 20.5 million bushels to 109.9 million during the same period. The crop was hand planted and cultivated in 1870, but by 1900 a mechanical planter was used on a few Texas farms.

Oats, the second leading crop in both production and for animal feed, flourished in the Western Cross Timbers and the Red River Rolling Plains, as well as in the black prairie areas. The land devoted to oats grew from 238,000 acres in 1879 to 847,000 acres in 1899. Other grain crops — such as grain sorghums (23,000 acres in 1899), wheat (1,207,947 acres in 1900) and rice (8,700 acres in 1899)—grew in Texas during the Gilded Age, but the king crop was cotton.

John Spratt, an economist, writes of a Bell County farmer who told in 1899 of a decrease of wheat in that county over preceeding ten years from 84,267 to 20,936 bushels. In that same period cotton increased from 9,217 to 37,473 bales. The Bell County farmer attributed this change in crop growth patterns to the railroad, which brought in cheaper flour than could be grown and furnished a market for a staple crop. The farmer saw the switch to cotton as sensible; so does Spratt. A similar pattern took place all across the state.

Spratt believed the move to cotton production a good one because cotton was less susceptible to drought than any other crop, it exhausted the soil the least, it produced the largest cash price, and it was the most adaptable to extensive agriculture which could utilize best new farm machinery. Moreover, the move to cotton specialization harmonized with the Gilded Age drive for economic specialization. A farmer, like his city cousin, wanted commercially made products, aimed to accumulate a cash balance, and desired to expand his share of the market. These activities demanded commercial specialization, long-term credit, and larger farms. Cotton seemed the crop for success, and production grew from 350,670 bales (922,000 acres harvested) in 1870 to 2.5 million bales (6.9 million acres harvested) in 1900. In 1870 the value of grains in Texas was $25.2 million and cotton $36.1 million; in 1890 the value of grains was $70.8 million and cotton $139.6 million. Texas farmers agreed that cotton was the "money crop."

But cotton did not bring prosperity. Tenant farming increased. Probably no matter what crop the farmer chose despair and tenant farming would have followed. He needed long-term credit to break the share-crop system and controlled markets, larger farms if he were to compete with new machinery, and some way to control interest rates and rising land prices. Thus, the rise of commercial agriculture and industrialization, not cotton, were the villains that wed the farmer to depression. In value of dollars to the state and to persons employed in allied industries cotton was by far Texas' most important product.

Industry never rivaled agriculture as the dollar-producing ingredient in the late-nineteenth-century Texas economy. Although non-agricultural production increased in Texas, industrial growth did not keep pace with national industrialization. In 1900 the national per capita value of manufactures was $171.00, up $62.00 from 1870; in Texas manufactures per capita grew from $14.00 to $39.99. The nature of industrial growth changed, however. In 1870 flour and grist mills totaled one third of the value of Texas manufacturing. The next five industries were sawed lumber, processed beef, carpenter and building trades, blacksmithing, and slaughtering. The economy in 1870 was that of a self-contained village, with a community producing all that its citizens needed. In 1900, however, industry had grown to $90.4 million in value; lumbering became the leading industry; followed by cottonseed mills and then flour milling which had concentrated in larger mills in urban areas. Like agriculture, industry moved with the completion of railroads from a self-contained village industry to commercial specialized production. Railroads and agriculture made industrial growth possible. A look at a major industry in 1900 can show how.

In 1880 important innovations were sweeping through the cotton-ginning industry. Steam replaced animals as a power source for gins, and mechanical feeders were installed, thus eliminating the need for men to rake seed cotton into the gin stand. Most of these improvements came from new entrepreneurs who discovered that tenant farmers could not afford to build their own gins and would not combine to erect collective ones. These entrepreneuers, frequently planters, by 1880 had improved the gin presses, moved them inside a gin house, and began ginning neighbors' cotton for fixed prices. Soon public gins sprang up in the larger towns and cities, and a major segment of the cotton industry was born.

The industry grew phenomenally. In 1882 it was reported that 1,200 gins operated within the state; four years later in the U.S. the industry reported a 50 percent increase. The 1900 census listed 4,514 gins in Texas that averaged baling 589 bales of cotton each, or 34 percent of the nation's total cotton crop. For the farmer these new gins saved him 20 percent of the cost of processing his cotton, and he paid $5.00 per bale for ginning, baling, and ties in 1870 and $2.00 for the same service in 1900. Gins were easily loaded on wagons and moved to new areas and their spread along railroad tracks pulled Texans from East to West Texas. In 1865, gins served the farmer; in 1900 they served the entrepreneur.

These town gins spurred the growth of urban Texas, too. They brought to a community needed capital and to the workers needed jobs. The 1890 U.S. Census failed to list all Texas gins. However, the 572 gins reporting claimed a total value of $1.6 million, including land and buildings, and employed 2,703 workers full or part time, at $356,463 in yearly wages. Most employees worked only the four months of ginning season. Consequently, the average wage gins paid to employees was lower than that of other industries. In 1890, a clerk earned $195.00 per year, a skilled operator $123.00, and unskilled women and children around one-half the latter figure. By 1900 gins claimed $9.2 million in aggregate capital, a six-fold increase that undoubtedly caused a like increase in wages and in urban employees.

An increase in gins caused the growth of a kindred enterprise—the cotton compress. As L. T. Ellis pointed out, the purpose of compression was to aid in and lower the cost of transportation of bales of cotton. Consequently, early gins and compresses probably operated inside the same buildings, but by 1865 the compress industry developed as a separate business. By 1868, Galveston boasted of two compress companies. The larger of these, the Southern Compress Company, capitalized at $800,000, had compressed 150,000 bales in 1865. Its competition, the Planters Cotton Press Company advertised that it compressed between 700 and 800 bales of cotton each day, and by 1875, three more companies moved into Galveston to compete for the compression trade.

Compresses and gins could be dismantled quickly and easily, placed upon a flat car, and moved along a railroad to a new site.

Wherever new railroad tracks went settlers followed and planted new cotton fields. These in turn attracted gin and compress companies. And railheads became cities and crossroad gins aided rural settlements. In 1874, for example, Houston had one compress company; in 1886 six companies, with an aggregate value of $500,000, flourished there. By that year compresses also operated in Austin, Belton, Corsicana, Dallas, Denton, Fort Worth, Jefferson, Palestine, Sherman, and Waco, and probably in other smaller cities. The 1890 census listed over forty compress companies serving shipping areas throughout the state.

Cotton and railroads moved other industries into the interior of Texas. In 1885 the American Oil Trust instituted the use of cotton oil tank cars, and the cotton oil mill industry was born. Before the railroad six oil mills existed in the state and paid farmers from five to ten cents per bushel for cotton seed. In remote areas farmers used the cotton seed for feed for cattle, for fertilizer, or discarded it. In 1890 with railroad expansion and the development of cotton oil tank cars, the U.S. Census listed 103 oil mills. Four years later it was estimated that farmers earned around $6 million from the sale of seed to these mills. By 1900 cotton oil mills, valued at $7.9 million, employed 2,478 workers, who earned $830,766 annually. Mills, therefore, joined compresses and gins in being a sizable financial asset to urban areas. Probably, by 1900, businessmen who engaged in cotton processing industries had investments of around $25 million in Texas agribusiness.

The processing industry only constituted part of the story of cotton and the industrial economy. Clearly the transportation industry relied on farming and cotton. In 1913, 50,000 bales of cotton entered the city of Galveston each day. Galveston, the largest cotton port in the world, handled 4 million bales of cotton that year. Its workers sent 3.8 million of those bales, valued at $251 million into the export trade. The buying, selling, loading, shipping, storing and classifying of this cotton was the economic blood that flowed through the city's veins. To make sure the cotton flowed smoothly, the city needed merchants, bankers, lumbering and construction firms, insurance and investment companies, labor unions, and many other industries. These organizations and individuals, thus, drew much of their profits, wages, and capital from agricultural production. Farmers knew this, and as they became less prosperous they resented others profiting off their products more and more. When agricultural reformers condemned middlemen, saying that "neither do they reap nor do they sew, but grow rich off the toil of others," they added urban dwellers to the list that included cross-roads merchants and transportation companies.

Processed cottonseed by-products having no commercial value in 1860 and unlisted as a significant industry by the census of 1870, ranked second only to lumbering in the industrial economy of Texas in 1900. That year cottonseed by-products were valued at $14 million and lumbering enterprises contributed $16.2 million to the state's economy. The growth of the lumbering industry followed the railroads. Sawmills, like gins and compresses, could be transported from area to area as railroads opened up new forests to cutting by improving transportation.

In 1870 the lumbering industry was located in deep East Texas around Orange and Jefferson counties, extending northward to Harris County. The yearly production in 1870 was slightly over 100 million board feet. Lumbermen sent the cut logs from the piney woods down the Sabine and Neches rivers to large commercial mills located in Orange, Beaumont or Houston, and from there by water transport to coastal towns. Small sawmills served local communities. On rare occasions ox-wagons hauled sawed lumber to frontier settlements, but lumber transported overland increased in price up to twenty times its coastal value. Consequently railroad expansion lowered the transportation cost of and opened up new markets for lumber products, particularly after settlers moved to the treeless plains.

From 1875 to 1900 lumber products led all other freight in tonnage transported by Texas railroads. Until at least 1880 Texans used all the lumber the state's mills sawed. By 1900 entrepreneurs sent Texas lumber products to other states and overseas, and that year alone Texas railroads shipped almost six million tons of lumber products, which made up 25 percent of the total freight tonnage of railroad companies.

Most of this lumber still came from the piney woods area—that 68,000 square miles of the Bowie, Harris, and Orange county triangle. There large mills, such as the Kirby Lumber Company, the state's first multimillion dollar industrial concern, had a capacity of 400 million board feet annually. Most firms, however, were smaller than the Kirby Lumber Company, and one result was a proliferation of small companies.

The producers of Texas in 1900 had moved from cotton industries to the rough processing of bulky raw products — timbering, flour milling, cotton ginning, compression, and milling. Less than 1.6 pecent of the population were listed as an industrial labor force. Many Texans believed that prosperity demanded that more workers be hired for non-agricultural industries. The question was how to attract industries into the state.

Industrialization demands fuel and ore. Texas before Spindletop had neither. Although authors of guide books on Texas wrote gloriously of coal deposits and iron ore of highest grades in their areas, none seemed to appear. As each new vein of coal was discovered — the first important ore was in Stephens County in 1879 — local newspaper editors described deep veins of bituminous coal that ran for miles, contained little sulphur, and could be used for industries needing high grade fuels. In reality Texas coal deposits were usually sparse, thin-veined, and contained high sulphur and slate content.

Inferior coal could drive trains. As soon as railroads entered an area they bought from local mines, if any, and by 1880 engines had converted from wood to coal. That year, at Coalville in Palo Pinto County, a sizable vein was discovered, and a strip mining industry grew there. The operators sold their coal to the T&P. A labor dispute, involving the Knights of Labor and the operators, closed the Coalville vein five years later. After several attempts to reopen, the mining industry moved to Thurber, also in Palo Pinto County, and a subsidiary company town of the T&P operated there until the early 1920s.

Coal production aided industries that could use cheap low-grade fuels, such as brick and clay products, as well as railroads. The demand for the fuel caused the annual value of production of the mineral to increase from $1 million to $5.3 million during the period. Coal led all other minerals in production, although salt mining — in particular the Grand Saline Plant that opened in 1889 — is the longest-lived Texas mineral industry. An iron industry could not develop without good native coal. Transportation would have been too costly. Nevertheless, some foundries smelted iron in East Texas, and the state prison at Rusk produced $10,000 worth of iron that went into the new state capitol. Other mineral ores were scarce too. Despite rumors of precious minerals and legends of lost mines, prospectors made no discoveries in Texas. In the early eighties newspapers reported copper deposits in Baylor County. Those too existed only in rumor.

The natural resource, then, that was to remake the state was not iron, coal, copper, nor gold, but oil. Since De Soto's men returned from Sabine Bay, Texans knew that their state contained petroleum. Pools or small gas pockets were accidently discovered throughout the nineteenth century. In 1880, at Brown County, three wells produced a hundred barrels a day. In 1891, "The Greatest Shallow Oil Field in the World" flourished, said the Chamber of Commerce in Shackelford, Hicks County. This early oil production was used primarily for medicine or lubricants. Then in 1894 an artesian company hit oil sand at 1,030 feet in Corsicana. Two years later a well produced twenty-two barrels a day. By 1900, wells in Corsicana flowed 836,000 barrels yearly, a glut on the market. Oil flowed everywhere ruining the countryside and alienating townspeople. Indeed the first regulatory law, in March 1899, dealing with oil fields came from the wastage of the Navarro wells. In 1897, J. S. Cullinan, a Pennsylvanian, agreed to build a refinery (the forerunner of Mobil) in Corsicana. The refinery processed 1,500 barrels of crude oil daily in 1901, and the modern oil industry was born.

But Spindletop caused the industry to grow to manhood. A. F. Lucas, hunting for oil, found the pool at Spindletop on January 10, 1901. The well spurted oil at the rate of 70,000 to 100,000 barrels daily, compared to the 6,000 barrel production of the greatest other United States producer. That year Texas chartered 491 oil companies, valued at $239 million. The modern age for Texas flowed in. Agriculture would now take second place to a fossil fuel, but the skeletons for industrial Texas were formed before Spindletop. The discovery merely fleshed out the industrial base.

Rural Texans saw the growth of urban areas as a threat to their way of life long before oil helped cities to grow. In 1878, the Worthy Master of the State Grange, W. W. Lang, called "great cities . . . plague-centers of the social system" and a place where "Depravity finds friendship." Lang attacked the cities partially because he identified them as centers of middlemen, prospering at agriculturalists' expense. He unconsciously, perhaps, explained another reason for rural opposition to urban Texas by calling up farmers to join the Patrons of Husbandry so that a rural environment of fellowship and fun could develop and counteract the lure of the city to the young of rural Texas. Texans worried about keeping "them down on the farm" prior to World War I.

The nineteenth-century Texan believed in what later historians called the myth of the yeoman farmer. The myth existed in this country from colonial times to the present day. It found its roots in a veneration of agriculture that flowed through the writings of Greek and Roman philosophers and the writers of the Renaissance. In America such famous agriculturalists as Thomas Jefferson and John Taylor of Caroline exalted the role played by yeoman farmers in a democracy. In the mid-nineteenth century agricultural periodicals seized upon what earlier writers had cited as the glories of farming and embellished upon them. Texas rural newspaper editors and such agricultural publications as *The Texas Farmer* joined this mainstream of agricultural thought. The extent to which editors of the journals discussed the myth signified a defensive reaction. They wanted to assuage farmers' growing doubts about the importance of agriculture in the state's economy and to discredit the increasing belief that one farmed in America only if he could do nothing else.

By the 1870s leaders of agricultural organizations, such as W. W. Lang, dispersed the myth of the yeoman farmer to their less knowledgeable rural contemporaries. The myth contained several tenets. It began with the thesis that agriculture was the only means of earning bread blessed by God. A Grange lecturer for the Texas Patrons of Husbandry told farmers in 1878 that "Tilling the soil is the only occupation of Divine Origin. God commanded man to till the soil." Furthermore, in addition to a divine role, the farmer was an essential cog in the industrial machine. The Waco *Daily Examiner* in May 1874 printed a bit of doggerel for its farm readership that pointed out that all of the professions and occupations would wither economically without farm prosperity because, "The farmer, he must feed them all." All other professions depended on farming went the myth, but the farmer needed no one. His economic independence gained from the land ensured democracy. Thus, explained a southern agricultural periodical, "if the idea can be established that labor is noble and the tiller of the soil is nature's true nobleman and the peer of anything human, the permanency of free institutions is a fixed fact." The Texas farmer by the 1870s, had a stereotype of an agrarian life — a happy yeoman, who guided the religious and political destiny of America.

There were opposite correlations to these assumptions. If agriculture were good and natural then the city was evil and unnatural. The Texas Grangers consequently felt secure in warning fellow farmers that cities "are hot beds of vice and nurseries of extravagance and harmful fashions," places filled with people who did not reap or sew, but lived off the toil of others. Indeed, said one committee of Texas State Grange in 1878, cities spawned revolutionaries who challenged democratic America.

Looking back from a largely urbanized America, late-nineteenth-century Texas seems not urban at all. The four largest cities in Texas — San Antonio, Galveston, Houston, and Dallas — were very small in comparison to present Texas cities.

Rural Texans probably found the attraction of the different cultural and entertainment opportunities to be a lure of the city. They also found the economic opportunities of the cities alluring. The cities needed craftsmen and laborers as the population grew. In 1878

*Burke's Almanac* listed for Houston five foundries, two compresses, three breweries, six planing mills, two candy factories, two soap factories and a grain elevator in addition to saddleries and blacksmith shops. Two years later the author spoke of $50,000 weekly poured into that city's economy by these and similar businesses. These enterprises meant not only wages for workmen but men with limited capital and some skills could found a competitive business. A list of San Antonio industries in the 1880 U.S. Census would seem to verify such an assumption. Of seventy-odd industries census takers cited in the Alamo City, ten were blacksmithing establishments, employing twenty-nine males, three females and ten children. Leather works — boots and shoes — with ten businesses, and saddles and harnesses — six establishments — were the next largest enterprises. These small, self-contained manufactories promised equality of opportunity to craftsmen.

Rural Texans lost in the struggle to retain control of the state because ultimately the city offered too many economic and cultural attractions. A city's growth rate might slow during the depression years — the Dallas population dropped in 1893-94 — yet the overall growth curve continued upward. Each depression worsened the farmer's economic condition, and unlike the city dweller, he did not recover once the depression ended. Something was wrong with the world if God's chosen failed. The issue for rural Texas was how to correct the imbalance, restore the farmer to his favored social and economic position, and continue as the backbone of democracy. The answer, farm leaders thought, to turn back the lure of the city and to improve their truly wretched economic condition would be in an organization of farmers.

The Patrons of Husbandry was the first national farm organization. Oliver Kelley, an employee of the United States Department of Agriculture, toured the South in 1866 and witnessed the despair and backwardness of the Southern farmer. He had previously considered the need for a national organization that would bring together people of a like interest in preserving rural America. After his return to Washington, D.C., he met with William Saunders, the Director of the Department of Agriculture's Divisions and Grounds and a man of great prestige in agricultural circles, and together they decided to create a new organization — one which admitted women, thus embracing all the family, and one which dedicated itself to curing only the ills of the farmer and did not concern itself with other classes. The ritual, begun in 1866 and modeled after the Masons, did not take final form until 1869, when Kelley left Washington and went into Minnesota to recruit new members.

When hard times struck rural America in 1870, the Grange began to grow very rapidly. Lecturers, paid from fees they collected, scrambled across the countryside recruiting members from depressed areas. These lecturers promised too much from an organization that had too little power and that was too decentralized to bring about concerted collective actions. Nevertheless, by the time it had peaked in 1875, the organization touched the lives of 750,000 farmers.

In July 1873 in Bell County, the first local Grange in Texas was born. The following October, the State Grange was organized in Dallas. The Patrons of Husbandry enrolled 40,000 members by 1876, dropped to 9,000 by 1879 and then rose to 13,402 members in 1884. The membership declined thereafter, until it totaled only 473 members in 1904. For the farmer the Grange offered a four-fold plan to stop the onslaught of industrialism: better education, social interchange, diversification of crops, and economic cooperation. In short, the Grange wanted the farmer to remain self-sufficient at a time when he was moving toward commercial agriculture and a one-crop economy. The Patrons' goals built into the organization its ultimate failure.

The first important Worthy Master of the Texas Grange, W. W. Lang, was a conservative redeemer Democrat and ever-hopeful politician. He emphasized education and crop diversification, urging farmers to plant less cotton, more cereal and food crops, and through local lectures and study in subordinate Granges learn more about scientific agriculture. He urged the organization not to fight for railroad regulation or to form their own local cooperative stores. He told farmers they needed both merchants and railroads and not to make war on them.

Under his tutelage Grangers organized fairs that demonstrated scientific farm techniques, authorized plans of study of scientific agriculture, sponsored social gatherings, founded experimental farms, and encouraged crop diversification. Undoubtedly these rural and educational activities were a major contribution of the Grange to rural Texas. They helped to ameliorate the loneliness of farm life, particularly for women who would participate in bimonthly meetings, and the Grange Hall was a place to sing songs, to train speakers, to create libraries, to read agricultural newspapers, and to meet fellow farmers in an atmosphere of friendship and learning. After Lang left the State Grange in 1880 such activities continued.

But the Texas farmer wanted more economic rewards more quickly than social or educational activities could eventually offer. He failed to diversify his crops because cotton brought money and money brought security. Thus, he wanted to increase his profits by decreasing the profits of middlemen — railroads and merchants. Consequently from the very beginnings of the organization, dirt farmers demanded that their leaders push for the regulation of transportation and the founding of cooperative stores. Despite Lang, then, the Patrons fought for Article X defining the railroads as public carriers in the Constitution of 1876 and pushed for railroad regulation by means of a commission throughout the Gilded Age.

Patrons created economic cooperatives, too, even though Lang opposed them. Based upon reports of successes of such enterprises in the Old Northwest, Texas Patrons tried to found cooperative gins, warehouses, an iron foundry, and flirted with the idea of manufacturing farm implements. But they lacked the capital to undertake or to make a success of such enterprises. Instead they concentrated upon organizing local cooperative stores which could challenge the local merchants by selling at lower prices and which could market their membership's cotton. These schemes enlisted an ally in Archibald J. Rose, who became the State Lecturer in 1875 and in 1880 succeeded to Worthy Master of the organization.

Rose served the organization during its declining years as president of its Texas Farmer Publishing Association, its Real Estate and Immigration Association, its Texas Mutual Fire Insurance Association, and as Secretary of the Texas Cooperative Association as well as Worthy Master. He envisioned a network of local Grange stores, serving subordinate Granges, marketing and buying through the Texas Cooperative Association.

The Association, based in Galveston, was to operate on the Rochdale plan, a scheme devised in England and endorsed by the National Grange in 1876. According to this plan a member paid cash for his necessities and received a rebate at the end of the year. By selling only at retail prices, the Association would not alienate local merchants by instituting price-cutting wars. The "pay-as-you-go" plan was to be a way for tenant farmers to escape the clutches of a credit economy and sharecropping, and collectively to curb monopolistic practices of merchants. In 1883, the Texas cooperative Association sales aggregated $560,282.16, and it handled 16,045 bales of cotton for 150 Grange stores. The high point of the agency's operations was 1883. It could not deny members credit because farmers must have credit until the fall harvests. Furthermore, by extending credit to customers, the agency replenished supplies with credit. When hard times hit in the drought years of 1885-86, farmers could not pay bills and neither could the agency. Moreover local stores faced a similar problem. They extended credit to local Grangers who had to have it and demanded in turn credit from their wholesale agency—The Texas Cooperative Association. The undercapitalized Association verged on bankruptcy from 1886 on. Finally, in the 1890s, a shell of its former self, The Texas Cooperative Association filed bankruptcy proceedings amid charges of malfeasance and quarreling between directors and creditors.

The reason for the failure of the Texas Cooperative Association emphasized why the parent organization, the Grange, failed. The Association based its philosophy upon a self-sufficient farm and upon a farmer who paid cash. Its propaganda pamphlets told farmers to tighten their belts, avoid credit for a few years, diversify their crops so they were not victims of the fluctuations in prices of the cotton market, and they and their children would escape tenant farming and enjoy prosperity. Presumably, the Grange Hall would provide a social life and educational opportunities for rural families. Thus, the evils of city life would be avoided when the children earned economic independence and social prestige in rural Texas. These ideas were anachronisms in the modern world as the country and Texas drove toward economic specialization and urban life. Furthermore, the Grange never considered politics, until the Hogg campaign, either as a viable alternative to or as support for economic solutions to the farmer's problems. Another Texas farm organization, one that surpassed it in both numbers and radicalism, made no such error—The Texas Farmers' Alliance.

Actually the Alliance, like the Grange, professed to be apolitical. But from its very beginning in 1877, the Alliancemen, as the members were called, talked more about politics in their meetings than did ever the Grangers. Partially this increased political awareness stemmed from Patron failures and partially from the nature of the early Alliance organizations themselves. Between 1870 and 1880 Texas farmers pushed west from Fort Worth into the treeless plains and the marginal lands of the Cross Timbers. There they joined in voluntary associations that varied from vigilante groups to social institutions — schools, churches, Masonic lodges, Granges. Lampasas County was in the mainstream of this westward flow; 1,344 people lived there in 1870 and 5,421 in 1880.

In September 1877 Lewis Chavose and John R. Allen called a meeting of a new voluntary association called first the Farmers' Reliance and later the Farmers' Alliance. One member suggested that this new organization, the only voluntary social group in the north of the county, become a Grange and join with two others to the south and east to form a County or Pomona Grange. A. P. Hungate, one of the members, replied that he opposed the self-help approach of the Patrons, and the new organization should "employ the whole foundation of the Grange as a single corner stone of a grand social and political Pallace *(sic)* . . ." Political issues always divided Alliance members. And in 1878, when some of the Lampasas Alliancemen supported the Greenback Party, the first local lodge died.

William T. Baggett, a school teacher and a member of the Grange as well as the Lampasas Alliance, moved to Poolville in Parker County. He took a copy of the Alliance constitution and immediately organized a school and a Farmer's Alliance. From Parker County the Alliance gospel spread to Jack County and then to Hamilton, Parker, Wise, Coryell, and back to Lampasas counties. Local lecturers-organizers, paid out of the organizational fees, enlisted farmers into the movement. The frontier was receptive to their plea. The Cross Timbers, sparse in vegetation and in rainfall, seemed to be the end of the path for those who followed the Western Star. Here Texans, unsure they could conquer the arid West, felt that they must organize to claim the financial successes the westward movements promised. They were receptive, therefore, to the lecturers' message that through the Farmers' Alliance economic grievances could be solved and political wishes made known to reluctant legislatures.

The Alliance did not sweep the rest of the state, however. Many thought that it would wither away in 1881-82. Some Texans believed that it would remain a secret lodge, using old Grange ritual, passwords, secret signs and social events to recruit members into a fraternal organization. Others could see little difference in the Alliance proposals for economic cooperation — stores, gins, warehouses, for example — and those ventures tried by the Grangers. Furthermore, the success of the Texas Cooperative Association limited the Alliances' growth.

In August 1883 only thirty of the more than 120 sub-Alliances were active, and the State Alliance had almost ceased to exist. Frontier economic conditions worsened that year. The next year, January 1884, William Garvin, the state President, chose his neighbor, S. O. Dawes, to revitalize the Alliance. As a "traveling lecturer" Dawes toured the state, recruiting new members, restoring the fire to old ones. He was not afraid of politics nor of attacking with vigorous speeches monopolies and middlemen. He found a receptive audience among farmers discouraged by a not too responsive government and by an inability to control the markets from their homes that railroads made for their crops. The Alliancemen accepted the concept of credit, unlike the Grange, and encouraged their cooperative organizations to let needy members charge goods. Between

1884 and 1885, 200,000 farmers across the state joined the Alliance, and the Grange collapsed.

In 1885 forces other than lecturers drove the organization toward politics. Throughout West Texas in the heart of Alliance country small farmers fought ownership of land by foreign syndicates and the fencing of large tracts. These farmers created political parties to oppose cattlemen. In some cases — Jack County for example — the insurgent groups and the local Alliances were the same. The Prohibition party also lured Alliancemen away from the Democratic party. Some state newspapers, such as *The Dallas Morning News*, feared the two organizations might unite. As unlikely as that merger probably was, the endorsement of prohibition by the Alliance President and two official Alliance papers made political insurgency respectable.

The major reason for increased insurgency, however, among farmers was the cordial relations that developed between the Farmers' Alliance and the Knights of Labor. In 1885, after the Knights seemingly defeated Jay Gould's proposed wage reduction for rail employees, the organization grew to include about one-half of the laborers in the state. That year the Knights sent representatives to the State Alliance meeting, and the organization pledged cooperation with each other. By 1886, some local lodges of the two organizations pledged cooperation with each other, and founded joint cooperative ventures, and more importantly, endorsed local political candidates. These same lodges urged fellow Alliancemen to support boycotts that the Knights called against the Mallory steamship lines, and that spring some Alliance leaders maintained that working class solidarity was so important that farmers should feed the Knights then striking the Gould railway system. This support continued, even after the Knights resorted to violence, and the majority of both the newspapers and political leaders in the state condemned the strikers. The strike ended unsuccessfully for the Knights of Labor in May 1886. The labor organization died shortly thereafter. The Alliance move into politics did not.

In 1886 a drought began. Cotton plants withered in the fields. The despair of farmers grew. That summer a drought-relief bill passed Congress, and Grover Cleveland, a Democratic President, vetoed it. His veto further disillusioned some Texas farmers with the existing political structure. The Alliance leadership, divided over political insurgency, now found itself with a membership also divided over the need for independent political action. S. O. Dawes, anxious to keep the organization from dividing over the issue of politics, proposed that the Alliance be education, debating political issues if necessary, but that Alliancemen combine with other farmers who agreed with their political views and as individuals form anti-monopoly parties. Thus the "Dawes Formula," as Lawrence Goodwyn called the compromise, kept the Alliance together; yet it redefined the limits of Alliance political activities. Now the issue became not should the Farmers' Alliance enter politics but rather how should political power be used.

In August 1886 the State Alliance met in Cleburne. The meeting was divided between members who supported direct political action and the Knights of Labor and those who wanted the organization not to endorse third party politics or any other organization. Both factions supported cooperation. The political activists controlled the convention, and passed the Cleburne demands, seventeen legislative resolutions that would aid laboring classes in their fight against "arrogant capitalists and powerful corporations." Conservatives particularly opposed one resolution that called for a national meeting of all laboring groups to discuss collective action of laboring classes. By a vote of 92-75 the convention approved of the Cleburne demands. Conservatives decided to organize their own Alliance, one that was not partisan. Some Alliance leaders, fearing a total collapse of the leadership structure, suggested a compromise whereby they would take the issue of politics back to sub-Alliances. Finally three officiers of the organization were to resign, and the Chairman of the Executive Committee, Charles W. Macune, would call a new state meeting in Waco in January 1887. The delegates would report back from the local lodges. In short nothing was settled. The Cleburne meeting would occur again.

Charles W. Macune, a moderate, presided over a divided convention that met in January. The insurgents believed that the rank-and-file supported them; the conservatives were grimly determined to remain loyal Democrats. Macune did a magnificent job of pacifying both groups. Now thirty-six, his career would include within the next five years posts as business manager of the State Exchange, president of the Southern Alliance and editor of the *National Economist,* its newspaper. Never enthusiastic about third-party politics, he would nevertheless support the Populist Party. Waco in 1887 may have been his finest hour in the Alliance movement. That day he announced that he had contacted the Louisiana Farmers' Union, and a merger of this group with the Texas Alliance would be the beginnings of a national organization (the Farmers' Alliance and Co-operative Union of America, usually called the Southern Alliance) which could bring increased political power to southern farmers through group pressure on the National Congress. Furthermore, he proposed an Alliance Exchange, capitalized at $500,000, that would institute a sweeping program of cooperative marketing and purchasing within Texas. Both factions rallied to his suggestions. And the first crisis passed. But in 1888, the division would open once again as cooperation and political endeavors failed. By that time the Texas Alliance had spread its ideas into the rest of the South and had moved into Kansas. By then, too, the Alliance Exchange dream had ended.

The half-million-dollar corporation, the largest in Texas, would be able to compete with the capitalist establishments, said Macune. In 1886, immediately after the Waco meeting, the Alliance applied to the state for incorporation of the Exchange and asked Texas cities to bid for its location. Dallas won with a promise of $100,000 plus a lot. The membership chose a twenty-five member board to direct the new Exchange. Macune accepted the post of business manager, at a salary of $1,800 per year, and in the summer of 1887 the new corporation began. It opened its doors in a new four-story building that cost $45,000 or one-half the Exchange's operating capital. Macune promised to buy from wholesale houses what the membership needed and sell their cotton directly to the market. The Exchange would replace the need for middlemen. Since Dallas failed to deliver the $100,000 promised, the Exchange, short of capital, soon extended credit to its members.

Unlike the Texas Cooperative Association, this new agency formalized its credit policy. Macune asked that each County Alliance poll its members and determine their needs for the next year. The cost of these goods was to be estimated, and the members of the Alliance would sign a joint note equal to each member's needs for the year. This promissory note would be sent to the Exchange, and Macune would allow the County Alliance to draw supplies against them. The farmer, thus, would write his own crop lien, and the power of the crossroads merchant would be broken. The Exchange assumed that it could discount these notes with banks for operating capital.

Texas banks refused to accept the notes. The Exchange, with only $18,000 in capital, could not finance all its members. Thus when the notes came in with farmers' orders for the coming season, the Exchange received $400,000 worth of supplies on its credit from wholesalers and manufacturers, citing the joint notes as collateral. Soon creditors became wary over the large indebtedness and the small amount of liquid funds of the Exchange. The major creditors met with Macune, and they agreed that all 300,000 Alliance members would be assessed $2.00 each. Less than ten percent of the membership paid. Creditors and signers of joint notes became alarmed. Rumors flew that the Board of Exchange mishandled, possibly embezzeled, several hundreds of thousands of dollars. After all, was it not a half-million dollar corporation, asked Alliancemen? And when the membership failed to respond to the call for an assessment, the Exchange declared bankruptcy, destroying also plans for Alliance mills, factories and a university.

The Exchange and the Texas Cooperative association both failed from a lack of capital and an overextension of credit. Macune and Rose maintained that their enterprises had not cost the farmers monetary losses but rather had saved them money by forcing down prices of commodities needed by farmers. Nevertheless, the failures of these agricultural enterprises disillusioned the respective organization's members and caused the Patrons' and Alliances' demise. Texas farmers abandoned the Alliance after the failure of the Exchange. The Grand State Alliance ceased to exist in reality by 1890, and the state would boast of no organization devoted exclusively to agricultural interests until the twentieth century.

All Texas farmers did not abandon their demands in 1890, however. Rather they moved into organizing a new vehicle, the People's Party. This organization included blacks as well as whites. The Grand State Alliance declared itself to be a "white-man's organization" in 1881. Yet in 1886 Robert M. Humphrey, a white minister in Houston County responded to appeals of black farmers and organized the Colored Alliance. Early this organization contented itself with forming trading associations and alliance exchanges. By 1891 more militant and now with sub-alliances outside of Texas, Humphrey called a series of cotton picker strikes. White alliance newspapers admonished their black counterparts urging them not to cause labor strife between the races. The proposed strikes failed in Texas, although one did succeed in Arkansas. The white farmers' reaction was not as fierce as might be supposed, partially perhaps because the Colored Alliance posed no social threat to whites. "We do not want to eat at their tables, sleep in their beds," said Humphrey, "neither ride in cars with them." This separate but unequal stance encouraged southern Populists to try to incorporate the black into the third party.

From 1890 to 1896 until fusion with the Democratic Party destroyed them, the Populists fought for a general reform of the abuses of industrialism. The crusade was more than an agrarian one. But the farmers were the backbone of the movement in Texas. Thus, by 1900, agriculturists had come a long way since 1876. Originally located only in the eastern part of the state they moved West, broke new grounds, increased production of crops, and along with railroads, gave urban areas an economic reason for being. Farmers moved from self-contained to commercial agriculture and joined organizations to enable them to compete in the businessman's world. These organizations brought them precious little economic relief. They did exert considerable influence on the state's and on the nation's legislatures to pass statutes that ameliorated industrial excesses. It was doubtful that an income tax, a federal reserve system, railroad regulatory agencies, or commodity credit legislation would have ever passed either Congress or state bodies unless Grangers and Alliancemen kept the issues alive.

Texas seemed ready for the twentieth century as the farmers' movements ended. Spindletop meant that oil would replace cotton as the basis for the Texas economy. Petroleum would in a way be as susceptible to market prices as was agriculture. Yet the mineral would bring capital to the state, hasten the growth of cities, encourage industrial development, and lay a base for the rapid development caused by World War I and II. Thus, the family farm, as the frontier, saw that way of life passing as the nineteenth century closed.

*Cotton Picking, painting by Oscar Berninghous.*
— Eugene C. Barker Texas History Center, University of Texas

# 7

## Texas in the Progressive Era, 1900-1930

*Robert S. Maxwell*

As Texas entered the twentieth century, winds of change and reform affected the Lone Star State as well as the entire country. The Progressive Movement was nationwide and influenced all levels of government plus economic, social, and educational institutions. Texas was not a leading progressive state but many or most of the reforms advocated by progressive leaders became part of the Texas system during the three decades from 1900 to 1930. Much of the pressure for change came from individuals or organized volunteer groups rather than the political leaders with the result that as much progressive legislation went into effect during so-called conservative administrations as under avowed progressives.

Texas was not without reform traditions. During the previous decade James Stephen Hogg had led in enacting antimonopoly legislation and in pushing antitrust actions in the courts. John H. Reagan, as chairman of the Texas Railroad Commission, had set a standard for effective railroad regulation. Alexander W. Terrell became identified with the demand for reform in the convention and election system of the state. None of these men established lasting political organizations so their influence was largely personal and temporary.

In 1900 Texas was a state of three million people, more than 80 percent of whom lived on farms or ranches. No city boasted as many as 60,000 population. Changes in the recent growth pattern revealed that San Antonio was the largest city, closely followed by Houston,

*GOVERNOR JAMES S. HOGG, First native-born governor of Texas.*

Dallas, and Galveston in order. Before the end of the year, Galveston — beautiful, rich, proud Galveston — was devastated by a mammouth hurricane and tropical storm. In the city more than 6,000 people perished and thousands more fled inland, never to return. Galveston, which had once been the largest city in the state and the largest cotton port in the world never recovered fully from this disaster. Its leadership role passed to other cities more fortunately located on higher ground.

The economy of Texas at the turn of the century was based on farming and ranching with cotton the chief cash crop. Lumbering led among manufacturing enterprises and by 1900 Texas sawmills reported a cut of one billion board feet of lumber per year. This made Texas one of the leading lumber-producing states in the union. To a large extent the growth of the lumber industry depended on the development of the Texas railroad network. By 1901 the railroads of the state reached 10,000 miles of mainline track and first rank in the entire country.

The year 1901 was also the date of the great revolution in the oil industry and in the pattern of Texas economic growth. Prior to this time petroleum production was only a modest industry with Corsicana, which produced about 900,000 barrels per year, the center of the industry. Texas production was only about 5 percent of the United States total, and the entire industry's refining and marketing pattern was based on scarcity and selected use.

Then on January 10, 1901 (a date as important in Texas history as the Alamo) Captain Anthony F. Lucas brought in the great gusher at Spindletop. Described by contemporaries as rising more than 150 feet, it poured out a great stream of oil estimated up to 100,000 barrels a day. It took Lucas and his crew nine days to cap the gusher and channel its black gold into tanks, ponds, and emergency reservoirs. New companies organized to exploit the discovery and new millionaires appeared overnight. From the Spindletop field such major oil producers as Texaco, Gulf, and Sun emerged to challenge the previous monopoly in the industry held by Standard Oil. By 1902 Texas production had reached 18,000,000 barrels of oil per year and Texas had become the number one petroleum-producing state in the nation.

In politics, the people of Texas seemingly ignored this economic revolution as much as possible. A series of Democratic governors — Joseph Sayers, Samuel W. T. Lanham, Thomas M. Campbell, and Oscar B. Colquitt — each served two two-year terms with little change in the status quo. Campbell was, perhaps, the most progressive of the quartet but a series of moderate reforms took place during the tenure of each, whether progressive or conservative. During the Sayers and Lanham years the legislature passed pro-labor measures which exempted labor unions from antitrust laws, outlawed blacklists, enacted wages and hours laws for special industries and an act regulating child labor. In 1904, after having no state banks for decades under the state constitution of 1876, the voters approved a constitutional amendment which authorized the establishment of a state bank system, and thus removed the long dead hand of Andrew Jackson from economic control of the state. The next year the lawmakers created a Commission of Banking and Insurance, directed by Thomas B. Love.

Perhaps the most important reforms passed under Lanham were the Terrell election laws. This legislation, first passed in 1903 and revised in 1905, required a primary election for any party that polled 100,000 votes or more at the last general election, set a statewide time for primary elections, and stipulated the requirements for voting in both the primary and general elections. Later legislatures plugged omissions in the laws and provided for a second (run-off) primary if no candidate received a majority of votes in the first election. Thus, the Democratic Party would always hold primary elections but minor parties (in Texas this included the Republicans) could hold primaries or continue to use the convention system if they chose.

Unlike the primary election laws of such progressive states as Wisconsin and California which broadened popular control and democratized the election process, the Texas legislation reduced and restricted voting. A constitutional amendment in 1902 required a poll tax of $1.50 to $1.75, paid early in the year, as a prerequisite for voting. The residence requirements included one year in the state, six months in the county and often sixty days in the precinct. These provisions eliminated many poor people, especially blacks, Mexican-Americans, and transients. Further, the leaders of the Democratic Party deliberately excluded non-whites from voting in the primary. Not for a number of decades, and series of Supreme Court decisions, were blacks in Texas able to break through these barriers and participate in the Democratic primary elections.

Regarded by his contemporaries as the most able and most liberal of Texas governors since James S. Hogg, Thomas M. Campbell won the governorship in 1906 and served until 1911. He vigorously strengthened the state's antitrust laws and pushed their enforcement. During the Campbell administration the attorney general prosecuted some 135 antitrust suits including a new case against the Standard Oil Company. Incidentally, Hogg who had retired to private law practice after his governorship was in on the ground floor at the Spindletop oil strike and was one of the organizers of the Texaco Company. At his death in 1906 Hogg was a multimillionaire and his fortune provided the foundation for numerous philanthropies and good works which have identified the Hogg family in Texas through the twentieth century.

Campbell continued the reform of the state's tax system, pushing through the legislature a "full rendition" law in 1907 and the creation of a state tax board. He also began the task of modernizing the Texas prison and ending the pernicious convict lease system. After a legislative committee described prison conditions as almost medieval — guards whipped or shot inmates almost at will, abused women prisoners, and on occasion resorted to torture — Campbell took action. With legislative approval he appointed a board of three prison commissioners to manage the prison system. The board improved food, medicine, and sanitary facilities, and largely abolished wearing of stripes.

In other fields, Campbell pushed for regulation of insurance companies, an issue that had made headlines in New York and other progressive states. The result was the Robertson Insurance Law of 1907 which set up comprehensive codes for the various classes of insurance and limited premiums and related charges. The law also required that the companies invest 75 percent of all reserves set aside to cover Texas policies in Texas securities. This resulted in twenty-one insurance companies, including many large national ones, withdrawing from the state. They protested that there were not that many sound investments available in Texas securities at that time. The long-range effect of this legislation was to make Texas a haven for local and often wildcat insurance companies which plagued the state for the next fifty years. A more constructive reform under Campbell was the establishment of a state insurance program to protect the deposits in the newly authorized state banking system. This excellent principle worked well for a time until it suffered from mismanagement in the 1920s. On the national level similar guarantees were not established until the organization of the Federal Deposit Insurance Corporation in 1933.

Campbell also supported higher standards for the public schools and greater freedom for local school boards to levy additional taxes to meet increased needs. In the area of local government he pushed for a larger degree of home rule for cities and more direct democracy through the inclusion of initiative, referendum, and recall provisions in new city charters. Though hailed as a leading progressive, Campbell's reforms were essentially moderate and followed the pattern of progressive legislation in other states. His administration did little to shift the burden of taxation from the general property tax or to mitigate the discrimination and disenfranchisement of many of the minority groups in the state.

Campbell's successor was Oscar B. Colquitt, an experienced politician who had served in the state legislature and as railroad commissioner. In the election of 1910 Colquitt entered the Democratic primary with four other candidates in which the chief issue was state-wide prohibition. Colquitt favored local option and aligned himself against the prohibitionists. He proved to be a colorful and capable campaigner and gained a sizable following. In the balloting Colquitt won a plurality of votes and thus gained the Democratic nomination. He easily triumped in the general election in November.

The question of prohibition by 1910 had become a leading issue in each election and tended to becloud other problems before the electorate. A statewide constitutional amendment for prohibition narrowly failed (by 6,000 votes) in the summer 1911, but this setback only caused the dry forces to redouble their efforts. Though regarded as a conservative Colquitt was not opposed to the moderate reform program that characterized Texas during the Progressive Era. He brought an end to the convict lease system, improved the state hospitals and established a training school for delinquent girls. He also supported laws promoting factory safety, new legislation restricting hours of work for women, and laws regulating child labor. In 1913 Colquitt proposed and the legislature passed a workmen's compensation law, placing on industry the financial burden for industrial accidents. This measure was a popular progressive reform in many states, and the Texas law followed the lead of Wisconsin in this field.

Colquitt inherited a state deficit of almost $1,000,000 and the new programs and institutions required additional funding. Though he had campaigned for economy and a respite from crusades, he was forced to support a general state tax increase. Indeed, state expenditures in Texas more than doubled in the ten years from 1904 to 1914.

The two United States Senators from Texas during these years were a study in contrasts. Charles A. Culberson had served as attorney general and governor before assuming his Senate seat in 1899. He was high-minded, a moderate progressive, and personally reticent. In his long career in the Senate Culberson rose to be minority leader of his party but ill health forced him to resign this duty. In his later years he was frequently absent from the floor of the Senate but his prestige, seniority and many friends kept him in the Senate until after World War I.

Joseph Weldon Bailey was quite the opposite. Born in Mississippi he migrated to Texas as a young man and immediately began to practice law and politics. He was tall, handsome, with a musical voice and a bent for high-flown oratory. He won a seat in Congress in 1890 and advanced to the Senate in 1901. A conservative in the Progressive Era, Bailey opposed most reforms on both the state and federal levels. He devoted his position and considerable talents in behalf of friends and corporate clients, his favorites being the Standard Oil Company and the Kirby Lumber Company. As could be expected, Senate committees frequently investigated him for conflicts of interest and corrupt practices. So notorious did Bailey become that muckraking journalist David Graham Phillips attacked him in an article entitled "The Treason of the Senate," which appeared in *Cosmopolitan* magazine. Despite these charges Bailey won reelection in 1907, but he found that he was out of step with both the times and his party. Harrassed by continuing revelations of misconduct, Bailey retired in 1913. To his friends Joe Bailey was the greatest man in Texas who had been unjustly accused. His opponents, and these included eventually much of the press, saw him as a conceited and pompous charlatan whose callous disregard for ethics and integrity in government made progressive reform more difficult. Appropriately, the people of Texas replaced Bailey in the Senate with prohibitionist and moralist Morris Sheppard.

Perhaps the most powerful figure in Texas during the Progressive Era held no political office. Colonel Edward M. House (the title was honorary) was a wealthy Austin businessman and planter. At an early age he had shown skill in organizing and manipulating campaigns and elections. Having no personal political ambitions, he helped direct Jim Hogg's 1892 campaign for reelection to the governorship. A small, thin, quiet man, House was a master of detail and knew the value of being first in the field to get commitments from local leaders. In 1894 he pushed Charles Culberson to succeed Hogg as governor and then secured Culberson's advancement to the United States Senate. In turn, he selected and successfully managed the campaigns of Sayers and Lanham for the governorship. In his correspondence House gleefully wrote about "our crowd" and their control of state elections. Among his close associates were congressman Albert S. Burleson, attorney Frank Andrews, lawyer Thomas W. Gregory, and South Texas political boss James B. Wells. Never a friend of Joseph Weldon Bailey, House was able to keep him at arm's length but at the same time avoid a direct confrontation with the popular Senator.

House was not unprogressive. He favored a uniform primary

*The Galveston seawall and beach some ten years after the hurricane destroyed the island city.*

system and direct election of U.S. Senators. In Texas he urged greater support for the University of Texas and Texas A&M College and reforms in state penal and charitable institutions. In 1912 House wrote a novel, *Philip Dru: Administrator,* which he published anonymously. If the hero's proposals and programs reflected House's own thoughts, the Colonel would favor a graduated income tax, elimination of extremes of wealth and poverty, labor representatives on all corporation boards, old age pensions, woman suffrage, a new federal banking system, and a curbing of the powers of federal judges. The book did not prove to be a best seller and relatively few people read it. However, among those who read and were influenced by *Philip Dru* were Woodrow Wilson and Franklin D. Roosevelt.

By 1908 House had despaired of William Jennings Bryan as a Democratic presidential candidate and he began a search for a more attractive personality whom he could support and help gain the presidency. After investigating several other public men, House's quest led him to Governor Woodrow Wilson of New Jersey, a scholar and former president of Princeton University. House was not the earliest advocate of Wilson in Texas; that honor would go to Thomas B. Love and perhaps Cato Sells. But House became a Wilson backer before the New Jersey governor visited Texas in October 1911 where he spoke at the State Fair in Dallas and in Fort Worth. Once committed, House bent every effort to achieve success for his candidate and soon House's experience and political expertise became apparent both in Wilson's Texas office and the national headquarters in New York. From their first meeting both Wilson and House held favorable impressions of each other and soon the two developed a warm friendship and mutual admiration. Despite Senator Joseph Bailey's opposition, the Wilson men controlled the 1912 state convention and sent a solid corps of Wilson delegates to the National Convention at Baltimore. In typical fashion House did not personally attend the convention at Houston but steered it to a successful conclusion by careful advance planning and a series of notes and messengers.

At Baltimore the Texas delegation, the immortal forty they called themselves, stood firm for Wilson through the stress of forty-six ballots. Not only did they have no second choice but Texans did missionary work among other delegations promoting votes for Wilson. Again House was not present but was on his way to Europe after sending notes on strategy to Wilson and key convention figures. After his victory, Wilson regarded Burleson, Gregory, and especially House as the architects of his nomination. With Wilson's election in November the president-elect conferred with House concerning cabinet appointments and other positions in his administration. The colonel announced that he would move to Washington but declined to accept an official position for himself. He recommended Burleson to be postmaster general, David F. Houston (former president of the University of Texas) to be secretary of agriculture, and a little later Gregory to be attorney general. With these and a number of lesser appointments Texas, especially the House Democratic group in Texas, wielded a strong hand in the Wilson administration.

In the meantime the people of Texas made history apart from the legislative halls. Galveston dug itself out from the debris of the great storm. The existing city government virtually disappeared as a result of the disaster and leading citizens organized a commission form of city government. The commission, composed of five highly qualified elected officials, divided the responsibilities among the members according to each's area of expertise. This innovation, which directly linked authority and responsibility in a small board, proved popular and other cities throughout the country copied the plan. Determined that Galveston would not become another Indianola, the commission undertook to build a seawall to protect the city from future Gulf storms. The great wall rose seventeen feet above high tide and extended more than ten miles on the south side of the island. A broad paved boulevard paralleled the top of the wall the length of the beach. The commission then raised the elevation of the populated part of the island and lifted 2,300 structures from five to eight feet.

In 1902 the U.S. Army Engineers deepened the harbor channel at Galveston to thirty feet which was regarded as a mark of confidence in the city and enabled Galveston to revive as a great cotton port. Shortly the street railway company electrified all routes in the system and retired the mules. By 1911 the city completed a permanent causeway to the mainland, inaugurated interurban service to Houston, and celebrated the opening of the Galvez Hotel. Prominent residents, such as the Sealy, Kempner, Moody, and Rosenberg families, contributed heavily to the restoration of historic and cultural landmarks of the city and the development of scientific enterprises and medical facilities. Though never again to rival Houston and Dallas as the metropolis of Texas, Galveston had recovered from the 1900 disaster to a large extent through the efforts of its own citizens.

At the same time the city of Houston made major changes and improvements in its transportation facilities that affected not only Galveston but the entire Gulf Southwest. From its first establishment in 1836, A. C. and John K. Allen, its founders, had insisted that Houston was "at the head of navigation" of Buffalo Bayou. The stream did admit small steamboats that traveled up to Houston in favorable weather. But like other Texas rivers, Buffalo Bayou was unpredictable. It had too much water at some seasons and not enough at others. Trees, snags, logs and sand bars impeded navigation. Clopper's Bar at Morgan's Point and the larger Red Fish Bar in Galveston Bay were further barriers. City leaders made some progress toward improving navigation during the late nineteenth century but the dream of a deepwater port at Houston still seemed far away. But with the advent of Thomas H. Ball in Congress in 1897 the drive for the "Port of Houston" and a convenient turning basin within the city took on new momentum. Aided by Horace B. Rice, Jesse H. Jones, and Ross Sterling, among others, Ball pushed the project at every session of Congress. The creation of a Houston and Harris County Navigation District made it possible to provide matching funds and continuing supervision that Congress demanded. The work went forward more rapidly and the success of the project was assured. November 10, 1914, saw a great celebration for the formal opening of the Houston Ship Channel, which made Houston a deepwater port and provided a permanent route to the sea. The Port of Houston sparked the growth of the city to become a major metropolis, the largest in the South and Southwest, and the port eventually became the third largest in the United States. At the same time, almost as a footnote to the Houston story, both Beaumont and Orange also formed navigation districts and achieved deepwater port status by 1916. All of these developments advanced oceangoing capabilities for the East Texas mainland but diminished further still the position of Galveston as Texas' principal port.

The period from 1900 to the First World War were bonanza years for the Texas lumber industry. Three times during this era lumbermen reported a cut of more than two billion board feet and the average cut for these years was more than one and one-half billion. These were peak times for such lumber tycoons as John Henry Kirby, Henry J. Lutcher and William H. Stark, Thomas L. L. Temple, Joseph H. Kurth, W. T. Carter and John Martin Thompson. To meet the demands for transportation Texas railroads extended into every part of East Texas and a myriad of short lines and tram roads criss-crossed between the mainline roads in every county. The pattern of the owner-dominated company town, where workers traded at the company commissary with company-issued merchandise checks, continued during the entire period and, indeed, would not end until World War II. Organized labor's efforts to form unions among the lumber workers failed without exception although work-

*Lumbering operation at Jefferson, around 1919.*
— Jefferson Carnegie Library, photo by Harvey Moore

ers were able to get the work day in the industry shortened from eleven to ten hours.

Concern over the rapid depletion of this timbered empire caused conservationists to predict a lumber famine in Texas within twenty years. W. Goodrich Jones, a Temple banker and leading tree enthusiast, sought to persuade timber owners that good forestry practices were also good business. He urged a program of selective cutting, sustained yield rotation, reforestation, and scientific management. After attending the White House Conference of Governors on Conservation where he met President Theodore Roosevelt and Chief Forester Gifford Pinchot, Jones organized the Texas Forestry Association in 1914. The next year the association, led by Jones, presented a comprehensive forestry program to the Texas legislature and lobbied for its passage. Jones became known as the "father of Texas forestry," and a champion of the conservation of natural resources in all forms.

In the petroleum industry, producers developed refining facilities at Beaumont, Port Arthur, and Houston which brought some order to the chaotic conditions of the Spindletop field. New discoveries at Sour Lake, Humble, in the Panhandle, and in Wichita and Archer counties expanded the area of oil production and more than made up for the decline of Spindletop due to loss of gas pressure. As of World War I, however, the legislature had made no serious effort to regulate or conserve petroleum production in this, the largest and fastest growing industry in Texas.

In contrast, the Texas Railroad Commission (TRC) carefully regulated the state's railroad network in the interest of Texas manufacturers and shippers. Though the federal Interstate Commerce Commission had jurisdiction over interstate rates, the Texas Commission exercised sole control over intrastate rates and services in the Lone Star State. Beginning about 1900 the TRC fixed freight rates between Texas towns well below the interstate rate for comparable distances. As a result manufacturers and wholesalers from New Orleans and Shreveport, who had previously competed on equal terms with merchants from Dallas or Houston, now were priced out of the market. An extreme case quoted freight rates on wagons shipped from Dallas to Marshall, a distance of 148 miles, at 37 cents per 100 pounds. The interstate rate for a similar wagon shipped from Shreveport to Marshall, a distance of forty-two miles, was 56 cents per 100 pounds. As could be expected traffic from the Louisiana cities to Texas dried up.

This brought litigation in behalf of the Louisiana shippers in the federal courts. Eventually after years of hearings and appeals, the

U.S. Supreme Court handed down an historic ruling known as the "Shreveport Case." The high court directed that the TRC could not discriminate in favor of Texas shippers as opposed to out of state shippers and ordered that intrastate rates be made uniform with interstate rates wherever they conflicted. The long-range effect of the Shreveport Case was to transfer effective jurisdiction over the Texas railroads to the Interstate Commerce Commission. Thus, for a time, the Texas Railroad Commission had few duties to occupy its time.

The year 1914 was a critical year for the people of Texas as well as the world at large. The ongoing Mexican Revolution caused concern and not a little panic among South Texas residents. President Wilson's policy of neutrality and "watchful waiting" angered Governor Colquitt, who wanted federal troops stationed along the Rio Grande to protect citizens and property. Numerous small raids by Mexican bandits triggered reaction and reprisals by Texas Rangers and sheriff's posses. In the turmoil that followed, Anglo groups killed some Mexican-Americans who lived north of the river. Colquitt demanded that the army be sent into Mexico to kill or capture the bandits. Wilson rejected the governor's demands at that time although in 1916 the president sent General John J. Pershing on a punitive expedition into Mexico.

The outbreak of World War I in August 1914 caused shock and fear among the people of Texas. The overseas market for cotton disappeared and international sales of Texas lumber collapsed. Governor Colquitt sought both state and federal assistance for the suddenly depressed cotton farmer and when neither the Congress nor the legislature responded to his demands, the governor blamed Wilson and denounced him as the "greatest failure in history" and predicted that he would be retired in the next election. By the summer of 1915, however, Allied needs for all kinds of materials produced a lively boom for farmers, lumber manufacturers and oil refiners.

The year 1914 also produced a new face in the Texas political gallery. James E. Ferguson was born in Bell County into the family of a rather poor but enterprising Methodist clergyman. His father died when he was only a young boy and he worked on the family farm and attended local schools. He entered Salado College (a preparatory school), where he studied history, literature, political theory, as well as Greek and Latin. In a generation in which many public men had only a smattering of education, Ferguson had a background of academic training. Though he never attended a university he was better educated than many of his contemporaries, and he was far from the "farmer Jim" pose that he later adopted in his political campaigns.

By 1914 Ferguson had worked on the railroad, run a farm, studied law and passed the bar examination, and had become president of the Temple State Bank. Though he had actively supported candidates in a number of races, he had not run for election until he announced for governor in late 1913. He argued that the voters were tired of the constant prohibition agitation and promised to veto any act dealing for or against alcoholic beverages that came to his desk. The important issue, he said, was the problem of land tenure. Pointing out that tenants operated almost two-thirds of the farms in Texas he proposed that the legislature restrict the "take" of landlords to one-fourth of the cotton crop and/or one-third of grain crops. He also talked of land reform — redistribution of farm lands to the actual farmer — but remained vague on specifics and later dropped the issue. Ferguson was a charismatic leader; he spoke well and was always on the attack, never on the defensive. In rural counties he related his farm background and regularly used folksy, earthy expressions to identify himself with his audience. He lauded the "boys at the forks of the creek" as the real foundation of Texas democracy.

In the 1914 primary election Ferguson's chief opponent for the governorship was Thomas H. Ball, Houston lawyer and former congressman. He was successful, well-known, progressive and a prohibitionist. Though Ball began the campaign with the advantages of money, recognition, reputation, and organized political support, he was no match for Jim Ferguson. "Farmer Jim" launched a furious campaign making more than 150 speeches and denouncing Ball as a plutocrat who "voted dry but drank wet" behind the closed doors of the Houston Club. He carried on such an unending assault of slander and charges against Ball that the Houstonian was kept on the defensive and rapidly lost support. In spite of a last minute effort to secure endorsements in behalf of Ball from President Wilson and Senator Culberson, Ball's campaign workers knew that the campaign was in shambles and their man faced a humiliating defeat. Ferguson won the primary election by more than 45,000 votes, and easily won the general election in November.

There is sometimes a fine line between the progressive reformer and the self-serving demagogue in American politics. Jim Ferguson was a bit of both. He presented himself as a progressive and a man of character and decision. He spoke of his farm tenant bill as a reform, in keeping with the national progressive tradition as were the other planks in his platform. In the platform convention he resolutely faced down former Senator Joe Bailey and later he successfully opposed and denounced the Ku Klux Klan. Soon after the election Ferguson made a trip east, where he met with Wilson and assured the president that he supported the administration's Mexican and neutrality policies. Later he visited Colonel House, who was pleased with the prospect of cooperation and concluded that Ferguson would be a "satisfactory" governor.

During his first term, Ferguson largely fulfilled that expectation. He pushed through the legislature his farm tenancy bill, but the attorney general did not vigorously enforce it and the United State Supreme Court eventually, in 1921, struck it down. Under Ferguson the legislature passed a compulsory school attendance bill, appropriated more money for rural schools, and opened the door for local districts to provide free textbooks. The same legislature increased funds for the University of Texas and Texas A&M College.

At the urging of his neighbor, W. Goodrich Jones, also a banker in Temple, Ferguson proposed the establishment of a State Department of Forestry to supervise conservation work in the state. After intense lobbying the friends of conservation saw the bill passed and Ferguson signed it into law. Thus, the Texas Department of Forestry (later renamed the Texas Forest Service) came into being in 1915 and began its task of protecting the great forest lands of East Texas and reforesting the cutover lands in the wake of the bonanza lumbermen. The department grew to become a strong, professional, non-political agency that has effectively promoted practical conservation in Texas for some seventy years.

During these same years, however, Ferguson began to display the same proclivities that eventually led to his downfall. He had state funds deposited in the Temple State Bank and other banks in which he had an interest. These "pet" banks paid the state no interest on the substantial accounts deposited with them, but the same banks lent the governor more than $140,000 at favorable rates. Ferguson also became embroiled in a controversity with acting University of Texas President William J. Battle. The conflict began over items in the university budget and expanded over the issue of tenure of certain faculty members who had been active in the 1914 political campaign in support of his opponent. Ferguson became further irritated when the University Regents selected a permanent president, Robert E. Vinson, without consulting the governor.

In the 1916 campaign Ferguson won renomination and reelection rather easily and Texas Democrats again supported President Wilson in a hardfought campaign and narrow victory. Soon afterward, Ferguson returned to his quarrel with the university, charging that it was "disloyal." He filled vacancies on the Board of Regents with his own men but still could not force the board to fire Vinson, remove some six faculty members, or curb the student

*GOVERNOR JIM FERGUSON delivers his inaugural address to the Texas Legislature.*

— Austin-Travis County Collection, Austin Public Library

newspaper which was outspoken in its criticism of the governor. Finally, in June 1917, he emphasized his displeasure by vetoing the entire university appropriation. Attempting some compromise, the regents, including the new appointees, did dismiss the six faculty members who were the objects of the governor's ire but refused to yield on other issues. Regent Will C. Hogg (son of the reform governor) took the lead in rallying regents, alumni, and friends to resist domination by the governor. Ex-regent George W. Brackenridge offered to underwrite the expenses of the university from his personal funds if the legislature was unable to override Ferguson's veto. In addition to the University ex-students association, the Texas equal Suffrage Association and the Women's Christian Temperance Union joined the fight against the governor. A number of legislators began to prepare impeachment charges including a new charge that Ferguson had received $156,000 during the campaign of 1916 from unknown sources and for which he refused to account.

The Speaker of the House called for a special session of the legislature to meet early in September 1917. The Travis County Grand Jury about the same time indicted the governor for misappropriation of public funds. Confident that he could explain away the charges, Ferguson issued his own call for a special session (thus giving legality to the Speaker's call) in order to consider a budget for the university. Once in session the House proceeded without delay to impeach Governor Ferguson on twenty-one articles, most of which were related to misuse of public funds. The Senate then convicted him on ten of the charges and not only removed him from office but also prohibited him from holding office in Texas again. In a last effort to forestall impeachment Ferguson resigned on September 24, but the Senate proceeded with the conviction and removal the next day. As other historians have pointed out, the legislature did not impeach and convict Ferguson because he vetoed the University's appropriation, but if he had signed that bill the anti-Ferguson forces would not have united against him and he probably would have been able to complete his term.

William P. Hobby succeeded Ferguson as governor and at once appointed several new regents to the university board after the Senate rejected Ferguson's last appointees. The new governor approved the university budget and the reconstituted board reinstated the ousted professors. The University of Texas did not emerge from this conflict with an enhanced reputation but at least the institution had beaten off a determined threat of domination by an aggressive and popular governor.

While the people of Texas concentrated on the struggle involving Ferguson, the legislature and the university, the United States went to war with Germany. President Wilson called on all Americans to support the war effort 100 percent and the great majority of Texans responded. Although Governor Ferguson expressed some criticism of the administration's mobilization policies including the draft, his successor displayed whole-hearted cooperation. The Texas delegation in Washington, with the exception of Jeff McLemore, followed Wilson's lead and loyally backed his wartime program. Colonel House, who for three years had served as Wilson's advisor on political and economic questions, now became his personal advisor on foreign policy and frequently went on diplomatic missions as his trusted emissary. Gregory as attorney general and Burleson as postmaster general had a large hand in developing wartime policy on the home front.

Texas became a major center for training troops for the conflict. Thousands of young men went through basic training at Camp McArthur (Waco), Camp Logan (Houston), Camp Bowie (Fort Worth), and Camp Travis (San Antonio). In addition there were a number of officer training schools and aviation fields located in the state. Men from all parts of the country made their first acquaintance with the Lone Star State during basic training at a Texas camp. Almost 200,000 Texans served in the armed forces through volunteer enlistments or the draft. The 36th Division, Texas National Guard, made outstanding contributions to the campaigns on the Western Front in Europe.

Governor Hobby took the lead in promoting the war effort in the state. The State Council of Defense (established in May 1917) assisted in the five great war bond drives, organized "four-minute-men" groups for speaking tours, and cooperated with the Federal Food Administration to persuade families to conserve meat, wheat, sugar, and other essential foodstuffs. As in other states Texans saw a rapid inflation of prices which more than doubled by 1919. The War Industries Board fixed the price of finished lumber which brought an outcry from the East Texas lumber barons. On the other hand, the board did not fix the price of cotton which continued to advance to more than fifty cents per pound. This brought a charge of favoritism from the wheat producers in the northern states.

Hobby also followed the Wilson administration in securing enforced conformity. He called a special session of the legislature in 1918 which enacted a series of laws similar to the federal sedition, espionage, and enemy alien acts. It became a state offense to criticize the United States government or its officials, the flag, soldiers, uniforms, or to oppose the war effort. The legislature also sought to deny the vote to all foreign-born people who were not fully naturalized and did require that all teachers be citizens. Hobby vetoed the legislative appropriation for the German department at the University and most high schools dropped German from the secondary curriculum. Caught up in the anti-German spirit the University regents fired a number of alien faculty members as well as the well-known antiwar advocate Professor Lindley M. Keasbey.

The war fervor had even uglier manifestations. A race riot in Huntsville killed at least seven people and a larger outbreak in Houston resulted in the death of seventeen. As an aftermath of the Houston melee the army court-martialed eighteen soldiers of the 24th Infantry (black regular army unit) and hanged thirteen for their part in the uprising. The county councils of defense became vigilante groups in some counties, threatening, whipping, or beating persons of German background or with German names who refused to buy war bonds, were suspected of violating the Food Administration regulations, or even had declined to join the Red Cross. These excesses of zeal and intolerant super-patriotism were often tragic. But in this Texans paralleled the drive for conformity in other states that had large populations of mixed ethnic background. Texans' behavior regarding civil rights during the war was neither the best nor the worst in the United States.

The war years saw the success of the prohibition and woman suffrage crusades. Led by the Anti-Saloon League the dry forces had pushed prohibition on a local option basis until by 1911 most counties were dry or partially dry. The metropolitan centers, however, continued to have legal liquor sales and open bars. Prohibition forces had succeeded in having a statewide constitutional referendum submitted to the voters only to be defeated by a narrow margin. Subsequent efforts for resubmission failed in 1914 and 1916.

The coming of the war in 1917 gave the drys a new opportunity and additional arguments. In a drive to "clean up" the areas around the newly established army camps and protect the recruits from evil influences, the Texas legislature passed a law prohibiting the sale of alcohol within ten miles of any military camp. At the urging of chief food administrator Herbert Hoover, Congress passed a wartime prohibition act to save food. Shortly afterward Congress approved the 18th Amendment to outlaw the manufacture, sale, or possession of alcoholic liquors and the Texas legislature promptly ratified it. In May 1919 voters approved a state constitutional amendment which at long last made Texas totally dry.

The question of woman suffrage largely paralleled the prohibition issue. The Texas Woman Suffrage Association had been active since 1903 and had sought repeatedly to persuade the legislature to submit a constitutional amendment for woman suffrage to the state's voters but without success. By 1917 most western and some eastern states had adopted woman suffrage, but all southern states had ignored this progressive reform. Texas women, led by Mrs. Eleanor Brackenridge and Mrs. Minnie Fisher Cunningham, continued the crusade pointing out the illogic of fighting a war for the expansion of democracy abroad when almost one-half of the adult population was disenfranchised at home. Some of the more militant women organized a branch of the National Woman's Party (NWP) and brought Alice Paul (NWP president) to Texas to speak. Her tactics, however, were too confrontive for most, and the state Equal Suffrage Association issued a statement disclaiming support for militancy. There was, to be sure, some opposition to suffrage among the women of Texas. Led by Mrs. James B. Wells, wife of the South Texas boss, they organized the National Association Opposed to Women's Suffrage. They distributed thousands of letters and pamphlets warning of Negro domination and socialism if votes were given all women.

Again, America's entrance into the war changed the situation. Though Governor Hobby had not been an advocate of woman suffrage (he had not been a prohibitionist either), he took the lead in 1918 for the passage of a bill to allow women to vote in primary elections. This passed easily and, as Texas was a "one party" state, this provided substantial enfranchisement without the delay of a constitutional change. As could be expected, women throughout the state formed "Hobby Clubs" to work for the governor's reelection. At the same time they supported Annie Webb Blanton for the office of State Superintendent of Public Instruction. She won and became the first woman to hold statewide office in Texas.

Hobby then proposed a constitutional amendment to allow women to participate in all elections. But at the same time he urged the permanent disenfranchisement of all aliens who had not completed the naturalization process. The legislature put the two proposals into the same resolution and when it was submitted to the people, strong opposition from South Texas resulted in its defeat. Shortly afterward (June 1919), Hobby called a special session to consider the Nineteenth Amendment to the federal constitution providing for nationwide woman suffrage. The legislature promptly approved it, and Texas became the first state in the South to ratify the Woman Suffrage amendment.

Hobby had won election to a full term as governor in 1918. Though described as a colorless and "quiet" person, he proved to be an able and effective campaigner who had supported Wilson's war policies as a loyal, dry, progressive Democrat. His opponent in the Democratic primary was none other than James E. Ferguson. Despite his conviction and ban by the Senate, Ferguson had managed to obtain a court order to have his name placed on the primary ballot, and he campaigned with his usual vigor and charisma. Aided by the newly enfranchised feminine vote Hobby triumped easily, polling more than 400,000 votes. But more than 200,000 Texans voted for "Farmer Jim," indicating that they discounted his impeachment which they saw as a "hatchet job" by the university.

The postwar years were a time of upheaval, readjustment and reaction in Texas. The people took seriously the proclaimed threat of bolshevism and linked labor unions and civil rights advocates with the radical menace. Union demands for collective bargaining and stabilization of wages at wartime levels were labeled as un-American. In Galveston, a prolonged dock strike led to repeated violence and Hobby eventually placed the city under martial law. Businessmen organized "Open Shop Associations" and the state's press denounced any union activity. Returning black servicemen demanded an end to segregation, which set off a new series of riots, beatings, and burnings. White supremacists alleged that black soldiers had become infected by communism, or socialism, or some other ism. Violence against blacks flared in Longview and continued until Hobby sent in the state guard to restore order. The attorney general subpoenaed the records of the National Association for the Advancement of Colored People (NAACP), and a crowd stood by while a mob beat up a black NAACP official on the streets of Austin.

The continued discontent and unrest prompted former Senator Joseph Weldon Bailey to reenter public life. Denouncing unions, feminism, prohibition, miscegenation, creeping socialism, and the centralizing tendencies of the Wilson administration, Bailey sought to lead an anti-Wilson delegation to the Democratic national Convention at San Francisco in the summer of 1920. Thomas B. Love and other Wilson men thwarted this effort by controlling the local and state conventions, sending a solid slate of delegates who favored William G. McAdoo (Wilson's Secretary of the Treasury and his son-in-law) for the presidency. Bailey then entered the 1920 race for governor demanding a return to states' rights and a revival of "Jeffersonianism" as he defined it. In opposition, Pat M. Neff and two other pro-Wilson candidates entered the primary. Neff, a successful Waco lawyer, was a moderate Democrat who neither drank nor smoked but demonstrated his progressivism by campaigning in an automobile, the first gubernatorial candidate to do so. Neff effectively defended the Wilson administration and the reforms enacted in Texas under Hobby. In turn he assailed Bailey's antiwar stance, his questionable record as a senator, and his desire to turn back the clock of progress. In the first primary Bailey held a slim lead, but in the run-off Neff won handily by more than 75,000 votes. This was an unusually dirty, vicious, mudslinging campaign and marked the last political effort of Joe Bailey and the end of his influence. Most Texas Democrats applauded his departure.

The postwar years also saw a further expansion and maturing of the Texas oil and gas industry. New discoveries at Ranger and Burkburnett prompted the legislature to pass an oil and gas conservation measure and place the petroleum industry under the supervision of the Texas Railroad Commission. Thus, though the commission did not change its name, energy, not transportation, became its chief responsibility. Further discoveries at Luling and the Yates field in the trans-Pecos region, plus the comeback of Spindletop due to new techniques after a period of declining production, sent Texas oil production by 1927 over the 200 million barrel per year mark. Both the legislature and the Railroad Commission took care not to burden or retard the development of the state's number one industry. Tax policies were not burdensome, pipelines spread under generous interpretations of eminent domain, and the TRC regulation of production practices was lenient.

Neff entered office as a law and order champion promising to curb what he called the "worst crime wave" in the history of the state. He called for a constitutional convention to modernize the state's basic charter plus a series of changes in the administrative system designed to strengthen the hand of the governor. The legislature, however, declined to take any action on either question. Neff did cope with a major rail strike by declaring martial law, and sending Rangers to key points to break the strike. He also pursued a tough pardon and parole policy, abolishing the Board of Pardons and making his own investigations.

On the constructive side, Neff promoted conservation of natural resources and established the beginnings of the state park system. He also championed the "good roads" program and worked for the expansion and improvement of the highway system. This is not to imply that the roads in Texas were good during Neff's administration. In fact, there were not 10,000 miles of paved roads in the entire state until ten years after Neff left office.

In the meantime, Galveston, now largely recovered from the direct effects of the devastating storm of 1900, developed into a popular seaside resort. While state and county officers more or less enforced prohibition laws in other parts of Texas, in Galveston the bars remained open. Most hotels and night clubs had well-equipped casinos for gaming and Post Office Street became infamous for its available ladies. These attractions plus its fine beach and deep sea fishing made Galveston a "fun" city (spelled SIN by the fundamentalists of East and North Texas). A succession of governors and attorneys general, though giving lip service to law enforcement, largely left Galveston alone until after World War II.

During Neff's administration there arose a far more sinister threat to the state than "fun on the Gulf." In 1915 Colonel William J. Simmons reestablished the Ku Klux Klan, and it spread throughout the South and Southwest. Under the promotional efforts of Edward Clarke and Mrs. Elizabeth Tyler, the Klan organized chapters in Houston, Beaumont, Dallas, and many smaller cities. Soon hooded klansmen began a campaign of violence against blacks, Jews, immigrants, Roman Catholics, and indeed anyone who did not conform to their notions of morals and proper social behavior. In February 1921 Kleagle George B. Kimbro led a party who whipped and tarred and feathered a Houston attorney because "he had the wrong kind of clients." In Dallas, exalted Cyclops Hiram W. Evans condoned or perhaps participated in the seizure and branding of a black hotel bellhop with the letters KKK on his forehead. In all there were more than fifty cases of Klan violence during 1921. By the next year organizer Clarke estimated Klan membership in Texas at between 75,000 and 90,000. Hiram W. Evans, a Dallas dentist, rose to become the most powerful Klansman in Texas. He advanced rapidly from Kleage to Cyclops, to Titan, and Kligrapp (national secretary) and finally to Imperial Wizard. It was Evans' policy that the Klan should devote its time and funds to political action on the state and local levels and should deemphasize vigilante action and violence.

The technique of the Klan under Evans was not to form a separate party but to back a friendly candidate in the Democratic primary. The most important wide open election in 1922 was for the United States Senate, and Evans was determined that a candidate friendly to the Klan be chosen. Charles A. Culberson had held the seat since 1899, but since he was old and ill, most observers expected him to be retired. The Klan backed Earle B. Mayfield, a member of the Texas Railroad Commission and a fellow Klansman. A surprise entrant in the Senate race was James E. Ferguson. "Farmer Jim" had waged a one state race for president in 1920 on the American Party ticket, but now he returned to the Democratic Party and won a place on the ballot. The first primary race was bitter and vitriolic and resulted in Mayfield and Ferguson running first and second in a five man field. Culberson finished a poor third and thus bowed out of public life after a career of more than thirty years. In the runoff Mayfield won by some 44,000 votes, largely because of superior organization and a large war chest. In addition to the senatorship, Klan-backed candidates won a number of local races and perhaps a majority in the 1923 state legislature. Evans was jubilant over the successes of the Klan's political venture and looked forward to 1924 and the contest for the governorship.

Hiram Evans and the Klan were not the only people in Texas who looked forward to the gubernatorial race in 1924. Jim Ferguson found a way to circumvent the Senate ban on his holding state office —he would have his wife run for governor. Miram A. Ferguson, born in 1875, had up until this time shown little interest in politics but had preferred to remain in the background, running the household and raising their two daughters. Now she entered the Democratic primary for the governorship with Jim Ferguson doing most of the campaigning. His slogan, "two governors for the price of one," rallied old Ferguson supporters: small farmers, tenants, laborers, and anti-prohibitionists. After a rather bitter internal struggle, Evans led the Klan to throw its support to Judge Felix D. Robertson of Dallas. Judge Robertson advocated "100 percent Americanism, tougher law enforcement, prohibition, and marital faithfulness." With all the fervor of earlier days Ferguson swung around the state denouncing Robertson as the puppet of Wizard Evans whom he regularly identified as the "Grand Gizzard." In another low-level, mudslinging, name-calling campaign with each speaker seeking to be more racist than the other, Robertson was no match for "Pa" Ferguson's invective and "Ma" Ferguson won in the runoff primary by almost 100,000 votes. In November she overwhelmed Republican Dr. George C. Butte, former dean of the University of Texas Law School.

In the second Ferguson administration, Miriam Ferguson, with her husband always at her elbow advising on each issue, pursued a conservative course. In a direct blow at the Klan she secured a law prohibiting the wearing of masks in public places. She cut funds for free textbooks and arbitrarily removed some books from the available list. She reduced the University of Texas by vetoing a number of line items which left a number of departments without funds. She also vetoed a prison reform bill. But "Ma" Ferguson did pursue a liberal policy regarding pardons and paroles from the state prison. She decried the apparent fact that the great majority of people convicted of violating the prohibition laws were poor, often members of a minority race, while wealthy Texans violated the laws at will and even drank imported liquors at the private clubs in Galveston, Houston, or San Antonio. In a proclamation published in the *Ferguson Forum* (the family newspaper) she offered a $500 reward for the conviction of any person with property worth $5,000. In the two years of her term she issued more than 2,000 pardons, paroles, and extensions, more than 800 of which went to prohibition violators.

"Ma" Ferguson's administration, however, did not escape charges of graft and scandal. The press accused "Pa" of selling pardons and indeed, Jim Ferguson acted as attorney for many successful applicants for pardons and paroles. Attorney General Dan Moody charged that many of the highway contracts had been awarded to friends illegally and some were fraudulent. He was able to bring suit to cancel a number of such contracts. These charges led to her defeat in the next election. But the state had not heard the last of Miriam Ferguson. She would return to serve yet another term as governor during the Great Depression.

Dan Moody succeeded Mrs. Ferguson as governor and gave the state four years of competent, progressive leadership. He reorganized the state highway department and regularized the method of awarding road building contracts. He reformed the prison system, setting up a Prison Commission and ending the *ad hoc* granting of pardons. At his recommendation the legislature authorized the office of state auditor and the regular auditing of state accounts, which began the modern fiscal controls system of the Texas state government. Other Moody proposals such as constitutional changes, increased appointive powers for the governor to give him greater control over his administration, and the creation of an effective civil service system were not able to overcome the legislature's ingrained resistance to change. Young (35), university educated, an effective speaker, and experienced attorney, Moody easily won renomination and reelection in 1928 against nominal opposition.

The year 1928 was also a presidential election year and a critical one for Texas Democrats. The control of the national party was in the process of shifting from the South, with its conservative, rural, states' rights philosophy to a more dynamic stance led by northern urban centers, organized labor, ethnic immigrant groups, and social justice advocates. Alfred E. Smith, Governor of New York, led this coalition of urban Democrats and appeared certain to win the party's nomination and wage a strong campaign for the White House. Smith, a second generation Roman Catholic Irish immigrant, marginally educated and anti-prohibitionist, was anathema to most Texas conservative Democrats. As a result the state saw the strange alliance of Moody, the Fergusons, and the Ku Klux Klan (now declining in influence) joining in opposing the nomination of Smith in the National Democratic Convention held, ironically, in Houston. After Smith won the nomination, Moody remained in the party and urged Texas voters to support the ticket "from top to bottom." A majority, however, bolted and followed former governor Colquitt who organized "Texas Democrats for Hoover." As a result Herbert Hoover, the Republican candidate won the 1928 election, carrying the electoral vote of Texas for the first time ever. The same year Tom Connally retired Klansman Earle B. Mayfield from the U.S. Senate after one term.

The Moody years were generally prosperous ones for the people of Texas. Population grew and urban population increased at a rate of more than 50 percent. The number of automobiles multiplied so that by 1930 there was a car for every five people. The petroleum industry continued to expand under the benign eye of the Texas Railroad Commission. The discovery of immense pools of oil in East Texas by C. M. "Dad" Joiner in 1930 set off a new oil boom reminiscent of Spindletop.

The lumber industry, however, declined in the postwar decade. As more and more companies exhausted their timber holdings of old growth mature pine they ceased operations and moved elsewhere, often to the Pacific coast. Through the twenties both logging and sawmilling were depressed, and there were regularly more experienced loggers and sawyers seeking work than there were jobs. Critics predicted that Texas would soon become a lumber importing state. The Texas Forest Service (expanded in 1928 by Governor Moody) added state parks, improved fire protection, and established a pine seedling nursery. These conservation measures did not halt the closing of mills which had cut out or done much to preserve the few remaining stands of mature pine timber. But, aided by the long, warm, wet growing season that characterizes East Texas, the Texas Forest Service had an important effect on the development of a vigorous second-growth forest in East Texas during the next generation.

By 1930 Texas had almost doubled in population, reporting almost 6,000,000 people with 41 percent living in cities. Among major cities Houston led with 292,000; Dallas had 260,000 and San Antonio had 231,000. Galveston was no longer listed as a major city, but with 53,000 population it had recovered from the losses in the great storm at the turn of the century.

In considering Texas from the turn of the century to the Great Depression, certain conclusions are in order. Though during this period Texas elected no great governors, Campbell and Moody were near-great and set a high standard for integrity and accomplishment. Jim Ferguson was easily the most controversial, but the election of Mariam Ferguson was a transparent charade. On the national scene Joseph Weldon Bailey stirred much excitement, but his influence was mostly destructive. Probably Colonel House was the most influential Texan in Washington, but he was not quite as important as his memoirs implied. On the home front, the bravest people were the citizens of Galveston, the most enterprising were the people in Houston who built the Ship Channel, the most fortunate were those at Spindletop, and the most unfortunate were those who fell afoul of the Ku Klux Klan.

One "error of omission" of this period has continued to cost Texas dearly. This was the failure of the state administration and legislature to make effective use of the talents, expertise, and special knowledge available at the University of Texas and Texas A&M College. Although there were specialists in many fields who could assist in solving the problems of the state, no one sought their contributions. Indeed some governors "made war" on the university which forced the institution into an adversary relationship. Instead, there should have developed a partnership between state and university to promote the upbuilding of Texas.

# 8

## Contemporary Texas

*Donald W. Whisenhunt*

The story of modern Texas has been a time of movement forward into a stronger and more influential role in national affairs. Texas is a large state with a diverse and growing population and with natural wealth to rival many nations of the world. These characteristics would suggest that it should be a natural force in national affairs, but the middle half of the twentieth century was not one of Texas' finest hours, and the progress that was achieved in this period was not easy.

Texas in the period from 1930 to the 1980s was something like the awkward adolescent — knowing that it was almost grown and with an increasingly important role to play as an adult but somewhat reluctant to take that final step toward adulthood. But, like the adolescent, the transition to adulthood and responsibility was delayed because of the reluctance of those already in positions of power to admit the new participant because it would dilute the influence of those already there.

The problems Texas found in the last step to maturity were common to many states. The Texas that gained independence in 1836 was overwhelmingly Southern in background and philosophy. After independence many Texans were disappointed that political considerations prevented immediate annexation to the United States while others were quite happy for Texas to remain an independent republic. When statehood finally came, most Texans regarded themselves as Southerners even if they were not slaveowners. The majority of

*AMARILLO — a growing city in the Texas Panhandle.*

Texans readily followed the rest of the South into secession. The political considerations of Reconstruction divided many Texans. The growing importance of the western portions of the state brought tension regarding political power. Texans were angry about the farmer's declining position in society, but many of them could not align themselves with the Farmers Alliance or Populist Party because of race.

Texans, furthermore, have long had an inferiority complex in the national picture. They have been characterized as bumpkins with no cultural heritage or tradition. They are considered crass *nouveau riche* who use their money (all Texans are oil or cattle millionaires, after all) to exert influence and maintain a power base. Many outsiders think of Texas as a land of deserts and cactus dominated by cows and oil wells. Texans overcompensated for the feeling of inferiority by boasting for so long that many Texans themselves came to believe the outrageous claims of the traditional "Texas brags."

Texans have regularly given lip service to a political philosophy on the one hand while they readily ignored it on the other. Texans, for example, have always been among the most vocal defenders of small government, states' rights, and local control while, at the same time, their actions undermined those concepts. They deplored and opposed government (especially federal) intervention in daily life while they were at the head of the line to get government benefits, whether they be relief in the depression or military bases in World War II and its Cold War aftermath.

Many Texans, of course, have been able to rationalize their actions to prevent conflict with their philosophy. The unthinking, on the other hand, simply ignored the contradiction and continued to take government benefits while condemning them at the same time.

The decade of the 1930s and the depression which dominated it exemplify this spirit very well. Economic hard times settled upon Texas like a fog that refused to burn away. Month after month and year after year, depression continued until it seemed after awhile as almost normal. No one wanted it, but the depression was so pervasive nationwide that it seemed little could be done about it.

In the aftermath, an attitude developed among many who lived through the era that Texas did not really suffer very much from the depression. Some historical studies of Texas, or of certain regions of the state, reported this attitude. A certain amount of Texas pride appears here because the statements were usually made in a comparative way: that Texas did not suffer as much as the cities of the North or the heavily industrialized areas of the North and Midwest.

Although regions of Texas can be found where the depression was not so severe, the facts do not support the claim that Texas did not suffer. Texas was not a highly industrialized state, to be sure, but the Great Depression was an all encompassing, not just an industrial, depression. Texas was hit hard by the depression, and it suffered as other places did.

Although most historians agree that the Stock Market Crash of 1929 was not the cause of the depression, it did cause many areas of the United States—Texas included—to recognize and acknowledge weaknesses in the nation's economic system. For two or three years Texans followed the lead of a majority of the nation in refusing to recognize the existence of a depression. President Herbert Hoover mounted a "confidence campaign" designed to prevent people from developing a mental attitude that would make problems worse. Most Texans gladly followed Hoover's lead, but when little more than platitudes came from Washington, many of them lost faith.

In the meantime, the extent and depth of the depression could not be ignored. Unemployment increased as business activity declined. Agriculture continued on the downward spiral that had begun immediately after World War I and it intensified in the thirties. Bank closings became epidemic. Government agencies at all levels began economy campaigns to reduce expenses, but in the process vital government services were often cut to the point of ineffectiveness. One of the most seriously affected was education. Public education was cut back in several ways. Teachers often were paid in scrip rather than money. Proposals were considered to close some of the colleges, but none of the plans was ever carried out. Without question public confidence in the future was severely weakened along several fronts.

Signs of hard times could be seen everywhere. As the agricultural crisis deepened farms were sometimes abandoned or were sold at auction for mortgage or tax delinquencies. Farmers burning cotton and corn for fuel was an experience that few believed they would ever witness in America, but it was being done in Texas. Milk was poured into sewers in Houston and Galveston as a protest against low prices and because sometimes it could not be sold at all.

Farmers dispossessed from their land for whatever reason—and many non-farm Texans as well—took to the streets and highways to shift for themselves as best they could. Some followed the fabled road west to California, where they believed fortunes could be made. Others were fearful of going too far from home and merely wandered from town to town in Texas looking for work. Transiency in Texas was a serious problem, not only because of wandering Texans, but

*Senate Majority Leader Lyndon Johnson, former President Harry S. Truman, former Vice-President John Nance Garner and Speaker of the House Sam Rayburn.*

— LBJ Library, Austin

*President Roosevelt, Governor Allred and Congressman Lyndon Johnson in Galveston, 1937.*

— LBJ Library, Austin

also because the Texas climate was attractive to people from other states who were also on the road. There is no way to know for sure how many people were homeless or the conditions under which they lived. Maury Maverick, later a congressman and mayor of San Antonio, toured Texas in 1932 to see for himself what was really going on. As he explained, he was permanently changed by what he saw, but his report to Governor Ross Sterling went virtually unheeded.

Relief for all Texans — transients as well as those who stayed at home — was a major question of the early years of the depression. Texans, believing that being in need was somehow a moral judgment of their character, were reluctant to ask for help — at least at first. Relief was considered by most to be a function of private charities — or local governments if some public agency had to be involved. In 1933 when the New Deal of President Franklin Roosevelt brought various relief and work agencies into being, some Texans still resisted, but by that time most recognized the extent of the crisis and were willing to take relief from most any source.

The decade of the thirties and its depression left a scar on the Texas psyche as it did on most of the country. Although many did not recognize it at the time, the decade brought changes to Texas that still remained fifty years later. Part of the problem was related to the dilemma of Texans faced with accepting change and participating in programs that were contrary to their philosophy.

Politically, Texas became more powerful on the national level during the thirties while the sophistication of state politics remained much the same. When the depression began, Dan Moody was governor. He had made a good reputation for himself as attorney general, but his approach to the depression was uninspired. Like so many others, he concentrated on the symptoms rather than the causes and did little to improve conditions for average Texans.

State elections in 1930 witnessed the return of the Fergusons to the political arena after several years' absence. Mrs. Miriam A. Ferguson, running as a surrogate for her husband, challenged Ross Sterling of Houston for the governorship. In a heated campaign, Sterling overcame the Ferguson challenge, but two years later essentially the same contest was replayed. Sterling was poorly equipped philosophically to be governor in a time of crisis. A big businessman himself (he was a former president of Humble Oil and Refining Company), he was quite similar to the Republican Hoover in his attitude about government action. Conditions did force him to modify his views to some extent, but state relief was limited at best. Like so many others, he had trouble understanding the depression, and little was done of a permanent nature to prevent or cope with another similar crisis.

Sterling's problems were unique since he had to contend with the mixed blessing of the East Texas oil boom. On the one hand, the discovery of a major oil field at Kilgore in 1930 should have been an unlimited economic blessing, but on the other hand, it created a crisis since the field was so large and production was unregulated. Within a short time the price of oil dropped to unbelievable lows and the lawlessness of the oil field became well-known. The stealing of oil — the so-called "hot oil" issue — finally forced Sterling to declare martial law in East Texas and to send in national guard forces to maintain order. The value of this natural resource was felt dramatically in World War II, but for the time being it was little more than a headache for the governor.

A major social issue was finally resolved at this time. Prohibition as a national experiment had been underway since World War I. It had created serious national problems throughout the twenties, and significant efforts were made to repeal the Prohibition Amendment to the national constitution. The wet-dry question had been a major issue in the 1928 presidential election and had been one of the reasons Texas had voted for Hoover. This matter was finally resolved in the 1932 election of Franklin D. Roosevelt to the presidency and Miriam A. Ferguson to the Texas governor's office.

Mrs. Ferguson came back and won the governorship for a second time over the hapless Sterling, who found himself in much the same political situation in Texas that Hoover was in on the national level. Mrs. Ferguson's second administration was very similar to her first in many ways, but the depression made things different for everyone. Mrs. Ferguson cooperated with the New Deal and was able to bring much federal money to Texas for relief and work projects.

In 1935 James V. Allred succeeded Mrs. Ferguson. Allred was considered the first progressive governor since James S. Hogg and was still remembered fondly by Texas liberals some fifty years later as the last progressive governor of Texas. Despite his talents, Allred was able to do little to ease the depression except to cooperate with the New Deal.

The decade was rounded out by the entrance of another figure on the state political scene who became an embarrassment to many Texans. In 1938, W. Lee O'Daniel, a flour salesman from Fort Worth who had made a statewide reputation with a radio program and a hillbilly band, startled the state by entering the race for governor and winning. Although he was a poor governor with little grasp of the subtleties of government, O'Daniel won reelection in 1940 and stayed in the governor's chair until 1941 when he won a special election to fill the Senate seat made vacant by the death of Morris Sheppard.

*Sixty thousand supporters were on hand for the inauguration of Governor W. Lee O'Daniel at the University of Texas football stadium on January 17, 1939.*

— Austin-Travis County Collection

On the national level, Texas did quite well in the thirties. Because of the seniority system and the Democratic tradition of Texas (despite its one lapse of voting for Herbert Hoover in 1928), Texas congressmen and senators moved into positions of leadership when Roosevelt came to power in 1933. John Nance Garner, a native Texan, was elected vice president with Roosevelt, and although he probably had more power as Speaker of the House during the Hoover administration, his position on the national ticket and in the new administration seemed to signal a new influence for Texans in national affairs.

The Texas power base in the New Deal, however, rested more in the important committee chairmanships held by Texans. Men like Senators Tom Connally and Morris Sheppard and Congressmen Hatton Sumners, Sam Rayburn, Wright Patman, Maury Maverick, and the young Lyndon Johnson were so visible and powerful that some Americans complained that Texans were dominating national affairs.

Texas, like the rest of the country, was aided by the efforts of the Roosevelt New Deal, but it did not fully recover from the depression until World War II brought economic demands never witnessed before. After the Japanese attack on Pearl Harbor, Texans quickly overcame their somewhat temporary pacifist and isolationist tendencies of the twenties and thirties, and supported the war effort in every way. Texans joined the various military forces in record numbers. Texas had the distinction of having the two most decorated soldiers in the war — Audie Murphy in the Army and Samuel D. Dealey in the Navy.

Like the rest of the country the Texas economy boomed during the war. Agriculture rebounded almost immediately as prices rose and demands hit new levels. Texas farmers responded to the patriotic need and to the opportunity for prosperity for the first time in twenty years. Although Texas was not highly industrialized before the war, the conflict brought new demands, and new industries—especially defense-related — began to spring up in Texas. The new demands for workers and soldiers significantly reduced unemployment. Many Texans continued their migration west to California, but it was a different type of movement from that of the "Okies" of the thirties. They were now welcome in California to work in defense plants. Even women began moving into the work force (including manual jobs like welding) as never before.

Texas was particularly successful in getting military bases located there—in part due to the political power of the Texas congressional delegation, but also because many parts of the state were well adapted geographically and climatically for military installations. Texans had the experience of World War I to draw on, and they were very successful in bringing government economic benefits to the state. Texans considered these efforts patriotic acts, but they were also quick to recognize the economic benefits they brought.

During the war and its immediate aftermath Texas remained loyal to the Democratic Party. Some Texans were even more Democratic than before because they blamed the hard times of the thirties on the Republican misrule of Herbert Hoover, a man they had supported but who had betrayed their trust. Many of them now regretted their previous action. Some Texans, to be sure, balked when Roosevelt tried to pack the Supreme Court in 1936 to protect his New Deal programs and when he broke the tradition of a president serving only two terms. Most Texans, however, believed that Roosevelt was responsible for economic recovery and they stayed with him and his party. Even in 1948 when the very unpopular Harry Truman appeared to be a sure loser against Thomas E. Dewey, Texans stayed with Truman and basked in the glory of his victory. Four years later, however, the situation had changed enough that Texas cast its electoral votes for a Republican for only the second time since Reconstruction. Some believed Texas supported Dwight D. Eisenhower because he was a native-born Texan, but the causes went much deeper.

During the forties, political leadership on the state and local level in Texas was little different than before. Almost any governor, admittedly, would have been better than O'Daniel who went on to the U.S. Senate in 1941. Coke Stevenson, his successor, was a competent governor, but he was of the old school of politics and was not really able to move Texas forward into the new world that existed after the war. His successor, Beauford H. Jester, was a relatively popular governor, but his term was cut short by his untimely death in 1949. Jester had the distinction of being the only governor to die in office. His death brought to the governor's office Allan Shivers, a man who would dominate Texas politics through the fifties — and beyond.

Texas continued its important leadership role in national affairs. Tom Connally, who introduced the resolution in Congress on December 8, 1941, to declare war on Japan, increased his importance during the war and in its aftermath as a leading spokesman on foreign affairs. The junior senator from Texas, on the other hand, was an embarrassment during much of the decade. W. Lee O'Daniel had won a special election to fill the seat of Morris Sheppard in 1941 and he was elected to a full term in 1942. For seven years, some people said, Texas had only one senator. That all changed in 1948, however, when Lyndon Johnson moved from the House of Representatives to the Senate.

Johnson had been elected to the House in 1934 as an avowed New Deal Democrat who used very effectively his reputation as the Texas administrator of the National Youth Administration. He had tied himself to Franklin Roosevelt, and it had worked well in his district in the Hill Country near Austin. Johnson made an abortive attempt to move to the Senate in the special election in 1941 but suffered a stinging defeat at the hands of O'Daniel. Johnson was ready to correct his campaign errors in 1948.

The 1948 senatorial election is probably the most famous (or infamous) of all Texas elections. Since O'Daniel chose to retire from the Senate, it was a wide open race. The two major contenders were Johnson and Governor Coke Stevenson. In the run-off Democratic primary, Johnson won by a mere 87 votes. Voting irregularities existed on both sides, but Johnson's reputation was forever tainted by the scandal and controversy surrounding the election. Despite this inauspicious beginning, Johnson, nevertheless, moved rapidly into leadership circles in the Senate and became the Democratic leader in 1952.

In the post-war era, Texas was able to maintain many of the economic gains it had made during the war. With Johnson and Rayburn holding major leadership positions, Texas power continued to grow. Since military preparedness remained the watchword through the forties and into the fifties, Texans flexed their muscles to keep military bases that had been established during the war and to bring other defense industry into the state.

Texas, like most of the country, was caught up in the Red Scare of the McCarthy era. As the senator from Wisconsin gained headlines for his communist hunting through congressional investigations, he was merely following the trail already blazed by Texas Congressman Martin Dies of Lufkin. Guilt by association, fear of subversion, and the banning of books in various public libraries in the state were among the issues that divided Texas. Where the Ku Klux Klan and prohibition had been major political issues in previous decades, now the fear of communist subversion replaced them in the late forties and early fifties.

The issue was very volatile in Texas. It seemed inconceivable to many Texans that anyone would refuse to answer questions before the Dies or McCarthy committees on the grounds of the Fifth Amendment unless he were guilty at least of sympathy with communists if not outright membership in the Communist Party. To force all Texans to declare their true positions and to ferret out subversives, the Texas legislature passed a law requiring a signed loyalty oath of all state employees and students in public colleges and universities. Despite grumbling and legal protests the oath was upheld in the courts.

Through the late forties, Texans gradually lost faith in Harry Truman as the nation's leader as he became more unpopular year after year. Texans voted for him in 1948, but it was probably more out of historical loyalty and the memory of what had happened in 1928 when they bolted the Democratic Party to vote for Herbert Hoover. Any number of issues caused Truman to lose his following in the state, but his strong stand on civil rights, including desegregation of the armed forces, was a major controversy in Texas. Scandals associated with the Truman presidency and the involvement in the Korean War also contributed to his unpopularity.

A major political shift came in 1952 when Texas voted Republican for the second time since Reconstruction and overwhelmingly supported Dwight D. Eisenhower. A major factor in that change was the leadership of Governor Allan Shivers, who strongly endorsed Eisenhower. The conservative-liberal division within the Democratic Party, long present under the surface, came into the open at this time. The progressive, or liberal, wing moved to establish a separate organization known as the Democrats of Texas (DOT). Throughout the next two decades the split remained although it was papered over at times, particularly when Lyndon Johnson moved into the presidency. The bitter differences began again with the unpopularity of the Vietnam War.

The shift to Eisenhower and the Republican Party in 1952 had much to do with the emotional "tidelands issue." The tidelands were the territory off the coast of Texas which were discovered after the war to be rich in petroleum deposits. During the New Deal, Secretary of the Interior Harold Ickes took the position that offshore minerals belonged to the federal government. The question was of little public concern at the time, but it became a white-hot issue in the late forties.

The issue came to the forefront in 1947 when the Supreme Court in a California case upheld Ickes' original position. Texas efforts, led by Governor Allan Shivers and Senator Price Daniel, to overturn the decision failed. Their arguments that the original status of Texas as a Republic gave it a claim to ten and one-half miles into the sea instead of the usual three was not convincing to the courts. A bill guided through Congress by Texans to give Texas legal ownership of the land through a quit-claim deed was vetoed by President Harry Truman.

The election of 1952 became a battleground on this question. Shivers and Daniel openly declared for Eisenhower when he supported the Texas position even though when first asked about his position Eisenhower apparently had never heard of tidelands and had no opinion. During the election the tidelands controversy became a classic case of states' rights. Moreover, supporters of the state position brought Texas school children into the controversy by claiming that Truman's veto took money away from Texas schools.

After Eisenhower's election the issue was laid to rest when the president repaid Texas support by signing quit-claim legislation pushed through Congress by Texas political leaders. The idea of the encroachment of the federal government into state issues did not go away as easily.

The fifties was a prosperous decade for Texas, despite a few soft spots in the economy. Federal money continued to flow into the state even while many recipients of federal largess openly denounced federal involvement in local affairs. More significantly, Texas became more industrial as major manufacturing companies discovered the favorable economic climate in the state and moved plants to major Texas cities. Texas became more urban as cities like Houston, Dallas-Fort Worth, and San Antonio took on characteristics like cities in the Midwest and Northeast. Although Texas held on for dear life to older rural values, the world and the state were changing. Although the term would not be coined for twenty years or more, the lure of the "Sunbelt" was already apparent as population continued to grow — to a large extent from inward migration from the north and east.

A major weakness in the economy that prevented Texas from being even more prosperous was the depressed condition of agriculture. Texas, like the rest of the nation, was beset with a problem never faced on such a scale before in human history. Farmers were far too successful. Their ability to produce more food and fiber than the world's economy could absorb caused a recurrence of the same disbelief that existed during the depression of the thirties. Many people were unable to understand how politicians could talk about overproduction while much of the world went hungry. It was little consolation to know that a time of Cold War brought such incongruities. Farm programs had started during the New Deal and began again on large scale under Truman. They grew and intensified under Eisenhower even though many Republicans denounced federal programs of the New Deal and the Fair Deal. Even so, farm programs of the Eisenhower administration were little different. Texas farmers benefitted in a significant way from the Soil Bank Program and other agricultural measures.

Texas agriculture was also dealt a severe blow in the fifties with a seven-year drought that was, in some ways, reminiscent of the Dust Bowl Days of the thirties. Beginning in 1950, year after year passed with almost no rainfall. Central and West Texas were most hard-hit, but no part of the state was spared. Certain areas had periods when it was not so severe, but generally Texas was in the grip of a severe drought until it finally broke in the spring of 1957. Eisenhower farm programs helped to ease the burden, but the danger that Texas land would be destroyed forever was the greatest fear. The return of dust storms on such a large scale throughout West Texas easily stimulated and perpetuated this idea.

The drought encouraged Texans to seek additional sources of water to protect farmers from nature's wrath. Expansion of irrigation from underground water on the High Plains was extensive in this period. Drilling techniques and water-finding methods had improved so much that areas once thought to be barren of underground water were now discovered to be rich in the precious liquid. The long-range impact of pumping such large quantities of water was noted by some, but the advantages of artificial rain were so great that the few voices of concern were ignored. Twenty years or more would pass before the seriously declining water supply became a matter of concern.

During the 1950s petroleum became the most dominant force in the economic and cultural affairs of Texas. The value of the oil reserves allowed Texas to avoid both sales and income taxes when other states were forced to use them to supplement state revenues. As a result property taxes—and most other forms of state taxes—remained among the lowest in the nation. The land given to the University of Texas for the Permanent University Fund and once considered virtually worthless, became some of the most valuable land in the state by the fifties. The university was well on its way to becoming the wealthiest public university in the world. Texas A&M University was able to share in the oil income through a quirk in the state constitution.

The importance of oil and gas to the state's economy caused the political system by the fifties to be dominated by petroleum interests. Political candidates were careful to be "right" on the issue of oil. Oil revenues were paying the major share of state government and few politicians were willing to challenge the dominance of oilmen. The oil depletion allowance at the federal level became a

*LYNDON B. JOHNSON is sworn in as President of the United States in 1963 aboard Air Force One at Dallas by U.S. District Judge Sarah T. Hughes. Among witnesses are Mrs. Johnson and Mrs. John Kennedy.*

— LBJ Library, Austin

"sacred cow" and a yardstick by which every politician was judged.

Politics, therefore, remained basically conservative during the fifties. Occasional progressive candidates appeared from time to time, but in most instances they were able to generate little statewide support. The exception was Ralph W. Yarborough. An Austin attorney active in progressive politics since the thirties, Yarborough made two unsuccessful bids for the governor's chair in the early fifties, but in the process he captured the heart of Texas liberals and became their spokesman and champion. In a special election in 1957, Yarborough was able to win a seat in the United States Senate. He replaced Senator Price Daniel who resigned after winning the governor's race in 1956. Some people believed Daniel left the security of the Senate to return to Texas to protect oil interests in the state. Yarborough was reelected in 1958 for a full six-year term and stayed in the Senate through the sixties until he was defeated in 1970 by Lloyd Bentsen.

In modern times, Texas has been susceptible to scandals of varying intensity; the fifties was such a period. One of the most notorious scandals involved insurance companies. Since Texas had very lax regulation of insurance companies, it was very easy for fly-by-night companies to operate without fear of violating the law. Since the law required only $25,000 in capital stock, many companies operated on the income they derived from selling new policies. Despite warnings from such people as Lieutenant Governor Ben Ramsey and the numerous company failures, little was done to correct the situation.

The rotten foundation of the insurance business finally was revealed with the bankruptcy of the U.S. Trust and Guaranty, and the I.C.T. Corporation that controlled seventy-two finance and insurance companies. The man who came to symbolize the corruption in insurance was Ben Jack Cage, head of I.C.T. When Cage left for Brazil with most of the company's assets, the state finally awoke to the problem. By then many Texans had been the victims of unscrupulous companies; the regulation that now came was beneficial to later generations but did little for the people already victimized. It did not help the prestige of the legislature when it was revealed that some of its members had been accepting bribes from various insurance companies.

The other major scandal of the decade involved the veterans land program. After World War II the state established a program to purchase land for resale to veterans at modest prices and reasonable interest rates. The program was designed to supplement the Federal GI Bill of Rights. The Veterans Land Board was composed of Land Commissioner Bascom Giles, Governor Allan Shivers, and Attorney General John Ben Shepperd.

Through a complicated fraud, Giles was able to circumvent the intent of the program to sell land to the state at prices much higher than it was worth and to resell it to veterans to their disadvantage. When the investigation revealed the fraud, Giles and several others were indicted and convicted. Shivers and Shepperd were not implicated in the fraud, but their reputations were tarnished by their association with Giles. Both of them decided to retire from public office at the end of their terms. Scandals, of course, were nothing new and would return again in the future, but by the end of the fifties Texans were looking more to national affairs again.

By the end of the decade, Lyndon Johnson was the best-known and most powerful Texan because of his position as majority leader of the Senate. Although he and Yarborough were not on the best of terms, they were able, most of the time, to suppress their differences for party harmony and for the benefit of Texas when they agreed on what was best for the state. Johnson and Sam Rayburn, the long-time Speaker of the House and Johnson's former mentor, had formed a partnership that dominated the Congress. During the first two years of Eisenhower's first administration, the Republican Party controlled Congress. Johnson was the Minority Leader of the Loyal Opposition. When the Democrats regained control of Congress in 1954, Johnson and Rayburn—but especially Johnson—cooperated with Eisenhower more than some of the most partisan Democrats liked. Johnson's control and manipulation of the Senate, as much as anything else, made possible the passage of many of Eisenhower's programs. Johnson's image as a party leader was somewhat tarnished by his cooperation with Republicans, but many people acknowledged that it was an act of statesmanship since without his cooperative leadership partisan differences could easily have caused the government to grind to a halt.

Johnson's position as a statesman somewhat above party differences gave him a national prominence that he might not have otherwise achieved. By the end of the decade Johnson had ambitions for the presidency, but by then he had to contend with the rising young senator from Massachusetts, John F. Kennedy, who had captured many people's imagination with his unsuccessful bid for the vice presidency at the Democratic Convention of 1956. Immediately thereafter Kennedy was a major contender for the Democratic nomination in 1960; he would be Johnson's major opponent should Johnson choose to enter the race.

Johnson did much in the last years of the fifties to broaden his national reputation and to disassociate himself somewhat from the "oil Senator" image he had carried for so long. Even though he was a Southerner, he was instrumental, along with several others, in the passage of the first federal civil rights legislation since the Civil War in 1957 even though it was a very mild and weak bill.

By the time Johnson declared himself a candidate in 1960, he had waited too long to counter the Kennedy bandwagon. Johnson understood how difficult it would be for him to win the presidency even if he should get the nomination. He was a Southerner, and no Southerner had been elected president since the Civil War. He attempted to associate himself with the West, but he still could not shake the Southern image.

To complicate matters for his personal career, his Senate term expired in 1960. To run for the presidency, he would have to vacate his seat in the Senate and give up his power there with no assurance of the presidency. The Texas legislature willingly moved to protect Johnson in the situation. For the first time and only time, legislation was passed allowing a person to run for two offices at the same time. When Kennedy unexpectedly tapped Johnson for the vice presidency—and he accepted to the surprise of most—Johnson was able to run for the Senate and the vice presidency at the same time.

Kennedy's choice of Johnson was controversial in many circles, but it proved to be a wise political decision. Texas went narrowly for Kennedy and made the difference in his election. Johnson was also elected to the Senate, but his candidacy in two races did anger many Texans and it inadvertently aided in the rise of a new politician in Texas — John Tower. Tower, Johnson's Republican opponent in 1960, was a little-known political science professor from Midwestern State University in Wichita Falls who was catapulted to state prominence and garnered more votes than any Republican in the state's history while still losing to Johnson.

When Johnson resigned his Senate position to take the vice presidency, a special election — one of the wildest free-for-alls in Texas history—was held to fill the vacancy. It was a winner-take-all election that brought forth seventy-two candidates, six of whom were considered serious contenders. Undoubtedly because of the attention he received as Johnson's opponent in 1960, Tower won the special election in 1961 and became the state's first Republican Senator since Reconstruction. This was something of a bitter pill for Johnson in that it diluted Texas' influence in Washington and made the liberal Democrat, Ralph Yarborough, the senior senator from Texas. Tower proved to have more staying power than anyone expected. Although he never authored any major legislation in over twenty years in the Senate, he moved into a position of power in the Republican Party and was able to win reelection in 1966, 1972, and 1978. Late in 1983 Tower announced that he would retire from the Senate at the end of his term in 1985.

Tower's longevity as a Republican from Texas was due to several causes, not the least of which was the support he received on several occasions from liberal Texas Democrats who were trying to build a two-party state by forcing extreme conservatives to declare themselves as Republicans and to leave the Democratic Party. This was a controversial tactic that some called "kamikazee politics," but it was a contributing factor in Tower's ability to stay in office.

By the end of the 1970s when Democrats were making a serious effort to defeat Tower, especially with the candidacy of Robert Krueger in 1978, Texas had moved much farther toward a two-party state than anyone had expected. It was in 1978 that Texas elected its first Republican governor since Reconstruction, the Dallas millionaire William Clements. Although that was the most dramatic event, it should be recognized that Texas Republican power had been growing through the sixties as urban and suburban areas began to elect Republicans to Congress in increasing numbers. Through the sixties and into the seventies, the Texas legislature was no longer the sole province of Democrats. Although Republicans were far from a majority in the legislature, their numbers grew steadily during these two decades.

Texas faced much the same turmoil in the 1960s as the country as a whole did. Although Texas was not the scene of major civil rights confrontations like Selma, Alabama, it did have its confrontations. Of course, Texas had been the origin of several major civil rights actions taken before the Supreme Court. For example, in 1944 in *Smith* v. *Allwright* the Supreme Court outlawed the Texas white primary, and in 1950 it ordered the integration of the University of Texas Law School in *Sweatt* v. *Painter*. When the Supreme Court ruled in 1954 that separate educational facilities were unconstitutional, Texans reacted in a diversity of ways, but a major portion of the population pledged to never accept integration peacefully. Although school integration moved slowly and other civil rights gains were painfully slow, Texas did move toward acceptance of the new way of things, even if there were pockets of resistance such as Tyler where the white community held out against school integration and the abandonment of racial symbols until a federal judge (the last federal appointment of Lyndon Johnson) with the unlikely name of William Wayne Justice forced it.

Like much of America, Texas did not understand the social upheaval of the sixties. To many Texans the young seemed to have taken leave of their senses as many of them adopted "hippie" lifestyles, and certain cities—particularly Austin—became magnets attracting the unusual and bizarre. The drug culture came to Texas, but authorities were unwilling to understand or accept it—so much so that for many years Texas had some of the nation's harshest laws for minor drug offenses.

Neither did Texas understand the objection of the young—and eventually of all ages—to American involvement in Vietnam. Many Texans believed that loyalty and support of the government should be without reservation. The fact that a Texan was in Washington and responsible for much of the American buildup in Vietnam made the issue even more complex. As was true in civil rights activities, Texas was not the center of antiwar protest, but it did, nonetheless, experience major demonstrations against American involvement.

Texas was undergoing much the same experience as other rural areas of the United States. It was rapidly becoming a major urban-technological-industrial state, but it had not given up its older, rural customs and philosophy, which were not suitable for the new world. Texans were anxious to benefit from the major technological changes taking place in the world, but they were not yet willing to admit that the world had changed and that any area that aspired to be a center of the new world would, by necessity, be required to change its way of looking at the world.

This problem was perhaps no better exemplified than with the assassination of John F. Kennedy. The situation was a complex one. John Connally, appointed by Kennedy at Johnson's suggestion as secretary of the navy, had resigned from his Washington post in 1962 to run for the governor's office. Connally seemed to symbolize a new era of Texas leadership. He was a younger Johnson in many ways, but he seemed different also. He attracted much attention and support in Texas and was able to win the governorship. The division among Texas Democrats became more intense, however, as the forces represented on the one side by the liberal Ralph Yarborough contended for control of the state with the Connally wing of the Democratic Party. Where Lyndon Johnson stood in the controversy was not entirely clear.

Certainly, Connally brought a new style of leadership to Texas and must be considered generally a good governor. He streamlined state government, led the fight for the Coordinating Board designed to bring some order to Texas higher education, and emphasized and promoted Texas tourism, to name only three of his programs.

With the approaching presidential election in 1964, John Kennedy knew that Texas was crucial to his reelection, particularly since his probable opponent, Barry Goldwater of Arizona, was so popular in Texas. He knew also that a feuding Democratic Party in Texas could lose him the state. At least, that seemed to be one reason that Kennedy made his ill-fated trip to Texas in 1963—to smooth over the differences in the state party for his own objectives.

The resulting events are well known. When Kennedy was shot and killed in Dallas on November 22, it pushed Texas directly into the national limelight in an unfavorable way. Many Americans believed Texas was responsible for the death, and some conspiracy theorists even suggested that Johnson had something to do with the assassination. The rise of an almost cult-like obsession with the Kennedy assassination kept Texas in the limelight for ten years or more. Although there was never any real consensus on who or what was responsible for the assassination and the method by which it was carried out, various persons who maintained an interest in the details for their own ends continued to come to Texas — Dallas in particular — and to put Texas and its culture under scrutiny. Even in the 1980s the controversy continued to be rekindled on occasion by some new theory or challenge to existing accepted facts. Without doubt, the scar of the Kennedy assassination would remain on Texas for many years to come — whether or not Texas should bear any particular special blame. Furthermore, because John Connally was wounded in the assassination, he became a national celebrity. He eventually left the Democratic Party to serve in President Richard Nixon's cabinet and even made an abortive attempt at the presidency as a Republican in 1980.

By the end of the sixties, Texas, like much of the country, was turning back to the right as the Connally actions showed. Some will argue that Texas never veered leftward in the sixties, but with Lyndon Johnson on the national scene, his overwhelming election in 1964 to a presidential term of his own, and the popularity of his social programs (War on Poverty and other neo-New Deal measures) it was quite difficult for conservative Texans to be heard. With the growing involvement in Vietnam and the increasing unpopularity of Johnson throughout the country, however, the momentum of progressive reforms slowed and the conservative voices were heard once again.

Although the Democrat, Hubert Humphrey, was able to carry Texas in 1968—possibly because of his association with Johnson—the trend toward conservatism was evident in Texas. In 1972, Texas went overwhelmingly for Richard Nixon, only the third Republican to carry Texas since Reconstruction. The reasons for the shift are difficult to assess. Texans, like the rest of the country, were weary and frustrated with the Vietnam experience; some who voted for Nixon probably believed he would take a harder line on the war with the objective of "winning" it while others believed he would disengage as soon as possible. Certainly, many Texans were attracted by his hard-line stand on "law and order" which seemed to be an answer to the decade-long period of social upheaval. Without doubt, many Texans were driven out of the Democratic Party by what they considered the radical politics of George McGovern, the Democratic candidate. Whatever the cause, Texans seemed by the 1970s to be turning their backs on the past and turning inward as much of America did.

The seventies proved to be a difficult decade for Texas. One of the most significant developments concerned petroleum. With the rise of the Organization of Petroleum Exporting Countries (OPEC), Texas was directly affected. When the oil embargo of 1973 ushered in a decade of uncertainity about energy, Texas benefitted at first. Shortage of petroleum and rapidly rising prices reaffirmed the importance of the vast oil reserves of Texas. Exploration and production of fossil fuels were so great that the state entered a boom period. State revenues increased year after year until the legislative session of 1983 when state lawmakers awoke to find that increases for existing programs and new state ventures would require tax increases. Oilmen had returned to their preeminent place in Texas social and political life. The discovery of new oil and the production of both old and new oil were so important that environmental regulations were challenged and efforts were made to give oil producers new rights. Rapidly rising prices of petroleum naturally caused a growing resentment among Texas consumers against all producers of energy.

Another major issue of the 1970s was an abortive effort to revise the state's one-hundred-year-old constitution. The document was an embarrassment to many Texans because it was so archaic and had been amended so many times. In 1971, after several unsuccessful efforts to get revision, the legislature called a constitutional convention made up of members of the 63rd legislature. The convention became so deadlocked over several issues, including especially the right-to-work issue, that it was unable to send any revisions to the voters. A new effort in 1975 did get several major amendments which amounted to constitutional revision before the public, but they were all rejected. Texans continued to amend the antiquated constitution several times every year or two without any general revision in sight.

By the time of its 150th birthday, Texas had come a long way from its humble beginnings. Without question, it had become a major political force in American affairs. Texans still had to live with a reputation that caused outsiders to view them as something of a cross between a romantic frontiersman and a buffoon or clown. Neither image was correct, of course, but they were hard to erase. By the 1980s, however, changes were beginning to occur, especially as more and more people from the Midwest and the Northeast migrated to Texas seeking economic opportunity supposedly offered by the so-called "Sunbelt." In some ways, the cycle seemed to have come full circle. Texas resembled the California of the thirties when "Okies" (a generic term that embraced persons from Texas and Arkansas, as well as Oklahoma) looked upon it as the promised land. When America faced the post-industrial era that saw the decline of the economic power of the Midwest and Northeast — especially in heavy industry such as steel and automobiles — more and more people looked upon Texas — and the South in general — as the new areas for opportunity and for starting over. So many people were migrating to Texas by the 1980s that several changes were occurring. For example, bumper stickers could be seen on Texas automobiles suggesting that if one were not a native Texan he might seek other places to live, a new term, snowbird, entered the Texas vocabulary to describe people migrating from northern states with heavy winters, and in some of the larger cities such as Dallas enough people had migrated from some areas to create small communities — the Michigan Club in Dallas, for example.

The challenge faced by Texas was immense. The state was not philosophically equipped to face urban life and massive population growth; its concepts of government and social service were still rooted in the nineteenth century. With its massive petroleum and other natural resources, Texas was quite attractive, but most people, in the state and out, had not faced up to the most serious natural challenge the state faced — a constantly declining water supply. There were many other challenges of a political, social, and economic nature that would provide a real test for the future. Given the state's record of recent political leadership, one could not be entirely optimistic about how the state would meet the new era. On the other hand, some people believed that a serious crisis or challenge would bring forth the leadership needed. Only time would provide the answer, but by then the direction of the state would already be set. Without doubt, the second half of the state's second century would be exciting.

# II

# The Texas Economy and People And Culture

*A farm landscape in the Texas Panhandle showing the diversity of Texas agriculture.*

# 9

## Texas: A State of Agricultural Diversity

*Garry L. Nall*

For almost three hundred years Texans have engaged in the formal production of food and fiber. From the initial missionary efforts by the Spaniards in the seventeenth century to the work of the agribusinessmen of the twentieth century, a transition from subsistence farming in a frontier region to a sophisticated commercial agricultural system in an increasingly urbanized society has occurred. With this change the willingness of farmers and ranchers from the Rio Grande to the Gulf of Mexico to adapt and to experiment has made Texas a state of agricultural diversity.

The agrarian efforts of the Spaniards in the eighteenth century laid the foundation for the formal organization of farming and ranching in Texas. In the missions established by those Europeans in eastern Texas and along the San Antonio River, elaborate agricultural operations emerged as priests sought to achieve self-sufficiency. Food crops were produced as Indians went to the fields to grow such items as corn, beans, Irish and sweet potatoes, cantaloupes, pumpkins, and sugar cane. Herds of hogs, sheep, goats, and cattle supplied meat, while horses and mules lightened the drudgery for the laborers.

Outside the confines of the missions, cattle appeared on ranges in eastern and southern Texas. Brought to the Western Hemisphere by Christopher Columbus, Spanish cattle, which were the forebears of the longhorns, made their way to Texas from Mexico in various ways. Those wild cows that the Frenchman, Louis de St. Denis, found in East Texas in 1714 were probably offspring from the animals that Captain Alonso de Leon herded to the Neches River Valley in 1690. Those that entered South Texas drifted northward across the Rio Grande in search of grass or were taken by settlers to Jose de Escandon's colony of Nuevo Santander in the 1740s. Regardless of the methods of their arrival, large numbers of cattle were grazing in the vicinity of Nacogdoches, San Antonio, and the Rio Grande Valley by the end of the Spanish era.

Lured by the availability of cheap land that the Spaniards had shown to be productive, Anglo-Americans followed Stephen F. Austin and other empresarios into Texas after 1821. As word spread that a family head could obtain a *labor* (177 acres) of farming land plus a league (4428 acres) of grazing land for a nominal filing fee, immigrants headed for Spanish, later Mexican, Texas in steady numbers. Within a decade more than one thousand families had received grants in the Austin Colony between the Brazos and Colorado rivers. Further land sales by other empresarios along the Lavaca and Guadalupe rivers as well as on the eastern border contributed to the arrival of 30,000 Anglo-Americans and 5,000 slaves by 1836.

In such a frontier setting, the pioneers went to work quickly to develop their farm units. Having come from a timbered region and believing that such acreage was more productive, most chose land from which trees had to be cleared before cultivation. From the initial settlement, corn was the primary crop for both man and livestock, and if the weather cooperated, the growers harvested two crops each year. Such other staples as Irish and sweet potatoes, beans, peas, and melons grew well. Some farmers who had suitable land and an adequate labor force also raised sugar cane, tobacco, and indigo. While poultry, hogs, horses, mules, and milk cows were generally kept near the log houses, beef cattle, sheep, and goats grazed on the adjacent prairies.

Undoubtedly, the prospects of raising cotton attracted settlers to Texas, for small patches and large fields of the crop appeared very rapidly after their arrival. The first large planter, Colonel Jared E. Groce, who moved to the Austin Colony from Alabama with ninety slaves in late 1821, planted 100 acres of cotton the next spring. Within four years he had constructed a cotton gin, harvested 100 bales, and begun marketing his crop in New Orleans. Though Groce's operation was an exception, both large and small farm operators from the Sabine to the Brazos raised the commodity so extensively that when the Mexican official, Colonel J. N. Almonte, visited the area in 1833, he reported a harvest of 7,000 bales.

The momentum in agricultural expansion found by Almonte

continued at a more rapid pace until the Civil War. Even as Texans staged a revolution, created an independent nation, and achieved statehood, farm settlers primarily from the southern states rushed to Texas to take advantage of liberal land policies. Residents of the Republic received grants ranging from 320 acres at 50 cents per acre for family heads, and a homestead act in 1854 gave 160 acres for those who would reside on the property for three years. In 1858 lots ranging from 160 to 1,280 acres became available at $1 per acre. Within less than a quarter century such policies caused the population to rise from 35,000 in 1836 to 604,215 in 1860.

Almost one-third of the state's residents were slaves in 1860. Though the institution had grown rapidly after the revolution, its impact upon farm development was limited in that only 5 percent of the population owned any Negroes, and 60 percent of those controlled fewer than six. Actually, nearly half of the slaves toiled for only 2,163 planters, 10 percent of the slaveholders. Quite obviously, Texas was a state of yeoman farmers rather than large planters on the eve of the Civil War.

As immigrants flocked to Texas in the antebellum years, the pattern of agricultural production established during the colonial era continued. Corn remained the leading food crop over the entire state. In the Blacklands area of northern Texas and along the edge of the western frontier some farmers experimented with wheat. On the Gulf Coast several large planters began raising sugar cane during the 1840s. More importantly, cotton production exploded during the 1850s from 57,596 bales at the beginning of the decade to 431,463 ten years later, making the commodity the state's leading moneymaker.

New dimensions in the cattle industry emerged during those years after statehood. As settlers from the south brought their livestock with them and established stockfarms and ranches, a creolization process often occurred when their animals mixed with the Spanish cattle. With such developments causing the cattle population to soar to 4,500,000 by 1860, the groundwork for the first large ranch empires was laid. In South Texas, Richard King and Mifflin Kenedy began purchasing grassland. In northern Texas such cattlemen as John Chisum, Dan Waggoner, George Webb Slaughter, and Oliver Loving ventured into the Cross Timbers region with large herds in search of acreage. Though New Orleans served as the chief market for most of these stockmen, prospects for large profits caused a few Texas cattlemen to drive their animals northward to Illinois or westward to California.

Sheep raising also grew during the 1850s. Partially as a result of the promotional activities of George Wilkins Kendall, who brought the livestock to the Hill Country north of San Antonio, immigrants from Scotland, England, Germany, Mexico, and other parts of the United States moved to Texas to become sheep ranchers. While some of these settlers brought their own animals, large flocks were driven from the Ohio Valley and the midwestern states.

The eruption of the Civil War virtually halted agricultural growth. As men left home to fight with the Confederate army, women, children, and slaves went to the fields to raise food for both the military and civilian population. Even though an extensive trade through Mexico developed, cotton production declined. During the initial years of the war, cattlemen prospered as prices paid in New Orleans and Memphis tripled after the army contracted for approximately 200,000 head of Texas longhorns. However, when Union forces seized the Mississippi River in 1863, the trade ended, forcing Texas to look for buyers in the western areas of the Confederacy.

Farmers struggled to recover from the effects of the war for almost a decade. In that portion of the state where cotton and slavery were dominant, the shortage of money and the loss of a labor force caused the plantation system to give way to tenancy. Land values plummeted, and foreclosure sales caused changes of ownership on much of the property in East Texas. Production of the primary food crop of corn increased almost immediately, but cotton did not reach the antebellum level until 1873.

As the residents in eastern Texas and southern Texas coped with the effects of the war, forces emerged that led to the elimination of the frontier. When the conflict ended, the line of settlement extended from Clay County on the Red River to Kimble County in the Hill Country and then to Val Verde County on the Rio Grande. Within thirty years the elimination of the Indian barrier, the extermination of the buffaloes, and the construction of a railroad network opened the farthest boundaries to ranchers and farmers.

Dramatic changes in the cattle industry served as a catalyst to the settlement of western Texas. As cattlemen realized that the demand for beef in the urban North had driven prices to as much as $50 per head, they proceeded to round up herds of unclaimed longhorns in southern Texas and elsewhere and launched the trail-driving era. For two decades after the war as many as seven million head of Texas cattle went up the Chisholm and Western trails and their branches to railheads in such Kansas towns as Abilene, Newton, Ellsworth, Wichita, or Dodge City. From those points livestock shipments went to Chicago or Kansas City for slaughter, to farmer-feeders in Iowa, Illinois, or Missouri for fattening, to Indian reservations for consumption, or to ranges in the Northern Plains for finishing. With very limited expenses, trail-driving cattlemen made vast fortunes.

Such success caused cattle raisers to look westward for grassland. This resulted in the establishment of the range cattle industry in which herds were driven onto the open domain for fattening before being marketed. By the early 1870s the Ikard Brothers, the Harrold Brothers, and Dan Waggoner had reached the vicinity of the Wichita River. In 1876 C. C. Slaughter moved his livestock even farther westward to the headwaters of the Colorado River and the southern rim of the Caprock. That same year Colonel Charles Goodnight became the first large operator in the Panhandle country. Very quickly western Texas became an important grazing domain.

This influx of the livestock producers did not go unnoticed in the eastern United States or in the British Isles. Indeed, as word spread that quick profits were being made in such enterprises, a rush to invest in large cattle ranches created an economic boom between 1881 and 1885. Outfits like the Matador, the Spur, the Rocking Chair, the LX, the XIT, and numerous others appeared. Such rapid growth signaled the end of the range cattle industry as competition for grass forced cattlemen to seek protection through landownership. Unfortunately, the boom turned to bust as drought struck and prices declined. For many of the poorly managed companies, bankruptcies followed. Others lingered on for a few more years until smaller ranch operators or farmers arrived.

Not far behind the cattlemen came the railroads. Though the construction of such lines as the Houston and Texas Central and the International and Great Northern had been important in linking the towns of eastern Texas in a north-south direction by the 1870s, the building of the Southern Pacific, the Texas and Pacific, and the Fort Worth and Denver railroads stimulated farm settlement in southern and western Texas. Besides offering easier access to the unsettled areas of the state, the railroads engaged in land sales promotion campaigns and assisted the settlers in the establishment of their homesteads. Furthermore, the development of a statewide railroad network gave Texas livestock and crop producers access to markets throughout the world.

The enhancement of marketing capabilities for Texas farmers and ranchers signaled the beginning of a transition from an agricultural system that was primarily subsistence to one essentially commercial. During a period of approximately sixty years from 1870 to 1930, technological and scientific advances increased the productive potential on farms over the state. Improvement of animal-drawn

*A citrus grove in the Lower Rio Grande Valley of Texas.*

gang and sulky plows, planters, drills, cultivators, headers, and binders as well as the introduction of steam and gasoline tractors added to the amount of acreage an individual farmer could handle. The distribution of improved seeds and plants heightened crop yields. Along with the extension of the railroads, the construction of roads and highways as automobiles and trucks became available expanded transportation opportunities. Even as these and other changes occurred, the old and the new systems operated side by side.

Corn, oats, and sorghum were consumed primarily on the farms and ranches and did not become commercial crops during the era. As had occurred repeatedly in previous frontier areas, corn was the first crop planted as settlers moved into western Texas because of its popularity as a food as well as the ease in planting and harvesting it. However, farmers soon learned that the crop did not do well in arid conditions. Consequently, the major center of production remained in the eastern half of the state, where rainfall usually averaged thirty-five inches annually. Acreage devoted to the crop continued to rise after the Civil War until a plateau of five million was reached around 1900, making corn second only to cotton in annual land usage among the commodities grown in Texas. With Yellow Dent, Surecropper, and Mexican June as leading varieties, the low average yield of 19.2 bushels per acre for the period 1909 to 1926 caused Texas to rank fortieth in production in the nation.

Statewide, oats ranked second in importance to corn as a livestock feed. With the Blacklands of North Texas as the leading area of production, acreage grew from 238,000 in 1879 to 1,846,000 in 1919 as significant planting of the crop extended westward across North Texas to the Edwards Plateau and the Northern High Plains. The prevalent variety, Red Rustproof, offered good winter grazing in all areas except the Northern High Plains, where climatic conditions restricted farmers to the growing of spring oats.

Farmers in the arid regions of Texas found the drought-resistant sorghums more dependable. Originally from Africa, the sorghum variety of Chinese sugar cane, now called Chinese Amber, was first planted in the state on the Comanche and Brazos Indian reserves in Throckmorton and Young counties in 1857. By 1890 giant milo maize and Blackhull Kafir, both of which a missionary, Reverend H. B. Pratt, had brought to South Carolina from Colombia, had become the most popular sorghums. From these, Dwarf Yellow Milo had emerged as the dominant grain sorghum in the state by 1905. That same year the Texas Agricultural Experiment Stations at Chillicothe and Lubbock began research that led to the introduction of feterita, hegari, and Sudan grass. An indication of the importance of sorghum primarily as livestock feed became evident as acreage increased from 23,000 in 1879 to 1,701,000 by 1929.

Among the commodities that became important commercially was wheat. Growing such soft winter varieties as Little Red May, which was brought from Missouri before 1850, and Mediterranean, which was introduced in 1870, farmers in the Blacklands region of North Texas annually planted approximately two-thirds of the state's acreage in the crop until World War I. However, as the Turkey and Russian hard wheat, which grew well in subhumid areas, became available, production shifted westward, so that an extensive plowup of grasslands in the 1920s made the High Plains the center of heaviest wheat concentration. By 1931 more than 4,500,000 acres were being planted in wheat.

Cotton's supremacy as a commercial crop continued after the Civil War. Though the eastern half of the state remained the major area of production for sixty-five years after the conflict, cotton followed the farm population westward to the extent that it had become significant on the High Plains by the 1920s. The increase from 532,000 bales gathered from 922,000 acres in 1870 to 4,037,000 bales taken from 16,138,000 acres in 1930 reflected the impact of such expansion. By 1925 Texas farmers annually harvested approximately 36 percent of the nation's cotton and 20 percent of that grown in the world.

As such expansion occurred, several problems inevitably arose. While Texas Stormproof did well in eastern sections of the state during the 1880s, the selection of varieties that would grow satisfactorily elsewhere constantly confronted the producers. Through research efforts of such men as Alexander D. Mebane of Hays and Caldwell counties, types suitable to areas below the Caprock, such as Mebane Triumph, became available prior to 1900. On the High Plains scientists developed Westex in 1920. Furthermore, the perennial problem of locating harvest hands led growers in the Lubbock area to construct both slot and finger-type sleds in 1926. Despite such successes, the failure to curb the spread of the boll weevil that had crossed the Rio Grande in 1892 kept cotton farmers challenged throughout the era.

Farmers in eastern and southern Texas turned to speciality crops after the Civil War. Among those that received attention was sugar cane. With the commodity growing on more than 5,000 acres on approximately forty-five plantations, the area that included Brazoria, Fort Bend, Matagorda, and Wharton counties had become known as the Sugar Bowl of Texas by 1880. Without the assistance of slaves who had supplied the labor in the antebellum years, such planters as Colonel E. H. Cunningham and L. A. Ellis in Fort Bend County began leasing state prison convicts in 1879. As production spread with this help, thirty sugar factories were grinding cane by 1893, and Cunningham had erected the first large refinery for processing raw sugar at Sugar Land. Though Texas would rate third among the sugar-producing states in the nation by 1899, poor weather conditions and the elimination of tariff protection virtually ended production by the eve of the First World War.

Though some rice had been grown in Texas as early as 1850, commercial production did not begin until 1886. That year three transplanted Louisianians, Edgar Carruthers, Louis Bordages, and Dan Wingate, planted two hundred acres near Beaumont in Jefferson County. Within the next two decades several developments contributed to a rapid expansion of the commodity. During the 1890s promotional efforts made by the Southern Pacific Railway and other companies lured a large number of potential rice farmers to the area. Furthermore, Joe E. Broussard, who constructed the first rice mill in the state, also established the first irrigation system for the crop in 1891. With the use of steam-powered water pumps, flood irrigation from bayous, rivers, and wells spread rapidly. In addition, Seamann A. Knapp, who had worked for an Iowa land developer on the Texas Gulf Coast, visited Japan in 1899 for the United States Department of Agriculture and returned with the Kiushu rice. The introduction of this short-grain variety along with Honduras long-grain rice provided growers with two excellent producers. With the expansion of the crop along the Gulf Coast from the Louisiana border to the Guadalupe River, farmers had planted 275,000 acres by 1912, making Texas the second largest rice-growing state in the nation.

Though oranges had been produced in the Galveston vicinity as early as the 1840s, the planting of approximately 910,000 orange trees during the first decade of the twentieth century in the area along the Gulf Coast from Beaumont to Brownsville launched the commercial citrus fruit industry in Texas. With leaders such as John Shary and Charles Volz breeding the citrus trifoliata stock with Satsuma, Washington navel, and Dugat oranges along with Duncan grapefruit, fine groves appeared. Unfortunately, severe freezes in 1910-11 and 1916-17 destroyed so many trees that growers from Beaumont to Corpus Christi did not bother to continue production. Consequently, Hidalgo, Cameron, and Willacy counties in the Lower Rio Grande Valley emerged as the only major citrus fruit region in the state due to their mild climate and ability to irrigate from the Rio Grande. By 1929, 85 percent of the 5,000,000 citrus trees were grapefruit, particularly the white and pink varieties, with the remaining 15 percent divided among oranges, lemons, limes, and tangerines.

Truck farming first achieved commercial status around 1900. Beginning with the growing of potatoes in the vicinity of Dallas and Houston, onions near Cotulla and Laredo, and tomatoes at Athens and Jacksonville, vegetable sales were scattered over the state until about 1910. However, with the construction of irrigation canals along the Rio Grande near Laredo and in the Lower Rio Grande Valley as well as the drilling of wells in the Winter Garden region south and west of San Antonio, South Texas emerged as the primary vegetable area in Texas. In the earlier phases of production, onions, particularly the Bermuda, led all others in sales until surpassed by cabbage in the 1909-10 season. Lettuce, carrots, beets, spinach, broccoli, turnips, and others also became important. Of the 101 counties in Texas that marketed truck crops in carlots during 1930, farmers in Hidalgo and Cameron counties in the Lower Rio Grande Valley shipped the most.

The growing of peaches and pecans for commercial purposes developed during the era. Though a large number of farmsteads included orchards with such fruits as apples, apricots, cherries, pears, plums, and figs, large-scale planting of peach trees began in the 1880s in the eastern half of Texas and expanded rapidly after the development of a refrigerator car for fruit in 1893. With the Elberta as the leading variety, production reached the high level of 4,621,000 bushels in 1919. Like peaches, extensive sales of pecans began around 1900. Especially prolific in Central Texas, the native or seedling varieties, which usually were shelled for marketing, outnumbered the improved papershells, which were products of the initial grafting efforts by such men as E. E. Risien of San Saba. With a ten year average of 22,700,000 pounds during the 1900s, Texas remained the leading pecan-growing region in the nation.

The commercial agricultural system that had developed in Texas received a jolt with the arrival of both the Great Depression and the Dust Bowl in the 1930s. Sharp declines in commodity prices, an inability to raise crops without rainfall, and the impact of the New Deal programs of the Franklin D. Roosevelt Administration all contributed directly and indirectly to long-range shifts in Texas farming and ranching. Indeed, this era of hardship served as the transitional phase to the modern structure of Texas agriculture.

Since the depression years, trends emerged that reshaped rural Texas. Between 1935 and 1980 the number of farm units declined from 501,014 to 186,000 as the percentage of rural population fell from approximately 59 to 17. As this occurred, the average size of a

Texas farm rose from 274.6 acres to 744 acres. However, even with the decrease in farms and ranches, crop and livestock receipts grew from $367 million in 1940 to $10 billion in 1979, an indication of the tremendous enlargement of the state's productive capacity.

Technological and scientific changes influenced such growth. By the eve of World War II the move toward increased farm mechanization was underway with the replacement of draft horses and mules with tractors, giving farmers the capability of working more acreage through the use of multirow equipment. Furthermore, the introduction of self-propelled combines, balers, cotton pickers, cotton strippers, and other harvesters enhanced the farmer's efficiency. The decline in the number of hours required to produce and harvest an acre of wheat from 7.5 to 3.1 and an acre of cotton from 98 to 54 between 1940 and 1960 reflected the impact of such technological changes. In addition, crop production multiplied with the utilization of nitrogen and phosphorous fertilizers to stimulate growth as well as herbicides and insecticides to control destructive pests.

The expansion of irrigated agriculture after World War II also enhanced productivity. In 1939 most of the 895,000 irrigated acres were located along the Rio Grande, Pecos, Brazos, and other rivers and in the vicinity of the Gulf Coast. However, as drought and improvement in pump technology occurred, farmers tapped the Ogallala acquifer, and the High Plains emerged as the crop irrigation center in the state. Of the 7,800,000 acres watered by Texas farmers in 1979, 67 percent were found in that region.

Such technological and scientific changes assisted in the maintenance of cotton's position as the leading commercial crop in Texas after 1940. Even as metropolitan expansion in the Blacklands and Coastal Bend areas caused a decline in acreage traditionally devoted to the commodity, the production of approximately four million bales remained steady as the High Plains, where 80 percent of the crop was irrigated, became the major production site. With short-staple Stormproof and long-staple Acalas as the leading varieties, mechanical pickers and strippers virtually eliminated hand harvesting after 1960. Once gathered, a decline in storage loss before ginning became available in 1975 with the introduction of the module, which could press ten bales together. In six of the eight years between 1973 and 1980, Texas farmers received in excess of $1 billion from cotton lint and seed production.

Wheat's role as a major crop continued after 1940. Grazed by cattle during the winter months, the harvested commodity maintained second place as an income producer until surpassed by sorghum in 1954. The Northern High Plains' position as the center of wheat raising was enhanced with the spread of irrigation in the area during the 1950s. With hard winter wheat planted almost exclusively, such varieties of the Turkey strains of Westar, Comanche, and Wichita and the Blackhull strains as Tascosa and Caddo were sown extensively. Improved semidwarf varieties, such as TAM W-101 and Sturdy, emerged as the most popular during the 1970s. Though the High Plains continued as the region of heaviest wheat concentration with approximately 44 percent of the state's 6,800,000 planted acres and 48 percent of its 5,200,000 bushels harvested in 1980, evidence of a resurgence of wheat growing appeared in the Blacklands of north central Texas, where approximately 17 percent of the state's total acreage yielded 25 percent of its production that year.

Sorghum emerged as the leading feed grain in Texas as a result of scientific and technological advances. Originally grown for use on the farm, the success of scientists at the Texas Agricultural Experiment Stations at Chillicothe and Lubbock in reducing the plant's height on the eve of World War II permitted combine harvesting and thus commercial production. This breeding change coupled with the irrigation of this drought-resistant crop caused yields to double. However, when hybrids became available to farmers in 1957, a production explosion occurred. With further research in genetic combination for higher yields, disease or insect resistance, and drought tolerance, farmers in the High Plains, where the major irrigation of milo was found annually, gathered 4,500 pounds per acre, while dryland producers in the Rio Grande Valley, the Coastal Bend, the Blacklands, and the Rolling Plains usually obtained 3,000 pounds per acre.

After World War II rice remained a major commodity along the upper and central Gulf Coast. In the growing of long- and medium-grain rice, farmers sow, fertilize, and spray their crop with airplanes and harvest with large combines. Though Texas led the nation in production for approximately thirty years prior to 1974, competition for water to use in flood irrigation in the highly industrialized and urbanized region threatened the state's ability to continue raising the usual half million acres of rice.

Corn production declined for almost thirty years after World War II. Though the crop had been a major food and feed commodity since the state's founding, the emergence of irrigated grain sorghum created such competition that acreage fell from five million in 1942 to approximately 600,000 by the late 1970s. However, when grain sorghum prices increased sharply in the mid-1970s, a resurgence in corn production occurred as cattle feeders turned to the less expensive commodity for use as both a grain and silage. By 1980 more than 70 percent of the 117,000,000 bushels produced was grown on the High Plains.

Besides these basic field crops, other commodities received attention on Texas farms after 1940. In 1964 Holly Sugar Corporation erected a sugar-beet processing plant at Hereford in Deaf Smith County. Since that time farmers in the immediate vicinity have planted approximately 20,000 acres and harvested yields of 350,000 tons yearly. Sugar cane, which was abandoned as a commercial crop in 1923, reemerged in the 1970s in the Lower Rio Grande Valley, where approximately 32,000 acres annually yielded in excess of 900 million tons.

Though grown by Texas farmers during the 1930s, soybeans did not become significant for another twenty years. First raised for commercial purposes in the irrigated area on the High Plains, production spread to northeast Texas and the Coastal Prairie as farmers were attracted by the lack of government restrictions and the high prices paid for the commodity. With one-half of the acreage located in the Coastal Prairie, Texans planted 860,000 acres in soybeans in 1979.

Numerous other field crops attracted farmers throughout the state. Such small grains as rye, oats, and barley were planted annually in most areas. The Spanish and Florunner varieties of peanuts grew so successfully that Texas usually ranked third nationally in production. In the South Central Coast area, flax-seed was raised for linseed oil. On the High Plains sunflowers made their first appearance in 1975 and periodically served as a substitute commodity on grain sorghum or cotton farms.

The pattern established prior to 1930 for fruit and vegetable production continued with a few exceptions. With approximately eight million citrus fruit trees in South Texas in 1980, the Ruby Red accounted for 84 percent of the grapefruit grown, replacing the pink and white as leading varieties, and the early and mid-season oranges outnumbered other types. Texas became the fifth largest grower of fresh vegetables in the nation with the addition of the production in the irrigated areas of the High Plains to that in South Texas.

As crop diversification occurred, beef cattle remained the leader in livestock production. In the readjustment that took place after the collapse of the cattle bonanza era in the 1880s, beef production developed on a cow-calf basis on both large and small ranches as well as stockfarms across the state. With the introduction of such British breeds as Durham, Angus, and Hereford, along with the Brahman from India, cattlemen succeeded in improving animal quality. Efforts in crossbreeding such cattle and the utilization of artificial insemination practices produced the Santa Gertrudis, Beefmaster, and several exotics. As farmers in eastern Texas turned worn-out cotton farms to grassland, the number of cattle climbed from approximately seven million in 1940 to 16,600,000 in 1975.

Growth in cattle numbers increased rapidly with the appearance of the feedlot industry. Centered on the High Plains, where large supplies of grain sorghum existed, feeding pens capable of holding thousands of animals were erected. When enthusiasm for such ventures became extensive in the late 1960s, a boom began that culminated in the marketing of 4,412,000 cattle from 1,533 feedlots in 1973. The emergence of the feedlot industry reenforced the position of Texas as one of the leading beef cattle states in the nation.

San Angelo, located on the Edwards Plateau, served as the center for sheep and goat raising in Texas after 1930. With 10,829,000 head of sheep in 1943, production declined as drought and low prices for mutton and wool hit the industry. By the mid-1970s the sheep and lamb population numbered approximately 2,500,000; Angora goat production reached a peak of 4,222,000 animals and 28,710,000 pounds of mohair in 1966.

As Texas farmers and ranchers marketed $10 billion worth of agricultural products in 1979, they reached a new plateau in a process that had begun three hundred years earlier. With the utilization of both natural and human resources, a sophisticated agricultural empire had emerged from a primitive farming system. As worldwide demand for food and fiber grows in the future, the diversity of the state's agricultural production will invariably assist in meeting the challenge.

# 10

## Texas Railroads

*Donovan L. Hofsommer*

The steamcar civilization arrived late in Texas. By the end of 1850, when the railroad mileage of the United States stood at 9,021, Texas boasted nary an inch of track. That changed, however modestly, in 1853 when the romantic sounding Buffalo Bayou, Brazos & Colorado Railway completed twenty miles of construction between Harrisburg and Stafford's Point. Additional expansion prior to the Civil War was negligible; only 407 miles were in service in 1861. Meanwhile, four rail lines were already pushing across Iowa and another in Missouri had connected Hannibal, on the Mississippi River, with St. Joseph, on the Missouri River. National mileage stood at 30,626. Texas clearly languished by comparison, but the situation soon would change. Because of its immense size, strategic location, as well as its agricultural and commercial potential, Texas eventually would emerge as the state with the largest rail mileage.

Aside from that noteworthy fact, the railroad history of Texas is typical of most western states. Railroad boosterism became vociferous criticism; branch lines, short lines, and interurbans were built to serve communities off the trunk roads; railroad companies engaged in colonization projects as well as agricultural and industrial development; the railroads suffered with their constituents during the Great Depression and labored gloriously during World War II; streamlined passenger trains in Texas offered a brief hope in the losing battle against the automobiles and the airplanes; and, railroads adjusted to the realities of mega-mergers and modal competition.

*Locomotive No. 1 at Brownsville, around 1905. This was part of the St. Louis, Brownsville and Mexico Railroad.*
— Texas Southmost College Library, Brownsville, Texas

*Railroads were still being used for whistle-stop campaigning in Texas when President Harry S. Truman visited the state in 1948. Shown with him is U.S. Senate nominee Lyndon B. Johnson.*

Although there was a brief flirtation with the notion of government-owned railroads, the Texas rail net was constructed principally with private funds. There were, of course, the usual inducements to promote construction or to encourage location of a line to or from particular communities. These included bonuses of various types; land for right-of-way, stations, and facilities; and, for a short period, state bonds. The most important public aid came in the form of state lands, granted in the amount of 32.1 million acres to several aspiring carriers.

Because of these inducements, but more importantly because of the westward movement and the burgeoning national economy, railroad construction fairly boomed during the decades of the 1870s and 1880s. At the end of 1889, the state claimed railroad mileage of 8,486. Much of this trackage radiated inland from eager Gulf Coast ports that were engaging in classic urban economic imperialism; from construction of transcontinental, Gulf-to-Rockies, and strategic north-south arteries within the state; and, from initial "fleshing out."

These lines both reflected and encouraged mass migration westward, promoted a rapid increase in agricultural production, and prepared the way for a subsequent industrial development. In 1870, the state's population stood at 818,579; two decades later it was 2,235,527. Twenty cities in 1890 had a population of 4,000 or more and ten claimed numbers in excess of 10,000. Preeminent among these were Austin, Dallas, Denison, El Paso, Fort Worth, Galveston, Houston, Laredo, San Antonio, and Waco; all boasted two or more railroads or were junction points. Railroad transportation guaranteed for these communities and others, as the network was expanded, subsequent growth of population and trade. Additional benefits accrued to the lucky cities or towns that found themselves established as railroad division points or shop locations.

The state would eventually grant more than 700 charters to railroad companies, but that impressive figure belied the reality of the giant regional systems that took shape and became crucial to the transportation needs of Texas before the turn of the century. These included the Atchison, Topeka & Santa Fe Railway, Chicago, Rock Island & Pacific Railroad, Fort Worth & Denver City Railway, Missouri, Kansas & Texas Railway, Texas & Pacific Railway, and the Southern Pacific Company. The Santa Fe, Rock Island, FW&DC, and the MK&T operated, in general terms, on a north-south axis, the T&P with an east-west origination, and, the Southern Pacific had the luxury of a transcontinental line plus a route from the Red River to the Gulf. Each of these important companies had formed their respective rail grids in Texas through original construction and/or acquisition of previously independent railroads.

Texas was thus joined to the rest of the country through a series of important connections. Each section of the state had rail service before the twentieth century began, although the majority of lines were east of the 100th meridian. Central West Texas and the Panhandle continued to yearn for more adequate rail transportation and, indeed, the state's system would not be complete for some years.

Texans like many other Americans got caught up in and participated in the rise of Populism during the 1880s and 1890s. Not surprisingly, Texas railroads received the regulation that the Populists demanded. They called it reform, but rail managers warned that regulation would drive capital from the state. Both sides tampered with the truth. Nevertheless, Texans, much like agrarians across the land during the Gilded Age, were understandably concerned with pooling, rebates, absentee ownership, and railroad involvement in politics.

These concerns manifested themselves in the state's constitution and in the antirailroad hysteria led by James S. Hogg and his admirers. The Texas constitution, several times longer than the document fashioned for the nation nearly a century earlier in Philadelphia, was adopted in 1876. Article X contained numerous sections related to railroads. Included was the declaration that railroads in Texas were "public highways." It also affirmed that every railroad company must "keep public office in the state" and further ordered that no Texas-chartered railroad could consolidate with a "foreign" company (one chartered in another state). This forced interstate carriers to establish expensive and redundant subsidiaries with offices in Texas. The Missouri, Kansas & Texas, with headquarters in St. Louis, was obliged to establish the Missouri, Kansas & Texas of Texas with duplicate facilities in Dallas and the Chicago, Rock Island & Pacific, with general offices in Chicago, created the Chicago, Rock Island & Gulf, headquartered in Fort Worth.

The collision between the railroads and their agrarian constituents was probably unavoidable. Agrarians continued to perceive themselves as independent and self-sufficient when the country was rapidly becoming industrialized and more complex. They saw the railroads as providers of transportation vital to economic and social advancement, but their owners and managers saw them as investments—vehicles for profit. In any event, the steamcars were immediate and highly visible symbols of change. Consequently, they served as a lightning rod for farmers and small businessmen alike.

The love-hate relationship between the carriers and their Texas constituents continued into the twentieth century. Expanding urban areas as well as underdeveloped rural regions continued to complain about "railroad abuses," but at the same time they clamored for more rail service. The arguments put forward had a familiar ring: immigration would increase, schools and churches would be built, business enterprises of all sorts would spring up, transportation costs would be reduced, and the value of property would be appreciated. The quality of life was reckoned in direct ratio to the distance that one lived from a railroad and its station. Nevertheless, investors worried about the "business climate" in Texas, and railroad managers recalled hard lessons they had learned earlier by pushing lines ahead of the frontier.

Meanwhile, the principal carriers—and even some of the smaller ones—engaged in extensive colonization efforts. They sought to advertise the state in a variety of ways and produced a prodigious supply of pamphlets and flyers that ballyhooed the area. Many hired immigration agents who made contact with prospective emigrants, accompanied them aboard special homeseeker excursions, and arranged to move them to their new locations aboard "zulu" (emigrant) cars. One carrier, the Texas & Pacific, even built what was called the "Immigrant's Home" along its line at Baird. Some newcomers were recruited from abroad but most carriers sought emigrants from the northern states. The FW&DC, for instance, focused on Iowa.

The railroads, of course, were indulging their self-interest as they provided various services to attract additional population along their lines. Self-interest also motivated their agricultural development programs. Nevertheless, that which benefitted the railroads also benefitted those who lived in the service area. The Santa Fe and the Rock Island, for examples, actively labored to educate their agricultural constituents in several ways. They advocated new crops such as pinto beans, oats, peanuts, sorghums, and wheat; improved methods of tillage, marketing, grading, and packaging; and soil conservation. Several companies operated demonstration trains and even more hired agricultural representatives. Dairy agents from the St. Louis-San Francisco spoke to farmers in West Texas regarding "proofmethods of feeding, the care of dairy cows, and economical milk production." The Santa Fe promoted experimental acres; the Texas Midland established a demonstration farm at Terrell and the St. Louis, Brownsville & Mexico did the same at San Benito; the Rock Island assisted cotton farmers in the matter of soil building and erosion prevention; the International & Great Northern hired a plant breeder to develop a new variety of Bermuda onion; and the Rock Island held "farm prosperity" Chautauquas. The Gulf

Coast Lines and the Southern Pacific both popularized the Rio Grande Valley with homeseekers parties and the SP urged the creation of a canning industry there. Not simply interested in the farmer and his techniques, two railroad presidents, James E. Gorman of the CRI&P and William B. Storey of the Santa Fe, helped to form the National Congress of Boys and Girls Work Club.

For those railroads that dared thrust lines to or ahead of the frontier there were opportunities for townsite development. Count Joseph Telfener's high-sounding New York, Texas & Mexico was responsible for many of the towns between Rosenberg and Victoria; the T&P for Abilene, Sweetwater, and Colorado City; the Kansas City, Pittsburg & Gulf for Port Arthur; and, the Wichita Falls & Northwestern for Burkburnett. Among a half-dozen such projects, Roaring Springs was the premier townsite of the Quanah, Acme & Pacific Railway. These ventures appreciated the value of all properties, whether they were owned by the railroads or not, made money for their promoters, and enhanced and accelerated the process of settlement.

The railroad companies were somewhat slower to engage in industrial development programs. However, there was a natural and understandable symbiotic relationship between the carriers and the shippers they served. For instance, the construction of railroads in East Texas gave rise to the timber and forest products industry. Other industries such as rice and sugar-cane processing and meat packing similarly began with the establishment of reliable rail transportation. The state's rail lines also brought an increased volume of inbound manufactured goods as the Texas economy matured. Some companies, the Texas & Pacific and the Katy among them, were early and energetic exponents of industrial development, and shortly after the turn of the century, these companies, as well as the Santa Fe and the Frisco, established formal industrial departments. Particular growth occurred at the important Gulf ports, especially Galveston and Houston, where shippers could take advantage of an expanding rail network as well as coastal and interoceanic steamship transportation.

The railroad companies benefitted immensely after 1900 from traffic generated by the booming petroleum industry. Some railroads, like the Southern Pacific, were fortunate to have existing lines through what became important "oil patches;" others, such as the Santa Fe, were obliged to build branches in order to tap them; and, still others, the Wichita Falls, Ranger & Fort Worth, for example, were built specifically to serve the new industry. The carriers handled generous shipments of equipment as well as crude and re-

*This Fort Worth and Denver train with boxcars of grain sorghum is typical of the use of railroads to transport Texas farm products.*

fined products. The railroad companies themselves became important customers for the petroleum companies when they converted their locomotives from coal to oil and later when they replaced steam with diesel.

The development of short-line railroads in Texas mirrored the national pattern. These were built for several reasons: to haul logs or some specific commodity, to link areas that had been ignored by the trunk roads with the outside world, and, of course, to make money for their promoters. Still others were constructed by or for a particular shipper. Even as this is written there are still twenty short-line railroads in Texas aggregating 683 miles of track. They range in size from the one-mile Texas Transportation Company—an electric operation that serves Pearl Brewing in San Antonio—to the 243-mile Houston Belt & Terminal, an important switching company owned by several railroads serving Houston. The average length of these lines is 34.1 miles, but if the HB&T is excepted the average drops to 23.1.

The rise and fall of the state's interurban electric railway network likewise reflected the national pattern. Interurbans offered several advantages: they could provide clean, convenient, and frequent service; they could offer lower rates; they could be built rather inexpensively; and they often could turn a profit for their owners. Eventually Texas boasted almost 500 miles of interurban lines with the Dallas-based Texas Electric Railway emerging as the largest among eleven companies operating within the state. The era of electric traction was brief, however, and half of the Texas mileage disappeared before World War II with the rest shortly thereafter.

The last great construction boom in the state—and perhaps the last such boom in the country—occurred on the High Plains of West Texas. Railroads heretofore had exercised only a halting interest in the area. There were a few lines, owned by the Santa Fe, Fort Worth & Denver City, and the T&P, but it was not until after the recession following World War I that the carriers were energized to expand their operations there. It all began in 1923 when a "paper" railroad, the Texas Panhandle & Gulf, announced a grand plan to connect the two regions of its corporate namesake. Impressive projects were then proposed by the FW&DC, Rock Island, Santa Fe, T&P, Frisco, and even the Quanah, Acme & Pacific. These, in turn, sparked additional studies, rumors of studies, and still more "paper" railroads. The Fort Worth & Denver City finally emerged with permits for more new miles than the others, but the remaining challengers continued to press their studies. A total of 1,536 miles of new railroad were constructed in Texas between 1922 and 1933, much of it in the

Panhandle-Plains area. Individual projects were completed later, but the Texas boom was effectively ended by 1931, the victim of the Great Depression — and changed transportation circumstances.

During the 1930s Texas railroads suffered not only from the effects of the depression and dust storms but also from increased modal competition. The economy eventually improved and the winds abated, but the railroads would never again experience the near-monopoly status they had enjoyed earlier. Two examples will suffice to illustrate the change. Dougherty, a new townsite spawned by railroad construction in Floyd County, was one year old in March 1929; the largest delegation to attend its birthday party arrived from Lubbock—by automobile. On August 16, 1925, the *Fort Worth Record* devoted its front page to endorsement of a railroad project; the entirety of page two, however, was given to articles dealing with automobile sales, traffic jams, and advertisements for Paige & Jewett, Willys-Overland, and Essex motor cars. Autos and buses ate into local rail passenger revenues and trucks nipped at the less-than-carload freight business. The railroads responded by backing legislation designed to regulate motor transportation and establish weight limits on trucks. They also gathered statistics on motor vehicle accidents and urged strict enforcement of traffic laws. It went for naught. Their lack of success in meeting this competition coupled with the general economic dislocation led the carriers to abandon 891 miles of railroad between 1932 and the end of the decade.

Hard times softened somewhat the longstanding conflict between railroaders and customers. Each suffered but the natural and close friendship finally stood in stark relief as they struggled to survive. For their part the railroads reduced rates on food, feed, and outbound movements of livestock, and shippers took advantage of these concessions. Railroads also hauled drinking water to drought-stricken communities and carload commodities for the Red Cross under "free tariffs."

The depression finally passed, but was replaced by yet another struggle, World War II. The carriers, happy to say, were remarkably able to handle the flood of traffic that came to them as a natural consequence. With the threat of U-boat attack precluding coastal shipments, entire trainloads of crude and refined petroleum rolled out of Texas over the Texas & Pacific, Katy, and other lines. These trains ducked in and out of sidings as they shared the overburdened tracks with troop trains, MAIN trains (military equipment), in addition to the usual flow of high-speed passenger and freight trains as well as the humble locals. The Southern Pacific was even obliged to institute commuter runs for the purpose of moving laborers to and from shipbuilding sites along the Gulf Coast. It was not without difficulty but the railroads performed well. They handled 90 percent of the wartime freight volume and 97 percent of military passenger traffic. Indeed, it was their finest hour.

When the war ended, Texans quickly reaffirmed their love affair with the automobile. Local passenger trains and interurbans were early casualties. However, the carriers fought hard to retain long-haul passenger business and the attendant mail and express revenues. They spent millions of dollars for shiny new streamlined trains —diesel powered with stainless steel and air-conditioned cars. These included the Fort Worth & Denver City's *Texas Zephyr* between Denver and Dallas; Rock Island's *Twin Star Rocket,* linking Minneapolis with Houston; and Santa Fe's *Texas Chief,* serving Galveston from Chicago. The Dallas-Houston route was served by three SP trains—the *Owl, Sunbeam,* and *Hustler*—and one representing the FW&DC, the *Sam Houston Zephyr.* Perhaps the most competitive corridor was that between St. Louis and San Antonio, where the Missouri Pacific and the Texas & Pacific jointly sponsored the *Texas Eagle,* handling through sleeping cars from New York and Washington and offering connections for Mexico City via the *Aztec Eagle.* San Antonio also greeted the *Texas Special,* another fine train from St. Louis handling New York and Washington Pullmans, sponsored by the Katy and Frisco. Queen of them all may have been Southern Pacific's *Sunset Limited,* linking New Orleans with Los Angeles via Houston, San Antonio, and El Paso. This jewel featured sleepers and chair accommodations as well as lounges, diners, and coffee-shop cars. Such luxury trains raised rail travel to its most elegant level, but the streamliner era passed quickly—a victim of the interstate highway system and jet aircraft. Amtrak assumed responsibility for the interstate rail passenger system on May 1, 1971, but retained only skeletal operations in the Lone Star State.

The railroads faced increased modal competition for their freight revenues in the postwar years, too, but in this area they were far more successful than in the passenger field. They prospered naturally from the vast expansion of the petroleum, petrochemical, and chemical industries and from the general Sunbelt boom. Yet they were also responsible for much of this economic expansion as each company actively sought to locate industries along its lines. The Southern Pacific, for instance, led the nation's carriers in locating new industries during 1959 and for many years averaged a net gain of one per day. The carriers also pioneered in the creation of industrial parks—fully planned properties developed for manufacturing, distribution, and sometimes retail and service centers. Several roads, including the Cotton Belt, Santa Fe, SP, Missouri Pacific, and Houston Belt & Terminal were particularly energetic in this regard. These activities generated jobs and traffic and made Texas increasingly attractive from a business point of view.

Texas remains number one in terms of railroad mileage and is served by seven class-one carriers in addition to a host of smaller lines. The primary rail tonnage originating in the state includes nonmetallic minerals, chemicals, farm products and food, petroleum products, and lumber and wood products. Primary commodities terminating in Texas include farm products, nonmetallic minerals, coal, chemicals, and other bulk materials. The railroad companies themselves are important employers; over 29,000 Texans were employed by them in 1982. Texas railroad companies have been and will continue to be involved in the movement toward mega-mergers, but the state's general network of lines is not likely to be dramatically affected.

The past is truly prologue. Texas railroads of tomorrow may be expected to play an important role in the development of the state —just as they have in the past.

*The Greer era got Texas highways "out of the mud" and into superhighways. Downtown Houston on an Interstate 45 interchange, Buffalo Bayou in the foreground.*

— Highway Department photo

# 11

## Highway Development: A "Concrete" History of Twentieth-Century Texas

*John D. Huddleston*

Texas' highway transportation system presently ranks as one of the nation's best. Federal interstates, designated state highways, and rural farm-to-market roads link the semiarid regions of West Texas with the East Texas piney woods and join the Panhandle Plains with the Rio Grande Valley. Statistically, the state's expansiveness dictates the need for a comprehensive network of roads. For instance, a traveler journeying from El Paso to Orange would drive approximately 860 miles to traverse the state. A similar driving trip north would take the sojourner into the Wyoming heartland. While the New England visitor could view several of the smaller states in a single day, a traveler could, at present driving limits, spend two working day equivalents on Texas' roads. How did a state as vast as Texas with her many topographical and geographical divisions attain a superior highway system? The answer lies in both the history and politics of the Lone Star State.

Historically, the Indians, Spanish conquistadors, Mexican authorities, and eventually the Anglo-Americans traversed Texas' primitive trails. As in the case of the *El Camino Real* stretching from San Juan Bautista on the Rio Grande to Nacogdoches in East Texas, most early roads were only vaguely designated paths linking Texas' few towns and shallow fording points on her many rivers. Nevertheless, these routes proved invaluable in the region's settlement. Road transportation also played a significant role in the 1836

Revolution. After destroying the Alamo defenders, Mexican President Antonio Lopez de Santa Anna's armies moved into East Texas in an attempt to drive out forcibly the remaining Anglo-Americans. There, in an area devoid of towns and roads, the Mexican columns bogged down in that which Mexican General Vicente Filisola described as "endless and everlasting mud." The wearied and frustrated column under Santa Anna then served an easier prey at San Jacinto for Sam Houston's Texan Army.

Transportation remained a continuing source of difficulty from the Republican years through the Reconstruction era. Although authorizing an ambitious road-building plan, the Texas national government virtually possessed no funds for internal improvements. Most roads were no better than trails of cleared brush, dusty in the dry months and quagmires in the rainy season. Conditions remained unchanged after Texas entered the American union. From 1845-1861, increasing Indian depredations did result in the United States Army establishing a line of forts across the North and West Texas frontier. Roads eventually developed to serve areas protected by these fortifications. With Texas outside the major theaters of conflict during the Civil War, the state sustained little physical damage. However, the Union blockade of the Confederate coastline forced much of the normal coastal trade inland and proved, once again, the existing inferiority of Texas' roads. In the aftermath of the war, the Republican Reconstruction leadership actively promoted railroad, not highway, development for the state.

Throughout the closing years of the nineteenth century, road construction and maintenance remained the sole responsibility of local governments. Although acknowledging the poor quality of Texas roads, the state government took refuge behind a cloak of post-Reconstruction poverty. Officials generally claimed that Radical Republican graft had placed extreme burdens on the state. The state government remained incapable of financing road work, and both industry and agriculture suffered. There existed a vicious circle — because of poor roads, resulting poverty; because of poverty, poor roads. Despite an obvious need, all legislative efforts to establish even a modicum of state control failed for the next dozen years. The legislature authorized county road taxes in 1883 and county road bonds in 1903 but steadfastly refused any move toward state control.

By 1910 the automobile clearly had passed from its novelty stage. Texas county registration figures showed 14,286 vehicles within the state and projected approximately 200,000 motor vehicles in Texas by 1917. The automobile represented a transportation challenge different from the railroad. For railroads, the track by necessity preceded the rolling stock. In the case of the automobile, the rolling stock came first and necessitated adequate track. To promote this point, the Texas Good Roads Association organized in 1911 and conducted educational programs statewide. The federal government served, however, as the major catalyst toward state assumption of road construction and maintenance. In 1916, Congress passed a national highway act and pledged matching funds for all states. A codicil to the act declared that no state could receive assistance unless it had a central highway agency to coordinate road building. Therefore, in 1917, the Texas legislature finally acquiesced and established the Texas Highway Department. Ironically, a federal monetary inducement, and not statewide road considerations, led to the formation of a state road agency.

In the immediate years after 1917, the Texas Highway Department operated under a number of handicaps. The first three road commissioners did not personally cooperate to the degree that their successors would. Each commissioner cultivated a cadre of loyal supporters within the road agency, and incompetent employees usually were not removed for fear of offending one or more of the commissioners. Personal partisanship existed, and bureaucratic inefficiency resulted. The First World War proved another debilitating factor. On the very day Texas Governor James Edward Ferguson signed the state highway bill into law, the United States Senate approved President Woodrow Wilson's proposed declaration of war against Germany. By September 1918, the United States Highway Council, a federal wartime agency, had declared a virtual moratorium on all work not related to the war efforts. Until the war's termination, most road work ceased. Finally, many counties continued to build roads. The 1917 road law granted the state only the loosest supervision over county road activity. Counties continued to plan, grant bids, and expend funds for road construction. The state simply reimbursed counties for their road related expenditures. Before a coordinated system of state highways was possible, this procedure would have to end.

Although world peace and a change of road commissioners solved a major part of the state road agency's problems by 1919, county road building represented a long-term problem of the severest magnitude. Until 1924, the state seemed unable to deal effectively with the situation. However, in that year, the counties finally overstepped their authority. State law divided automobile registration fees between the counties and state and provided that the state's share would be used for road maintenance, previously a sole function of county governments. Several disgruntled county tax collectors refused to remit the state's percentage of fees and obtained an injunction against the law. The state Court of Civil Appeals dissolved the injunction and ruled that the legislature possessed the function of both building and maintaining highways through agencies it so designated. The legislature clearly intended, the court ruled, that the Texas Highway Department rather than the counties should administer the system. Ironically, the state gained the upper hand only because of the counties' monetary greed.

While state officials rejoiced over the favorable judicial ruling, other observers recognized a far greater danger to road development. In 1924, political strife within Texas over the Ku Klux Klan paved the way for former Governor James (Jim) Ferguson's return to power. Although impeached and permanently disbarred from office in 1917, Jim Ferguson promoted the gubernatorial aspirations of his wife, Miriam Amanda Ferguson. Previously a housewife by occupation, the generally reserved Mrs. Ferguson filed for office as an anti-Klan candidate. Realistically, however, she served as a proxy for her husband. After a vigorous primary campaign, Mrs. Ferguson swept to victory over her Republican opponent in November 1924. Like most politicians, the Fergusons had developed a vast following of supporters, and those followers provided assistance in anticipation of holding offices in the subsequently elected administration. The Fergusons quickly rewarded their partisans with hundreds of agency positions. As the largest state agency, the Texas Highway Department seemed particularly vulnerable to blatant political manipulation. The agency led all southern states both in motor vehicular registrations and in total road expenditures. This large monetary commitment invited intervention. Few procedures had been established since the state attained full responsibility for road maintenance. Conceivably, the Fergusons could institute, and then exploit, a lucrative road maintenance program. In addition, the legislature in 1923, had established six-year, rotating terms of office for the three-man road commission. Mrs. Ferguson inherited the privilege of appointing an entirely new road commission. Given these circumstances, many observers feared the possible consequences of Jim Ferguson's return to power.

Rumors of mismanagement quickly centered on the Ferguson-appointed commissioners. After an extensive investigation, Attorney General Daniel J. Moody filed suit in late 1925 against several road construction companies. The suits alleged that the highway commissioners had allocated contracts for hundreds of miles of work and that numerous irregularities existed. For example, the

American Road Company contract with the highway commission provided that the firm be paid on a monthly basis for a two-course application of asphalt, irrespective of whether or not the company chose to apply a second course. Moody also charged that these contracts had been allocated without competitive bids or bonds and that former Governor Jim Ferguson, the commissioners, and the contractors had illegally planned, met, and negotiated exorbitant and wasteful contracts. These suits revealed the naked truth concerning the Ferguson-controlled road agency. The highway commissioners had initiated correspondence with their personal friends in the road construction business and then negotiated multimillion dollar contracts with companies so small, in some cases, as to be unable to fulfill their obligations. Most of the contracts had been allocated on a cost-plus 10 percent basis, so few if any contractors sought to hold down expenditures. On a cost-plus basis, escalating costs meant higher company profits. In each case, either the offending company settled out of court and voluntarily returned excessive profits, or the court ordered restitution to the state. These suits saved Texans hundreds of thousands of dollars and propelled Attorney General Moody into the political limelight.

Continuing allegations of wrongdoing fueled a growing anti-Ferguson movement in late 1925. Two of the three highway commissioners resigned, and rumors of mismanagement also clouded the state prison system and textbook commissions. With political observers calling for Mrs. Ferguson's removal, Attorney General Moody gained in credibility as a potential gubernatorial replacement. Hailed by the *Dallas Morning News* as "the Moses capable of leading the people from the political wilderness," Moody soon announced for the position. Undeterred by these events, the governor also cast her bonnet back into the gubernatorial race. After a bitter campaign, Dan Moody defeated Mrs. Ferguson in the Democratic primaries. Since Texas was essentially a one-party state, Moody would be elected governor in November 1926. Anti-Fergusonites and good road advocates expressed delight in the prospects of a Moody governorship.

Although temporarily vanquished by the voters, the Fergusons continued to wreak havoc with the state road program. In late 1926, the United States Bureau of Public Roads suspended all federal aid monies to the Texas Highway Department, pending a thorough investigation of Ferguson-initiated monetary shortages. Even after Moody's inauguration, Jim Ferguson continued to intrigue against the road department. For instance, in April 1927 Mr. Ferguson alleged that the chief officer of the road agency, State Highway Engineer Robert A. Thompson, had illegally drawn a second salary as a consulting engineer for the City of Dallas. In an ill-founded effort to further embarrass the Moody administration, Ferguson supporters in the legislature also forced a special investigation of the agency in 1928. These actions cast considerable doubt on a Moody-appointed road commission which diligently attempted to restore order to the state road program.

Despite the Fergusons, Moody supervised a complete administrative overhaul of the state road department. The governor appointed able and ethical men as commissioners, and he personally convinced the United States Bureau of Public Roads to lift its aid suspension on the Texas highway agency. Yet the governor's insistence that a comprehensive state road policy be adopted must be cited as his most significant contribution to Texas' road program. Moody appointed a Citizens' Advisory Committee in November 1928 to formulate Texas' future highway program. To all observers, financing posed the greatest single barrier to long-term development. The pay-as-you-go, biennial appropriations process seemed inadequate for a stable road program. A whimsical or unsympathetic legislature could effectively cripple Texas' program by either denying or restricting appropriations and, in the process, force the federal road bureau to reinstate its aid suspension policy. Without a fixed income independent of the state legislature, the Texas Highway Department would remain, many argued, a pawn in the hands of petty politicians.

State Highway Commissioner Ross Shaw Sterling of Houston, advocated a massive bond issue to provide long-term funding with deferred payment. Since the state constitution generally forbade the creation of debts, Sterling proposed a constitutional amendment to legitimatize a $350 million bond issue. State Representative Leonard Tillotson, author of the 1917 bill creating the state highway agency, and other good road advocates opposed a bond issue and recommended doubling the 2 percent per gallon gasoline tax. Most also felt that the legislature should be retained as the financing agent of the road program because despite the legislature's political deficiencies, only it could sustain enough leverage over the highway department to insure the judicious expenditure of the state's monies.

The question over road bonding clearly divided Texas' leading highway advocates. While a significant minority favored the issuance of bonds, a majority opposed the Sterling bond plan. Conservatism held the people's fancy, and politicians throughout Texas echoed the public's disdain for extensive governmental activity. The decentral-

*Road work in Lee County using an ox-drawn scraper in the early 1900s.*

— Texas Highway Department

ized, creaky, and expensive structure of state government virtually insured limited activity and the rejection of expensive governmental policies, such as the multimillion dollar road program Sterling advocated. Prominent Texans remained unwilling either to see the road department freed from the tutelage of the legislature or to see the state abandon the fiscally conservative pay-as-you-go monetary policy. Even Governor Moody refused to endorse the bond proposal. With good road advocates divided among themselves, the Forty-first Texas Legislature, meeting in 1929, could not agree on any financing plan. Moody had to call the legislature into special session just to get a biennial road appropriations for 1930-31.

Inevitably, the question of highway financing entered into the 1930 gubernatorial primaries. After due consideration, Governor Moody declined candidacy for a third term, citing personal and professional reasons. In May, former Governor Miriam Ferguson declared for the position. One week later road commissioner Sterling also announced. His decision surprised few political observers. The chairman had traveled extensively throughout the state and addressed numerous professional and civic organizations. If successful as a candidate, Sterling could promote his multimillion dollar bond issue. In all, eleven candidates filed in one of Texas' most exciting gubernatorial primaries. Focusing on the corrupt nature of previous Ferguson rule, Sterling promised a business-like and ethical administration. For their part, the Fergusons criticized Sterling's road commission record and predicted that the potential graft and waste associated with a bond issue would "make Teapot Dome look like thirty cents." Despite trailing Mrs. Ferguson in the May primary, Sterling defeated her in the August runoff. Ross Sterling, road bond advocate, would be Texas' next governor.

The collapse of the nation's economy, which began in New York on October 23, 1929, did not immediately affect Texas. Since there had been comparatively little industrial development within the state, there occurred none of the massive unemployment and crushing fear which pervaded the industrial North and East. Relatively few Texans owned corporate stocks, and a majority of Texans—the farmers—had lived through commodity price crises before. Texan morale and fundamental concepts of society essentially remained unchanged, despite the market crash. Thus Sterling felt Texas could pursue a highway bond plan even as the rest of the nation slipped into the Great Depression. The state highway commission's 1931 seventh biennial report, which Sterling had prepared, supported the concept of road bonding. The report endorsed a ten-year building program to be financed through a compromise, combination bond issue and pay-as-you-go biennial appropriation plan. A $200 million bond issue would be retired through the motor fuel tax and would be used both to supplement present construction funds and to reimburse the counties for funds expended on the state road system since the creation of the department.

By the time the legislature convened to assess the combination bond issue and biennial appropriations proposal, many Texas counties had suffered financial difficulties. The state constitution enjoined only the state, and not the counties, from deficit spending. For years, virtually every county had liberally adopted massive bond issues. Despite large interest debts on these bonds, the counties prospered while the economy remained solvent. As the Great Depression's economic effects arrived in Texas, most counties faced the specter of financial chaos and extensive bond payment defaults. Just as states will appeal to the federal government for aid, so too did Texas' counties appeal to the state for assistance. The choice for the legislature and the governor increasingly became either to save the counties or to finance a long-term road program. Both objectives could not be simultaneously satisfied. While the Texas Senate concurred with the governor on the necessity of a bond issue, the House of Representatives twice refused to endorse a bond amendment which would have stimulated the state's sagging economy by providing road construction related jobs. Governor Sterling, on the other hand, as a conservative businessman could not accept any relief measure designed solely to alleviate county and local governmental financial obligations. At odds within itself, the state government appeared incapable of coordinated action against the depression.

Inevitably, the failure of the legislature and governor to provide economic leadership, the ever deepening depression, and widely publicized legal battles between Texas and Oklahoma over the shared cost of several Red River bridges insured that highway politics would become the focal point of the 1932 Democratic primaries. In mid-February, realizing that citizen discontent heightened her chances of regaining the governorship, Miriam Ferguson announced for the position. Initially, most political observers greatly discounted the former chief executive's chances. Preoccupied with the economic scene, Governor Sterling filed for reelection several months later. Seven other candidates eventually filed in a race reminiscent of the last gubernatorial primary. During the campaign the Fergusons opposed a bond issue and stressed a relief measure for the counties. Criticizing the Sterling-appointed highway commission, Jim Ferguson cited allegations of misconduct and waste and promised a wholesale removal of Sterling appointees if his wife were elected. Sterling shocked his supporters by abandoning temporarily any public support for a bond issue. The governor emphasized his business-like and self-professed progressive administration, as compared to the Ferguson's previous misrule. After leading Sterling by a surprising 106,000 votes in the May primary, Mrs. Ferguson won the August runoff by only 4,000 votes. Mindful of the 1925-26 Ferguson-initiated road scandals, good road advocates and highway employees feared another round of rough-and-tumble Texas politics in which the highway agency would become a reluctant participant.

Despite his fiscal conservatism, Governor Sterling could no longer ignore the persistent appeals of county officials who urged him to act decisively against the depression. Therefore, in late August, less than one week after his reelection defeat, Sterling called the Forty-second Texas Legislature into special session to consider state assumption of county road indebtedness. When the special session passed such a bill, Sterling promptly signed the measure. The law required the state to assume all interest and equities of county road districts and to reimburse these governmental units for expenditures on the state road system. The law further diverted one-fourth of the gasoline tax fund to a "County Road District Highway Fund" and established a board to oversee reimbursement procedures. The passage of this law thus represented a final defeat for road bond advocates. With county indebtedness in excess of $100 million, a bond issue of any significant size remained out of the question.

While highway officials greatly feared the monetary effects of the legislature's actions, the Fergusons remained the immediate problem of the road agency. The Sterling-appointed commission escalated the allocation of available highway monies before Mrs. Ferguson's inauguration while publicly reassuring all parties that its actions were not politically motivated. Privately, officials candidly stated their intense dislike of the Fergusons. In an effort to block allocation of road contracts, Jim Ferguson filed suit and received a temporary state injunction against the road commission. However, in December 1932, the state filed a general demurrer against the temporary injunction. This action, in essence, allowed the road commission to allocate hundreds of thousands of dollars of federal emergency work relief funds before Mrs. Ferguson came to power. As soon as she entered office, Governor Ferguson began a concerted attempt once again to control the Texas Highway Department. Although the commission had allocated virtually all available construction monies, the department still could serve as a source of patronage for her political supporters. The governor first asked the legislature to investigate allegations of financial wrongdoing and waste by the commission. After two weeks of testimony, the legislature could find only an approximate one hundred dollar shortage within the department's multimillion dollar budget. A Del Rio, Texas, section foreman had illegally padded his payroll account. The money had been repaid, however, and the employee discharged. Although rebuffed in her attempt to discredit the commission, the governor soon inaugurated a new program to control it. In February 1933, Governor Ferguson announced the nomination to the road commission of Frank L. Denison, a long-time Fergusonite and a road contractor who had been investigated during the 1925-1926 road scandals. After heated debate in the Texas Senate, Denison's appointment failed to receive the necessary two-thirds vote for confirmation. In an unprecedented move, the governor requested the Senate to reconsider the nomination and argued that a simple majority vote rather than two-thirds legally would suffice. When the Senate again refused the appointment, the governor presented Denison his papers as commission chairman in defiance of the Texas Senate. Attorney General James V. Allred then filed suit to block Denison from sitting with the highway commission. The incumbent road commissioners also greeted Denison with cold indifference when he visited the highway building at Austin.

The Fergusons eventually redirected their attack and forced an elective highway commission bill through the House Committee on Highways. The bill provided that five commissioners would be elected in the November 1934 general election and take office in January 1935. Until then, the existing road commission would be abolished and interim members appointed by the governor. When anti-Ferguson forces in the House amended the bill to leave the commission's status unchanged until the 1934 general election, the Fergusons soon lost interest. With the failure to confirm Denison or to pass an elective commission bill, the Fergusons could try only one other ploy to control the Texas road agency. If they could not control the department from within, then why not influence the agency by controlling the federal bureau which monitored the activities of the state agency? In August 1933, United States Congressman Fritz Lanham of Dallas began promoting his brother Frank V. Lanham for the federal government position of Senior Highway Construction Supervisor for Texas. In this post, Lanham would exercise enormous supervisory power over the Texas commission. In fact, Frank Lanham had served as the chairman of the Texas Highway Commission in 1925-1926. The road scandals of Mrs. Ferguson's first gubernatorial administration occurred, in large measure, because of Frank Lanham. Now the Fergusons hoped to bring the Texas road commission again under his control. After private messages and meetings with federal officials, Texas good road advocates successfully blocked the Lanham appointment.

Rebuffed at every turn, the Fergusons chose not to seek reelection in 1934. Texas Attorney General James Allred's election lulled good road advocates into a false sense of security since the governor-elect had a long history of supporting road development. They obviously had no way of anticipating that Allred and his associates would try, as the Fergusons had, to manipulate highway affairs. The governor appointed new commissioners, who in turn replaced the road department's chief engineer and many subordinate employees for political reasons. Even worse for the agency, Governor Allred proposed a three-million-dollar diversion of highway revenues into a newly created old-age assistance fund. Supporters of the department predicted that the agency would suffer massive deficits, lose thousands of workers, and forfeit federal aid. Editorials in many of the state's newspapers ridiculed the governor's alleged statement that "eating is more important than riding" and wondered if many good road advocates agreed with the governor's logic. Facing intense public pressure, the legislature eventually declined to address the governor's proposal and pursued an independent road program. It created the Texas Department of Public Safety and transferred the State Highway Patrol from the highway department to the new agency. The legislature also passed Texas' first driver's licensing law, which certified three million Texas drivers. Yet the law failed to include a provision for the examination of new drivers. The Forty-fifth Legislature rectified this serious omission, passed a workmen's compensation program for road agency employees, authorized Texas centennial roadside markers, and inaugurated the state's present roadside beautification program.

Despite politics, the Texas road program actually prospered during the depression. By 1937, the state highway department had completed all the work originally planned when the agency was created. In the worst of the depression, the agency had pursued a vigorous construction program. In the period, 1935-39, approximately $100,000 a day or $6,500 per mile had been expended. However, numerous problems remained. With the road system expanding, maintenance expenditures declined to the point of endangering the entire system. Sectional interests also hampered the state road agency's construction efforts. Officials throughout Texas wanted highways built for their constituents. By 1939, an average of forty-five delegations appeared before each monthly highway commission hearing. To avoid charges of favoritism, the commissioners gave each delegation a complete hearing and judiciously divided available funding between the competing interests. So common had the practice become of rewarding all comers that by 1940 the road commission had designated future construction projects for the next fourteen years. Traffic safety also became an increasingly complex problem. As vehicular density and speed mounted, the Texas Highway Department had to reevaluate its construction and maintenance procedures. In the 1930s the road agency's engineers pioneered the concepts of flat slope roads with shallow ditches and wide-surfaced road shoulders. The agency also introduced graded and longer curves into its procedures to facilitate increased vehicular speeds.

The constant uncertainty of Texas politics represented a continuing enigma more serious than maintenance, sectional interests, or traffic safety for the road program. In the 1938 Democratic primary, politics and showmanship produced Wilbert Lee "Pass the Biscuits Pappy" O'Daniel, a Fort Worth businessman and radio personality as Texas' next governor. Snubbing legislators and relying heavily upon an unofficial cabinet of business advisors, the political neophyte governor alienated the state's top politicos. As a result, O'Daniel quickly underwent a rude political lesson at the hands of a recalcitrant Forty-sixth Legislature. With one of the three road commissioners retiring, the governor nominated his close friend and business adviser, Carr P. Collins of Dallas, to fill the vacancy. Noting that Texas' governors from Jim Ferguson to James Allred had respected an unofficial precedent of appointing road commissioners from separate geographic areas of the state, senators pointed out that North Texas already had regional representation on the commission. Since East Texas would be denied representation when the outgoing commissioner retired, it made perfect sense to senators of that section that the governor once again select from their area. The Senate rejected the Collins nomination, forced the withdrawal of a second nominee, and refused confirmation of a third gubernatorial choice. O'Daniel finally relented and nominated the East Texas road advocate, Brady P. Gentry of Tyler. The Senate then acquiesced to the governor's new found wisdom.

With the war in Europe nearly a year old, Texans in 1940 faced the prospects of a no-holds-barred gubernatorial race. The state highway program might again prove a major issue of the primaries since included among the four candidates opposing O'Daniel's reelection bid were former Governor Miriam Ferguson and former Texas Highway Commissioner Harry Hines of Dallas. Texas good road advocates, as well as the road agency's "old guard," certainly did not welcome the Fergusons' return. Under usual circumstances, Texas' road advocates would have endorsed wholeheartedly the candidacy of a former highway commissioner. However, Harry Hines had earned the wrath of many individuals and organizations for his significant role in Governor Allred's manipulation of the road agency. Therefore, Hines' 1940 campaign did not attract much support despite the fact that the candidate had compiled an extensive list of alleged supporters during his road commission years. On election day, with Governor O'Daniel sweeping 54.3 percent of the vote, Hines and Mrs. Ferguson finished third and fourth respectively. Apparently, Texans had lost their fascination for highway politics. The 1940 primary marked both the last time a highway commissioner made a serious bid for the governor's post and the final political retirement of James and Miriam Ferguson.

By late 1940, the possibility of America entering World War II loomed ominously. Federal officials designated thousands of miles of completed and planned roads to be of strategic military importance. Of these, Texas held 6,375 miles, or more than any other single state. Massive federal aid insured that the Texas highway construction and maintenance program boomed throughout 1941. With the onset of war, the Texas road commission quickly canceled all non-strategic highway work and volunteered complete road construction units for the war effort. The road department zealously supported the military and even criticized publicly the United States Manpower Commission when that agency listed road maintenance and repair workers as draft deferrable civilians. The road commission promised not to use the ruling to harbor "draft dodgers." By 1944, the commission proudly reported eighteen hundred employees in uniform and lamented the loss of two dozen employees killed or held as prisoners of war.

The war effort greatly disrupted the state's previous construction and maintenance program. Federal prohibitions on asphalt usage severely limited the agency's maintenance capacity. The legislature, therefore, ordered the road department to reduce speeds throughout the state to prevent the road system's deterioration. Restricted speeds, in turn, led to reduced gasoline sales, which even more adversely affected the agency by dropping gasoline tax revenues significantly. With an uncertain monetary future and an approximate 30 percent shortage in personnel, the department struggled throughout the war. Innovation became a hallmark of the agency. For instance, since rubber was in short supply, in early 1943 the department conducted tubeless tire tests on previously tubed tires. Although the tests were not successful, they proved to be significant in the postwar development of the tubeless tire.

Despite the problematic times, the road agency planned for the future. Officials realized that the wartime curtailment of the regular construction and maintenance program and increased military traffic would necessitate an enormous postwar road program. However, a successful program would have to raise millions of dollars just to qualify for matching federal assistance. To do so, the legislature liberalized its highway funding policies and even authorized county governmental units to contribute funds to the state road department, if they chose to accelerate local road construction in the postwar era. With federal aid, increased biennial appropriations, and possible county assistance, the agency would realize sufficient funding. A second fundamental issue to the success of the postwar program involved guaranteeing the agency's finances. Despite federal prohibitions against the practice, previous legislatures had considered the state highway fund as fair game for raiding. Therefore, road proponents introduced an antidiversion constitutional amendment in the Forty-ninth Texas Legislature. Supported by Governor Coke Stevenson and the Texas Good Roads Association, the bill would permanently freeze the statutory distribution of the motor fuel tax, driver's license fees, and automobile registration fees. After bitter debate, the legislature submitted the proposal to the people. In November 1946, Texans adopted the amendment 231,834 for to 58,555 against. After three decades of politics and war, the state road department had been granted a guaranteed income.

The end of World War II and the adoption of the antidiversion amendment inaugurated a new era in Texas' highway development. No longer distracted by purely political considerations, able and judicious men under the leadership of State Highway Engineer Dewitt C. Greer guided the road agency. A gentle, learned man, with tenacious organizational ability, Greer sagaciously promoted the Texas Highway Department fortunes for over four decades. The state's farm-to-market systems, begun in 1949, and her participation in the 1956 federal interstate program stand today as enduring achievements to all postwar good roads advocates and especially to Dewitt Greer. Graced with dynamic leadership and a nondivertible income, the state road agency remained free from the political entanglements which clouded its first thirty years. Even Republican Governor William Clements' 1978 victory and subsequent appointment of the state's first Republican Party road commissioners failed to embroil the Highway Department in controversy. Texas' road program had matured into one of the nation's finest.

*Another big Texas gusher "The Texas Chief" blowing in in 1919, in Burkburnett, Texas.*

— Photo courtesy J. C. and W. F. Reynolds, Wichita Falls

# 12

## Black Gold: Oil Development in Texas

*Bobby D. Weaver*

"Texas Oil Era Fading: Declining production threatens century of prosperity" screamed headlines in the *Dallas Morning News* on Sunday, December 19, 1982. The article went on to point out all the benefits accruing to the state from petroleum production. "Oil has given birth to the largest corporations in Texas, spawned vast private and public fortunes and created the industry that pays more taxes than any other in the state." All this is true. The economic growth of Texas in the twentieth century is closely linked to the growth of the petroleum industry, but perhaps sounding the death knell of that industry is a little premature. Maybe investigating the history of the petroleum industry in Texas might put the present dilemma in more perspective.

Previous to the twentieth century, petroleum production in Texas was negligible. As early as the 1860s small oil discoveries were made near Nacogdoches and later in the San Antonio area, but they were hardly worth noting. Then in 1895 a small field was discovered near Corsicana. A refinery was even built at Corsicana, but by the end of 1900 the state's annual production stood at only 836,039 barrels. This small beginning represented a unique addition to the state's economy, although few recognized its potential.

Texas in 1900 was a decidedly rural state with agriculture dominating the economy. Over 82 percent of the total of three million Texans in that year listed their residences as rural. Manufacturing was a miniscule portion of the economy. Newspapers were filled with land advertisements and agricultural related news. The state's wealth was considered to be composed of cotton, cattle, and land.

Texas did not enter the twentieth century in 1900. For Texas, the twentieth century exploded into life on January 10, 1901, when the Lucas No. 1 blew in at Spindletop, near Beaumont. The state's growth and development changed course at that moment. This first major oil discovery in Texas flowed wildly for six days at an estimated rate of 75,000 barrels of oil per day before it was capped. Thousands rushed to see the sight and rampant speculation in oil properties developed. An estimated $11,000,000 was actually invested in the field, but total capitalization was almost $232,000,000, prompting some newspapermen to name the field "Swindletop." This spectacular beginning of the petroleum industry in Texas set the tone for most of the subsequent discoveries in both the areas of production and investment.

Petroleum production jumped to 4,292,658 barrels in 1901 and in 1902 Spindletop alone accounted for 94 percent of the state's oil production with 17,421,000 barrels. Leases on the 240-acre Spindletop salt dome were so small that many were just barely large enough to contain a derrick. Wells were drilled so close together that there was hardly any room to work, and there seemed to be no end to the black gold.

Within three years of the Spindletop discovery, the salt dome formations lying in a 150-mile radius of Beaumont were being drilled. Fields like Sour Lake, Batson, and Humble boosted production. The fantastic gushers in the Gulf Coast area soon created an unprecedented oil glut that attracted worldwide attention. At one point, in 1901, oil sold as low as three cents per barrel while drinking water for oil-field workers cost five cents a cup.

The petroleum industry was in its infancy in 1901 when the Spindletop discovery electrified the world. Technology was crude and most of the industry business activity was conducted by independent oil operators with limited financial resources, but unlimited ingenuity and nerve. That situation has remained a consistent part of the oil industry, particularly during any particular phase of discovery and early development.

Within months of the Spindletop discovery, the process of converting the petroleum business from small independent operations to large corporate control had its beginnings. Both Gulf Oil Company and the Texas Company were organized at that time. Gulf operated through several subsidiary companies, including the J. M. Guffey Petroleum Company and the Gulf Refining Company of Louisiana. The present company was incorporated under a Pennsylvania charter in 1922. The Texas Company was founded by J. S. Cullinan, who had built the original Texas refinery at Corsicana. He called his company the Texas Fuel Company and in 1902 reorganized the corporation as The Texas Company. Both these companies, along with the Sun Oil Company of Pennsylvania, were instrumental in developing pipelines, building refineries, and establishing export facilities in the Port Arthur-Beaumont area. These activities, which began as early as 1901, were responsible for ultimately creating a major industrial region along the southeast Texas Gulf Coast.

Meanwhile, in 1911, another giant in the oil business, Humble Oil Company, was formed by a group of Houston investors. Later, as the Humble Oil and Refining Company, it became an affiliate of Standard of New Jersey. Humble built gigantic refining facilities in the Houston area and expanded its production and pipeline activities to every part of Texas. These giant corporations and a host of smaller oil companies were instrumental in increasing Texas manufacturing output by 200 percent within a decade of the Spindletop discovery.

The seemingly inexhaustible supply of inexpensive oil produced along the Gulf Coast had the effect of stimulating more use of petroleum as a fuel. In 1901 major railroad lines, including the Houston and Texas Central, the Gulf, Colorado, and Santa Fe and the Southern Pacific began converting the coal-burning locomotives to oil burners. Within a matter of four or five years nearly all coal-burning locomotives in Texas had converted. The example of the railroads was soon followed by steamship companies, particularly those operating in the Gulf of Mexico and the Carribean. Additionally, numerous small manufacturing concerns scattered throughout the state began using petroleum products as a fuel. The availability of this cheap new fuel began to attract new industries to the state. Thus, by 1910 the enormous 200 percent increase in Texas manufacturing could either be traced directly or indirectly to the petroleum business.

The spectacular beginning of the oil business along the Gulf Coast prompted the development of "oil fever" throughout Texas. Oil men fanned out over the state with a gleam in their eyes that only vision of immense wealth can evoke. In 1902 a field was discovered at Brownwood and some small production developed in Jack and Montague counties. Then, between 1902 and 1907, another major field was discovered at Petrolia in Clay County near Wichita Falls. But nothing of the magnitude of the Spindletop discovery developed.

Then in 1910, attempts at drilling water wells on the Waggoner Ranch in North Texas west of Wichita Falls produced a showing of oil. In later years, W. T. Waggoner was quoted as saying, "Damn the oil. I wanted water." But he got oil. By mid-1911 that major discovery centered around the town of Electra in western Wichita County. Although this boom generated instant comparisons to Spindletop, it was only a prelude to the discovery destined to rival Gulf Coast activity both in production and in unbridled speculation. The boom at Burkburnett, on the Red River just a few miles north of Wichita Falls, began with a discovery well on July 29, 1912. Within three weeks fifty-six drilling rigs were operating on the Burkburnett townsite and within a few months the town became a forest of derricks.

Meanwhile, sporadic activity was taking place farther south near the little town of Ranger. An oil showing was found, but it was not until late 1917, when local citizens convinced the Texas-Pacific Coal Company to drill a well, that significant production became evident. This discovery caused Ranger to mushroom from a population of 1,000 to 30,000 within one year. Once again, the pattern of unchecked production and wild speculation created a chaotic situation.

The Ranger boom instigated widespread wildcat activity which within a year produced a similar boom at Hogtown a few miles south of Ranger. The discovery well which blew in on September 2, 1917, on the Joe Duke farm created instant pandemonium. Whereas, the Ranger boom was largely controlled by one firm, the Texas-Pacific Coal Company, which quickly changed its name to the Texas-Pacific Coal and Oil Company, the Desdemona boom, as Hogtown came to be called, was conducted by numerous independents owning small leases. Their activity soon outstripped storage capacity creating a tremendous loss of oil. At one point traffic on the DeLeon to Desdemona road was blocked by a three-foot-deep stream of oil flowing across the road. Gas was vented in the Desdemona field so indiscriminately, either as a nuisance or in the form of pressure to cause gushers to blow for the benefit of potential investors, that within two years all wells stopped flowing and had to be put on the pump. By 1920 both Ranger and Desdemona had already passed their peak production and their oil output was in a steep decline.

During 1918 and 1919 North Central Texas fell deeper and deeper in the clutch of oil fever. Exploration expanded in ever widening circles from the centers at Ranger and Desdemona on the south and Electra and Burkburnett on the north. Those activities developed production throughout the region, but none was more spectacular than the boom at Breckenridge. It was touched off by the No. 1 Chaney, which came in within the townsite of Breckenridge on February 4, 1918. Within months, over two hundred rigs rose within town limits and less than five years later some 2,000 rigs could be counted from the courthouse roof. Breckenridge, like all the other booms, rose and fell within five years or so.

Nevertheless, by 1920 Texas had gained the reputation of being the "El Dorado" of oil seekers. The state seemed to be floating on a sea of oil. Petroleum production that year neared 100,000,000 barrels valued at over 300 million dollars while natural gas began assuming some importance as it produced over $7,000,000 in revenue. In 1920 there were over twenty refineries either operating or under construction in North Central Texas and probably more than twice that number along the Gulf Coast. The industry was even starting a move toward conservation by building gasoline processing plants that utilized natural gas to make gasoline thereby saving some of the gas that was usually vented or flared. Although the spectacular booms captured the popular imagination, oil men were working to stabilize the industry, but the massive finds hampered any effective control over the activity.

The decade of the 1920s witnessed an increase in the tempo of petroleum activity in Texas. It began with discoveries near Mexia in 1920 and 1921 that soon escalated to boom proportions. The production there was along the Mexia fault zone which produced an area called the "Golden Lane." The "Golden Lane" was only about one-half mile wide, but it extended for many miles in length along the fault zone causing an area of extremely closely packed oil wells. Many of those wells flowed 18,000 to 20,000 barrels a day. Further south, but still on the fault line, a large field developed at Luling in 1922. The following year, production was found at Powell, near Corsicana, on the northern end of the fault zone, and later various other finds boosted production all along the zone.

Meanwhile, discoveries in the Panhandle between 1918 and 1926 opened another petroleum area for Texas. This region also had the distinction of developing into the largest gas field in the world. It began with a gas well, the Masterson #1, completed on December 13, 1918, about thirty miles north of Amarillo. Steady activity throughout the region gradually defined the outlines of the field which stretched 115 miles across the Panhandle with an average width of twenty miles. The first oil well in the field was not drilled until 1921, but, the real boom developed in 1926 with a 10,000 barrel a day oil well in Hutchinson County. That touched off such excitement and drew so many oil men to the area that the town of Borger was founded in the midst of the field in March 1926.

The Panhandle field attracted numerous gasoline plants that utilized the casinghead gas available in such enormous amounts. By the mid-1930s the forty-three such plants in the Panhandle produced

*Oil storage tanks at the Port of Houston, Texas.*

over 50 percent of the total of natural gasoline made in Texas. The vast amount of unmarketable gas residue coming out of the natural gasoline plants soon attracted a large carbon black industry. Beginning with one plant in 1927, within ten years the area was producing 97 percent of world production of the material. Additionally, twenty-four pipelines ultimately left the Panhandle field carrying fuel as far north as Chicago and Minneapolis.

As the Panhandle oil and gas reserves were being proven in the 1920s, great discoveries were being made in other parts of West Texas. Beginning with a small discovery during 1920 in Mitchell County near Colorado City, the vast petroleum resources of the Permian Basin began to come to light. The area which encompasses over 76,000 square miles eventually produced ten major oil fields. Towns like Colorado City, Big Spring, Midland, Odessa, and Pecos were transformed by an influx of oil-field workers. McCamey changed from a sleepy cowtown to a booming city of 10,000 in a few months. Crane County organized a county government which is a considerable feat when it is considered that as late as 1918 there were only fourteen citizens in the entire county. Iraan was founded and boomed due to the great Yates field production. West Texas found wealth and attracted a population on the strength of the Permian Basin oil discoveries during the 1920s.

One of the major benefits to Texas that developed from the West Texas discoveries was the economic boost given to education in the state. Much of the land in the Permian Basin area had been set aside to assist in supporting the University of Texas. There seemed little hope that income from the property would ever amount to any significant amount. Then, beginning in 1926 when the Permanent University Fund received five million dollars in oil-related revenue from its West Texas land holdings, all that changed. Every year since then that figure has risen, making the University of Texas one of the wealthiest in the nation.

During the 1920s as western Texas from the Panhandle on the north to the Permian Basin on the south was developing as the major petroleum-producing area in the world other activities were taking place within the state. The already proven areas continued to produce large amounts of petroleum. Many of the older fields were expanded or rejuvenated. Perhaps most spectacular was the second Spindletop boom that developed in 1925. All this activity resulted in Texas becoming the leading oil-producing state in the United States in 1928. The Lone Star State has continued in that position since that time.

The twenties was a period of remarkable growth for Texas. New manufacturing plants were built in record numbers. Lumbering, sulphur production, meat packing, and public-utility companies doubled and redoubled their sizes. Thousands were attracted to the state to increase the population to almost six million, double the amount of 1900. But the state was still 59 percent rural at the end of the decade.

Despite the growth of general industry in Texas, the oil and gas industry was the greatest factor in economic growth in the state during the decade of the twenties. By the end of the decade annual oil production tripled that of 1920 with production standing at 300,000,000 barrels annually while the natural gas produced doubled in value to $15,000,000 annually. In 1919 there were forty-three refineries operating in the state with a combined capacity of 277,000 barrels daily; by 1928 there were 101 with a total capacity of 750,000 barrels daily. In 1918 there were 3,116 miles of trunk pipelines; during 1927 and 1928 over 5,500 miles of pipeline were laid in West Texas. All this activity added to deposits in Texas banks, built skyscrapers, stimulated retail trade, and enriched Texas farmers and ranchers through rents and royalties. It is little wonder that the rest of the nation looked on Texas with a certain amount of awe and legends of the "Texas millionaire" began to grow.

The story of Texas petroleum activity up to 1930 is a spectacular drama involving fantastic discoveries, great fortunes, and sweeping changes. It is the stuff from which novels are written and movies are made. It would seem that the state had exhausted itself of the ability to astound the world with spectacular oil discoveries, but that was not the case. On October 3, 1930, the #3 Daisy Bradford was brought in near Overton in East Texas by an experienced wildcatter who had been working in Oklahoma. He was Columbus Marion "Dad" Joiner. Once again thousands rushed to a new discovery area and "the boom was on."

The East Texas operation was conducted by hundreds of independent oil men. They drilled wells as quickly as they could and produced them as heavily as possible. By the end of 1931 the East Texas fields around Kilgore and Longview contained 3,732 completed wells and in the next year 5,652. The situation led to massive overproduction. The price of oil tumbled lower and lower until at one point it reached ten cents a barrel. Early in April 1931 the Texas Railroad Commission began trying to control the amount of production in the field. After various hearings they set allowable oil production at 400,000 barrels a day. Most producers either ignored the order or filed lawsuits to stop any control over their activity. By mid-1931 the field was producing over 800,000 barrels a day, and the price ranged from ten to twenty-five cents a barrel.

The situation in East Texas was getting out of hand. Factionalism began developing between the operators who wanted to regulate production to raise the price of oil and extend the life of the field and those who opposed regulation in order to make a profit while they could. The federal court case of *MacMillan* v. *Railroad Commission of Texas,* decided in July 1931, effectively tied the hands of the Railroad Commission by declaring that it could control physical waste but could not regulate economic waste. Accordingly, Governor Ross S. Sterling, former president of Humble Oil and Refining Company, called a special session of the legislature and enacted laws covering every conceivable kind of physical oil waste. Meanwhile, the threat of violence erupting in the oil fields of East Texas became so great that Sterling took drastic action. On August 15, 1931, he declared the East Texas oil fields under martial law, put the area under the authority of General Jacob F. Wolters, and shut down all oil and gas wells in the area.

This incident marks the beginning of serious concerted efforts on the part of the state to develop a conservation program for its petroleum industry. A month after the wells were shut down they were started up again under Texas Railroad Commission regulations. It was not until December 1932 that a federal court ruled the martial law incident unnecessary. The troops were removed, but even then the governor kept most of them in the area as commissioned law-enforcement officers. During the period of martial law there was a dramatic rise in oil prices that convinced the majority of the operators that regulation was in their best interest. However, circumventing the Railroad Commission regulations continued in East Texas for a number of years. After the dramatic events of 1931 and 1932 the Railroad Commission has gradually achieved control over production of petroleum throughout the state. That agency's efforts toward conserving this valuable natural resource has done much to maintain a healthy economic petroleum industry.

The great oil booms with their fantastic production, lawlessness, and production of amazing wealth ended with the discovery of the East Texas field. Many areas have developed fields since then, but a general control over the activity by the Railroad Commission and responsible oil operators have tended to stabilize the industry. There are still great fortunes made in the petroleum business and an aura of romance definitely surrounds it, but those first thirty years or so of "flush production" have colored the industry.

The petroleum industry has continued to make great strides in technology. During the years of the great booms, 1901-30, most of the wells were in the 3,000 to 4,000 foot depth range. The equipment used had not materially changed since the 1860s. Today it is not unusual for wells to be completed at depths exceeding 20,000 feet and 10,000 to 15,000 foot wells are common. Petroleum geology was not even a science when Spindletop blew in 1901. Now not only has geology gained tremendous knowledge of likely petroleum producing areas, but technology such as seismograph techniques allow oil men to predict rather accurately what lies beneath the surface.

Offshore drilling has become a reality since World War II. The continental shelf in the Gulf of Mexico has developed into a major oil-producing area for Texas. Once again sophisticated technology, particularly directional drilling techniques, have made this possible.

Perhaps the greatest impact that petroleum has made on Texas is in the area of product development. Up until the 1930s the primary petroleum products gradually shifted from an emphasis on kerosene and lubricants to gasoline plus some notable side products such as carbon black. During World War II the petroleum industry began to develop the petrochemical industry, which has mushroomed into the largest manufacturing entity in the state. The petrochemical products produced are almost endless. They include thousands of variations of plastics, synthetic rubber, thousands of chemicals, fertilizers, dyes, and numerous other products. Manufacturing centers for this vast industry have grown up in the Gulf Coast areas of Beaumont-Orange-Port Arthur, Houston, and Corpus Christi, Odessa in the Permian Basin, and Borger in the Panhandle.

The story of petroleum production in Texas since 1930 has been one of continuous development of already existing proven areas. In the mid-thirties the Goldsmith field in Ector County expanded Permian Basin production as did the great Spraberry find of 1948-49 in Midland County. Oil production continued to rise in the state to peak at 3.5 million barrels in 1972. Production has steadily dropped since then to 2.5 million barrels a day in 1981. At the same time that production has fallen, proven reserves of oil within the state have dropped from 12.14 billion barrels to eight billion barrels and proven reserves of natural gas have dropped from 95 trillion cubic feet to 50.5 trillion cubic feet. Predictions indicate that the trend of steadily dropping production and amounts of proven reserves will continue. All this indicates that the pattern of heavy production followed by a steady decrease in activity developed in all the boom towns has been transferred from that localized situation to the state as a whole.

In the years following the big East Texas boom, the state of Texas became the largest oil-producing area in the world. Associated with that tremendous activity was the work of the Railroad Commission, which stabilized the price of oil by limiting production. This made oil the most dynamic force in the Texas economy. In 1981, among the one hundred largest companies in the state, fifty-nine of the top revenue generators were petroleum related. More than half of Texas' industrial production is either directly or indirectly related to the oil business. Twenty-five percent of the Texas gross product of goods and services are produced by petroleum related activities.

In addition to their economic control, petroleum-related businesses, in late 1982, employed 500,900 people or roughly one out of every twelve non-farm workers in the state. But, that is only the direct effect on the population because for every ten jobs created in the oil and gas industry another thirty-seven jobs are created in other sectors of the economy. Every $100,000 paid out in oil and gas worker wages generates more than $1,000,000 in state economic activity. Thus, any increase or decrease in petroleum activity in Texas has a profound effect on all aspects of the state's economy.

The state and local governments in Texas have also prospered from the effects of the petroleum industry. The oil and gas business has become the state's largest single taxpayer. During 1982 the industry payments amounted to 27.4 percent of all state collections. This sum amounted to $2.3 billion in production taxes. The industry also pays more local and corporate franchise taxes than any other business in the state. This flood of wealth into the state coffers provided numerous benefits to Texans in the areas of transportation, education, and numerous other areas without the state having to impose additional taxes such as the state income tax so much enjoyed by many other states.

Nowhere does the impact of petroleum activity become more apparent than when it is compared to agriculture. When Spindletop blew in at the turn of the century, Texas had a population of slightly over three million, which was 83 percent rural. Thus, agriculture dominated the state's economy. In 1980 petroleum income in Texas totaled thirty billion dollars, while agriculture accounted for only ten billion dollars. During the same time period the urban population increased to 80 percent of the total, while the rural population decreased to 20 percent and one out of every twelve Texans became involved in oil-related work. Thus, during the first eighty years of the twentieth century petroleum became the giant of Texas' economic and population growth which has in turn contributed heavily to the reversal in roles of the urban and rural populations.

The sad fact is that all this growth has created a processing industry in the state whose demand has outstripped domestic production capabilities. The result has been a growing rate of importation of foreign oil to supply the refineries and petrochemical complexes in Texas. This, for the first time, has tied Texas very closely to the international economic situation. To keep the industry alive we are forced into a dependency on foreign oil which also negates the traditional role of the Railroad Commission in controlling the price structure of the industry. Texas is entering a new era.

Petroleum production in Texas will not cease tomorrow. It will continue for years to come, but at a gradually decreasing rate. The technology and expertise developed in the Texas oil fields will continue to be a big business as the international oil business demands help in its development. Texas' petro-chemical complexes will continue to operate, but at a more subdued rate as they come to rely more and more on imports. All this in turn will decrease tax bases for local and state government entities. The legacy of Texas oil has done much to build a mystique surrounding the state as well as building a sound economic base for future growth. The future of the industry lies under a cloud of uncertainty. But judging from its past performance, petroleum should play an important role in Texas for decades to come.

# 13

## Looking Better Every Year: Apparel Manufacturing in Texas

*Dorothy D. De Moss*

Clothing is one item which is close to all Texans all the time; yet rarely has the contribution of the apparel industry to the recent growth of the state's economy been appreciated fully. Beginning before the turn of the century with a few firms producing work clothes and red flannel underwear for the local market, the industry today is composed of almost 800 companies employing more than 74,000 Texans who manufacture a wide variety of garments and accessories for consumers throughout the world. Most important, the manufacture of such clothing and related products has been a statewide phenomenon. Factories are located in smaller communities and towns as well as large cities and have had a vital and beneficial impact on local economies. Among the numerous clothing producers are many whose origins are exclusively within Texas and whose home offices remain in the state. The rise to prominence of these early pioneer firms is an inspiring story of tenacity, courage and creativity.

The modern-day apparel story really began in 1897 with the founding of the Finesilver Manufacturing Company of San Antonio, the oldest Texas apparel manufacturer still in operation today. The firm, led by Abraham Finesilver, a European immigrant, prospered steadily during the years of World War I from its production of men's work clothes and uniforms for the army. By the end of the 1930s the company had established a strong business relationship with the J. C. Penney chain of stores and steadily grew under the leadership of Mervin Finesilver, son of the founder.

At the same time, the expansion of the petroleum industry, the dramatic increase in urbanization and industrialization in the state, and the construction of a better transportation system had motivated the founding of a number of new companies in Dallas, Fort Worth, El Paso, and San Antonio. These pioneer Texas apparel makers were to become prominent national leaders in the production of women's dresses and sportswear, men's work clothes and leisure wear, and children's playclothes. Such firms as Lorch, Higginbotham-Bailey-Logan, Marcy Lee, Farah, Juvenile, Kingston, Justin McCarty, Williamson-Dickie, Haggar, Donovan, Page Boy, and Nardis began as small family-owned businesses led by entrepreneurs who desired to produce quality garments priced competitively with those sold by eastern producers and which would satisfy the regional tastes and seasonal needs of the Southwest. Few of the founders had any previous manufacturing experience, having worked primarily as retailers, wholesalers, jobbers, and salesmen. Several of the early manufacturers were recent immigrants from Europe or Lebanon who were especially eager to participate as producers in a free enterprise system. Most used the private corporation technique of organization in their early history. This business procedure insured a condition of strong family control and resulted in a record of continuity of ownership and longevity of existence for the Texas companies which is practically unknown in the volatile national garment industry.

Many of the early entrepreneurs chose to establish their clothing factories in Dallas during the period 1909-38 because the city already was the important distribution center of the Southwest. Of the firms, the Lorch Manufacturing Company has proven to be the most exceptional, since it is the oldest privately owned women's apparel company in the United States. Its founder was August Lorch, a native of Germany who came to Texas as a young man in 1892. After achieving success as a peddler and then the owner of several drygoods stores, in 1909 he made the important decision to settle in Dallas in order to open a wholesale jobbing business specializing in ladies apparel. In 1924, Lester Lorch, son of the founder, encouraged his father to have the company enter the manufacturing field. Soon the firm was producing the inexpensive cotton house dress so popular with women in Texas because of its attributes of being cool and crisp-looking.

When the economic crisis of the early 1930s plunged the industry into the doldrums, Lorch and other Dallas manufacturers were alert to the possibilities of increased national sales for the low-cost house dress. They gave the cotton garment extensive new styling and conducted advertising campaigns in northern markets emphasizing its novelty, variety, and above all, economy.

While sales volume and profits increased for other Dallas firms, the Higginbotham-Bailey-Logan Company also prospered. This firm, organized in 1914 by Rufus W. Higginbotham, A. H. Bailey and W. L. Logan, Jr., began as a wholesale distributing house, but began to manufacture "Paymaster" work overalls for men and "Virginia Hart" wash dresses for women shortly after World War I. The company often has been referred to as the "apparel university" of Dallas because it served as the training ground and "graduate school" for a number of young men who later founded their own apparel manufacturing enterprises. Under the guidance of A. H. Bailey, the firm greatly expanded its manufacturing operations to include dresses, underwear, ties, slacks, overalls, shirts, millinery, and children's clothing.

Contemporary with developments at Higginbotham-Bailey-Logan was the growth of the Marcy Lee Manufacturing Company founded by Lester Lief and Ernest Wadel. Lief was an "alumnus" of Higginbotham-Bailey-Logan who had begun the Marcy Lee company in Tyler in 1923. Wadel, a distinguished chemical engineer, returned to that city, his hometown, in 1925 and decided to join Leif in the apparel business. Shortly thereafter they moved their firm to Dallas in recognition of the growing market potential of the city and its excellent transportation facilities. Like most other Dallas clothing makers, Marcy Lee's prosperity in the 1920s and 1930s was based upon the production of cotton wash dresses, better dresses made from rayon, and sportswear.

During the same period of time occurred the growth to national prominence of a Dallas apparel maker whose name became synonymous with the phrase "fashion creativity." In 1927 Justin McCarty left Higginbotham-Bailey-Logan to form his own business. McCarty, a native Texan, soon produced not only "Mary Lou" cotton dresses, but more expensive "Justine" street dresses. Sportswear became another of McCarty's interests when, in 1939, he introduced a new line under the "Sportess" label. He later added the "Justmoor" coat and suit line. McCarty put emphasis on hiring proven designers to create simple, classic garments and, in elaborate advertisements, sought the patronage of college-age sorority coeds.

Like Lester Lief and Justin McCarty, John B. Donovan was also a former Higginbotham-Bailey-Logan employee who went on to become one of the pioneers of women's fashion in the Dallas market.

His move to create a new company in 1930 during a worsening economic depression was typical of the courage and expertise displayed by most of the Texas apparel manufacturers. Donovan perceived the strong demand for sportswear as well as the cotton house dress, and quickly introduced a "Don-A-Tog" collection of casual and separate playclothes and slacks. It featured a special "Texas look" and became nationally known for its styling and workmanship. Much later, in 1957, Albert J. Galvani, a graduate of the University of Chicago and a twenty-year employee of the Reliance Manufacturing Company, became president and owner of the company whose name was changed to Donovan-Galvani. Under his leadership the firm continued to produce high-quality garments, reflecting "champagne styling at working girl prices" and using double knit polyester for its sportswear separates.

The outbreak of World War II in Europe greatly affected the women's apparel industry in the United States. Shipments from Paris or the eastern apparel producers were delayed and there was an increased demand by consumers for practical clothing to be worn when working in defense plants. To capitalize on the new opportunities for a national market and on the "Rosie the Riveter" phenomenon, twenty-eight local manufacturers formed in 1942 the Dallas Fashion and Sportswear Center, now the Southwest Apparel Manufacturers Association. This aggressive trade organization bought ads in national fashion magazines, published its own magazine, sponsored elaborate style shows, established a school of design at Southern Methodist University and expanded the size and number of apparel markets held in Dallas. The center continually emphasized that Dallas manufacturers offered a fashion timeliness to women of the Southwest, particularly meeting the needs of the early spring and mild winters of the South.

Special articles in *Woman's Wear Daily* during the war underscored the special sense of cooperation and helpfulness which existed among Dallas clothing producers. This sense of friendliness and esprit-de-corps was unusual among apparel manufacturing centers such as New York City, Chicago, or Los Angeles. This distinctive attribute of cooperation came to a remarkable culmination when five of the manufacturers — Lorch, Marcy Lee, Justin McCarty, Donovan and Nardis — bought a cooperative advertisement in the February 1942 issue of *Mademoiselle* magazine. The ad featured photos of Texas "playsuits" and fashion sportswear from all the companies, and emphasized the picturesque themes of the Southwest. Such an advertisement was extremely rare in the national experience and delineated the Texas producers of ladies garments as being enterprising, astute, and foresighted. Their wartime efforts greatly expanded the national recognition of Dallas as an apparel center.

The record of growth of the leading women's apparel manufacturers in Dallas during the war obscured somewhat the remarkable success of another clothing firm in the city, the Page Boy Maternity Fashions Company. Because its founders were young women, the three Frankfurt sisters, and because it produced garments designed for a special purpose, Page Boy constituted an unusual and distinctive chapter in the broad history of the Texas industry.

Elsie Frankfurt graduated from Southern Methodist University in 1938. That same year she found herself analyzing with dismay the appearance of her pregnant older sister, Edna Frankfurt Ravkind. As Elsie later recalled, "she looked so horrible I had to do something." Prior to World War II pregnant women's choices for fashions were limited to wearing either clothing several sizes larger than normal, or wraparound dresses which had no shape. To solve this dilemma Elsie, an excellent seamstress, made a special skirt and jacket outfit for her sister. So many expectant women in Dallas inquired where they might purchase such an attractive ensemble that the two sisters decided to manufacture and sell the outfit. They pooled their resources and opened a small shop in the Medical Arts Building in downtown Dallas. Another sister, Louise Frankfurt Gartner, known as "Tootsie," also joined the enterprise.

The Frankfurt sisters chose the name Page Boy after the medieval trumpeter whose fanfare proudly announced the birth of an heir. Together they produced garments which soon sold to prominent mothers-to-be in Dallas, Atlanta, New York, and Chicago. From the very beginning the Frankfurts decided to sell their rather expensive dress to the higher income, fashion-conscious woman. In 1940 they opened their first retail store outside Dallas in Beverly Hills, California, and attracted immediate attention from such expectant Hollywood stars as Alice Faye, Joan Bennett, and Loretta Young. All design, cutting and sewing still was done in the cramped rear quarters of the Dallas retail shop. With the onset of the nation's postwar affluence and baby boom the company greatly expanded its retail operations in Texas and California. Elsie Frankfurt, attractive, smart, and single, became a national celebrity in a period predating the women's liberation movement. In 1951 she was chosen to become the first woman member of the prestigious Young Presidents Organization.

The history of Dallas as an apparel manufacturing and marketing center also was highlighted by the rise to prominence of a menswear corporation which today has become the largest privately owned clothing company in the United States — the Haggar Company. The founder of this significant organization was Joseph Marion Haggar, who was born in Jazzin, Lebanon, in 1892. At age thirteen he left his poverty-stricken family to migrate to Mexico and thence to the United States. He held a number of jobs, including that of a salesman for an overalls company. In 1926 he took the dramatic step of beginning his own men's pants business in Dallas.

Contrary to trends in the eastern menswear apparel centers, the depression years were growth years for the Haggar Company. Its founder established a one price merchandising policy and refused "to haggle" with a retailer. Haggar also became the first pants manufacturer in the country to introduce the concept of straight-line production. Concurrently, J. M. Haggar made the decision to decentralize manufacturing by establishing factories away from Dallas in Greenville and Waxahachie. The rationale behind this policy was to tap the labor pool in small Texas communities where many women resided who were skilled as homesewers but had no employment opportunities. In the late 1930s the company began to advertise in national trade publications. These advertisements were some of the first to use the term "slacks" in describing trousers which should be used by a man in his leisure or "slack" time. After the attack at Pearl Harbor, Haggar, like many other apparel makers, shifted more than half of its output to the production of combat garments and uniforms for the army.

Closely paralleling the success story of the Haggar Company was the development of another menswear producer, the Williamson-Dickie Manufacturing Company of Fort Worth. Beginning as a modest-scale operation involving thirty-three workers, it grew to be a worldwide organization employing thousands, and is today the largest producer of matched sets — work shirts and pants — in the nation. The firm grew up amidst the expansive railroad, stockyard, meatpacking, and petroleum industries of Fort Worth. In 1922 conditions were ripe for Charles Nathan Williamson and Emmett Eugene Dickie to found an apparel company which would meet the increasing demand for heavy-duty work clothes needed by the growing number of oilfield and agricultural laborers of the area. The two men were distant cousins and natives of central Texas.

After purchasing an overalls company, they reorganized it into the Williamson-Dickie Manufacturing Company and relocated on West Vickery Street, where the home office remains today. C. Don Williamson, son of the founder, joined the firm and gradually assumed responsibility for most policy decisions. In honor of E. E.

Dickie the company adopted the nickname "Dickies" for its products, which was later superimposed over a horseshoe emblem to form the firm's official label.

During the Great Depression budget-minded Americans continued to buy the durable Dickies cotton work clothes and overalls. Like other manufacturers in the Dallas-Fort Worth area, Williamson-Dickie became heavily involved in the production of military uniforms when World War II began.

Six hundred miles to the west of the Haggar and Williamson-Dickie factories there arose to prominence another menswear manufacturer which was destined to become one of the largest and most controversial in the Texas industry, Farah Manufacturing of El Paso. It began in 1920 as a tiny, family-run business producing work shirts. Within fifty years it had grown to be the city's largest single private employer with 12,000 workers statewide.

Mansour "Frank" Farah, a native of Lebanon, opened his apparel company with the assistance of his wife Hana and his two sons, James and William. The company concentrated on the production of denim pants, made from cotton grown and manufactured in the El Paso area. After the death of the elder Farah in 1937, James became president and "Willie" maintained equipment and experimented with new machinery. When World War II broke out production quickly converted to the manufacture of combat trousers for the army and the Farah company became the only clothing manufacturer in Texas to win the Army-Navy "E" flag for excellence as a war plant. The postwar period saw a rapid increase in the population of El Paso and in the size of the Farah company.

The existence in San Antonio of a large population of skilled low-cost needleworkers of Mexican heritage was the primary reason for the founding there in 1923 of the Juvenile Manufacturing Company, now Santone Industries. In early years the firm, under the leadership of Morris Scherr, produced hand embroidered, fine batiste dresses for infants and toddlers. It later expanded its product line to include boyswear, menswear, and ladieswear. Harold Scherr, son of the founder and a graduate industrial engineer, led the company during its dynamic growth years.

Because of World War II the number of apparel firms statewide increased in number, producing a wide variety of items. Many firms which secured federal contracts for uniforms were able to modernize factory machinery. Most producers greatly broadened their national sales connections. There was a growing recognition throughout the country of the quality of Texas-made sportswear. By producing such specialized garments as slacks for wartime work, maternity fashions and children's clothing, the firms demonstrated an astute ability to adjust production in order to meet new market needs.

In the immediate postwar years, Texas apparel executives embarked upon energetic programs involving national advertising campaigns, technological innovations, and expansion of plant facilities. During the 1950s, particularly, pioneer Texas apparel manufacturers decentralized their operations from the large urban centers by constructing new plants in smaller Texas towns. This arrangement met the mutual economic needs of both parties. The communities desperately wanted new payrolls to offset a business decline caused by the loss of population to the cities during the war. Garment company owners increasingly needed to locate a larger supply of skilled workers willing to work as sewing operators. Often the small towns would offer building space, rent subsidies, tax exemptions or payment of utilities in order to lure settlement. From Greenville to Robstown and from Corsicana to Sweetwater, the flood of new apparel-manufacturing plants gushed across the Texas economic landscape to engulf most outlying communities. Such decentralization effectively blunted any labor union efforts at organizing apparel workers in Texas.

One word, "showmanship," characterized the efforts of most Texas-based ladies apparel firms in the immediate postwar period. Manufacturers sponsored the establishment of the "Dallas Alice" award to be given for excellence to the top four designers of Dallas-created clothing. Local producers made use of merchant conferences, fashion clinics, and appearances by national personalities to publicize the city as a national fashion and sportswear center. Companies expanded the size and focus of the five, week-long apparel markets held in the city for retailers during the year. Blending cotton with the new synthetic fabrics, firms such as Lorch, Justin McCarty, and Donovan-Galvani produced sportswear geared especially for the working woman and new suburban lifestyle.

Demographic and economic changes also had a great impact on the menswear and boyswear industry of Texas. Such producers as Haggar, Williamson-Dickie, Farah, Finesilver, and Juvenile benefitted greatly from the high net-migration of population of the 1950s and 1960s. Aggressive, competitive, and resolute in their actions, these longtime manufacturers used national advertising campaigns in major publications and in the new medium of television to extol the comfort and low price of their products. They also emphasized the development of new technology and management techniques. The introduction of new styles of dress slacks made with wrinkle-resistant fabrics, likewise, brought increasing success and attention to these firms. Several of the companies underwent dramatic geographic expansion by building new manufacturing plants in the southern states as well as in South Texas. Williamson-Dickie established factories in British Honduras, now Belize, and along the border with Mexico.

The event which helped establish Dallas as the market center of fashion and to ignite the growth of the Texas apparel industry was the completion in 1964 of the Apparel Mart building. Located adjacent to the Stemmons Freeway in the midst of a bustling merchandise market center, it is the world's largest wholesale fashion market under one roof, having 1.8 million square feet of space in six stories with nearly 2,000 separate showrooms. The Great Hall, a magnificent central atrium which is the focal point and core of the building, was designed especially for elaborate fashion shows. It vaults sixty feet to the roof, with balconies, fountains, trees, gardens, tapestries and art pieces. Today the Mart attracts approximately 80,000 buyers annually and its women's market show in August will lure more than 18,000 buyers, making it the most well-attended one-week market in the United States.

Development by the pioneer apparel firms during the period 1930-1980 was greatly encouraged by the existence of a conservative economic philosophy which discouraged any meaningful unionization of workers. Labor unions, such as the International Ladies Garment Workers (ILGWU) and Amalgamated Clothing Workers of American (ACWA), now the Amalgamated Clothing and Textile Workers, found it particularly difficult to arouse and sustain membership in the small communities where factories were established after World War II. Many workers there were grateful for their employment, felt a close relationship with management, and had no familiarity with the historic ideals of trade unionism in the apparel centers of the eastern United States.

A major strike in Dallas in 1935, union protests in San Antonio in 1936 and in 1954, and abortive efforts in Fort Worth in the 1950s all failed. After the 1947 passage of the Taft-Hartley law, Texas became a right-to-work state and work places were prohibited from requiring union membership. Clothing manufacturers steadfastly maintained that there was no need for unions if the proper management-employee relationship was established. Company leaders, in effect, blunted the appeals of the ILGWU and ACWA by noticeably bettering the pay, hospitalization, insurance, and vacation opportunities given to all workers.

Most garment producers in San Antonio and El Paso have not found it necessary to establish factories in small towns in order to find adequate numbers of workers. A surplus labor force has existed in the two metropolitan centers since the war. Poverty and population pressure in the northern provinces of Mexico motivated many women workers, both legal and illegal, to seek higher wages available to sewing machine operators in the two cities. Many female American citizens of Mexican descent were also in need of jobs.

Against this backdrop of labor relations occurred the widely publicized strike and national boycott conducted by the ACWA against the Farah Manufacturing Company in the years 1972-74. Correctly or incorrectly, the strike by one-fifth of the 10,000 Farah workers became a crusade for social justice, pitting Mexican-American employees against a company which they believed to be paternalistic, inflexible, and arbitrary in its actions. After twenty-one months of a nationwide consumer boycott of Farah products, an avalanche of adverse publicity, opposition by Catholic and Protestant leaders, and a devastating loss of profits, the company management was compelled to seek a settlement, and signed a three-year contract. This victory by the ACWA, however, was not followed by other labor union success. The strong enforcement of the right-to-work laws, the attrition and impermanency of the work force, the decentralization of factories, and the desperate financial needs of many employees discouraged organizing activity by apparel unions.

Enticed by the lure of low-cost labor and minimal corporate taxes, many clothing manufacturers departed from New York, Pennsylvania, and New Jersey in the period 1960-80 to relocate their businesses in Texas. Other entrepreneuers, having worked for older, established Texas companies were eager to establish their own firms. Many made use of the new synthetic, wrinkle-free fibers, as well as natural-fiber fabrics, to produce clothing for big chain stores such as J. C. Penney, Montgomery Ward, and Sears, as well as for the discerning, stylish consumer.

Among Texas companies organized in recent years, Prophecy, a contemporary sportswear fashion house which was established in Dallas in 1971, has compiled an outstanding record of performance because of its management expertise and creativity in design. The varied background and professional experience of the three founders, Carl Abady, Barry Miller, and Luigi Mungioli, provided a stimulating foundation upon which the successful business was built. Abady, president of the company, was a native of Cleveland, Ohio. Before coming to Dallas he served as national sales manager for a St. Louis clothing firm. Vice president Barry Miller was the son of a respected Dallas apparel manufacturer and was a graduate of the University of Texas at Arlington. Luigi Mungioli, a native of Italy, immigrated to Dallas, where he worked ten years for a firm specializing in garments made from Italian silk.

The three formed Prophecy, a private corporation, on an investment of $50,000 and focused on the production of fashionable sportswear and dresses for the younger working woman, who was no longer the junior-sized baby-boomer, but rather an independent-minded, liberated woman who desired contemporary styling. Specialty stores and better department stores made up the preponderance of the firm's sales accounts. A major reason for Prophecy's consistently high level of sales was the creative ability of the firm's vice president of design, Polly Ellerman, a fashion design graduate of Washington University in St. Louis. Her design emphasis was always on giving the professional career woman customer a realistic wardrobe with touches of fashion and excitement.

Many of the state's apparel companies, both large and small, supported the efforts and goals of major trade associations to promote the Texas clothing industry. The Southwest Apparel Manufacturers Association, a descendant of the Dallas Fashion Center, was the active spokesman for the ladies fashion manufacturers, while the Southwestern Men's and Boy's Apparel Club addressed the problems of its particular constituency.

Hard work, wise management, adequate capitalization, and good luck in predicting fashion trends have enabled Texas apparel manufacturers successfully to challenge the hegemony of the New York and California clothing centers. The national marketing of locally produced cotton house dresses during the Great Depression years, the manufacturer of new lines of sportswear accurately timed to the climate of the Southwest, the production of uniforms and ladies slacks during World War II, the decentralization of factories to smaller communities, the early adoption of polyester fabric for garments, and the upgrading of styling to capture a particular clientele are the hallmark events of the industry's first eighty years.

The future, undoubtedly, holds numerous challenges—especially the competition from the growing importation of foreign-made clothing produced by low-cost labor. Such a threat may be counteracted by the predicted continued growth of the state's young population during the 1980s and 1990s. Non-durable goods, such as clothing, will be in great demand by such a group of consumers. By means of creativity in policy and audacity in action the Texas apparel manufacturing industry will overcome its problems and achieve a notable record of success during the next sesquicentennial period.

*Remote wilderness area of Texas in the Big Bend National Park.*

# 14

## Conservation and Environmental Developments in Texas

*J. B. Smallwood Jr.*

Since colonial days Texans, like other Americans, have viewed the frontier as an area of opportunity, its resources to be exploited primarily for personal gain. The lovely woodlands, the fertile blackland prairies, the expansive High Plains, the arid grasslands of South Texas inspired an individuality and a sense of the grandiose that continued to motivate Texans into the twentieth century. Intensely committed to a proprietary control of natural resources, Texans have considered those resources inexhaustible, whether it was the timberland of the east or the underground water of the west. In the 1980s Texans still emphasized economic growth over ecological considerations, while the legislature placed low priority on conservation issues.

Prior to 1900 no organized conservation movement existed in Texas, partially because of the rural nature of the state and a legislature committed to a restrictive fiscal policy. Despite these handicaps, attempts to conserve some of the state's resources began in the first two decades of the twentieth century, but with the exception of the forestry, early conservation activities in Texas showed little cohesiveness.

In the early period of Texas conservation, forestry achieved the greatest success. In the years of the Republic and early statehood, Texans viewed trees, as did most other Americans, either as a nuisance to farming or a resource to be exploited. Spurred by activities of the national government in the first two decades of the twentieth century, especially the conservation crusades of Theodore Roosevelt and Gifford Pinchot, Texas moved toward a forest management policy. Passage by Congress of the Weeks Act of 1911 to promote forest-fire protection led in 1915 to the establishment, as a part of Texas A&M University, of the Texas Department of Forests, which in 1926 was renamed the Texas Forest Service (TFS). Because of opposition from lumbermen, lack of scientific knowledge, and inadequate financial support from the state, the agency accomplished little during the 1920s except its own survival.

Among the conservation issues confronting Texans, none has been more essential to their economic development and well-being than water resources. Water distribution in Texas is extremely uneven, creating an almost endless variety of water problems unique to each region. Concepts drawn from the Spanish, Mexican, and English heritage of Texas have also complicated formulation of a state policy governing water rights. The Spanish concept of prior appropriation gave the first user primary claim to water while the English tradition of riparian rights entitled landholders adjacent to the river first use of its water. Legal recognition by the state of both doctrines created endless conflicts over water rights, which the legislature attempted to deal with in the Irrigation Act of 1889. Passage of a constitutional amendment in 1904 permitting creation of special water districts indicated legislative reluctance to challenge the tradition of local control over water policy, although the act did enable localities to develop more unified and comprehensive water programs.

Creation in 1909 of a Reclamation Engineer's office represented the first official consideration of water resources by the state. As part of the Irrigation Act of 1913, the Texas legislature formed the Board of Water Engineers (BWE) to collect data, make biennial reports to the governor, and to suggest water legislation. The agency had no authority to enforce water policy or to develop a comprehensive water plan. In 1917 Texas made further attempts to cope with water management, when voters approved an amendment permitting the state to create river authorities and to divide the state into as many water districts as needed for various purposes. In the same year the legislature also adopted the Texas Water Code, authorizing the BWE to adjudicate water right controversies. The law also negated any riparian rights that had been unused for three consecutive years, touching off an intense controversy between riparian and appropriation users.

Developments during the 1920s laid the basis for future water programs in Texas. The state Supreme Court opened the way for state water development projects when in 1926 it asserted the state's authority to control storm and flood waters while authorizing the BWE to control appropriations for water projects. In 1929, by establishing the Brazos River Conservancy and Reclamation District, the legislature set a pattern for future water management.

Some of the earliest interest in conservation among Texans concerned wildlife preservation. Although the legislature passed several game laws prior to 1890, there was little organized support of means for enforcement of such laws. By 1895 concern among certain groups over the decline of the Texas fish and oyster population spurred the legislature to create the Office of Fish and Oyster Commissioner. Although there was much public resistance to the activities of the commissioner as well as lack of legislative support, by 1900 some Texans recognized the need for fish and game legislation.

Development of the oil industry, expansion of agriculture, and urbanization during the twenties created threats to Texas wildlife, but the Office of Game, Fish, and Oyster Commissioners (OGFOC) possessed little enforcement power prior to 1927. In that period, however, the agency did inaugurate a program to both stock game and fish that were in decline and to develop game preserves, resulting in significant increases in some game and fish varieties. In 1929 the legislature replaced the OGFOC with the six-member Game, Fish, and Oyster Commission (GFOC).

Since its inception in the 1920s the Texas parks movement has remained troubled and weak. When Texas began to initiate a state parks program, it suffered from having already relinquished most of its public lands. While other states could call on their often extensive public domain for parks development, Texas had to rely primarily on the generosity of private donors or the parsimony of the state legislature. Responding to efforts by Governor Pat Neff in 1923, the legislature created a State Parks Board (SPB) composed of individuals serving without pay and charged with seeking gifts of land for state parks. The lawmakers failed, however, to provide financial support for maintenance of any recreation parks that might be created.

As early as the New Deal Era federal initiative, and occasionally federal pressure, provided incentives for conservation activities in Texas. The depression caused more people to recognize the interrelated nature of various conservation programs, such as water management and soil erosion. In 1935 the legislature established the Texas Planning Board (TPB) charged with developing a long-range program for managing the state's natural resources. Federal programs, such as the Civilian Conservation Corps, stimulated the activities of the Texas Forest Service, especially its educational program. The Great Depression also forced the lumbering industry to face two issues they previously had avoided: overexpansion and poor forestry management. Lumbermen and public officials alike increasingly regarded timber as a crop rather than an exhaustible resource, providing the basis for much of the southern pine industry so important to the East Texas economy in the 1980s.

As with most of the state's other conservation activities, the New Deal spurred interest in water development and conservation. New Deal support encouraged river basin developments modeled on the 1929 Brazos project. Establishment of multipurpose river authorities for most Texas river systems had removed water management from county and single-purpose districts by 1959. Through the Agricultural Adjustment Act and the Reconstruction Finance Corporation, the New Deal encouraged development of irrigation on the High Plains, but conflict soon developed between state officials and users over best use policy.

The Texas Planning Board attempted to prepare the first comprehensive water plan for the state, but ended by focusing on the lack of information on which to base such a plan. By highlighting the deficiencies in Texas water planning generally, the TPB laid the groundwork for future water planning activities. Many factors prevented Texas from developing a comprehensive water plan prior to World War II. Yet as early as 1938 a report to Governor James Allred expressed official concern about adequate future water resources for industry, irrigation, and personal use.

Parks and wildlife staffs experienced severe reductions during the depression years, while increased oil production and industrial wastes posed even greater threats to Texas wildlife. Federal legislation in 1937 made available federal aid for wildlife restoration bringing some improvement in Texas wildlife management. The Texas parks program also received a boost from the federal Civilian Conservation Corps (CCC) during the depression years, although the legislature failed to respond with added support. Only when federal authorities threatened to withdraw CCC aid did the state increase parks appropriations.

World War II had a profound effect on many aspects of Texas conservation activities. The war heightened public awareness of the importance of forest conservation, while pressure created by rapid expansion of water use highlighted the need for a coherent water plan for Texas. During the war both state and federal authorities attempted to develop a desirable water policy, but Texans remained suspicious of federal efforts except when directly affected by floods. In 1944, near the end of World War II, the Texas Water Conservation Association (TWCA) was formed, composed primarily of businessmen, government officials, and water engineers. It endorsed a statewide water conservation program, calling for wise management of groundwater as well as educational programs focusing on future water needs. During World War II wildlife conservation efforts suffered from financial cutbacks as well as from pressure on land for cattle raising and from increased industrial pollution. State park development essentially ceased during the war.

The period from the end of World War II until passage of the National Environmental Protection Act of 1969 represented a significant stage in the history of Texas conservation and environmental policy. In that period activities by both public officials and private groups reflected an increasing awareness of limitations on the state's natural resources. They publicized the need for planning and conservation to meet the resource requirements of the future. As in other areas of the United States, the 1950s and 1960s saw the subtle evolution among Texans from the older conservation ethic to the newer principles of environmentalism, with its emphasis on quality of life as well as wise use of resources for development purposes. The two postwar decades provided much of the foundation for the flurry of conservation and environmental activity in Texas during the 1970s and 1980s.

An adequate supply of usable water for agriculture, industry, and cities emerged as critical to the economic prosperity of the state as Texas became increasingly industrialized and urbanized after the Second World War. Concern over water supply led Governor Allan Shivers in 1952 to appoint the Statewide Water Resource Committee. Responding to the committee's report, the legislature passed several measures related to water management but avoided the question of long-range water planning by establishing the Texas Water Resource Committee to make further studies and recommendations. Opposition by those fearing loss of control over their water sources prevented adoption of any state or federal water management plan, leaving water development planning to local authorities or to the U.S. Corps of Engineers by default.

Critics of the Board of Water Engineers' lack of aggressive action demanded its reorganization, although its ineffectiveness stemmed largely from lack of authority. In 1962 the legislature reorganized the BWE, replacing it with the Texas Water Commission (TWC). During Governor John Connally's administration (1963-69), the TWC became the Texas Water Rights Commission, with the planning function being transferred to the Texas Water Development Board.

During the postwar decades the High Plains experienced increasingly critical problems of adequate water supply for its flourishing agriculture. Recognizing the need for control of groundwater usage, in 1949 the Texas Water Conservation Association sponsored appropriate regulatory legislation. Again opposition by groups fearful of losing absolute control over their water supply, especially irrigators on the High Plains, defeated TWCA's attempts to develop a comprehensive water code for Texas. A compromise resulted in the Underground Water District Act of 1949, which encouraged a more orderly approach to pumping but did little to alleviate the problem of excessive withdrawal. To allieviate the increasingly critical water problems on the High Plains in 1968, the Texas Water Development Board proposed the grandiose Texas Water Plan (TWP). Appealing in its very size to a certain Texas mentality, the most controversial aspect of the plan provided for the importation of water to the arid High Plains of West Texas from the wetter regions to the east. Environmental and fiscal critics of the plan responded by organizing a campaign to prevent its funding.

Although water supply often affects water quality, pollution of water resources can derive from many causes. In 1961 the legislature created the Texas Water Pollution Board. Ineffective because of lack of adequate funds and staff, it was replaced in 1967 by the Texas Water Quality Board (TWQB), but that agency still lacked lab facilities to document cases against polluters.

In the postwar years increased activity by both state and federal governments characterized Texas wildlife conservation. Beginning in the 1930s, wildlife conservation in Texas followed mainstream conservation policies, emphasizing a more scientific approach. Supporters of such efforts generally did not resist federal regulations as had advocates of forestry and water conservation. The GFOC renewed its efforts to promote conservation education, becoming in 1951 the Game and Fish Commission (GFC). Hunting for urban Texans remained, however, the province of the more affluent, since land pressures and the lack of public lands prevented development of hunting areas for persons of moderate means.

In an attempt to consolidate some conservation activities and to strengthen the ailing public parks program, Governor Connally obtained the merger of the GFC with the State Parks Board in 1963 to create the Texas Parks and Wildlife Department (TPWD). After the war the parks program continued to suffer from insufficient funds, although in 1946 the legislature provided $240,000 for maintenance and improvement of the state's parks. Several studies during the 1940s and 1960s made by both official and semi-official organizations reached a similar conclusion: Texas parks were pitifully underfinanced.

With the passage of the National Environmental Protection Act (NEPA) in 1969, federal action provided great impetus for conservation in Texas. NEPA prodded state officials to consider environmental issues more seriously, but also engendered resentment and resistance both from state officials and the general public. While the issues involved in Texas environmental policy were highly complex, interrelated, and almost limitless, after 1970 concern focused on several major areas: land-use management, energy, water issues, air quality, and wildlife, and recreation issues.

Most environmental questions touch the all-important areas of land-use management, a sensitive and controversial subject for many Texans. Texans, like most Americans, have considered land a commodity to be used for economic development. Officials charged with management of the state's natural resources traditionally viewed their responsibility as one of achieving maximum economic benefit from those resources, although by the 1980s some officials gave more attention to environmental protection. Bob Armstrong, commissioner of the General Land Office (1971-82) claimed that techniques were available to provide orderly development without serious damage to the state's renewable resources. Other public officials, such as state senator Fred Agnich of Dallas, asserted that Texas needed a land-management policy but doubted that the tradition of individualism in the state would permit the adoption of an effective one.

In the 1980s the General Land Office, Texas Coastal and Marine Council, and the Texas Forestry Service held primary responsibility for land-use planning, although other agencies directly affected land use management. The critics claimed there was little coordination or cooperation among these groups and that conflicts of interest often prevented effective management of land resources. Despite the general suspicion of land use planning among Texans, the Governor's Division of Planning Coordination (DPC) declared in 1974 that land-use management was critical to an effective use of the state's natural resources.

Even though the state legislature rejected several suggestions after 1970 to establish statewide plans to regulate land use in environmentally sensitive areas, state officials evidenced growing concern for land-use management. Various government agencies produced many excellent studies concerning land-use problems, but the reports generally ignored the essential issue of enforcement, crucial to the success of any plan. The heightened interest in land-use man-

*Road through the piney woods of East Texas.*
— Photo by Edward C. Fritz from *Sterile Forest*

agement represented not only a genuine concern about environmental problems but also the realization that the state faced possible federal action. While the state inched toward an awareness of the need for land-using planning, the prevailing ethic in Texas remained one of growth psychology only dimly influenced by environmental concerns.

In the period since World War II, the Texas Forest Service, alone among Texas conservation agencies, has developed land-use policies that recognize the interrelationship of forests, climate, soil, wildlife, and water. Despite the success of the Texas Forest Service, its policies drew increasing criticism by the 1970s. Environmentalists objected to the monoculture produced by reforestation for timber only. They argued that it destroyed the ecology of the region and was harmful to other conservation objectives, such as wildlife preservation and recreation.

Next to land-management planning perhaps the most critical environmental concerns among Texans have been those associated with the production of energy; yet in the late 1970s Texas had no comprehensive energy policy. Both the worldwide energy crisis of 1974 and the depletion of oil and gas reserves, the state's major energy sources, dictated the need for a coherent energy policy. Three state agencies directly affected energy policy: the Railroad Commission, the Governor's Office of Fuel Allocation, and the Governor's Division of Planning Coordination, although decisions by other agencies often influenced that policy. In addition, conflict between public and private development presented a major problem. Only the legislature could determine the relative roles of the private and public sectors in electric, oil and gas, and coal production, as well as encourage experimentation with less proven sources of energy, but state officials complained of getting little guidance from the legislature.

Of the various problems associated with energy production perhaps none received more attention in the 1970s than strip mining of coal. Despite some successful examples of land restoration following strip mining in East Texas both bureaucrats and environmental critics continued to call for more specific policies concerning restoration. Texas also lacked laws governing the mining of uranium. The commissioner of health complained in 1974 that his department suffered from lack of authority to deal with health hazards associated with open-pit mining of uranium as well as from inadequate funding for radiation control and solid-waste disposal.

While historically the Texas Railroad Commission has had primary responsibility for regulating production of oil and gas, federal action directly affected state policy. Many environmental issues impinged on the production of Texas oil and gas. Among these were environmental protection of coastal waters during exploration and production of oil and gas on the continental shelf as well as the water requirements and water pollution problems associated with petroleum production.

After 1974 the Texas government became more actively concerned about energy policy. In 1975, the legislature authorized the appointment of a Governor's Energy Advisory Council charged with developing comprehensive plans for the state's energy needs. Consisting of representatives of energy-related industries, this council was later replaced by the Texas Energy Advisory Council, chaired by the lieutenant governor. This group, which included many holdovers from the Governor's Energy Council, had done little by the early eighties.

While in 1978 Texans voted to tax-exempt solar and wind-powered energy devices, little else had been done to encourage development of other alternate energy sources except for nuclear power. Growing resistance to the construction of nuclear power plants and the problem of nuclear waste disposal placed the future of that source of energy in doubt. Texans, while somewhat more aware of energy-related problems since 1974, did little to reorient their thinking away from traditional supply sources.

By the early 1980s most authorities recognized that water would most likely be the primary limiting factor in the state's economic development. Perhaps the most critical problems facing many Texans by the 1980s was the management of groundwater usage. In the late 1970s groundwater provided 90 percent of the public water supply systems and approximately one-third of the water used by industry, while irrigation utilized nearly 85 percent of all groundwater pumped in the state. Texas groundwater problems fall into four categories: declining supplies and rising costs, deterioration of water quality, losses of spring and stream flows, and coastal subsidence.

While declining groundwater supply affected all the heavily populated areas of the state, it was most critical to the people of the High Plains, who faced the possibility of their highly productive agricultural area reverting to semidesert. By 1978 High Plains agriculture constituted 65 percent of the total value of Texas crop production. Attempts to alleviate the situation on the High Plains reflected many of the factors relevant to solution of Texas water problems. While the state maintains legal authority over surface water, legal ownership of groundwater is associated with land ownership. According to Texas courts, a landowner has absolute authority to extract groundwater from his property without regard to the effect on others.

The controversial Texas Water Plan continued to engender both enthusiastic support and militant opposition. In 1969 and 1976 TWP opponents achieved major victories at the polls by defeating proposals supportive of the project, which represented major victories for the emerging environmental movement in Texas. Nevertheless, influential leaders and politicians still promoted the idea in the late 1970s, while West Texans continued to believe that changing technology and worldwide demand for their products would make the plan acceptable. On the other hand a 1983 study by the Texas Water Resources Institute predicted that, unless the area immediately instituted rigorous conservation measures, by the year 2030 the 5.9 million acres of irrigated land would be reduced by almost two-thirds. Such a drastic reduction could cause significant repercussions to the Texas economy. It remained to be seen if Texans would accept radical changes in the traditional ethic affecting water policy or if they would reap the consequences of that ethic.

Water quality became an increasingly critical issue during the decades of the 1960s and 1970s. Even though the legislature had endorsed the Texas Water Quality Act in 1967, seven years later the executive director of the Texas Water Quality Board (TWQB) declared a need to develop a state water quality policy. Only in 1970, under pressure from the national government, did the state begin to file suits against water polluters, leading to conflict between the national Environmental Protection Agency (EPA) and the TWQB over application of federal standards for water quality. In 1978 the legislature added over one hundred amendments to the 1972 Clean Water Act to make the water supply more stable and safe; yet by 1980 many communities had not met those standards because voters refused to provide necessary funds.

Officials recognized coastal subsidence as a serious matter in the Houston-Galveston area by the 1970s. In the Houston region local authority had its greatest success in handling groundwater problems associated with subsidence, after the legislature in 1975 authorized creation of the Harris-Galveston Coastal Subsidence District (HGCSD). Through use of the pumping permits, the district had significantly reduced the rate of subsidence by 1978. Despite numerous legal challenges from those affected by these restrictions, the Texas Supreme Court upheld rulings favoring the district's action. HGCSD remained the most effective state agency managing groundwater in the late 1970s. Under the exegisis of the situation, Texans had begun to alter, however slightly, their individualistic approach to use of groundwater resources.

The question of navigation on Texas rivers and harbors has led to a conflict over policy in many areas of the state. Lack of a clear navigation policy brought constant conflicts between navigation districts and other state environmental agencies, especially over dredging and spoils disposal. One project that continued to stir controversy into the 1980s was the proposal to canalize the Trinity River for barge navigation to the Dallas-Fort Worth region. Just as the Trinity project seemed on the verge of success, a group of environmentalists and fiscal conservatives organized opposition to it, defeating in 1973 a local bond referendum necessary to obtain federal funding.

The nature of Texas rivers has made periodic flooding a serious problem in much of the state. Torrential rains at the semi-arid headwaters of Texas rivers often swell the dry streambeds, rushing seaward where they overload the lower, wetter reaches of the river. Texans have used traditional methods of physical restraint—levees and dams—to try to prevent damage from flood waters. Neither the state nor local governments have done much to prevent residential or commercial construction in flood-prone areas, but in the 1970s some groups began to advocate flood plain management through zoning. While a few public officials endorsed the idea, most Texans and their leaders continued to cling to the right of an individual to use his property without restriction. That philosophy often resulted in greater losses of property and life from flooding and greater public expense in trying to hold back nature's rampages.

The coastal zone of Texas represents an area where almost all aspects of water resources issues interconnect. Because of rapid population growth and industrial sprawl, the Texas coast has become one of the state's most critical areas of land and water-use problems. The multifarious issues associated with the coastal areas have received considerable attention since the late 1960s. Concern about bays and estuaries led the Texas legislature in 1969 to request an investigation of coastal resources. The resulting studies indicated the fragmented nature of planning for water management in the coastal area, especially those policies that affected water supply and water quality in the bays and estuaries. By 1971 the legislature had taken tentative steps to preserve the ecology of the coastal area, especially as it was affected by the freshwater inflows from rivers and streams. The legislature strengthened the state's authority over this matter in 1975. The Federal Coastal Zone Management Act of 1972 pressured Texas to establish the Texas Coastal Management Program (TCMP), which influenced the legislature to pass several acts concerning resource protection in the coastal zone.

Developments during the 1970s focused attention on the need for greater coordination of the various agencies associated with Texas water policy. In 1977 the legislature combined the Water Development Board, Water Quality Board, and Water Rights Commission into the Texas Department of Water Resources (TDWR), charged with planning for all water developments in the state. Despite recognition of state responsibility in water planning, Texas formulated no effective statewide plan, because consensus did not exist among Texans concerning the goals of water resource development in their state. By yielding to local perspectives and authority concerning water development, state officials retarded statewide planning. Critics accused TDWR in the 1980s of protecting agribusiness and industrial users, petroleum and lignite operations, and sports fishing at the expense of proper water management. The agency's challenge was to set priorities on future uses of water in Texas or to determine how all water users could be served at the same time.

In the area of air-quality control Texas began to develop a program only in the early eighties under prodding by the federal government. Created in 1965 the Texas Air Control Board claimed by 1974 that it had reduced pollution from identifiable sources but argued that it faced the difficult task of discovering the source of many other pollutants. EPA accused Texas agencies not only of minimal enforcement of federal air-quality regulations, but of greater laxity in enforcement than most other states. Texas businessmen criticized the federal agency's arbitrariness and rigidity. While EPA and TACB quarreled with each other, Texas environmentalists accused both agencies of excessive leniency in enforcement of air-pollution controls.

In the early 1980s slow economic growth reinforced antiregulatory attitudes in the state concerning air-quality control; however, opposition had also grown against increasing pollution from new plant construction, especially along the Gulf Coast. By 1983 Texans had yet to develop a coherent philosophy concerning air quality or even a firm commitment to the principle in general. Planning and control had only begun.

Park development and wildlife management remained in the 1980s one of the less successful programs in the Texas conservation movement. By the 1980s the GFC turned more toward management of wildlife on state owned or leased land, but critics, nevertheless, continued to complain that the state emphasized law enforcement to the detriment of wildlife management. Clearly, Texas wildlife still faced many threats in the decade of the eighties.

During the 1960s and 1970s the legislature provided more substantial support for the parks movement in several ways. In 1969 the lawmakers created the Texas Conservation Foundation, charged with encouraging private donations of park lands, and with administering such areas until the state could find a use for them. Providing more substantial funding for parks in 1972 through the Dedicated Parks Fund, the legislature followed in 1979 with additional funds for park acquisition.

In the 1970s and 1980s environmental and conservation groups, such as the Sierra Club and the Texas Nature Conservancy, actively promoted preservation of land for parks development. As the trend toward urbanization continued in the eighties, the inadequacy of the Texas parks system became increasingly evident. Although in 1980 Texas had 105 state parks, it still ranked far behind most other states in park area per capita. Texans not only pressed into their overcrowded parks, but fled to support the excellent park resorts in neighboring states.

That pressure from the federal government encouraged increased state activity about environmental issues was clearly reflected in a 1974 report from the Governor's Division of Planning Coordination concerning "Natural Resource and Environmental Agencies in Texas." Of the twenty-six state agencies concerned with some aspect of environmental issues, several indicated their resentment of federal pressure and their fear of federal action if the state did not develop its own environmental policies. The report from the Texas Water Quality Board expressed clearly both the resentment of federal regulations as well as the growth psychology of many Texans, declaring that in meeting water quality standards established by the Federal Water Quality Act of 1972 Texas should do nothing adversely to affect its economic development.

A change in the public's view of the environment, along with federal pressure, doubtless prompted this evaluation of Texas environmental agencies. The report revealed a fragmented approach to environmental issues. While the agencies generally agreed that Texas needed a more comprehensive approach to environmental problems, they admitted that effective interagency communication was generally lacking. To achieve a more unified approach to these problems, most agencies recommended increased coordination and cooperation, while allowing each agency to retain its independent status.

Even before passage of NEPA Texas had taken some tentative

steps toward improving coordination of its environmental policy. As a result of water-management recommendations made by the Texas Research League (TRL) in 1967, the legislature authorized the governor to establish interagency councils to coordinate planning among related agencies. Governor Connally created the Interagency Council on Natural Resources and the Environment (ICNRE) to coordinate activities of conservation and environmental agencies. The ineffectiveness of ICNRE indicated that most agencies are unwilling to relinquish voluntarily any of their independence to a central coordinating body. Doubtless, fear of losing agency independence as well as rivalries among the agencies contributed to this reluctance to change significantly the way Texas approached environmental issues.

In 1977, the Natural Resources Council (NRC) replaced the ICNRE as the chief coordinating body for policies and activities concerning the state's natural resources. Abolishing the Natural Resources Council in 1981, the government established the Texas Energy and Natural Resources Advisory Council. Clearly, state officials had been actively searching for an effective administrative mechanism throughout the 1970s for managing the state's natural resources. Whether the organization in place by 1983 would prove sufficient to handle the problems of the future remained to be seen.

Several factors influenced the history of conservation in Texas and continued to affect environmental developments in the state throughout the twentieth century. The belief in the unlimited riches of nature and man's right to exploit that largess without restriction motivated Texans as it had other Americans. Regional perspective remained a hindrance to statewide conservation planning, more so in Texas than in most other states because of both size and geographical diversity. Only after 1900 did significant groups or state officials begin to seriously advocate any conservation policy for the state, with the turning point in public awareness concerning conservation in Texas coming in the 1920s. Not until the 1960s, however, did the various public agencies and private groups concerned with conservation begin to cooperate in limited ways, but the conservation movement in Texas remained fragmented. It had yet to achieve real unity in 1983. In addition, political consideration still influenced appointment of personnel to the various conservation agencies and boards. Political interference in policy decisions continued to complicate the development of conservation policy, while financing for such programs remained generally low.

Since 1900 Texas conservation efforts have generally emphasized use-type of conservation, designed to manage resources primarily for the most effective economic exploitation. Achievements in Texas environmental programs have usually occurred with support from powerful economic groups that considered certain policies beneficial to their interest. In the 1960s environmentally oriented organizations emphasizing ecological and non-material aspects of conservation became more active in Texas. They have figured significantly in many environmental issues: pressing for a Big Thicket national park, supporting a more effective state park system, opposing various water projects, and actively pursuing various projects of local and statewide concern. As Texans entered the eighties they confronted many critical questions concerning the management of their environment. The policies they supported, or failed to support, would have significant, perhaps crucial, impact on the quality of life as well as the prosperity of those who lived in the Lone Star State.

# 15

## Texas Women at Work

*Fane Downs*

The dominant Texas images are masculine and the archetypes are male. In the public mind a typical Texan is an Anglo rancher, oil man, or wheeler dealer; he is tough, resourceful, just a tad ruthless, and above all, a self-reliant individualist. This framework for describing and understanding Texans omits the majority of Texas men who are neither Anglo, ranchers, oil men, or wheeler dealers — but who, of course, may be individualists — and all of Texas women. Moreover, Texas history is sometimes chronicled as the providential triumph of American political and cultural institutions over inferior ones. This point of view overlooks the stories of the supporting cast and the "losers." Again, women are virtually absent.

The history of Texas women, when it has emerged, is principally collections of the exploits and contributions of outstanding or unusual women. While these stories are significant, and certainly interesting, the larger story of everyday, average women is missed. The potential topics of women's history are rich and varied, both in time period and subject matter. This essay will deal principally with women's work in three eras of Texas history — hunter, agrarian, urban — recognizing that such approach omits consideration of other important topics: women's roles in creating community and state institutions, or women in politics, to name but two.

Perhaps three centuries ago a group of Karankawa women searched for food where today a group of modern high tech women scientists and pilots are preparing for space flight. These three cen-

*Pioneer Texas woman in a typical early Texas home.*
— Eugene C. Barker Texas History Center, The University of Texas, from the papers of the Joseph E. Taulmans

turies reveal an incredible variety of women's experiences stemming from change over time, geographic location, and class, ethnic, or racial identity.

The history of women in Texas reaches far back in time to the prehistoric hunter cultures. As this way of life was transformed into regionally distinctive patterns, broad culture groups emerged in Texas. In each, women were integral to the social and economic survival of the clan, band, or tribe. Among the nomadic gathering and hunting coastal Karankawa, women gathered roots, berries, and nuts in season and hunted smaller animals. The Comanche women prepared the game brought down by the men. Women of the Caddo peoples of East Texas performed most of the agricultural labor. Although men helped prepare the fields, women planted, cultivated, and harvested the crops of corn and beans; later, they prepared the food for storage or consumption. Women also gathered nuts and several varieties of wild fruits in the forests. The agricultural economy of the Caddo people of East Texas provided an economic base sufficient to allow a differentiation of tasks and status. Although women did not possess delegated authority, they might exercise considerable influence within kinship or tribal groups. Female chiefs were rare as were women religious leaders; however, older women might have influence by virtue of their supernatural power.

Indian women likewise had the principal responsibility for household tasks — preparing and storing food, making clothing, gathering and administering medicinal herbs and manufacturing pottery, baskets, and other household utensils. In several tribes women erected the shelters. Karankawa women constructed their huts using a dozen or so willow poles which were covered with woven mats and skins; these circular structures were ten to twelve feet in diameter and housed seven or eight people. Plains Indian women had a more arduous task of homebuilding. A family's teepee made of buffalo hides could weigh nearly three hundred pounds and was held up by sixteen to eighteen poles of over fourteen feet in length. The women could erect or dismantle and pack the teepee in about half an hour.

Observers who frequently commented that Plains Indian women seemed to be slaves while their husband relaxed in camp failed to recognize the gender-based division of labor. Men served as leaders and hunters — "breadwinners" — while the women bore and tended the children and accomplished a wide variety of household chores. They were submissive and subordinate to the men but were equally responsible for the well-being of the group. As important as Indian women's economic functions were, their familial functions were even more essential. Mothers had primary responsibility for the children for several years until their training was shared by other tribal members.

Life for Texas Indian women was frequently hard and hazardous. Infant mortality was high and disease common. Food supplies were sometimes precarious and enemies often threatened. The intermittent, yet vicious, war for possession of Texas took its toll on the lives of Texas Indian women resulting ultimately in the destruction of a way of life which had been well-adapted to a time and place. The Indian women who survived this war for conquest of the land did so by escaping Texas or by incorporating into the Spanish-Mexican culture.

As frontier women, Indians had a distinct advantage over their later Hispanic and Anglo counterparts. They had a large kinship network and significant support groups; living in bands, clans or tribes provided sufficient social community in which they could live securely. They did not experience the isolation and loneliness which was such a factor in the lives of some later frontier women.

Frontier life for the subsistence farmers and their families differed in many respects from that of the Indians. Hispanic immigration into Texas from northern Mexico resulted in the establishment of missions, presidios, towns, farm and ranches. Spanish-Mexican occupants while never extremely numerous nevertheless left a Hispanic imprint on Texas. Anglo-American and European immigration into Texas began in the third decade of the nineteenth century. The early immigrants were principally farmers like their Hispanic counterparts. As settlement and settlers moved across Texas throughout the nineteenth century, patterns of life stayed basically the same. Even in the twentieth century, before the introduction of electricity, families in rural areas lived in a manner reminiscent of earlier times. In these subsistence agriculture areas in all parts of the state women's lives bore a startling similarity. For black, Hispanic, and white women, daily routines and annual rhythms varied little whether they were separated by several hundred miles or several decades.

Rural women's space and identity were defined by their functions as wife, mother, and housekeeper. While work and responsibilities were divided into those done by men and those done by women, life on farms did not permit a strict division. Men and women who could not or would not cross into one another's spheres risked a breakdown of the efficient functioning of the farm. But there were definite jobs, tasks, and responsibilities for each. Since women spent the major part of their time coping with household tasks, a survey of the variety of houses will show something of the challenge of housework.

Hispanic women lived in *jacales,* structures formed by placing mesquite or other poles upright, close together in the ground and covering them with hides, blankets, thatch, or plaster. These homes were roofed with dried reeds or coarse grass. In the later nineteenth century these houses were often patched with flattened tin cans. The floors were packed mud or clay; blankets served as doors and shutters. These huts were usually around 12′ x 12′; and although they appeared flimsy and primitive, they lasted many years. These houses were sparsely furnished with mats, a few chairs or benches, a table and a few kitchen utensils. Hispanic women in somewhat more prosperous families lived in adobe houses. These structures constructed of adobe brick were more weatherproof and easier to keep than the *jacales.*

Farm women of eastern and central Texas lived in log cabins, usually one room at first. It was common for families to live in the wagon, lean-to, or tent before the log cabin was erected. The houses had dirt or puncheon floors, a fireplace, beds or pallets, a few chairs or benches, table, cupboards to hold the few utensils and tools, and a trunk for personal possessions. In western Texas where trees were scarce and lumber unavailable, families lived in dugouts, semidugouts, and sod houses made of prairie sod brick. These homes, while they provided ample protection from the elements, were nightmares for the housekeepers. Dirt continually flaked off the ceiling and walls; moreover, heavy rains could cause the house to collapse. The furnishings included whatever had been brought in the wagon or subsequently purchased. These prairie dwellings, like the log houses, were transitory because as soon as they could afford it, the family acquired lumber and built a frame house. Those early, crude homes were small, crowded, dirty, poorly ventilated, and primitive. Only somewhat less primitive were the small frame houses in which twentieth century rural families dwelled before the advent of electricity and in which some still dwell. Small, box-like with little insulation, these structures were hot in the summer and cold in the winter.

Farm women had to maintain households with few conveniences or labor-saving devices. The availability and proximity of water was probably the most significant factor in a woman's work patterns. The family's water needs were considerable, and a woman might have to spend a great deal of time and energy carrying it—if her husband, sons, or daughters were not available. Women were ingenious in their conservation, recycling the water until it was consumed or so dirty as to be unusable.

Food preparation was a continuous full-time activity with women having responsibilities for growing as well as preparing, preserving, and storing the food. Most farms had a garden which was the province of women. Their husbands generally prepared the ground and the women then planted, cultivated and harvested the vegetable crops. Many families had fruit trees or access to wild fruit and nuts in the forests. Given the lack of refrigeration and distance from stores, one of the important chores was food preservation. The fruits and vegetables had to be either dried or canned. Canning on a wood stove in the summer was a dreaded, but necessary, job. The fruit or vegetables had to be canned when picked; thus canning was a constant activity while the crops lasted — usually something was ripening from June to September. The wood stove, while a friendly presence in the winter, contained a blazing inferno during canning. The water and sugar had to be boiled; then the fruit had to follow. The jars had to be boiled before the food was packed, necessitating more heat and wood. This process took all day for many days in the searing heat of summer.

Hispanic women prepared corn meal from corn grown in gardens they tended. Every housewife possessed a stone *comal* (griddle) and *metate* (which consisted of the metate on which the grain was ground and the *mano* with which it was ground). After the maize soaked, it was ground, then patted into flat cakes—tortillas—and baked on the comal.

Women also helped with butchering hogs, calves, or game, and jerking or salting the meat. They sometimes milked the cow, and nearly always made the butter and cheese. Further, they tended to chickens and gathered the eggs. It was not uncommon for women to have the use of the butter and egg money for their own purposes.

Cooking meals involved considerable labor and ingenuity. Many nineteenth century farm women cooked outside on an open fire or in the fireplace inside. The heat of these fires was difficult to control and cooking on them was hot and dangerous. Women cooked with relatively few utensils, equipment, and ingredients. The variety and quality of the meals is remarkable given the rather meager materials the women had to work with. Feeding the family was chore enough, but when harvest or roundup time came, women prepared food for all the hands. The neighbor women helped with these community feeds providing an enjoyable social occasion.

Except for one group of women, washday was not a time for socializing. For Hispanic women along the Rio Grande or San Antonio River washday occurred by the banks of the stream. Women brought their children and dirty clothes and spent the day toiling over the laundry and enjoying one another's company. For other women, however, washday was the most dreaded day of the week. Women made their own soap by mixing lye (obtained by pouring water and lime over fireplace ashes) and grease and boiling it until soap came. This obnoxious chore was best done outside with soapmaker standing upwind of the kettle. Washday necessitated many gallons of water and hot fires. Generally this was done outside. The laundress sorted the clothes—whites, colored, and work clothes—and washed and scrubbed each in turn. The clothes might be "punched" with a heavy stick in a vat of boiling water or they might be beaten on a bench or block as well as being scrubbed on a rub board. The heavy, wet clean clothes were then transferred to the rinse water where they were sloshed around. The laundress then wrung them, blued and starched them, and put them on the line, on the fence, or on bushes. The physical labor involved in washday was so great that washing machines and running water were the most ardently desired home improvements. Women eagerly anticipated their children growing into the chores. And there is at least one surviving dog-powered washing machine which worked well until the dog began to run away each Monday.

Washday over — with backs aching — women contemplated, perhaps with even more dread, the next day's ironing. Irons weighed six or seven pounds; they had to be heated on the stove and each lasted through about half a man's shirt. In summer, heat from the wood stove and the irons was nearly unbearable. Spending the day lifting seven-pound weights in the heat made women tired and old before their time.

Frequently women had to make the clothes as well as keep them clean and in good repair. Before commercial cloth was widely available in rural areas, women spun thread and wove cotton or woolen cloth. Women used their needlework skills to add personal touches to their clothes and homes. One of the well-known community gatherings for women was, and still is in some areas, the quilting party. Women frequently worked together on quilts accomplishing the work quickly and with pleasant social interaction. The quilt form allowed women to give free rein to their self-expression; and although designs were passed down from mothers to daughters, no two quilts were alike and all bore the imprint of their makers. Women exercised considerable ingenuity in their needlework; one creative quilt maker washed, bleached, and dyed 325 Bull Durham tobacco sacks and fashioned them into a red, white, and blue striped quilt on a muslin backing decorated with white stars on the blue stripes.

Women provided beauty for their homes; they also provided an atmosphere of love, nurture, and support for their children and husbands. Some women managed child-rearing along with their numerous other tasks very gracefully; others found themselves distracted and burdened by their children. They all eagerly anticipated the day when the daughters and sons were old enough to help around the place. Mothers worried about their children's health and safety and worked hard to keep them safe and well. Infant mortality rates in the nineteenth century were as high as 30 percent, and it was a rare mother who did not lose one or more of her children. Slave women's family life was a great deal less stable than that of free women. If their children did not perish at a young age, they might be sold to other owners; sometimes these separations were permanent.

Women worried not only about their children's health, but also about their own. The risks of childbearing were great and some women practiced birth control and abortion in order to limit the size of their families. Knowledge of contraceptive methods and abortifacients was apparently widespread so women could exercise some control over this most significant area of their lives. Even so, women experienced various debilitating illnesses and injuries connected with pregnancy and childbirth. They often feared childbirth because of the risks to themselves and the infants.

Many women experienced alienation, isolation, and loneliness on their frontiers and in their rural environments. The pioneer women on the leading edge of settlement missed their families and the company of other women. The anxieties of starting life in a raw, unpeopled area caused some women grievous stress; most, however, coped successfully with their loneliness and depression. Rural isolation was diminished by visiting and by such community events as dances, barn raisings, harvests, roundups, and Grange meetings. As Texas became more populated, women set about establishing schools, churches, and other agencies of civilization—thus reducing their own isolation considerably.

Women obviously coped well and ably in rural Texas; they were remarkably self-reliant and resourceful workers. Their work, sheer drudgery by the standards of any age, was essentially the same as that of their mothers and grandmothers. Moreover, they found time to grace their homes with beauty and their communities with concern. While they experienced no marked change in male-female roles and dominance patterns, they did experience feelings of satisfaction and pride in their work and accomplishments. In most families women's work was valued and respected and not considered subordinate nor second-class. Women's obvious contributions to frontier and rural society were not "rewarded" by increased legal status nor

*Texas women work in sewing rooms in government-sponsored programs during the 1930s.*

— Austin-Travis County Collection

a significant relaxation of expectations of what was appropriate for women to do and be.

This discussion of farm women should not obscure the wide variety of life experiences of other women. Many women lived in small towns, some serving as teachers, seamstresses, laundresses, and shopkeepers. Some women lived at army forts as officers' and enlisted men's wives or as collateral support personnel. Other women lived as slaves on plantations or smaller farms and worked at a variety of tasks both in the fields and in the house. Their labor was not so different from that of other women, but their living conditions and chattel status made their existence markedly different from free Texas women. Slave women more often than white women worked in the fields and thus had to attend to their family's needs at night after their field work was done. Unlike free women, slaves were forced to work and risked severe punishment if they resisted. Slave women were subject to often brutal sexual exploitation by rape or forced breeding.

Work for wages was fairly uncommon among women in the nineteenth century. The 1860 census lists 58 women engaged in the lumber industry, 3 in fishing, 6 in cotton ginning, along with scattered others in the few manufacturing enterprises of those years. In 1870 some 5 percent of women over ten years old were listed as employed. Of these women almost one-half were engaged in agriculture, not surprising since Texas was 93 percent rural. Nearly one-fourth of the female agriculture workers were girls 10-15 years old. Ten years later the census again revealed that one-half employed women were engaged in agriculture; about one-third were girls 10-15. For those two censuses the other major employment category for Texas women was domestic service (46 percent in 1870 and 43 percent in 1880).

Other prominent jobs were laborers, laundresses, seamstresses, hotel employees, milliners, and tailors. In 1880 there were 16 women listed as clergy, 2 lawyers, 15 physicians, 6 bankers, 96 traders, 54 government employees, 190 musicians and music teachers, 7 bakers, 12 boot and shoe makers, 7 wagon makers, 3 jewelers, 8 cigar makers, and 18 textile mill operatives. Teaching had not yet been feminized as a profession; in 1870 there were 1,190 men teachers and 431 women; ten years later there were 2,710 men and 1,624 women. Carl Degler in *At Odds: Women and the Family in America* calls the process of women following their husbands out of the home into industrial and commercial workplaces the "first transformation" of women's work. This process is evident in Texas though the profoundly rural character of the state retarded the process somewhat.

As Texas moved through the twentieth century, its economy became increasingly modern and urban with predictable results for women. More women lived in towns and cities and engaged in a wider variety of occupations than before. Most married women did not work outside the home until very recently. Of course, a much higher proportion of black and Hispanic women have worked for wages than white women. Changes in technology have eliminated the back-breaking drudgery of housework, but higher standards of cleanliness and increased demands of nurturance and child care have not significantly reduced the time and effort women are expected to spend as housewives and mothers.

A study of occupational census data of 1920, 1950, and 1980 will reveal something of the extent of changes in Texas women's lives and opportunities. The women's labor force more than doubled from 1920 to 1950 and then increased nearly four times by 1980; further, the proportion of women working increased dramatically. The following figures show these changes:

| year | women employed | % of women employed |
|---|---|---|
| 1920 | 303,843 | 17.8 |
| 1950 | 720,531 | 26.8 |
| 1980 | 2,751,443 | 50.0 |

A study of classes of employment will show that women's working patterns and opportunities have changed somewhat, but with some concentrations remaining the same, as the graph below illustrates.

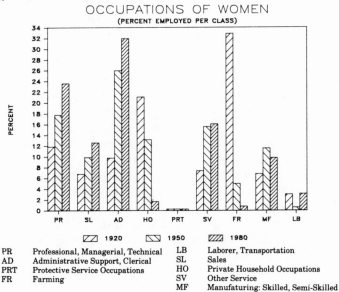

OCCUPATIONS OF WOMEN
(PERCENT EMPLOYED PER CLASS)

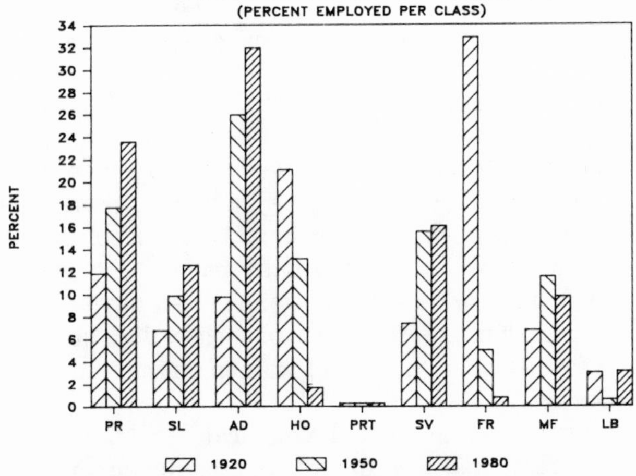


| | | | |
|---|---|---|---|
| PR | Professional, Managerial, Technical | LB | Laborer, Transportation |
| AD | Administrative Support, Clerical | SL | Sales |
| PRT | Protective Service Occupations | HO | Private Household Occupations |
| FR | Farming | SV | Other Service |
| | | MF | Manufaturing: Skilled, Semi-Skilled |

While the pattern of women's work has shown some changes, the percent of women to men in many occupations shows little change. The number and percentage of female workers in selected professional occupations will show interesting trends.

Professional, Managerial, and Technical Occupations

| | 1920 | | 1950 | | 1980 | |
|---|---|---|---|---|---|---|
| accountants | 259 | 7% | 2,507 | 15% | 28,718 | 41% |
| authors, editors, reporters | 209 | 18% | 1,222 | 41% | 4,603 | 50% |
| clergy | 72 | 1% | 369 | 3% | 781 | 4% |
| college profs | 438 | 34% | 1,670 | 26% | 12,496 | 34% |
| computer analysts | —* | | — | | 2,135 | 19% |
| dentists | 42 | 3% | 71 | 3% | 239 | 4% |
| dietitians | — | | 824 | 94% | 3,372 | 94% |
| engineers | 0 | | 248 | 1% | 4,231 | 4% |
| lawyers, judges | 52 | 1% | 226 | 3% | 3,672 | 12% |
| librarians | 177 | 86% | 1,983 | 90% | 8,250 | 85% |
| nurses | 3,265 | 96% | 16,843 | 97% | 56,582 | 94% |
| physicians | 133 | 2% | 365 | 5% | 2,393 | 10% |
| religious workers | 554 | 59% | 1,108 | 71% | 1,765 | 56% |
| social workers | — | | 1,323 | 67% | 12,672 | 63% |
| teachers | 26,050 | 81% | | | | |
| elementary | | | 31,698 | 90% | 140,711 | 83% |
| secondary | | | 10,795 | 55% | 29,632 | 61% |
| med tech | 367 | 87% | 2,108 | 60% | 19,566 | 69% |
| veterinarians | 0 | | 32 | 5% | 259 | 12% |

*Dash indicates absence of occupational category from census.

One of the most obvious findings is the heavy concentration of women as dietitians, librarians, nurses, teachers, and social workers over the six decades. It has been observed and documented in women's history that teaching and nursing have long been considered appropriate women's work as extensions of their roles as mother and nurturer; thus it would seem equally natural for women to be dietitians and social workers. Since women also have been considered the protectors of the moral values of society, it is not surprising to find a significant concentration of women as religious workers—though not clergy.

The percentage of women in the medical, legal, and theological professions has remained low, except as technicians or assistants. There has been a significant increase in the percentage of women physicians, lawyers, veterinarians, and scientists. Less dramatic gains occurred in dentistry and engineering. Newer professions are showing fairly high concentrations of women; computer analysts and programmers are frequently women. The most dramatic change of male-female ratio is in accounting. It would appear that women have made significant inroads into professional, managerial, and technical occupations in the last sixty years.

This picture, however, is not the same for all Texas women. In this class of occupations for 1980 the percentage concentration by race is as follows: Hispanic 14 percent, black 17 percent, and white 27 percent. Black and Hispanic women are heavily concentrated in teaching and nursing.

Women's participation in sales and clerical occupations has increased in the last half-century. For 1950 and 1980 the clerical category is the most heavily feminized of all others except for private household occupations; in 1980 almost one-third of employed women were in administrative support and clerical jobs.

The chart below shows the percentages of women employed in selected sales and clerical occupations.

Sales and Clerical Occupations

| | 1920 | | 1950 | | 1980 | |
|---|---|---|---|---|---|---|
| insurance sales | 201 | 5% | 1,758 | 12% | 11,103 | 29% |
| real estate agents | 411 | 6% | 1,313 | 17% | 20,049 | 48% |
| retail sales | 17,667 | 29% | 66,738 | 39% | 250,128 | 67% |
| retail dealers | 2,164 | 4% | 20,461 | 19% | 36,849 | 29% |
| bank tellers | — | | 1,016 | 43% | 23,559 | 90% |
| bookkeepers, cashiers | 7,512 | 38% | 41,748 | 73% | 121,558 | 90% |
| file clerks | — | | 3,423 | 86% | 18,087 | 87% |
| secretaries, typists | 13,608 | 87% | 63,680 | 94% | 314,088 | 99% |
| teachers' aides | — | | — | | 20,205 | 93% |
| telephone operators | 6,381 | 92% | 17,267 | 96% | 17,964 | 91% |

The sales and clerical occupations are heavily female with some categories having in excess of 90 percent women. The explosion in office work in the last four decades has provided new employment opportunities for women, making work more attractive than when the options were more limited. It would appear that white, Hispanic, and black women have all benefitted from this expansion of jobs. Percentage distribution among classes of employment for those three groups is as follows for 1980: sales occupations, Hispanic 11.6 percent, black 7.2 percent, white 13.9 percent; clerical occupations,

Hispanic 25.9 percent, black 22.2 percent, and white 35.3 percent.

Women have been heavily represented in service occupations, and some of these occupations are still almost exclusively female—domestic servants, cooks and kitchen work, hotel maids, counter workers, waitresses, practical nurses, and laundry workers—reflecting the availability of women with few skills needing employment and their willingness to work for low wages. Industrial and factory jobs for unskilled persons have not always been readily available to women either. Black and Hispanic women are heavily represented in service industries. In 1980, 84% of the private household workers and servants were black and Hispanic. Selected service occupations with numbers and percentages of women employed in them are as follows:

Service Occupations

| | 1920 | | 1950 | | 1980 | |
|---|---|---|---|---|---|---|
| housekeepers, chambermaids | 3,553 | 94% | 10,232 | 94% | 35,228 | 84% |
| launderers | 3,468 | 73% | 7,839 | 97% | 7,557 | 68% |
| servants | 64,262 | 82% | 86,990 | 96% | 32,761 | 96% |
| waitresses | 3,207 | 40% | 33,818 | 85% | 62,544 | 84% |
| bartenders | 0 | | 514 | 14% | 6,883 | 51% |

Perhaps the most salient fact about private household occupations today is that they employ fewer than 2 percent of all employed women, reflecting the increasing array of jobs available for women. Traditionally, women have preferred virtually any work for pay rather than as household servants because of the confining nature of the work, hard toil, and low pay.

Women have worked in a wide variety of skilled and semiskilled manufacturing jobs. While they were and are concentrated in a few industries, they are represented in a large number of "non-traditional" occupations. Selected craft and manufacturing occupations for the three census reports reveal some patterns.

Craft and Manufacturing Occupations

| | 1920 | | 1950 | | 1980 | |
|---|---|---|---|---|---|---|
| bakers | 130 | 6.00% | 623 | 15.0% | 2,993 | 52% |
| carpenters | 13 | .04% | 368 | .6% | 1,325 | 2% |
| mechanics | 3 | .02% | 685 | .8% | 1,506 | 1% |
| paperhangers | 3 | .80% | 135 | 10.0% | 441 | 27% |
| dressmakers | 6,937 | 99.00% | 8,882 | 98.0% | 4,794 | 94% |

| | | | | | | |
|---|---|---|---|---|---|---|
| lumber, furniture mfg. | 246 | 2.00% | 1,000 | 13.0% | 1,810 | 15% |
| textiles, apparel mfg. | 1,274 | 31.00% | 7,964 | 72.0% | 45,765 | 95% |
| food ind. | 1,205 | 32.00% | 3,096 | 21.0% | 5,694 | 24% |
| metal ind. | 38 | .70% | 246 | 4.0% | 6,403 | 18% |
| electronic eqpt assemblers | — | | — | | 6,963 | 80% |

Women again are concentrated in "traditional" industries associated with food and clothing. The reasons for this are likely the wage scale and skill level. In 1980 national wage figures revealed that the highest proportion of women workers was in textile and apparel industry and that this industry ranked lowest in hourly wage level of fifty-two industries. Strikingly, the lowest proportion of women was employed in coal mining in which the hourly wage ranked the highest of the fifty-two. Generally, the greater the proportion of women in the occupation, the lower the wages.

Women make up over three-fourths of the workers in a relatively new industry, electronic equipment assembling plants. However, the percentage of women engaged in manufacturing as skilled and semi-skilled workers has increased only marginally since 1920 (14 percent to 17 percent), and the percentage of all employed women working in these areas has remained nearly steady in the last thirty years. Among blacks and Hispanics the percentage of working women in manufacturing is 14 percent and 18 percent of the black and Hispanic female workforce as compared to 7 percent white for 1980.

In some respects the changes in women's employment patterns are not surprising. There has been a dramatic decline in the percentages of women employed in private household and farming occupations. The major shifts have been into clerical and sales occupations with significant gains registered in professional and managerial jobs. The service sector has likewise increased.

In *At Odds* Carl Degler suggests that while the second transformation has resulted in the adding of large numbers of married women to the workforce, old occupational patterns persist. Texas bears out his conclusions; gender-segregation in the workplace is quite marked with some occupations strongly feminized as noted earlier in this essay. Likewise these occupations tend to be those characterized by lower wages than the male-dominated occupations. The following graph illustrates the ratio of women to men in classes of occupations.

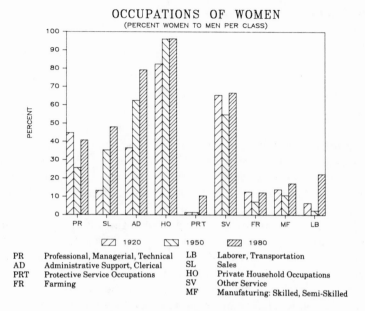

OCCUPATIONS OF WOMEN
(PERCENT WOMEN TO MEN PER CLASS)

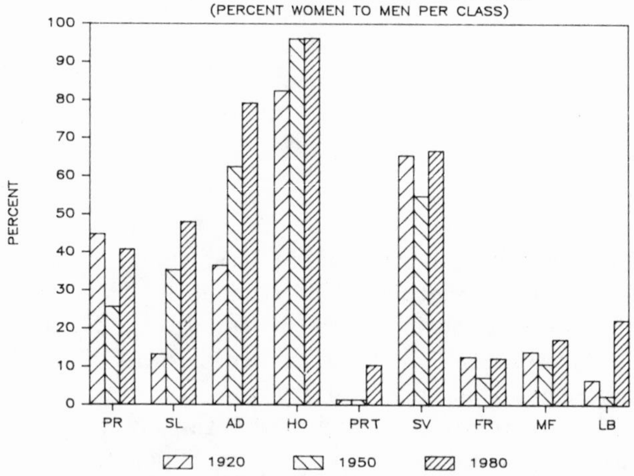


| | | | |
|---|---|---|---|
| PR | Professional, Managerial, Technical | LB | Laborer, Transportation |
| AD | Administrative Support, Clerical | SL | Sales |
| PRT | Protective Service Occupations | HO | Private Household Occupations |
| FR | Farming | SV | Other Service |
| | | MF | Manufaturing: Skilled, Semi-Skilled |

The composition of the female work force has changed dramatically in the past twenty years. Not only has the number of employed women increased significantly (in Texas from 1,051,404 in 1960 to 1,609,357 in 1970 to 2,751,443 in 1980), but the number of working mothers has likewise increased. In 1980 in Texas 48 percent of women with children under 6 were in the labor force; moreover, 63 percent of women with children 6-17 years old were in the labor force. Younger women have moved into the labor force in great numbers also.

Another common pattern is that women bear a disproportionate share of the unemployment, reflecting the types of jobs they hold and perhaps their tenure on the job. The following figures from January 1983 reveal that women had a higher percentage unemployed in every race category.

| | male | female |
|---|---|---|
| total | 7.8% | 9.6% |
| black | 14.1% | 14.4% |
| Hispanic | 12.5% | 14.5% |
| other minority | 7.6% | 12.1% |
| nonminority | 5.6% | 7.4% |

Women remain vulnerable to economic cycles and will remain so as long as current economic patterns persist. Over one-third of the families with children below poverty level were headed by women, which is consistent with the national patterns. The number of families headed by a woman with no husband present increased from 284,260 in 1970 to 467,362 in 1980.

Nationally women's earnings are 59 percent of the median for men; this ratio has remained virtually unchanged for two decades. There is no reason to suppose that the wage differential varies for Texas since the other employment statistics are comparable. Although earnings increase with the increase in the number of years of schooling, women at every level of educational achievement lagged far behind men's earnings. In a September 1982 study the commissioner of the Bureau of Labor Statistics observed that even the vast array of data does not reveal why women continue to work more in jobs that are traditionally female intensive, nor how much of their occupational choice may result from family responsibilities, nor how much of women's job choice and earnings may reflect discriminatory practices in hiring and promoting. But the facts are that for the United States and Texas, women in general earn less than men and that the jobs they hold command lower wages than the jobs held by men.

Texas women's lives have changed dramatically over the centuries. The transition from hunter to agriculture to urban ways has resulted in a significant change in women's work. Yet it appears that there has been little change in women's relationship to their families. Just as earlier women's work was integral to the smooth functioning of the family, contemporary women's work for wages is necessary for the family. Modern women, as surely as their Comanche or frontier ancestors, are the primary housekeepers and child-rearers, and are now frequently single parents. Although families are smaller today, women still carry out most of the household responsibilities. Women are a great deal more engaged in work for wages away from the home than in the past; moreover, their activities in political, civic, cultural, union, and church affairs have increased as well. Their economic and social contributions to families, to communities, and to the state are incalculable; and while their contributions are more visible today, they were no less essential and valuable in the past.

*William Goyens, Sam Houston and John Forbes with Col. Bowles at 1836 treaty-making with the Cherokees. Painting by Kermit Oliver.*

— Photo by Institute of Texan Cultures
Original at Texas Southern University

*Painting of "Chief" John Horse on a trek across Texas. This African was a member of an Indian tribe in the 1850s.*

— Photo by Institute of Texan Cultures,
painting from Texas Southern University

# 16

## Blacks in Texas

*Roland C. Hayes*

The existence of black people on what is now Texas soil dates back as early as the sixteenth century. They arrived with the first Europeans, continued to come in growing numbers for three centuries, and today constitute about 14 percent of the state's population. In those early days blacks came who were both free and slave. Free blacks came from Spain with the explorers, while those who came as slaves were captured mostly from West Africa and were brought to the Spanish-controlled territories during the slave trade era to dig for gold.

Around the 1520s, as more and more explorers came from Europe looking for gold and fame, history records the presence of blacks among those expeditions. One such man was Estaban, sometimes referred to as Estabenico (Little Stevie) by his companions. He was a Moor from North Africa who came with Captain Dorantes of the Narvaez Expedition and was one of the four survivors who, with Cabeza de Vaca, finally made their way across Texas to Mexico. Estaban was adept at making friends with the Indians and speaking their dialects; he played an important role in the first exploration in Texas. Records indicate that during Coronado's expedition of 1540, several Negroes accompanied him in his exploration across New Mexico and western Texas. In 1751, two Negro men were with the Frenchman Blancpain when he established an Indian trading post on the Trinity River in Texas. Friar Juan Augustin Morfi's 1777 census of San Antonio showed 151 Negroes among the population of that town. When Baron De Bastrop tried to secure a land grant from the Mexican government in 1805 to bring in colonists, he brought three Negro servants with him and established residence in San Antonio. When the United States purchased the Louisiana Territory in 1803, the Spanish declared that any slave who crossed the Sabine River into Texas was automatically free. Many slaves escaped and settled in the forests of East Texas, many joining friendly Indian tribes. The annals of history show the contributions of black women as well as men, such as a young black girl, Kian, who helped her mistress, Jane Long, through a difficult winter in 1819 on Bolivar Peninsula. The relationship was more amiable than one would expect, and they remained friends throughout the rest of their lives.

The purchase of the Louisiana Territory in 1803 opened up good farm land for cotton production. Cotton was becoming a very important economic crop, and there was a strong move to raise it in Texas. What Texas now needed was settlers.

Moses Austin came to San Antonio in 1820 seeking a land grant from the Spaniards for the purpose of bringing in colonists. Moses died before he could carry out his plans, but they were completed by his son, Stephen. The Austins supported the philosophy of slave labor, probably because they were from slave-holding states. Nevertheless, most of the colonists brought slaves and adhered to the southern states' way of life, i.e., large farms supported by large slave labor forces. Not all blacks who came at the time were slaves. Some free blacks came just as others came, seeking opportunities to acquire land.

Under Mexican law a freedman had all the legal and political rights of citizenship. He could own land, amass wealth, hold office, marry whom he pleased. The frontier society of pre-Texas generally accepted any individual on his personal merit without reference to race. The historical records show there were no strong social bars against intermarriage. This was true even of the Indian, who was in this period the low figure on the social scale.

As more and more southern Americans migrated to Texas, the southern culture and mentality became dominant. Small skirmishes between proslavery and antislavery factions took place. Blacks were on both sides of the issue since some blacks owned slaves while others were themselves slaves.

Americans who migrated to Texas had to live under Mexican law; one of the requirements was to abandon slavery. Since Texas was attractive to Southerners because of its potential for extensive cotton production, they could not expect to prosper without a large labor force. This was nothing new to them since the same conditions prevailed in the Southern states from which they came. There they had solved the problem by the use of slave labor. If they could not bring their slaves to Texas and have them protected as property under Mexican law, few would be enticed to Texas. The appeal of Texas was so great, however, that Southerners came with their slaves, legally freed them to comply with Mexican law, and continued to hold them in bondage on one pretext or another. The violation of the Mexican law in regard to slavery eventually led to the Texas-Mexican War in which Texas struggled to be free of Mexican control — resulting in the battle of the Alamo, San Jacinto, and Texas' independence.

Blacks who participated in Texas' struggle for independence were Hendricks Arnold, a noted guide of the period who fought in the Bexar campaign in 1835 and at San Jacinto; Greenberry Logan, who fought with Fannin at the Battle of Concepcion and Main Plaza in the heart of San Antonio; William Goyens, a wealthy man who lived near Nacogdoches; Sam McCullough, Jr., a free Negro from Jackson County, one of the first soldiers to shed his blood during Texas' struggle for independence; Peter Allen, who was killed with Colonel James Fannin at Goliad; Joe Travis, who was at the Alamo; and Dick the Drummer, who participated in the Battle of San Jacinto. There were many more blacks who helped in Texas' fight for independence whose names are still unknown to history.

The status of the Negro freedman changed sharply with the founding of the Republic. He could not remain in Texas and own land without special permission from Congress. Samuel McCullough, mentioned above, in spite of his contribution, had to file a petition with the Congress of the Republic of Texas, reminding it of his military service and asking permission to remain. This permission was granted in a number of cases to freedmen who had played important roles in the revolution. Others remained illegally, but the social attitudes changed more slowly than the laws and they were unmolested.

In 1845 Texas was admitted to the Union and was sympathetic and committed to the southern way of life. During the period before the Civil War, East Texas became very much like the rest of the South. Plantations developed that very much resembled those in the older states of the South, and there were a few planters who owned large numbers of slaves. Even so, the great majority of Texans — as was true of the South as a whole — did not own slaves. Nonetheless, Texas sentiment was overwhelmingly supportive of the plantation cotton culture with its heavy dependence on slave labor. Slavery was the accepted order and the status of the blacks deteriorated rapidly. The Civil War finally changed the law on the books.

The status of blacks in Texas, just as in all southern states, changed tremendously with the passing of the Thirteenth, Fourteenth, and Fifteenth amendments. These amendments wrote into the basic law of the land the rights guaranteed to blacks, but it has required a struggle on the part of black Southerners and their white friends and supporters to maintain them.

Reconstruction in Texas afforded blacks the opportunity to participate in the government at almost all levels, but that participation did not come and is not maintained today without tremendous struggle and sacrifice.

Blacks had observed life in Texas very closely and had some idea about how they wanted to pursue it as free people. For the sake of continuity we will look at specific segments, institutions, and categories of the black Texan's existence from Reconstruction to the 1980s.

Blacks in Texas live mostly in the eastern one-third of the state. This was the case during the antebellum days and continues to be true for the majority of the race into the twentieth century. This section of the state is composed of counties lying generally east of a line from Corpus Christi to Austin, through Waco, Dallas, and on to Denison. The Black Belt counties, about sixteen in number, are located mainly in the southeastern portion of this section.

There are several reasons why more blacks are found in the eastern part of the state. During the time when Texas was a part of Mexico, slaves were free people after escaping into Mexican territory, which then included what is now East Texas. East Texas contained large cotton plantations which had many slaves doing the work. Also, during the Civil War, Southerners in the east moved their slaves toward friendlier territory in the west as the Union began to win the war, hoping to keep their slaves and take them back when the South won the war. The South lost, and the former slaves stayed in that area (western Louisiana and East Texas).

Blacks proved to be successful farmers when given the opportunity and were left alone. East Texas had good soil for crop production and many blacks stayed and did quite well. Blacks in Texas, however, faced the same problems as newly freed blacks throughout the South. Set free with nothing, it was difficult to get a start in farming or in any other occupation. Rumors circulated for years that one of the Reconstruction programs would be to provide free land to blacks, but it never occurred. As a result, blacks either became day laborers on farms or they were caught up in the sharecropping system. They were able to stay alive and provide the basic necessities through sharecropping, but few tenants or sharecroppers were ever able to progress to the point of owning their own land. Those who did become landowners faced the problem of holding the property when the Jim Crow era began.

Until the end of World War II most black Texans lived in the rural areas. Better transportation facilities, better paying jobs and hopes for a better quality of life pulled a great number of blacks by the 1950s to urban centers, i.e., Dallas, Fort Worth, and Houston. Many also left the state for urban areas in the Midwest and Northeast. Today most native blacks of the state are just one generation away from the rural farm — somewhere in East Texas.

The one area where there is more recorded information concerning black contribution to Texas than any other is in politics and government. Statutes passed by the federal government at the close of the Civil War limited citizens' participation in all states which had participated in rebellion against the Union. Black men who had always been free and ex-slaves, along with Republicans, served in an effort to bring equality, law, and order out of chaos. The task was not easy. Many ex-slave owners and their sympathizers refused to accept the defeat of the slavery system and tried to practice "business as usual."

From 1869 to 1874 Union forces controlled political activities in the state. During this time, Norris Wright Cuney became a dominant figure in the Republican Party. Some of the other outstanding blacks who served were G. T. Ruby, W. Johnson, J. McWashington, C. W. Bryant, S. Curtis, M. Kendall, R. Long, and Shepphard Mullins. Between 1871 and 1895, there were three blacks elected to the Texas Senate and thirty blacks elected to the Texas House of Representatives. Two men of this period who made significant contributions were from the East Texas town of Marshall. David Abner, Sr., participated in the writing of the 1876 Texas Constitution and was one of the founders of Bishop College, and Meshack Roberts was one of the founders of Wiley College. J. Mason Brewer's book, *Negro Legislators of Texas* is a good source for more information about black participation in politics.

Blacks politically supported the Republican Party until the middle of the 1880s when the party adopted a "Lily White" attitude. The Democrats were not seeking black support. The Populist Party endeavored to capitalize on this situation but were not successful.

With the abandonment of blacks by the Republican Party,

*John Biggers, who established the art department at Texas Southern University in Houston, is one of Texas' leading artists.*

white Democrats embarked upon a systematic plan to remove blacks from the political process. Through law and extra-legal intimidation blacks became almost non-existent as far as government was concerned. Laws were passed excluding them from voting, holding office, and participating in political parties. Along with these changes, laws were also passed segregating blacks from whites in almost all aspects of daily life—education, residential neighborhoods, employment, social life. The era of "Jim Crow" was in full swing in Texas.

Thus, until the 1930s, black participation was almost nil in influential party politics. One of the ways white Texans prevented blacks from active political life was to keep them out of the Democratic Party, the only party that made any difference in Texas before the 1960s. Since a political party was considered a private organization that could control its membership, the legislature passed a law prohibiting black membership in the party. A test case in 1927, *Nixon* v. *Herndon,* brought a Supreme Court decision that the Texas law was unconstitutional since it violated the Fourteenth Amendment. The state law was repealed and membership in the party was left to local Democratic officials. They continued to exclude blacks from participation. The so-called "white primary" continued until the Supreme Court finally struck it down in 1944 in *Smith* v. *Allwright.*

For sixty-eight years, 1898 to 1966, blacks were absent from the Texas legislature. Curtis Graves and Barbara Jordan of Houston and Joseph E. Lockridge of Dallas were elected in 1966. By this time blacks had been won over to the Democratic Party—thanks to President Franklin D. Roosevelt. Today the black representation in the legislature has risen to thirteen (twelve in the House of Representatives and one in the Senate). More and more blacks are becoming politically astute and are judicially exercising their political rights.

The keys to protection from the ills of life was to get as much formal education as possible, a fact well understood by the newly freed slave. Blacks had to fight against great odds. Some whites opposed all education for blacks fearing it might reduce white control over black people. This general feeling caused little tax money from the state and local government to go toward black public education.

Blacks had to attend classes, when classes were taught, in churches, barns, and other rented buildings. The first black high school existed by 1890 and nineteen had been created by 1900, all in cities.

Southern white teachers refused to teach blacks, leaving the way open for black and white northern teachers to fill the void. In the beginning there were few qualified black teachers in Texas. Teacher institutes began in the 1880s to upgrade both black and white instructors. Salaries differed between the two races from 5 to 25 percent and remained that way until the 1950s. The black churches were the early allies in the education of blacks. Through their efforts whites joined blacks to improve educational opportunities for blacks in Texas. By the 1920s most towns with a black population of 500 or 1,000 could boast of having a black high school segregated from the white high school. From these schools came black leaders of today. Some of the more notable high schools and their locations include the following: H. B. Pemberton in Marshall; Emmett Scott in Tyler; Booker T. Washington in Dallas; L. C. Anderson in Austin; Phyllis Wheatly in San Antonio and Houston; and I. M. Terrell in Fort Worth. The teachers and administrators performed a labor of love to their pupils in nearly all black public schools from Reconstruction to today.

It was quickly realized that colleges and universities were needed to provide advanced training. Through self-help and philanthropic organizations, the following institutions developed: Paul Quinn Elementary-Secondary School, founded in 1872 in Austin and moved later to Waco; Wiley College (1873) Marshall; Bishop College (1881) Marshall; Tillotson College (1881) Austin; Mary Allen Seminary for Girls (1886) Crockett; Samuel Huston (1900) Austin; Jarvis Christian College (1913) Hawkins; and Texas College (1894) Tyler. The state-supported institutions of Prairie View A&M College and later Texas Southern University helped to sustain these efforts.

Segregated education was the accepted way in Texas between blacks and whites. The system began to change in the 1940s when blacks who wanted advanced training in the professions challenged the state's practice of forcing blacks to go to another state for training. In 1946 Herman M. Sweatt, a graduate of Wiley College and a World War II veteran attempted to register in law school at the University of Texas at Austin. When he was denied admission he filed suit in federal court. A district judge ordered his admission within six months unless an "equal" law school for blacks was made available. Texas reacted in a typically Southern fashion by immediately establishing a law school that eventually became Texas Southern University. Sweatt and others continued to press the issue of admittance to the UT Law School. Finally in 1950 in the case of *Sweatt* v. *Painter* the Supreme Court ruled that the separate law school was not equal and ordered Sweatt's admission to the UT Law School. Integration at the University of Texas had begun.

Once educational segregation in the graduate schools had fallen, undergraduate colleges in 1952 also began to integrate. 1954 was a benchmark year because of the Supreme Court's decision on integration in public schools. Total compliance with the decision took until the early 1980s in Texas. Education has proven to be the genie in the lamp, so to speak, for blacks in Texas. As opportunities present themselves, more and more blacks are able to take advantage of them because of formal training.

The one institution slaves were able to develop more fully than any other was the church. From the days of slavery, religion offered hope and solace for black people and was one thing whites could not take from them. Blacks adopted Christianity soon after their enslavement, and it became a major psychological support for them. Churches were and are the focal point among black people. They supported education and provided forums for discussion, outlets for frustration and an organizational structure for the development of black leaders. Baptists formed a clear majority, followed by Methodists. One unique characteristic of the church is its autonomy. Many blacks who have become successful in other walks of life received their training in the church. It has been a school without grades, a training ground for understanding the larger business world. Every community had or has one or two congregations.

Years ago when most blacks lived in rural areas, the church was the center of the black people's world. Today, when most blacks live in urban centers, this is not necessarily the case, although some churches have grown tremendously in size. Texas had produced some prominent black religious leaders: J. Gordan McPherson and Rick and A. C. Mount of the early twentieth century; Reverend Lacey Kirk Williams, who served churches in Marshall, Dallas, and Fort Worth and became president of the black Baptist Missionary and Education Convention in 1922; Reverend Caesar Clark of Dallas, Reverends Albert E. Chew, Nehmiah Davis, and Smith Carey of Fort Worth; and Marvin C. Griffin of Austin are just a few of the contemporaries following the black religious tradition.

Lodges generally rank close behind churches as important centers of social and civic affairs. One such organization is the Saint Joseph's Grand Lodge, AF and AM, along with Mount Olive Grand Chapter, Order of the Eastern Star, which were established on June 27, 1924. George B. Black, W. A. J. White, and W. M. White were the prime organizers. The Grand Lodge was moved to Austin in 1927. The present Grand Master, Marcellus J. Anderson, assumed the top position in 1960.

Lodges have filled a very important need in the black community, providing a protection most insurance companies and other organizations would not or could not fill. Lodge halls often doubled as recreation centers, schools, and churches. Several groups became public advocates of improved community health facilities for black people and supporters of other civic projects.

Since the days of slavery, blacks in Texas have found ways of entertaining themselves. Celebrations and holidays stemming from slavery to the present were causes to have a good time and enjoy one another's company. Births, weddings, family reunions and even deaths led to positive social activities. Christmas and New Year's are times to celebrate by having balls, dances, or parties. Christmas is a dual type of holiday, because like Easter, Mother's and Father's Day, it is a religious family time.

Probably the most patriotic day for celebration is the 19th of June (Juneteenth). Like the Fourth of July, it is a date of independence from oppression. Unlike other Southern states, blacks in Texas celebrate this day instead of the date of the Emancipation Proclamation since they were told of the freeing of the slaves in a different way. News of slavery being unlawful in those states in rebellion against the Union was not announced to slaves in Texas until June 19, 1865, when Federal officials arrived at Galveston. Until the 1950s it was a very special holiday for blacks. Today, it is being revived all over the state where there are blacks. Comanche Crossing and St. Mary's colony are two places where the tradition has always been strong.

Segregation among the races in Texas was very debilitating. It deprived a number of blacks the opportunity to ply their God-given talent and skill for the maximum remuneration. Some, however, were able to break the fetters of segregation and reach some semblance of proper recognition, e.g., Jack Johnson, boxer; Andrew "Rube" Foster, ball player; Blind Lemon Jefferson, Huddie "Leadbelly" Ledbetter, Teddy Wilson, Oscar Moore, Henry "Buster" Smith, Budd Johnson, Gene Ramey, Julius Bledsoe, musicians, and many others.

In the 1950s and 1960s Texas blacks joined with blacks across the South in support of desegregation efforts led by Martin Luther King, Jr., and other civil rights leaders. The struggle was long and hard — and often dangerous — for the participants. With the successes that came in breaking down racial barriers, the momentum developed for full equality. That has not been achieved by the 1980s, but many of the obstacles and barriers—both legal and social —have been broken, and blacks are more able than ever before to develop to their full potential and to make their mark on American life. A major task of all blacks — and all who truly believe in the American democratic process—is to remain on constant guard to be sure that the gains that have been made are not eroded or chipped away by those who would reduce blacks—and other minorities—to less than first-class citizenship.

Black people have contributed greatly to Texas. In the sands of time across this state their footprints are there; it just depended on where you look and who is doing the looking.

*Lorenzo De Zavala, Texas patriot and* ad interim *vice-president of the Republic of Texas. He was a native of Yucatan and was a member of the Mexican Constituent Congress and the Mexican Senate before moving to Texas.*

# 17

## The Tejanos of Texas

*Rodolfo Rocha*

Texas history is diverse. It is a history of people who sought to forge a way of life in a land full of promises. Among the numerous inhabitants have been the Amerinds, French, Germans, Anglo-Americans, and many others. For the most part, historians have ignored the contributions as well as the role that most of these people played in the *desarrollo* (development) of Texas, except for the Anglo-American role. Deletion can be attributed to the ethnocentricism of many Texas historians. Racial prejudice, rather than ignorance, however, has led to the omission of Tejanos (Mexican-Americans) from the annals of Texas. The pretext that Tejanos have played a minimal role in the *desarrollo* of Texas fails the test of time. Beginning with the Spanish, Tejanos have contributed *muchisimo* to the story of Texas.

By the end of the seventeenth century, Spain had extended its authority to the Texas frontier. French intruders worried the Spanish; they feared that Mexico's northern frontier was in jeopardy. Numerous priests wanting to extend their missionary work to Indians living beyond the Rio Grande also pressured Spanish authorities to establish missions in Texas.

The Spanish established five centers in Texas: Ysleta de Corpus Christi in West Texas, Nacogdoches in East Texas, San Antonio in central Texas, Goliad (La Bahia) along the Gulf Coast, and Nuevo Santander in lower South Texas. In each sector life was based on a patriarchal system where *ricos* lived in comfort while *pobres* lived a simple but harsh life. Short of adequate military protection, education facilities, and economic prosperity Spanish Texas had stagnated by 1821. Only the central and southern settlements showed some prospects.

Mexican control of Texas brought few changes. The Tejano population remained constant at about 3,500 and 4,000. The most memorable change came from the admission of Anglo-Americans to Texas. By 1830 they outnumbered Tejanos. The new immigrants concentrated in newly established townsites, while the older Tejanos settlers continued to live in larger *ranchos.* Accommodation, consequently, was minimal, for Tejanos and Anglo-American interaction was limited to the most prominent Tejano families. The lack of interplay probably explains why few Tejanos openly supported the Anglo-American war of independence in 1836.

Tejanos were caught in the middle when the war of independence erupted in 1836. The majority stayed clear of combat. In San Antonio and Goliad many became frightened and fled to East Texas or to *ranchos* in the country. Those who stayed maintained their neutrality, while some joined the insurgents. Most of the 160 Tejanos who joined the rebels fought under the leadership of Captain Juan M. Seguin. Tejanos fought at the battles of Concepcion and San Antonio in 1835 as well as at the Alamo and San Jacinto in 1836. Seguin's *rancho* served as a supply distribution center for belligerents. Two Tejanos, Jose Antonio Navarro and Francisco Ruiz, both of whom had long harbored revolutionary sentiments and had fought against both Spanish and now Mexican governments, were among the fifty-six signers of the Texas Declaration of Independence. Nonetheless, Tejanos were victimized by both sides. The Mexican Army maltreated Tejanos in San Antonio and executed one at Goliad along with James Fannin's men. Anglo-Americans even accused Tejanos who remained neutral in San Antonio of treason.

After independence Tejanos found themselves living amidst two nations. On the one hand, their social life remained traditionally Mexican (Spanish). On the other, they found themselves confronting an increasing white Anglo-Saxon Protestant population that viewed Tejanos with a growing animosity.

Privately, Tejanos continued to endure life much as they had during the Spanish and Mexican periods. *Ricos,* mostly former high-ranking officials and wealthy landowners, enjoyed a comfortable life style, though not an exorbitant one. They were either moderately or substantially secure with income from their stock and produce. Their children attended the few nearby schools or away in Mexico or Europe. Children then returned as physicians, druggists, teachers, or took positions as clerks in local government. *Ricos,* utilizing the politics of accommodation, became acquaintances of the new ruling class. Unknowingly, they became pawns of the new dominant society. *Los pobres,* on the other hand, endured a harsh life. Most pobres were mestizos. Living in *jacales,* they were day laborers, vaqueros, carters, and artisans. Most were dependent on agriculture or ranching for their livelihood, as a constantly depressed sector of the economy. Money was scarce and bartering existed as the base for exchange. A few managed to acquire land and farm for themselves.

Tejanos, both *ricos* and *pobres,* entertained. They celebrated frequently *con mucho gusto;* the people seemed always ready to find an occasion for celebration. They celebrated Mexican *fiestas,* especially patriotic days and numerous religious holidays, in particular *el dia de la Virgen de Guadalupe* (December 12). *Fiestas* were celebrated during weddings, birthdays, or baptismals. Most *fiestas* lasted several days with everyone pitching in to keep the party alive. Tejanos enjoyed dancing, especially *el fandango.* They also played billiards, watched cock fights, and participated in raffles and gambling. Several musical instruments including the fiddle, accordion, and guitar provided music at the *fiestas.*

As isolated as they must have felt, Tejanos continued to practice their religious beliefs. After 1836 most priests in Texas were Anglo-Americans who misunderstood Tejano culture and were indifferent to Tejanos. In central Texas Tejanos seemed to have had less religious experiences than those in the *ranchos* along the Rio Grande. As cut off as the *ranchos* may have appeared in South Texas, they never lacked the presence of *Diosito* (the Lord). People there were notably religious. Almost every evening there was a reading of the Bible and recital of prayers. Large size *ranchos* usually had a chapel where prayers and mass were held. Priests sporadically visited the *ranchos* and attended the official religious need of the Tejanos.

Because there were few Tejano doctors in Texas, most Tejanos relied on home remedies to cure illnesses. *Los ricos* usually relied on doctors, but the *pobres,* especially in the *ranchos,* went to see *curanderos* for help. *Curanderos,* mostly herb healers, prescribed various herbs for medication. For the most part, Tejanos, however, lived *una vida sana* (a healthy life).

Politically, Tejanos remained busy as they had in the past, though it became increasingly more difficult to exert power in Texas. In the 1840s at least four Tejanos served in the Texas Congress. Rafael de la Garza, a former justice of the peace and district clerk in Bexar, was elected to the House of Representatives. Two conservative friends of the *americanos,* Jose Antonio Navarro and Jose Francisco Ruiz, served in the Texas Senate. Juan Sequin, who had also fought for Texas independence, was elected to the Texas Senate, where he worked vigorously to pass legislation requiring that all Texas laws be printed in Spanish.

Tejanos also served in local offices during the Republican period. In the first elections held in San Antonio, Tejanos won control of the city council. Tejanos also won major elective offices including the county judgeship in Bexar County. Unfortunately, Tejano politicians represented the *rico* class, not the majority of the Tejanos, who were *pobres.* As a result, most Tejanos did not take politics too seriously. At the same time many Anglo-Americans felt that Tejanos should not be allowed to vote, but no concentrated effort to disenfranchise them occurred.

Well over 500 Tejanos applied for and received land grants from the Republic of Texas as provided under the Constitution of 1836 which granted land to all persons living in Texas on March 2, 1836. Others received land for their participation in the war itself.

As relations between Mexico and Texas deteriorated, life for Tejanos became more difficult. In 1842 Mexican armies invaded Texas, twice occupying San Antonio. During the forays, only Anglo-Americans were taken prisoners. Most Tejanos remained neutral and did not oppose the invading forces. A few Tejanos joined Anglo-American forces in ousting the Mexican Army. Many Anglo-Americans claimed that all Tejanos were traitors for not opposing the Mexican Army. Anglo-Americans perceived the exodus of well over 100 families with the Mexican Army as testimony of a Tejano conspiracy with Mexico. The Mexican invasion led to further distrust between Tejanos and *americanos.* Even Juan Seguin, long-time friend of the *americanos,* had to abandon his office of mayor in San Antonio and go into exile. Consequently, immediately after Tejanos left, their properties were confiscated without compensation.

The *americanos* brought to Texas their racist attitudes — their taste of "Manifest Destiny." Subsequently, they were hostile to Tejanos, whom they regarded as inferior. To most Anglo-Americans Tejanos were lazy, jealous, cowardly, backward, immoral and superstitious, never mind incompetent and inept. Much of the anger and resentment came from the atrocities of the war, especially at the Alamo and Goliad. A murder was avenged by a murder, a raid by a raid. Language barriers and differences in democratic experiences widened the gap. Because Tejanos did not demonstrate Protestant values, stereotypical ambitions, many *americanos* labeled them as "un-American." Tejanos also had prejudiced views of Anglo-Americans. They regarded them as arrogant, extremely aggressive, conniving and cruel. Politically and professionally they perceived Anglo-Americans to be unethical as well as dishonest. Because of their Roman Catholic beliefs they were suspicious of the Protestant conquerors. It appears that few Tejanos and Anglo-Americans were able to accommodate each other, that is, to work together. When they did, it occurred exclusively within the upper Tejano class. Along the Rio Grande very few Anglo-Americans settled, allowing Tejanos to retain control of their destiny for a while longer. On the eve of the American war with Mexico, in the four major settlements where Tejanos lived, their diminished influence was quite noticeable.

The war against Mexico in 1846 culminated two and a half decades of cultural conflict. Anglo-Americans, especially Texans, used the war as a rationalization to lash out their hatred against Mexicanos. Numerous acts of robbery, rape, and murder became commonplace in South Texas. Some Tejanos lost their land through fictitious law suits, sheriff sales, or dubious title transfers during the war.

The war brought a drastic change to Tejanos along the Rio Grande. Anglo-American soldiers stationed in the forts along the new frontier line remained after their tour of duty. Merchants moved into the area, first to supply army posts, later to serve the substantial Mexican populace in northern Mexico. Quickly, Anglo-Americans such as Charles Stillman, Richard King, and Mifflin Kenedy, acquired, mostly through suspicious title transfers, hundreds of thousands of acres of land. A few married into Tejano families and legally inherited large tracts of land. The newly arrived conquerors quickly demonstrated to the Tejanos their absolute power as they established themselves as rulers and executed the law to their advantage.

The loss of their land worried Tejanos. Anglo-Americans increasingly began to challenge Tejanos' land claims. In 1852 the Texas legislature created a land commission to clear land titles in South Texas. Due to lack of understanding of how the commission worked, Tejanos feared the worst. They viewed the action of the state legislature as a plot to take their lands. When the land commission began its work, Tejanos panicked. They organized demonstrations and rallies to protest the work of the commission. Some Tejanos thought of launching a separatist movement for South Texas.

Tejanos elsewhere became victims of the aggravation of war. In 1853 citizens in Austin sent into exile twenty Tejano families accused of horse theft. For that matter, all Tejanos were branded as horse thieves. The following year, city fathers in Seguin passed a resolution prohibiting Tejano peons from entering the city. Furthermore, Tejanos were prohibited from associating with slaves. In South Texas, periodically, Tejanos were required to have a pass to travel in Cameron County. Also, in 1857 Mexicans were prohibited from traveling in Uvalde County without a passport.

Strained relations between Anglo-Americans and Tejanos exploded into violence in the late 1850s. The first encounter occurred in the freight business in San Antonio. Tejanos hauled goods worth millions of dollars from the coast to San Antonio. Anglo-Americans began the "Cart War" when they sought to drive Tejanos from the freight business. But Tejanos undercut the rates. Subsequently, *americanos* resorted to a campaign of lawlessness, waylaying Tejano caravans, robbing and destroying their cargo. Several Tejano cartmen were murdered in the upheaval.

Two years later in 1859, the first major Tejano challenge to Anglo-American rule in Texas occurred in Brownsville. Juan N. Cortina led a paramilitary group of Tejanos in an effort to drive Americanos from South Texas. Cortina, heir to a large Spanish land grant, had in effect accommodated Anglo-American settlers when they first arrived in Brownsville. He had worked with them in Democratic Party politics. But, by the late 1850s, he had become resentful of their aggressiveness. He resented the abuse, insults, and the plundering of Tejano property. Seen as a growing challenge, several Anglo-Americans began to smear Cortina's reputation by continuously accusing him of cattle thievery. The animosity exploded on July 13, 1859, when Cortina witnessed a Brownsville city marshal pistol whip a Tejano acquaintance of the Cortina family. Cortina challenged the marshal's right to abuse the Tejano and, in the scuffle, shot the peace officer.

Cortina realized he would not receive a fair trial in Brownsville. Therefore, he hid at his family's ranch and organized a band of men, approximately 1,000 strong, and in September of 1859 occupied the city for several days. From his ranch Cortina issued a manifesto declaring himself a champion of the oppressed Tejano and calling for explusion of Anglo-Americans from South Texas. Anglo-Americans reacted by killing many innocent Tejanos in the area, most of whom were not involved in the conflict but whose land was coveted by *americanos.* Early in 1860 Texas Rangers and American soldiers drove Cortina into exile in Tamaulipas.

Cortina's support came from the oppressed poor, while upper class Tejanos, led by Francisco Yturria, organized a company of Tejano militiamen and joined lawmen chasing Cortina. Most of the Tejanos who resented Cortina were larger rancheros. In the early

1860s growing sectionalism in the South and Texas overshadowed the Cortina war.

The Civil War affected Tejanos just as it did everyone else in Texas. The Texas seccessionist convention met on January 28, 1861, at Austin. Of the 176 delegates, not a single one was Tejano even though they were in the majority in Starr, Hidalgo, Cameron, El Paso, Nueces, and Bexar counties. Approximately 3,400 Tejanos fought in the war, 2,500 in the Confederate army, 900 in the Union forces. Most of the Tejanos in the armies came from South Texas, the rest from the Bexar and Corpus Christi areas. Tejanos who joined the armies were actually following the actions of their patron. Many, however, were conscripted by the Confederate Army. They resented the draft since they were assigned to units commanded by Anglo-American officers who had no respect for Tejanos. To avoid conscription hundreds of Tejanos fled to Mexico, others merely claimed to be Mexicans and not United States (Confederate) citizens. Luckily, the Confederate government abandoned its assertive efforts to draft Tejanos. A few Tejanos who deserted their military obligations were shot.

Tejanos fought on both sides. Some Tejanos joined the Union Army when those forces occupied the lower Rio Grande Valley. They were led by Adrian Vidal, who served both the Confederate and later the Union Army. Most Tejanos in the Confederate Army served under Colonel Santos Benavides. Tejanos saw action in major battles of the war, including Gettysburg, Appomattox, and Chattanooga. At the Battle of Palmito Hill, Tejanos fought on both sides. Although Tejanos had done their share of fighting, when the war was over, their contributions were soon forgotten.

After the Civil War Tejano contact with Anglo-Americans increased tremendously. In South Texas the population doubled from 8,541 in 1850 to 14,959 in 1880. From the south Mexicans came seeking tranquility from the political upheaval caused by French intervention and the subsequent contest for power which finally led to the iron rule of Porfirio Diaz. From the north, Anglo-Americans came to escape the indignation of Republican Reconstruction. Other immigrants came to start anew. They brought with them their more recent resentment for the newly freed black man and memories of recent Indian attempts to free their lands from the encroaching American in the West.

Law and order collapsed in Texas, especially in the area where Tejanos predominated. The area from the Nueces to the Rio Grande became no-man's land as guerrilla warfare broke out. The absence of law and order in northern Mexico encouraged banditry. The influx of Confederate refugees along the border also kindled outlawry. Bandits raided both Tejano and *americano* ranches. Cattle rustling increased; law officials could not stop the brigands or they were themselves participants in the turmoil. When bandits murdered an Anglo-American, all Tejanos were suspected; any Tejano seen in the vicinity of the crime automatically forfeited his life. Anglos retaliated against all Tejanos, for in their eyes all Tejanos were bandits. The killing of a Tejano was thought not to be a crime. In 1875 a band of Mexicans (nationals) raided near Corpus Christi, Texas, and stole horses, robbed stores and several people, set several buildings on fire, killed a Tejano and several of the lawmen who were chasing them. In retaliation, Anglo-Americans in Corpus Christi launched a massive expedition against all Tejanos in South Texas. Peaceful farmers were murdered, accused of being members of the Mexican gang or, at a minimum, sympathizers. In Brownsville, a gang of Tejanos and Mexicans accused of rustling were lynched and their bodies displayed in the town plaza as a warning to others.

In West Texas, Tejanos also experienced difficult times. Tejanos suspected of committing a crime were summarily lynched. In 1877 Tejanos were denied their right to extract salt from beds near El Paso, a tradition dating back to the Spanish period. Tejanos, demanding respect for their rights as guaranteed by the Treaty of Guadalupe Hidalgo, demonstrated in El Paso. Several days of riots followed as Texas Rangers, lawmen, and other Anglo vigilante groups tried forcefully to exterminate Tejanos. A large number of Tejano families fled to Mexico.

The root of much of the turmoil continued to pivot around demands by Anglo-Americans for Tejano land holdings. Indian raids and banditry intensified the animosity between Tejanos and Anglo-Americans and compelled some Tejanos to abandon land holdings or to sell cheaply. In other cases Anglo-American squatters established homesteads without legal claims.

The "legal" displacement from their land either by legislative, judicial, or extra-legal means became increasingly difficult for Tejanos to accept. Tejano landowners took pride in their possessions. Increasingly they refused to yield their *tierras*. Unfortunately, proximity to the Mexican border gave a false sense of security. They relied on the existence of well-kept records on land grants and *prociones* to defend their titles. As they involved themselves in the litigation process, they realized that in order legally to acquire land, all heirs to a grant had to sign the title away. Land losses occurred anyway when extra-legal means, such as the killing of the head of the household and most of the older sons, occurred. Subsequently, widows were forced to sell their land. Another method of transferring land from Tejano to Anglo hands followed interracial marriages, a practice that had been employed by earlier *americanos* who came after the war with Mexico.

A most acceptable way for Anglo-Americans to establish themselves within the community was to marry into a wealthy Tejano family and adopt the pattern of social life used by many Tejanos; usually that meant becoming a patron. Because of the isolated cultural and economic conditions of the area, Tejanos became susceptible to political bossism. During the Spanish and Mexican periods, landowners executed almost complete authority over the lives of their laborers. The peon depended totally on his boss for economic survival. The patron met the needs of his workers. Consequently, a blind loyalty developed between the two parties. The social and economic ties transcended into the political arena. In the period after the Civil War, patron and Anglo-American employers became political partners — bosses — directing Tejanos in the electoral process. Tejanos obeyed as a gesture of their respect, loyalty, and trust in their patron or employer.

In the later nineteenth century several Anglo-Americans became political bosses by manipulating Tejanos. Prior to the Civil War Tejanos in San Antonio had been governed by Bryan Callaghan. After the war, Stephen Powers became the most powerful patron in South Texas. As a lawyer Powers quickly became a friend — a protector—of Tejanos. He rendered Tejanos assistance, particularly in land and cattle litigation. Gradually he earned the respect, loyalty and trust of Tejanos, who in return gave him political power through their votes.

By the latter part of the nineteenth century, Tejanos had lost direct influence in Texas politics. Some well-to-do family members such as the Santos Benavides from Laredo and the G. N. Garcias from El Paso were elected to the state legislature, but they did not champion issues, such as extra-legal abuses, of concern to the general Tejano population. Indirectly, wealthy Tejanos, influenced Texas politics by serving the Democratic Party. In the 1870s Tejano delegations attended county and state Democratic conventions. Tejanos also served in the Executive Committee of the Bexar County Democratic Party. Along the Rio Grande, they served in lesser county political positions. By the turn of the century, however, as the Anglo population increased, Tejanos lost ground, victims of gerrymandering. All Tejanos now were totally dependent on the political "freedom" which Anglo-Americans allowed them.

Tejanos occasionally held their ground against the dominant

*Irma Rangel, of Kingsville, attorney and first Mexican-American woman to serve in the Texas Legislature.*

political structure. On several occasions they bolted the Democratic Party. In the latter 1870s Tejanos denounced the Democratic leadership when their demands were ignored. When the San Antonio city council closed San Pedro Park to Tejano dances, they again withdrew support from the Democratic leadership. The Democratic Party in Texas faced an exodus of Tejanos in the 1890s when two San Antonio lawyers attempted to have a federal court disenfranchise Tejanos.

The 1910 Mexican Revolution was a movement by an oppressed people to rid themselves of the iron rule of an old ruling class and to establish a new social order. The revolution became the catalyst which moved Tejanos in South Texas to challenge the Anglo-Americans, who had displaced Tejanos from their lands. In 1915 Tejano social bandits led by Aniceto Pizana and Luis de la Rosa launched seventy-three raids in South Texas. The raids disturbed, but did not destroy, Anglo-American control. The social bandits, both lower and middle class Tejanos, attacked members of the predominant Anglo-American upper class killing some twenty-five of them. They also destroyed symbols of modernization, such as rail lines and irrigation pumping stations which had upset traditional patterns of life in South Texas. In retaliation, authorities and extralegal vigilante committees conducted a massive roundup of Tejanos, killing from 3,000 to 5,000, mostly innocent victims.

Political upheaval in Mexico at the turn of the century coerced Mexicans to emigrate to Texas. At first, the Mexicans were welcomed as laborers by the expanding commercial and agricultural sector of the state. Assuming that the new Tejanos would be submissive to exploitation, no regard for their safety was considered. The new Tejanos, however, quickly challenged working conditions in Texas. A series of labor strikes led by Tejanos rippled the state from 1901 to 1940. Tejanos struck the El Paso Street Car Company in 1901 demanding higher wages; in 1903 they struck the smelting industry also in El Paso; in the same year Tejano miners went on strike against the Texas and Pacific Coal Company in Thurber, also demanding higher wages and an eight-hour day; in 1919 Tejano laundry workers struck in El Paso; in 1938 Tejanos in South Texas attempted to organize workers in the packing sheds; also in 1938 Tejanos struck the pecan shelling industry in San Antonio. Unionization in Texas was Tejano-bred. These early efforts failed to achieve their goals as scabs along with the strong arm of the law broke many of the strikes. Elsewhere in the labor sector, Anglo-Americans dominated the skilled crafts. Yet, some Tejanos did manage to enter into several areas of work other than agriculture. A few became small entrepreneurs. They served the Tejano community as operators of Mexican food restaurants, bakeries, or herbal stores, and still others were street vendors.

Education was the most important objective that Tejanos fought for in the first half of the twentieth century. By the turn of the century, sporadically at best, school officials permitted Tejano children to attend schools designated for "Mexicans only," mostly primary grades in segregated campuses. School officials defended segregation maintaining that it was necessary to protect Tejano children from social prejudice of Anglo children. Segregation also prevented socializing of the two groups. Landowners, many of whom served on school boards, opposed educating Tejano children. They feared that the labor force would decrease as educated Tejanos moved to urban areas to work in factories.

Several Tejano groups expressed concern over limited access to education for their children. In 1910 Tejanos parents pulled their children from the public schools at San Angelo, Texas. They demanded better facilities for their children. In the 1920s and 1930s many Tejano organizations such as the League of United Latin American Citizens established pre-schools to teach basic English vocabulary. Also in the same period Tejanos took their plight to state courts demanding that as members of the "white race" they should not be segregated. Tejanos won at the local court levels but lost in appellate courts. It was not until the 1940s that federal courts intervened on behalf of Tejano school children. In the 1950s Tejano groups organized "back-to-school" drives using radio, newspaper, and church agencies to encourage parents to enroll all their children in schools. Organizations collected and distributed school supplies, shoes and clothing for needy children. In 1948 Tejanos won a judicial decision when the segregation of their children from Anglo children was declared unconstitutional. Later *Hernandez* v. *Texas* (1957) outlawed the practice in Texas of requiring Tejano children to repeat the first grade.

By the 1940s Tejanos had become more assertive, probably because they had again come to the defense of their country. Tejanos quickly answered the call of arms in 1941. They fought in all theaters of the war—North Africa, Europe, and the Pacific. Five out of the fourteen Texas Congressional Medal of Honor recipients were Tejanos. Jose Lopez of Brownsville won the Congressional Medal of Honor as well as the Azetc Eagle, the highest Mexican military honor. Unfortunately, participation in the war did not mean acceptance for Tejanos. In March 1944 a Tejano war hero was denied entrance to the Blue Moon dance hall in South Texas. Later in 1948 Felix

Longoria's remains were refused burial in Three Rivers, Texas. The mortician would not allow a Mexican to be interred in an all-white cemetery.

Tejanos made modest gains in the next thirty years. In the 1950s they won the right to serve on grand juries. A large number of Tejanos began to finish high school. Others, taking advantage of the GI Bill after having served in the Korean conflict, earned professional degrees in Texas universities. But a century after Tejanos had been American citizens, their rights, earned by the sweat of their brow and the blood of their military dead, still had not been accepted by most Anglo-Texans.

The 1960s was a decade of learning. Tejanos organized "Viva Kennedy Clubs" and for the first time participated enmasse in a national election. Shortly thereafter, two Tejanos, Henry B. Gonzalez and Eligio de la Garza were elected to the United States Congress. Reynaldo Garza became the first Tejano federal judge in the country. Dr. Hector P. Garcia, founder of the GI Forum in Corpus Christi, was named a member of the U.S. delegation to the United Nations.

Also in the 1960s Tejanos organized protest movements to bring to light abuses against their community. Young Tejanos in public schools and universities led by Jose Angel Gutierrez organized the Mexican American Youth Organization (MAYO). They confronted school boards demanding a meaningful education for their brothers and sisters. Using MAYO as a base, Tejano political leaders founded La Raza Unida Party, which eventually put up several candidates for state office, including the governor's seat. In 1972 Ramsey Muniz collected over 200,000 votes, almost forcing the election of the first Republican governor since Reconstruction. On a more conservative front, the Political Association of Spanish-Speaking Organization (PASO) used the established political structure to support Tejano conservatives for local offices.

The United Farm Worker Union led by Cesar E. Chavez began organizing in Texas in the late 1960s and early 1970s. Led first by Antonio Orendain and later by Rebecca Harrington, farmworkers, the poorest people in the state, hoped to improve their life in one of the richest agricultural sections of the state, the lower Rio Grande Valley.

By the 1970s Tejanos were working at putting into practice the gains made in the sixties. Increasing numbers of young Tejanos graduated from colleges and universities to become teachers, doctors, lawyers, and other professionals. A large number returned to the *barrio* to share their experiences with the greater Tejano population. Elsewhere, Patricio F. Flores became the first Tejano Bishop in the Catholic Church. However, too many Tejano veterans came home from Vietnam. Several earned the Congressional Medal of Honor, among them Freddy Gonzalez and Roy Benavides.

In the "Decade of the Hispanics" — the 1980s — Tejanos still face many serious problems in Texas. Politically they are under-represented and victimized by police brutality. Tejanos are still employed at low-paying jobs with little or no decision-making opportunities; two thirds are still at or below poverty level in Texas. Tejanos still face many obstacles in the education process, especially the newest Tejano immigrant — the undocumented child. Nonetheless, the 1980s promise expanded opportunities for Tejanos who have an extensive record of participating in the *desarrollo* of Texas. The road for Tejanos was arduous; the future, however, appears auspicious.

# 18

## Violence in Texas History

*Bill O'Neal*

Violence has played a major and colorful role in Texas history. From hard-riding Comanches to proud *conquistadores;* from deadly feudists to sixgun-wielding outlaws and Texas Rangers; from Depression-era criminals to modern roisterers packing Saturday Night Specials, violence became a tradition in the Lone Star State which has influenced Texan attitudes and enlivened the state's history.

Most other states endured frontier conditions for only a decade or so, but in Texas the frontier period lasted for half a century, from the 1820s through the 1870s. Indeed, Spaniards waged a losing effort to civilize Texas from the late 1600s until they were deposed in 1821, and gunfighters and family feudists continued to blaze away at each other until early in the twentieth century.

Why was Texas so consistently violent, even after it ceased to be a frontier? One answer pertains to the vast size of Texas: all western states are large, but Texas is especially so. Therefore there were that many more semilawless towns sporting saloons and bagnios where gamblers and other hardcases would congregate and inevitably clash; there were more cattle camps and ranches where tensions would erupt into range wars and bloodshed; there were numerous areas of forbidding countryside—from the Big Thicket to the Cross Timbers to the Big Bend country—into which fugitives could disappear. Also, the Texan fancied himself as the very embodiment of the frontier personality: Texans were filled with a sense of self-reliance, prone to settle their own difficulties abruptly, lethally, and without resorting to tedious legal procedures.

The most protracted violence in Texas involved Indians. By 1700 Comanches and their Kiowa cousins had adapted the horse culture, enabling them boldly to thrust aside previous Indian inhabitants and utilize much of West Texas as a buffalo hunting range. Comanches and Kiowas proved to be fierce and daring warriors, mounted astride swift ponies and skillfully fighting with lance and short bow.

When the Spanish ventured into *Comancheria* they clashed ineffectively with the superb Indian light cavalry. The Spanish boasted proud traditions as medieval warriors and as the *conquistadores* of Mexico and Peru, but they met more than their match in the Comanches of Texas. Comanches came and went as they pleased, riding even into San Antonio to steal horses and kidnap children for ransom, and their plundering raids stabbed deep below the Rio Grande.

The climax of the conflict between Comanches and the Spanish occurred in the late 1750s. In 1757 the Spanish constructed a mission and a presidio on the southeastern edge of *Comancheria,* beside the San Saba River. Within a year 2,000 Comanches struck the mission, killing soldiers and priests and burning the log mission. Again in 1758 Comanches raided the presidio, and Spanish authorities decided to retaliate with a full-scale invasion of *Comancheria.* By 1759 Colonel Diego Ortiz de Parrilla had organized an expedition of 600 men, more than either Cortes or Pizarro had commanded when they launched their respective conquests of Mexico and Peru.

But neither Cortes nor Pizarro faced horse Indians. As Parrilla marched north he decimated a village of Tonkawas — Indians who had played no part at the San Saba — but when he reached the Red River he enountered a massed group of tribes led by Comanche warriors. Parrilla was routed, and although he managed to retreat with little loss of life, the Indians seized his brace of cannon and supplies. Parrilla was court-martialed, but the Spanish had suffered a blow from which they never recovered. They had mounted an impressive expedition — certainly for an assignment on an eighteenth-century frontier — but this all-out Spanish effort met with defeat. From this time the Spanish were unable to thwart Comanche aggression, and the "Comanche Moon" would become a recurring period of death and destruction from northern Mexico throughout Texas. With impunity Comanche raiders slashed virtually unopposed, becoming increasingly contemptuous of the settlers they terrorized.

One of the main reasons Anglo-Americans were permitted to colonize Texas during the 1820s was that officials of Mexico hoped

*Indians attacking a wagon train at Beaver Creek, around 1864.*

— Institute of Texan Cultures
Engraving from Frank Leslie's *Illustrated Newspaper,* Sept. 24, 1864

that the Anglos could more successfully combat the horse Indians. At first Anglo settlements were too far southeast of *Comancheria* to cause serious conflict between the new Texans and the Comanches, but by the 1830s Anglo expansion began to result in frequent combat. And in the grim, fierce pioneers of early Texas, the ferocious Comanches and Kiowas found a resourceful and implacable foe.

These Texans were descendants of frontiersmen who had battled hostiles in Kentucky's "dark and bloody ground," and in Tennessee and Alabama. Reared on crude pioneer farms and witnesses since childhood of wilderness violence, these men and women were accustomed to a life of hardship and danger, and they brought to Texas the ruthless determination of American frontiersmen to remove obstacles to their progress by any means necessary.

Texans initiated the vicious wars against the horse Indians by moving into *Comancheria*, and the natives struck back with their usual ferocity, mercilessly torturing captives and mutilating the corpses of fallen enemies. Texans did not quail before this barbaric menace, but determined to eliminate it by sweeping the Indians from the plains. The ensuing forty years saw red and white Texans grapple in a brutual life-and-death struggle. A study of western clashes between Indians and white men revealed that Texas led all states and territories as the site of known fights with 846, while Arizona, the next most troubled area in this regard, was the scene of just over 400 Indian scrapes. Sixty-one Medals of Honor were awarded to United States soldiers who fought Indians in Texas after the Civil War.

The outline of the war for *Comancheria* is well known. In 1836 Comanches ventured east of their usual range to assault Fort Parker, perhaps because the Parker clan had wronged them in trade; a nine-year-old kidnapped child, Cynthia Ann Parker, became the mother of Quanah, the last great war chief of the Comanches. San Antonio's Council House Fight occurred in 1839, triggering Indian retribution to this treachery, a sweeping raid all the way to Victoria and Linnville, and white counterattacks at Plum Creek and the Colorado River. During the 1850s Texas Rangers and the United States Army struck deep into *Comancheria* and finally brought the horse Indians to the verge of defeat. But the Civil War erupted, the frontier forts were abandoned, and Comanches and Kiowas rebounded with terrible vengeance. West Texas continued to be ravaged for a couple of years after the war, as federal troops in Texas were utilized for occupation of an ex-Confederate state, rather than for protection of pioneer ranches and farms. At last the army again took the field, led by Colonel Ranald Mackenzie, the military's finest Indian fighter, and aided immeasurably by the Frontier Battalion of Texas Rangers. In 1874 when Mackenzie penetrated Palo Duro Canyon, the final Comanche refuge, *Comancheria* fell.

These major battles were classic confrontations between hard-bitten foes, but in between the landmark actions were scores of combats, year after bloody year, fought on a small but vicious scale. In 1835, for example, eleven warriors approached the central Texas log cabin of a Mr. and Mrs. Taylor, their two sons and two daughters. A dog barked but instantly was silenced by an arrow, and within moments the Indians opened fire on the cabin. Mrs. Taylor braved arrows and bullets to bustle her children across the dogtrot to her husband's location. When the warriors rushed the room two were slain, but before retreating they set the roof ablaze. Taylor wanted to surrender, but his resolute wife refused, clambered to the roof and — again ignoring missiles from the Indians — extinguished the flames with milk and homemade vinegar handed up by her daughters. Although two more braves were wounded, another nearly gained entry to the Taylor stronghold. But the resourceful Mrs. Taylor shoveled live coals into his face, and when he staggered away the battered war party gave up the attack.

In present-day Bastrop County in 1837, Mr. and Mrs. James Goacher were slain by Comanches, along with three of their children and their son-in-law; their married daughter and three grandchildren were carried into captivity. In 1842 four warriors executed a horse-stealing raid near present-day Cameron. Captain S. P. Ross and five other men pursued through the rain, but when they closed with their prey their powder was wet. A desperate hand-to-hand fight ensued, and all four raiders were killed. In 1851 Ed Burleson, Jr., led eight Texas Rangers into a scrap against sixteen Comanche warriors on the Nueces River. After several minutes of vicious hand-to-hand fighting nearly every combatant on both sides had been wounded. One Ranger expired, but Burleson killed the chief with a pistol and three other braves died on the field. The Comanches retreated, but Burleson's party was too mauled to pursue.

In 1855 a band of Uvalde citizens chased a Comanche raiding party, but when they closed the Indians wounded two men named Lakey and Bearmore. While the Uvalde men fell back, carrying Bearmore with them, the injured Lakey courageously covered their retreat — armed only with an empty revolver. Finally he fell with five arrows in his chest, but his comrades made it to safety. Two years later there were six raids into Bosque County, and 150 Comanches struck Johnson's Station, a stage stop housed in a double log cabin. A Mr. and Mrs. Evaness were wounded, but the six men and a woman managed to beat off their attackers. In 1858 Indians killed Mr. and Mrs. Joshua Jackson and their son and daughter in Lampasas County, while two men, a woman and three children were slain in a raid into Jack County. The next year another raid on Jack County saw two women and two children murdered, and a sweep into Parker County resulted in the deaths of John Brown and a Mrs. Sherman, after she was gang raped by the warriors. That same year three men and a woman were killed by Indians in Bell County, but in Young County when a Reverend Tacket and his trio of sons were attacked by twelve warriors, four braves were slain and the others routed.

A large Second Cavalry patrol, commanded by Major G. H. Thomas, was returning to Camp Cooper in 1860 when they located thirteen Comanche braves beside the Salt Fork of the Brazos. The cavalrymen struck just as the Indians were breaking camp and a running fight ensued. After three miles an old warrior, with suicidal courage, determined to hold the soldiers at bay while his comrade escaped. Expertly he began to fire iron-tipped dogwood shafts from his bow, twice wounding Major Thomas. The patrol pulled up and an interpreter called out a demand to surrender, but the Comanche shouted his defiance. When the soldiers moved in the old warrior was shot more than twenty times, but he fired arrows into three troopers, one of whom died. As the cavalrymen closed in for the kill, the dying Comanche wounded two more men with lance thrusts before collapsing.

In 1821 in Eastland County four sisters were captured and raped, and two were killed, while in Brown County hostiles attacked the wagon of Mose Jackson, shooting him to death and slitting the throats of his wife and three children. Burnet County suffered two murder raids in 1863: Waford Johnson and his wife and daughter died in one assault, and in the other attack three men were killed, although a survivor, the brother of one of the victims, drove off the Indians. Parker County was struck three times in 1864, and in one raid Mrs. Jane Smith and her two daughters died.

The following year a Mrs. Joy and her daughter were buggy-riding when three Indians attacked, beheading the little girl and also killing the woman. Mr. Joy took up the trail and caught his prey asleep in camp: he killed one with his rifle, then shot the other two to death with his revolver. In Llano a six-year-old boy was slain by hostiles, but his mother fought off the Indians and saved her other children. In 1866 ten sheepherders were killed by Apaches in El Paso County, but in Jack County Francis Long singlehandedly beat off a war party by effectively emptying two revolvers and a Spencer carbine.

On a drizzly day in 1867 two Brady area farmers named Miller and Morrell were driving a wagon loaded with corn when they were attacked by an ill-prepared war party. The braves, who had no horses or guns, sprinted toward them from a dense thicket. When Miller lashed his team into a jolting advance, his revolver dropped to the ground. An Indian seized it and opened fire, as his comrades launched arrows and spears and tried to throw large rocks in front of the wheels. Morrell emptied his revolver, winging two braves before killing another with his final shot. As the Indians fell back Miller and Morrell, bleeding profusely from multiple wounds, cut loose one of the horses and rode him into nearby woods. The Indians, their bowstrings slackened by the rain, refused to pursue into a thicket choked with cactus and underbrush. Morrell managed to crawl to a nearby creek, and after drinking he filled his boot with water and struggled back to his companion. A search party, sent out when the farmers did not return, found the grievously injured men unable to walk, clothes stiffened with blood. Miller had been wounded twenty-seven times, Morrell twenty-one, but both men eventually recovered.

That same year in Hamilton County, schoolma'arm Ann Whitney spotted a war party approaching her one-room building. She sent her pupils out the back way, but was trapped when the Indians surrounded the log structure. Firing arrows through the windows and between the logs, the warriors methodically made a pincushion of the 230-pound young woman. Indeed, in a two-year period from 1865 through 1867, 162 settlers were slain by Indians, 43 were kidnapped, and 37,000 head of livestock were carried off.

And the raids continued. In 1868 in Denton County six adults and two children died in one assault, a widow and five children in another, and nine people in another attack in Wise County. In 1870 in Palo Pinto County three cowboys returning from a Kansas trail drive were killed by a war party. The following year in Young County Britt Johnson and three other black teamsters were slain after a desperate battle with warriors. Another raiding party in the same area in 1872 came up against Henry and Willie Dillard; Henry fought like a wildcat, killing four braves, wounding several others, and felling five war ponies.

From 1874 through 1880 the Frontier Battalion backed up the army with attacks against ninety-seven hostile bands. For example, in 1874 forty Texas Rangers routed a party of Comanches. One old Indian squaw, who had fought ferociously alongside the braves, turned toward the onrushing white men and bared her breasts, to show that she was a woman. Without hesitation, however, she was gunned down—not only had she been observed engaging in combat, but Rangers were convinced that squaws were more cruel and merciless to white captives than the braves were.

The horse Indians of Texas thus were decimated or driven onto reservations in Oklahoma, and after 1880 fighting against Indians finally ceased. But other violent problems had not yet been quelled.

Following the bloody combat of the Texas Revolution and the Mexican War, violence between Anglos and Mexicans continued for decades. During the Mexican War, Texans too young to fight under Travis or Houston now could prove their manhood, now could demonstrate their courage and skill with weapons, now could seek vengeance for fathers or older brothers lost at the Alamo or Goliad, as well as for fellow Texans who had drawn the black beans in the deadly lottery ordered by Santa Anna in 1843. So young, adventurous Texans enlisted in the several companies of Rangers under Colonel Jack Hays and rode off into Mexico. Packing a brace of Colt revolvers, flaunting discipline and swilling whisky, they butchered so many Mexicans that they became known as *los diablos Tejanos.* (The U.S. Army adopted revolvers as a result of effective Ranger use during the war, and Southern soldiers picked up a piercing Texan war cry and later immortalized it as the "Rebel yell.")

In ensuing years the Texas Rangers would become a focal point of Mexican resentment. Indeed, Rangers were notorious for killing Mexican prisoners who "tried to escape" (admittedly many Anglo outlaws met the same fate at the hands of Texas Rangers). In 1875 the lethal Captain L. H. McNelly cleared up cattle thieving in the lower Rio Grande Valley with a climatic Ranger assault, after which the corpses of a dozen Mexican rustlers were dumped in the square at Brownsville as a typically unsubtle object lesson to other wrongdoers. As late as 1915 Rangers captured four Mexicans suspected of wrecking and robbing a passenger train near Brownsville; the prisoners were marched into the brush and shot to death. Although more than 400 members of the Texas Rangers have had Mexican surnames—an obvious indication that the famed law enforcement group has not been antagonistic to all Mexican-Americans—Rangers continued to foster deep hatred among Mexican Texans, and chicano parents long would instill fear in their children with pointed references to the detested *Rinche* (Rangers).

The greatest chicano hero in the Latin struggle against Anglo-Texans was the fearless, cunning, chrismatic bandit leader "Cheno"—Juan Nepomuceno Cortinas. Reared a *vaquero* in the border country of the lower Rio Grande, in 1859 Cheno Cortinas led a spontaneous uprising against *gringo* domination. Cortinas and his riders seized Brownsville and twice repulsed retaliatory forays. Finally Rip Ford and a hand-picked band of 53 Texas Rangers shattered Cortinas' 300-man force, killing at least 60 of the foe before Cheno beat a retreat into Mexico. Later Ford and his Rangers crossed the Rio Grande and again mauled a superior force led by Cortinas. Cheno, however, managed to stay at large in Mexico, and a nasty racial war ensued in the aftermath of his operations. (Cortinas became a wealthy Mexican official, but when the iron-fisted Porfirio Diaz ascended to the presidency of his country he arrested Cheno and ordered him to be shot. Ironically, the life of the old border raider was saved by the intervention of Rip Ford.)

The Salt War of 1877 was a chicano uprising against Anglo oppression. When, through political maneuvering, chicanos were prohibited from gathering salt at traditionally public deposits located 100 miles east of El Paso, the Mexican population was outraged. In San Elizario 500 armed men ran rampant, finally attacking Texas Ranger headquarters. The arrival of federal troops a few days later raised the siege, but after vengeful Rangers summarily shot two Mexicans the death toll stood at thirteen, with numerous wounded.

Killin' Jim Miller, who served two stints as a Texas Ranger and who wore a deputy's badge in Reeves County, expressed the callous attitude that was all too common on the nineteenth-century Texas frontier: "I have lost my notch stick on Mexicans that I killed out on the border."

Racial violence, of course, was not confined to Anglos in conflict with Mexicans. Negroes were the subject of frequent lynchings following the Civil War. Prior to the war, it was frowned upon socially to mistreat slaves, but during Reconstruction widespread bloodshed was common to keep the former chattels in subservience.

One of the most notorious incidents occurred in Paris a number of years after the Civil War. A Negro named Henry Smith strangled a four-year-old white girl because he had been beaten over the head by her father, a Paris police officer. Smith was arrested in Arkansas, and when word reached Paris a scaffold quickly was erected in a field near town. Upon the arrival of the prisoner's train at the Paris depot, he was seized by a number of men as several thousand citizens gathered around the scaffold. A telegram from the governor's office commanded that the lynchings be halted. The sheriff wired back: "Send your national guards down here to stop it if you want to have them killed. Nobody can stop it."

At noon a wagon carrying Smith made its way through the

crowd. The bound murderer was taken to the scaffold, where he confessed to his crime. Then the father of the murdered girl was handed a heated soldering iron, which he pressed across the prisoner's foot. Next he placed the iron higher and higher on Smith, who cursed his tormentor vehemently as the blistering soldering iron worked all the way up to his head.

Although the men shouted their approval, every woman except the mother of the dead girl left the grisly scene. At last a red-hot iron was rammed down Smith's throat, and he fainted. On-lookers then drenched the fallen man and the scaffold with gallons of coal oil. Soon the scaffold was ablaze, but when the ropes binding the Negro burned through, he sprang to the ground, only to be hurled back into the flames with pitchforks. Later his singed heart was preserved in a local saloon.

Such violence continued into the twentieth century. In Corsicana just after the turn of the century, a Negro named Hill insulted a Mrs. Younger, a white woman; promptly Hill was burned to death on the northeast corner of the courthouse square. There were brutal lynchings in Temple in 1915, Waco in 1916, and Galveston in 1917. In Shelby county in 1920 a young black man who had killed a white woman was lynched from an oak tree on Center's courthouse square. Eight years later, on the same site, another Negro murderer was hanged by another lynch mob. When the doomed man was asked if he had anything to say, he requested a drink of water. "Be patient," came the cold reply, "you can get all you want to drink when you cross the River Jordan."

Blacks found it difficult to retaliate in kind, but during Reconstruction Negro soldiers and members of the State Police occasionally turned the tables of violence against their oppressors. In Marshall, for example, two Negro officers killed a white adolescent, and in Groesbeck four black state policemen shot down a white man. At Fort Concho in 1878 black troopers of the Tenth Cavalry went on a rampage in ramshackle San Angelo after their sergeant was humiliated by civilians. The soldiers killed two and wounded several others, and a similar incident occurred in San Angelo in 1881. A quarter of a century later Brownsville, the scene of so much trouble between Anglos and chicanos, suffered a race riot involving black soldiers. And in 1917 tensions between white residents of Houston and the proud black 24th Infantry erupted in street fighting which produced seventeen dead and many other wounded; most of the casualties were white, and the threat of reprisal against the soldiers was so great that martial law had to be enforced.

After cowboys — a Texas creation — the most colorful and romanticized frontier figure is the gunfighter. Texas made an enormous contribution to gunfighter lore. A survey of 255 western gunfighters and 589 shootouts involving these men reveals that Texas dominated the action of frontier pistoleers. More gunfights—nearly 160—occurred in Texas than any other state or territory; no other western commonwealth was the arena of even half this many shootings. Most western states and territories saw widespread gunfighting activity for only a brief number of years before law and order prevailed: Kansas, for example, during the cattle town era, New Mexico during the bloody Lincoln County War, and Oklahoma during its lawless heyday as a refuge for outlaws. But gunfighters became active in Texas during the 1850s and continued to blaze away at each other until past the turn of the century.

In an efficiency rating of gunfighters, comparing the number of shootouts and killings of western shootists, ten of the top sixteen spent most of their careers in Texas. (The top sixteen with Texans italicized were: *Jim Miller, Wes Hardin, Bill Longley,* Harvey Logan, Wild Bill Hickok, *John Selman, Dallas Stoudenmire, King Fisher,* Billy the Kid, *Ben Thompson,* Henry Brown, John Slaughter, *Cullen Baker,* Clay Allison, *Jim Courtright, John Hughes.*) More gunfighters were born in Texas than any other state or territory, and more died in Texas than in any other state. The revolver was refined and popularized as a weapon in Texas; until that development, barroom brawlers and other men who found themselves in violent conflict resorted to the knife, since single-shot pistols were inadequate in a close fight (the frontier's premier knife-fighter, of course, was Jim Bowie).

The Reconstruction period produced bitter violence, and such young gunfighters as John Wesley Hardin and Wild Bill Longley; at fifteen in 1868 Hardin pumped three pistol balls into the chest of a former slave, and at the same age in 1867 Longley killed a black member of the Reconstruction troops in an exchange of shots. Hardin and Longley and many other Texans shot it out with occupation soldiers, members of Governor E. J. Davis' destested State Police, and ex-slaves. Longley would gallop into the midst of Negro street dances and other celebrations and fire indiscriminately into the crowd; he became known as "the nigger killer." In Lampasas the violence prone Horrell brothers took on the State Police in a local saloon, killing three of the four officers who came to arrest their brother-in-law. From 1873 through 1877 the six Horrell boys fought local law officers, Texas Rangers, and a range war with rancher Pink Higgins, with time out to battle through the "Horrell War" in Lincoln County, New Mexico. By 1877 five of the contentious Horrell brothers had been slain.

The Horrell-Higgins fray was merely one of seventeen range wars and family feuds which erupted throughout the Lone Star State. At least half of these private wars were conducted in the forested hills of East Texas or the Hill Country of Central Texas. Most of the people involved had migrated from hilly areas such as the Ozarks, where feuding traditions ran strong.

East Texas' Regulator-Moderator War during the 1840s squared off more than 150 men per side in two factions which defied the feeble peace-making attempts of the Republic government under President Sam Houston. The largest-scale private war in Texas was the Sutton-Taylor feud from 1867 through 1875. Assisting the Taylors were Wes Hardin and his cousins, the Clements boys; in 1873 Hardin helped to kill Sutton stalwart Jack Helm, sheriff of DeWitt County. Faction leader Bill Sutton attempted to avoid a similar end by fleeing to New Orleans, and in 1874 he boarded a steamer in Indianola with his young wife and child. But Jim and Bill Taylor caught up with him before sailing time, firing bullets into his head and heart as his horrified wife looked on.

Texas produced prominent gunfighters from the legendary Ben Thompson to the West's premier assassin, Killin' Jim Miller. There was the lethal King Fisher, Clay Allison, and John Selman, who numbered Wes Hardin and ex-Texas Ranger Baz Outlaw among his victims. Tall Dallas Stoudenmire tamed El Paso before dying there in a vicious fight, and the homicidal Cullen Baker terrorized northeast Texas before being slain in Arkansas—on his corpse were found four revolvers, a shotgun, three derringers, and six pocketknives. The famed Texas Ranger Captain John R. Hughes was a deadly left-handed marksman; when he was nineteen Hughes was so badly wounded in his right arm that he had to train himself to shoot with his other hand, and he became so proficient that few suspected that the "Border Boss" was not a natural southpaw.

Doc Holliday fought the first of his eight gunfights in 1875 in Dallas, and the following year Bat Masterson engaged in his inaugural shootout in a Mobeetie saloon. Henry Brown killed the first of at least five career victims in a Panhandle cattle camp in 1876. Eleven of Ben Thompson's fourteen gunfights were in Texas, and eight of Wild Bill Longley's dozen shootouts were in his native state. Ben Thompson, Wes Hardin, John Selman, Baz Outlaw, King Fisher, Sam Bass, Mannen Clements, and Longhaired Jim Courtright are among the noted western gunfighters who met their end in Texas shootouts.

Indeed, one of the West's most famous gunfights occurred in 1887 in a Fort Worth shooting gallery. With Bat Masterson at his side, gambler Luke Short clashed with former city marshal Jim Courtright. Longhaired Jim whipped out a sixgun and jammed it into Short's vest front, but Courtright's hammer caught on the gambler's watch chain. Luke palmed his own revolver and emptied it rapid-fire. The first slug smashed the cylinder of Courtright's pistol; two shots went wild; and three bullets tore into Longhaired Jim's right thumb, right shoulder, and heart. Courtright collapsed and died within minutes, but Short was released from custody on grounds of self-defense.

In 1879 Maurice Barrymore, father of Lionel, Ethel, and John, brought his troupe, the Warde-Barrymore Combination, to Marshall for a performance in the Mahone Opera House. That night after the show Barrymore and fellow thespians Ellen Cummins and Ben Porter were insulted in a restaurant by a drunken railroad detective, Big Jim Currie. Barrymore, an accomplished boxer, doubled his fists and approached Currie, but Big Jim produced a Smith and Wesson five shooter, plugged Maurice in the shoulder and mortally wounded Porter. Eastern newspapers severely castigated Texas in general and Marshall in particular, especially after Big Jim Currie won acquittal. As the local saying went, "In Harrison County steal a hog, get sent to jail; kill a man, get set free."

One of the legendary gun battles of Texas occurred in Round Rock in 1878. During the spring Sam Bass and his gang staged four train holdups in the Dallas area, but eluded a widespread manhunt until September. Bass planned to rob a bank in Round Rock, but one of his accomplices, Jim Murphy, betrayed the plan to the Texas Rangers in exchange for leniency. The town was swarming with lawmen when Bass, accompanied by Seab Barnes and Frank Jackson (Murphy dropped back on a pretext), rode in to case the bank. In a general store the three bandits gunned down two deputy sheriffs, but outside Barnes was killed in the streets by a Ranger. Bass, also mortally wounded, fell from his saddle but Jackson braved a hail of lead to put Sam back on his horse. The two made it out of town, but Bass forced Jackson to leave him beneath a tree, where he was found the next morning. Taken into Round Rock, he lingered in agony for two days, dying on his twenty-seventh birthday.

Texas' two deadliest shootouts produced four fatalities apiece. One took place in Tascosa in 1886. After midnight on a Saturday evening four LS riders tangled with townspeople, and following a wild gunfight in the darkness, three of the cowboys lay dead, alongside an innocent bystander. Dallas Stoudenmire was the central figure of the other tragic fight. Stoudenmire already had three shootouts in South Texas to his credit when he was appointed city marshal of wild and wooly El Paso in 1881. Within four days a man named John Hale shot Constable Gus Krempkau, and the new marshal charged up the street brandishing a revolver in each hand. He fatally wounded an onlooker, then shot Hale in the brain when John peered out from behind an adobe pillar. The dying Krempkau shot another of his antagonists, Jim Campbell, in the wrist and foot, whereupon Stoudenmire fired a bullet into his stomach. Mortally wounded, Campbell clutched his middle and gasped, "You big son-of-a-bitch, you murdered me." Three days later there was a nighttime assassination attempt against Marshal Stoudenmire, but Dallas and a companion whipped out revolvers and pumped eight slugs into their assailant. As the would-be killer dropped his shotgun and collapsed, other enemies opened fire on Stoudenmire from across the street. Stoudenmire ferociously charged with both guns blazing in three more El Paso shootouts before finally being slain in an 1882 saloon fight.

The most prolific assassin of the old West was Killin' Jim Miller. At the not-so-tender age of eight he warmed up to his life's work by murdering his grandparents in Evant, and when he was seventeen he shotgunned his brother-in-law while the man slept at his home near Gatesville. Among Miller's many victims was Sheriff Bud Frazer and, according to widespread rumor, Mannen Clements and Pat Garrett. In between murder assignments Killer Miller spoke at Methodist prayer meetings, served two hitches with the Texas Rangers, and dressed in a metal undershirt which twice saved his life in 1894 shootouts with Bud Frazer in Pecos. The first time Frazer shot Miller in the right arm. Miller began firing his revolver left-handed, but managed only to drill a by-stander in the hip. Frazer emptied his sixgun into Miller, felling him but producing no damage other than a few dents in Jim's steel breastplate. Eight months later Frazer again attacked Miller, shooting him in the arm and leg. But Jim stood his ground, popping away with a revolver as Frazer shot him twice in the chest. When bullets merely glanced off Miller's breastplate, Frazer's morale shattered and he fled. In 1896 Miller ended their feud by entering a Toyah saloon and blasting away most of Frazer's head with a shotgun.

For thirteen more years Miller continued to pursue his murderous inclinations. Cattlemen paid him $500, for example, to assassinate Lubbock lawyer James Jarrott, who had won several cases on behalf of area farmers. As Jarrott watered his buggy team near his farm, Miller drilled him in the chest from ambush. Jarrott stayed on

*Clyde Barrow and Bonnie Parker check over their "loot" following a 1930s-style "hold-up." Below is their death car riddled with machine gun bullets during an ambush by law officials just inside the Louisiana border.*

his feet, but Miller felled him with another rifle bullet. Somehow Jarrott struggled to his feet as Miller emerged from hiding. Miller triggered another round which tore into Jarrott's neck and shoulder and again knocked him down, but it took a fourth bullet to finish him. "He was the hardest damn man to kill I ever tackled," admired Miller.

Killin' Jim finally bushwhacked one man too many. In 1909 three men from Ada, Oklahoma, hired him to kill a competitor. Following the murder Fort Worth officials happily complied with extradition requests, and an angry Ada mob hung Jim and his three employers from livery stable rafters.

The gunfighter tradition continued in Texas during the twentieth century; the habit of frontier violence would not die. Family feuds persisted into the early part of the century, along with racial violence, and Texans continued to pack handguns and a touchy inclination to use them. During the Roaring Twenties more murders were recorded in Houston than in Al Capone's Chicago. Martial law was necessary to restore order in the oil-field turbulence of Mexia in 1922 and Kilgore in 1931.

The depression spawned the crime spree of Bonnie Parker and Clyde Barrow. The Barrow gang committed twelve homicides and numerous holdups, including several in Texas. Many older Texans today nostalgically relate having seen Bonnie and Clyde driving along some dusty back road as they eluded lawmen. In 1934, Texas Ranger Frank Hamer and Dallas County Deputy Sheriff Ted Hinton tracked the couple to Louisiana, where they were trapped and shot to death in a fusillade by a six-man posse. Their bullet-riddled Ford was displayed across Texas, and a 1967 film interpretation, *Bonnie and Clyde,* elevated the couple to the front rank of folk heroes.

World War II found Texans as willing as ever to bear arms; Texas A&M provided more army officers than any institution of higher learning other than West Point, and 7 percent of the men in uniform were from Texas, although the Texas population was just 5 percent of the United States total. Natives of Texas earned more than 10 percent of the Medals of Honor issued; Audie Murphy was America's most decorated combat soldier, while Commander Sam Dealey posthumously received more decorations than any other sailor.

Today Texans still consider it their right to slip Saturday Night Specials into their hip pockets (and purses!) when they patronize a favorite watering hole, and the homicide rate remains alarmingly high. The twentieth-century adolescent male in Texas proves his manhood on the gridiron. Football, a ritualized substitute for combat, is pursued with fanatical zeal by hordes of young Texans. The finest high school football in the United States is played in Texas, and as a consequence college recruiters from across the nation raid the Lone Star State of strapping young men, who, in an earlier time, would have marched off eagerly to fight Indians or Mexicans or Yankees or each other.

Thus Texans grudgingly have adjusted to a more peaceful period, clinging unconsciously to the volcanic individualism of generations of frontiersmen who carried arms and defended themselves and their property without hesitation. The violent ways of a proud and harsh people have not yet vanished, reminding us of a colorful if brutal past and rendering our present somewhat less safe than it might be.

*Celebration of the twenty-fifth anniversary of the ordination of Reverend C. J. Benes, October 28, 1915 at St. Mary's Catholic Church, Halletsville, Texas.*

— Archdiocese of San Antonio

# 19

## Battling Evil: The Growth of Religion in Texas

*John W. Storey*

Alexis de Tocqueville, that discerning Frenchman who criss-crossed the nation from New York to New Orleans in 1831, was struck by the strength of religion in the United States. There was "no country in the world," he remarked, "where the Christian religion retains a greater influence over the souls of men than in America." This observation would be just as fitting today, for recent surveys suggest that America is perhaps the most religious of the modern western nations. Studies completed by the early 1980s disclosed that 94 percent of all adult Americans believed in God, 68 percent belonged to a church or synagogue, 41 percent attended church weekly, 56 percent considered religion an important aspect of daily life, and 65 percent saw religion as the answer to many contemporary issues. This religious profile certainly would not apply to Texans of the early nineteenth century, and one wonders what de Tocqueville would have written had he ventured beyond the Neches River.

Early Texans of the 1820s and 1830s were generally indifferent to religion, and their moral behavior was censured by numerous observers. As a Presbyterian traveler lamented in 1836, the morality of "Texasians" was "Bad-bad! superlatively bad!!" Given the feebleness of organized religion in colonial Texas, such observations were not too surprising. Until March 1834 Catholicism was the official and exclusive faith of Texas, but the Roman hierarchy paid little attention to the spiritual needs of the colony. So prior to independence, worship facilities, whether Protestant or Catholic, were scant, church membership was negligible, and the Sabbath was more an occasion for fun and frolic than a time for contemplating eternal verities. "Sunday," wrote a female emigrant from Virginia, "is spent by most Texans in hunting and fishing and breaking wild horses."

Some Texans obviously preferred this secular atmosphere. In 1830 Ira Ingram, an early settler, remarked with pleasure that the region was free of "the shameless strifes and animosities" which usually accompanied "the cause of true religion." Ingram elaborated: "We hear no ravings, and see no rompings, or indecorous and indecent exhibitions under the cloak of a religious assemblage." Such nonsectarianism was no doubt reinforced by the activities of numerous charlatans in ministerial garb. It was common on the Texas frontier to encounter bogus men of the cloth who were more familiar with the rules of Hoyle than the Holy Scriptures and more fond of hard liquor than ecclesiastical routine. The problem became so acute that a group of Baptist, Methodist, and Presbyterian ministers in Houston organized "The Ecclesiastical Committee of Vigilance for Texas" in 1837. If the paucity of worship places and the general lack of piety in Texas deterred some prospective colonists, many others, lured by land grants and economic opportunity, easily adjusted. Colonel John Hawkins probably bespoke the sentiment of many early Texans. "I can be as good a Christian there [Texas] as I can here [Missouri]," he told Stephen F. Austin. "It is only a name anyhow."

For evangelical Protestants, of course, Christianity was much more than just a name, and conditions in Texas fired their missionary zeal. Here was a rugged country where they could battle evil, snatch the souls of sinners from Satan's grasp, redeem a wayward society, and establish lasting institutions to carry on the struggle. As historian William Ransom Hogan aptly put it, the Texas frontier was an arena in which Protestants could come to terms with "the Devil on his own ground." Consequently, in defiance of Mexican law, Methodist, Baptist, and Presbyterian preachers were furtively conducting religious services in Texas, usually in private homes, by the 1820s.

Sumner Bacon, a Cumberland Presbyterian, was in many ways typical of these early missionaries. Born in Auburn, Massachusetts, in January 1790, he soon ventured West as a soldier and surveyor in hopes of economic and social advancement. A religious skeptic, Bacon enjoyed theological arguments. In 1826 he and several friends attended a camp meeting near Fayetteville, Arkansas, intent more upon raising hell than seeking salvation. Dramatically, Bacon was converted, and the former scoffer then became an ardent disciple eager to share the gospel with Texans.

The Cumberland Presbyterians, growing out of the intense revivalism of 1800 in Tennessee, readily accommodated to frontier conditions. They abandoned Calvinistic determinism for free will, enthusiastically conducted camp meetings, and lowered the educational qualifications for the ministry. Even so, Bacon posed a dilemma for the Cumberlands. The thirty-six-year-old convert wanted to be ordained for the ministry, but he could hardly read or write. The Arkansas Presbytery, therefore, refused to ordain Bacon until he had improved his literary skills.

Although he never made substantial progress in his educational development, Bacon nevertheless journeyed in the fall of 1829 to Texas, where he tirelessly promoted the Cumberland Presbyterian cause. He held secret prayer meetings in San Antonio, Gonzales, San Augustine, and the Nacogdoches area. In 1834, as the first regular agent of the American Bible Society in Texas, he began an extensive distribution of Bibles, and in 1835 the Louisiana Presbytery in Alexandria reluctantly licensed him to preach. The Cumberlands were still distressed by Bacon's educational shortcomings, but the religious needs of Texas, along with Bacon's obvious zeal and dedication, prompted them to relax their requirements. As a result, Bacon now had authority to form churches, ordain elders, and administer the sacraments. In 1836 he established the first Presbyterian Church in Texas, and in 1837 the first Presbytery of Texas was launched. Although still young, Bacon's health failed after 1837. In January 1844 he died.

By the time of Bacon's death the Cumberland Presbyterians, along with several other denominations, had become firmly established in Texas. When the Lone Star Republic entered the Union in 1845, approximately 12.5 percent of the white population belonged to a church. In order of numerical strength, the leading religious bodies were Methodists, Baptists, Presbyterians, Catholics, and Episcopalians. Catholicism, despite its privileged status in the colonial era, was a negligible force in Texas until the late 1800s. There was little reason for the early settlers, most of whom were of Protestant backgrounds, to take Catholicism seriously, especially since church officials in Mexico generally neglected the Texas colony. Beginning in the 1840s, however, when the Reverend Jean Marie Odin assumed leadership of Texas Catholicism, the pattern began to change. Odin assembled a cadre of able priests who labored productively among a growing number of German, French, and Irish migrants. Still, San Antonio and Galveston would remain for many years the primary areas of Catholic influence.

In the 1840s and 1850s, meanwhile, the continued advancement of the larger Protestant groups was due to aggressive evangelism. Methodists, Baptists, and Presbyterians, especially the Cumberlands, relied heavily upon protracted camp meetings to arouse spiritual fervor. Playing upon the emotions, fiery evangelists vividly contrasted the horrors of hell to the joys of a heavenly paradise. Stirred by these graphic descriptions, "seekers" were often overcome by frenzy, to the distress of some Texans. Reporting on a Houston meeting in the fall of 1845, a critical observer remarked that "no pen or tongue could give . . . an adequate description of these riotous scenes—a person must see and hear in order to be convinced of their mad extravagancies. . . . [And] they call it a revival." Despite such disparagement, camp revivals, generally lasting two to four weeks, served both religious and social needs. They were a respite for the loneliness, monotony, and toil of rural and small-town Texas life. This was especially so for women, for whom the daily routine was exacting and tedious.

To maintain regular contact with scattered congregations, Methodists and Presbyterians used itinerant preachers, or circuit riders. There were advantages and disadvantages in this. A limited number of competent clergymen could minister to numerous isolated communities, thereby substantially extending denominational influence. On the other hand, the circuit system made it easy for congregations to be lackadaisical about making the necessary financial arrangements to support a resident pastor or attending worship services on a weekly basis. By contrast, Baptists, who outdistanced all other religious groups in Texas by the end of the nineteenth century, encouraged the obtainment of a resident pastor for each congregation. This was accomplished in many instances at the expense of educational requirements.

In addition to camp meetings and circuit riders, denominational newspapers were also important to Protestant evangelism, and religious editors were the precusors of a sort of contemporary electronic ministers. Similar to television today, the religious press of the 1840s and 1850s added a new dimension to denominational outreach. George Washington Baines, editor of the *Texas Baptist* from 1855 to 1861 and the grandfather of future President Lyndon Baines Johnson, understood this. An "ably edited, . . . neatly printed, and widely circulated" religious paper, he averred, enabled one to preach "week after week . . . to twice as many *thousands* as . . . to *hundreds* in any other way." The Cumberland Presbyterians were first in this field, commencing the *Texas Presbyterian* in November 1846. The Methodists quickly followed suit with publication of the *Texas Christian Advocate and Brenham General Advertiser* in 1847. It was 1855 before the Baptists issued the first copy of the *Texas Baptist,* the same year in which the Old School Presbyterians began *The Panoplist and Presbyterian of Texas.*

The usefulness of religious newspapers to evangelism in the 1840s and 1850s was exemplified by the work of Methodists among German Catholic immigrants. As was true elsewhere in North America, Protestants in Texas looked askance at Catholics, whose Christian fidelity and national loyalty were suspect. Patriotic and missionary zeal, then, coalesced when Texas Methodists embarked upon a concerted effort to convert these newcomers from Germany. The Methodists established missions at Galveston, the port of entry, Houston, and, eventually, New Braunfels, and in the mid-1850s they began printing the *Evangelische Apologete,* the only German-language paper published by Southern Methodists. That patriotism was a factor in these missionary endeavors was attested to by a promoter of the *Apologete.* "The only way to make these Germans good American citizens," he declared, "is to furnish them with sound protestant *[sic]* reading."

Aside from promoting evangelism, what was the impact of organized religion, which was well-established by the 1850s, upon life in Texas before the Civil War? As in so many other matters, Texas in its religious outlook was a part of the Old South. The state was predominantly Protestant. More importantly, Protestantism in Texas, as in the South generally by the 1840s, was of a conservative variety which emphasized personal frailties and stressed the need of individual regeneration. The emphasis was upon piety, a heartfelt awareness of God's presence, rather than ethics, the application of Christian ideals to daily life. This religious perspective reinforced individualism, strengthened the belief that one was responsible for one's self, and tended to overlook the corporate aspects of faith. As a result, Protestantism in Texas was neither as alert to social conditions nor as attuned to broad social programs as evangelical Protestantism in the North.

It would nevertheless be erroneous to conclude that Texas Protestants left society entirely in the lurch. Although not as broadly reformist as churches in the North, Texas congregations pursued objectives beneficial to society. The churches were civilizing influences, and there certainly was room for social refinement in the Lone Star region. Texans very early acquired a reputation for disorderliness and violence. A contributing factor to such behavior was excessive alcohol consumption. Public drunkeness was common, as Martin Ruter, a prominent Methodist missionary, observed in 1838. "Profaneness, gaming, and intemperance," he noted, were the "prevailing vices against which" Texans had "to contend." Clergymen in Texas subsequently were in the forefront of the temperance movement. In February 1839, William Y. Allen, an Old School Presbyterian, helped found the Texas Temperance Society at Houston. Former President Sam Houston, whose drinking habits were well known, was a featured speaker on this occasion. Sam Corley, an able Cumberland Presbyterian in northeast Texas, added his influence to the cause. Although the Texas legislature in the 1850s enacted some legislation dealing with alcohol, the war against John Barleycorn was just beginning. Many preachers would be satisfied with nothing less than total prohibition.

Education was another area in which the churches figured prominently. The various denominations in Texas valued schooling, despite relaxed educational standards for the ministry, especially among Baptists. The formation of Sunday schools, in which secular teachers often took the initiative, reflected the close tie between religion and education. Thomas J. Pilgrim, a school teacher and a Baptist layman, started the Texas Sunday School movement at San Felipe in 1829. William Y. Allen supported the effort, and there were Sunday schools in Houston, San Augustine, Nacogdoches, and Washington-on-the-Brazos by 1838. While primarily religious in scope, these schools often contributed to the broader intellectual development of a community. Flourishing Sunday schools tended to generate an interest in temperance societies, libraries, and educational institutions in general. The nonsectarian American Sunday School Union, for example, maintained libraries with over 1,000 volumes in Brownsville and Austin.

Motivated by religious concern, the churches also addressed the academic needs of elementary, secondary, and college students. And academies, institutes, colleges, and universities were an additional measure of denominational influence. Many of these institutions, which varied widely in scholastic respectability, failed after a brief time; several were relocated in more promising communities; some were consolidated; and all bore a distinct religious imprint. Clergymen generally doubled as administrators and faculty members. In January 1840 the Methodists opened, near LaGrange, the first Protestant denominational school in Texas, Rutersville College, appropriately named for Martin Ruter, much of whose career was devoted to education. Until about 1850 this was the state's leading educational center, but it declined abruptly thereafter. At Independence in 1845 the Baptists founded Baylor University, which quickly assumed a position of leadership. By the late 1850s this Baptist school was granting more degrees than all other Texas colleges combined. In 1886 Baylor was moved to Waco and consolidated with Waco University, which Baptists in central Texas had established on a coeducational basis in 1861.

These institutions of higher learning did far more than train future preachers. They cultivated civic mindedness by encouraging students to become involved in the political process; promoted academic opportunities for women, sometimes in a co-educational atmosphere; nurtured, within limits, a spirit of critical inquiry; and contributed to a declining illiteracy rate. Among whites in Texas, by 1860 illiteracy was under 4 percent for men and slightly over 5 percent for women.

With regard to slavery, the overriding socioeconomic issue of the 1850s, Texas Protestants again disclosed their Southern roots. With few exceptions, church leaders defended the peculiar institution, looked upon blacks as innately inferior, and later justified secession. In 1860 a Cumberland Presbyterian voiced the feeling of perhaps most Texans. "God in the creation of the Negro," wrote he, "I think, designed him for a secondary sphere in society that is a sphere of labor and servitude." This suggests that democracy was both a source of strength and weakness for Texas Protestants. It kept them responsive to the needs and subject to the prejudices of ordinary people. With church leaders and the laity of one mind, dissenting opinions on slavery were not readily tolerated. When Aaron Grigsby, pastor of the Cumberland Presbyterian Church in Jefferson, aired his abolitionist views on the eve of the Civil War, he had to flee because of harrassment. And in September 1860 Anthony Bewley, a Northern Methodist minister, was lynched near Dallas for allegedly encouraging slave uprisings in North Texas. Unrepentant, the southern Methodist press hinted that Bewley had gotten what he deserved.

In spite of its support of slavery, religion was generally a refining force in antebellum Texas. It brought neighbors together in worship, gave meaning to life, contributed to a sense of community, promoted sobriety, added impetus to education, encouraged thoughtful discussion of a wide range of temporal concerns, and helped bring order to an unruly frontier region.

By the time the Civil War began the Methodists, with 30,661 members and 410 church buildings, still easily surpassed all other religious groups in Texas. The Baptists, with approximately 500 congregations and 280 worship facilities, were a distant second, while the Cumberland Presbyterians, with 6,200 members and 155 places of worship, were next. The other denominations were all considerably smaller. In 1860 the Christian Church, which had experienced dramatic growth in the 1850s, had 39 churches; the Catholics, 33; and the Episcopalians, 19.

This configuration changed substantially by 1906. The Baptists, composing some 33 percent of the church-going public, surged past the Methodists, who now comprised approximately 27 percent of the state's worshippers. Slightly behind the Methodists were the Catholics, whose extraordinary advancement in the latter nineteenth century was due primarily to German, Czechoslovakian, Polish, and Hispanic immigration. The Christian Church, along with the Disciples of Christ, representing about 7 percent of the state's church membership, moved ahead of the Presbyterians, whose adherents numbered approximately 5 percent. Lutherans, Episcopalians, and numerous smaller bodies rounded out the pattern.

In large measure, the rapid growth of Baptists in the late nineteenth century was due to that denomination's appeal to blacks, who constituted a substantial element of the Texas population. In 1860 blacks represented slightly over 30 percent of the total population of 604,213; and in 1900 they comprised approximately 20.3 percent of the state's 3,048,710 residents. This sizable number of blacks simultaneously excited the missionary fervor and aroused the racial fears of white Christians. Emancipation posed a dilemma for churches across the South, and Texas was no exception. It had been common practice in the antebellum years for slaves to attend white churches, usually occupying the balcony or designated pews in the rear of the sanctuary. This arrangement had served a dual purpose: it satisfied the moral obligation of white Christians to share the Good News with the slaves, while at the same time dramatizing the blacks' inferior status. The outcome of the Civil War jeopardized this order. Should the freed persons now be encouraged to organize their own separate congregations or to remain in white churches? Pursuance of the latter course raised the additional issue of equality. Should blacks be invited to come down from the balconies, participate in church deliberations, and share authority with their former masters?

White churchmen in Texas, as elsewhere in the South, were not about to accept blacks as equals. That would have been far more revolutionary than emancipation. Still, white congregations were sharply divided during the early Reconstruction years over the retention of blacks. The debate among Texas Baptists was typical. In 1866, following a heated discussion, the Colorado Baptist Association voted to retain its black members, explaining that the former slaves lacked adequate "intelligence and education . . . to keep the doctrines and ordinances in God's work pure and unmixed with human error when unaided by the superior intelligence of the whites." While perhaps genuinely concerned about the spiritual welfare of blacks, Baptists disclosed deeper motives. Just as the antebellum church had often been a means of social control, exhorting slaves to be obedient and humble, so it would remain after the Civil War, shielding blacks now from the blandishments of northern politicians and Catholic priests. A Houston Baptist put it plainly. He argued in 1868 that the removal of blacks from white churches would render them "a prey to the combined evil of ignorance, superstition, fanaticism, and a political propagandism more dangerous and destructive to the best interests of both whites and blacks than Jesuitism itself." Self-interest, then, if not Christian duty, compelled the Houstonian to conclude "that our churches should retain the Negroes in their membership, and control their [blacks'] action so far as they [white churches] have a moral right to do so."

While the former masters wrangled, blacks settled the matter—they withdrew en masse from white-controlled churches, and in so doing tested and demonstrated their newly acquired freedom. Eager to be rid of white surveillance, blacks quickly forged their own religious institutions, and overwhelmingly their denominational preference was Baptist. A democratic polity and local autonomy probably accounted for this latter trend, inasmuch as such practices facilitated the creation of Baptist congregations. One authority, however, has even suggested that the affinity of blacks to the Baptist faith was due to baptism by total immersion, a practice which closely resembled various rituals of the West African river cults. The first black Baptist church in Texas was organized at Galveston in 1865. By 1890 black Baptists numbered 111,138 statewide, while the Methodists lagged far behind with approximately 42,214 followers. And in 1916 Baptists made up almost 72 percent of the state's 396,157 black churchgoers.

That religion was a vital aspect of life for Texas blacks is indisputable, but there is considerable disagreement regarding the exact function of the church within the black community. Was the church essentially a veneer for enduring elements of African culture? Was the black preacher, for instance, merely a latter-day witch doctor? Or was the black church an example of folk religion, perpetuating beliefs, practices, and superstitions which had little basis in historic Christianity? Or was the church an aggressive agency in the struggle for freedom? Were the spirituals really subtle protest songs, and was the minister a freedom fighter? Or did the church, serving a peo-

*First Baptist Church, Dallas, with a membership of 21,000, is the largest Baptist congregation in the world. Founded in 1868, the church has reflected the growth of Southern Baptists which has become the largest religious denomination in the state.*

ple afflicted by oppression and suffering, more nearly reflect the values of Jesus than the prosperous, secularized white churches? Or was the church an alternative society, providing opportunities of a religious, educational, social, recreational, and political nature denied to blacks in a nation controlled by whites?

Whatever its precise role, the black church in Texas was clearly a springboard for some able and ambitious blacks, an institution within which others developed and exercised leadership qualities, and for still others a refuge. In the 1870s Meshack Roberts, a former slave blacksmith and a Methodist lay reader, served Harrison County three terms in the state legislature. Sutton Griggs, a Baptist preacher, was a noteworthy author. Written between 1899 and 1908, his five novels depicted the shifting fortunes of Texas blacks at the turn of the century. Richard Henry Boyd, a former Texas slave who was a cowboy and a mill hand before turning to the ministry, rose rapidly through the black Baptist Convention eventually to become secretary of the National Baptist Convention. In 1897 he organized the National Baptist Publishing Board, which printed denominational literature exclusively for blacks. To the extent possible, Boyd believed blacks should control their own religious and educational endeavors. And Texas blacks did not go wanting for fiery evangelists. In the early twentieth century, J. Gordon McPherson, the "Black Billy Sunday," and "Sin Killer" Griffin battled evil as zealously as their white counterparts.

An issue of concern by the early twentieth century to blacks as well as whites was the saloon. The prohibition movement had steadily gained momentum in the late nineteenth century, and in Texas the churches, especially Baptist and Methodist, spearheaded the effort. In 1900 a prominent Texas Baptist, convinced the corner tavern was "the greatest curse" facing "our country," even applauded the hatchet-wielding antics of Mrs. Carrie Nation of Kansas. "It often seems that the only way to annihilate the saloon is to meet lawlessness with lawlessness," he rationalized. Significantly, the crusade against "demon rum" enabled many churchmen to see more clearly the social implications of their faith. By 1908, for instance, the Baptist General Convention of Texas recognized that the saloon was "so interlaced . . . into commerce, politics, society, and the administration of law" that it behooved the church to become more active politically and alert socially.

Contrary to popular assumption, the social gospel did come South. In Texas, Baptists early in this century, while remaining intensely evangelistic and quite conservative theologically, increasingly applied the Bible to society. And to Eugene Coke Routh, the associate editor of the *Baptist Standard,* a weekly publication distributed to Baptists statewide, there was actually "nothing new about" this, for Jesus Himself had given "examples of social service" in the parable of the Good Samaritan and in acts of compassion toward the needy. One of the more important exponents of social Christianity was a native Texan, Joseph Martin Dawson. Born in June 1879 and reared neared Waxahachie in the cotton belt of north central Texas, Dawson, a Baylor graduate, ministered to congregations at Lampasas, Hillsboro, and Temple before assuming the pastorate at the First Baptist Church in Waco in 1915, a position he held until 1946. Always interested in politics and sensitive to social ills, the young clergyman readily expressed preferences in electoral campaigns, openly supported political means to achieve worthy goals, and persistently reminded fellow churchmen that the Good News was for society as well as the individual.

In 1914, just before leaving the First Baptist Church in Temple, Dawson delivered the first formal series of sermons by a Texas Baptist on social Christianity. Subsequently printed in the *Baptist Standard,* these messages had an impact across the state. Disclosing a familiarity with the leading social gospel thinkers of the North, notably Walter Rauschenbusch, Dawson dealt with capitalism and "the masses of submerged industrial classes," child labor, the exploitation of immigrants, and women's rights. Later, during his ministry in Waco, Dawson grappled with racial justice. He denounced mob violence, rebuked the Ku Klux Klan, promoted interracial meetings, and shamed fellow Southerners for refusing to fund more adequately public schools for blacks. In 1927 he argued in a national magazine publication that blacks were being kept illiterate because of disgracefully low appropriations for black schools. This commitment to racial justice never flagged. In 1957 the seventy-eight-year-old minister appeared before a hostile state Senate committee in Austin to oppose pending legislation harmful to blacks, and the following year in *Christianity Today* he voiced disappointment in Governor Price Daniel, a fellow Baptist, for not pursuing a more enlightened racial policy.

Importantly, Dawson was not alone. By the early twentieth century there were institutional manifestations of social Christianity. In 1915 Texas Baptists created the Social Service Committee, which subsequently focused attention on disputes between land owners and tenant farmers, conflicts between labor and capital, the need for prison and child welfare reforms, prostitution, and the "craze for amusements and 'athletics.' " If fellow Baptists had misgivings about this social emphasis, the Social Service Committee did not disclose them. Indeed, in 1917 it exuberantly declared that "Jesus [Himself] was the great sociologist." These were heady times, and many Texas churches reflected the temper of the moment.

But the mood of optimism soon waned because of involvement in World War I and the virulent evolution controversy of the 1920s, led in Texas by fundamentalist J. Frank Norris, pastor of the First Baptist Church of Fort Worth, and the air of self-confidence was shaken by the hard times spawned by the Great Depression and the rise of Nazism and the eruption of global war in the 1930s. Nevertheless, the growth of social Christianity in Texas continued, even among conservative Baptists.

In 1950 the Baptist General Convention created the Christian Life Commission, an activist agency dedicated to applied Christianity. Professor Thomas B. Maston, whose long and distinguished career at Southwestern Baptist Theological Seminary in Fort Worth lasted from 1920 to 1963, was a prime mover in this development. Without ever losing sight of the individual or departing from a conservative theology, the seminarian, folksy in manner and style, used the classroom, a prolific pen, and personal involvement to expand the social vision of Baptists in particular and Christians in general. Under his leadership, ethics became a major field of study at the Baptist seminary, and by the late 1930s and early 1940s Maston probed the racial issue in courses on "Social Problems in the South" and "The Church and the Race Problem." Fort Worth became a laboratory, as Maston's students took field trips through black neighborhoods and examined various aspects of the city's race problem. Through his students alone, one of whom was Bill Moyers, a former aide to President Lyndon B. Johnson and presently a commentator for CBS Evening News, Maston's influence was enormous, but his reach was further extended by literary endeavors. He wrote nineteen books and hundreds of Sunday school lessons, pamphlets, articles, and columns in Baptist weeklies. Works such as *Of One* (1946), *The Bible and Race* (1959), and *Segregation and Desegregation* (1959), written at the request of Macmillan and Company, offered calm advice to Christians searching for answers to the troublesome racial issue.

Despite a career devoted to teaching and writing, Maston was no ivory tower scholar. He engaged actively in the quest for desirable change through such organizations as the Southern Regional Council, the NAACP, and the Fort Worth chapter of the Urban League. As Cold War fears mounted and the hunt for subversives intensified, these civil rights groups were often dismissed as communist fronts.

Even Maston was called a "Negro lover" and a communist dupe. Patiently, the seminarian responded. In 1947, for instance, he addressed a Fort Worth audience on "The Urban League and the American Way of Life," concluding that the league was based upon such humane American ideals as democracy and charity.

Maston's vision was mirrored by the Christian Life Commission, and the hallmark of this agency has been a practical application of Christian ideals. Its principal areas of attention since 1951 have been public morals, involving such traditional Baptist concerns as alcohol, gambling, and pornography; race relations; family life; economic matters, especially "issues involved in the rapid industrial growth of the South and the Southwest, the materialistic influences on the spiritual life of the Christian, [and] the stewardship of labor and management"; citizenship, pertaining to involvement in the political life of society; and relationships between church and state.

To its credit, this commission has never evaded controversial topics. Without being sanctimonious, it has forthrightly attempted to provide a biblical approach to difficult questions. The concerns of modern Americans have been the concerns of the commission. It opposed universal military training in the early 1950s, has consistently defended the Supreme Court in its desegregation rulings of the 1950s and its school prayer decisions of the early 1960s, sanctioned abortion under certain circumstances, promoted sex education, grappled with drug abuse, urged a settlement to the Vietnam conflict, upheld the principle "that people" were "more important than profit," insisted "that businesses take the necessary steps to eliminate pollution from the air and water," condemned "raw violence" and the exploitation of sex on television, advocated bilingual education, supported free public schooling for the children of illegal aliens, endorsed programs to rehabilitate Texas prison inmates, warned against political groups that shrouded themselves in the flag and claimed to be *the* voice of the Christian community, encouraged energy conservation, advised restraint "in wage and price increases and in our own consumption habits" as a means of dealing with inflation, and urged Texans in 1982 to approve a constitutional amendment allowing greater state aid for dependent children.

To a great extent, the Christian Life Commission has been an educational institution. It has served as a think-tank, studying issues and making position statements. But since the early 1960s it has also worked actively through the political process to influence public policy. It regularly lobbied the state legislature, offered testimony on specific issues to governmental committees, and encouraged local Baptists not only to vote but also to advise their state representatives of denominational sentiment. And the commission was quick to answer both those Texans who frowned upon such involvement by the churches in secular politics and those Baptists who fretted over such political activism. In 1961 it declared that "the principle of church-state separation has never meant in this nation that the Christians should not seek to influence the policies of the state to reflect a higher morality." Texas politics could hardly be lauded for reflecting "a higher morality," but the Christian Life Commission has certainly worked toward that end.

Among Texas Catholics, who were second in number only to Southern Baptists, there was by the mid-twentieth century a comparable concern for social justice. Most notably, this was exemplified by Archbishop Robert E. Lucey, who came to Texas as bishop of the Diocese of Amarillo in 1934. Seven years later he became the archbishop of the Archdiocese of San Antonio, remaining there until his retirement in 1969. Authoritarian and controversial, Lucey consistently placed the church on the side of the poor and the underprivileged. He championed labor's right to unionize and spurred employers to pay decent wages. Within his archdiocese, he would not allow the employment of non-union labor for church construction. "It would be a tragedy," he asserted, "if a Catholic building were constructed dishonorably on the blood and sweat of honest workmen." In the 1950s Lucey pushed for racial integration, encouraging Catholics to follow the example of Jesus and chiding those who fell short. Parochial schools in San Antonio were integrated several months before the landmark Supreme Court decision on school desegregation in 1954. And in the 1960s Lucey directed attention to the plight of migrant farm workers in the Rio Grande Valley.

As with Baptists, Texas Catholics institutionalized social action. Lucey challenged the priests under his authority to apply the gospel to society. "You cannot be silent, neutral, afraid to raise your voice," he exhorted them in 1964, "as though the hopes and the longings, the fears and aspirations of the suffering and exploited masses were none of your business." In 1969 Lucey's archdiocese created the Commission on Church and Society, an activist agency concerned with such matters as racial justice, housing, equality of economic opportunity, job development, and health services.

As illustrated by Baptists and Catholics, organized religion in Texas has not only grown stronger since the Civil War but has also assumed greater responsibility for society. And since the 1950s the impact of religion, albeit difficult to gauge exactly, has been evident in matters ranging from race to bilingual education to horse racing and parimutuel betting. Texas, for instance, while certainly not free of ethnic strife, escaped the bitter racial turmoil that rocked Mississippi and Alabama in the 1960s, and those church leaders who defended the Supreme Court and exhorted fellow Christians to measure up to the ideals of their faith deserve at least some credit for this. On moral issues, Texas churches can and often do exert considerable power.

But despite enormous advancement since the struggling days of Sumner Bacon, Texas churches cannot afford complacency. The number of church-affiliated Texans has declined in recent years. In 1971 over 56 percent of the state's populace belonged to a congregation. Dominating the scene were Southern Baptists, who composed 21.1 percent of the total, and Catholics, 18 percent. The United Methodists were a distant third at 7.6 percent, followed by Presbyterians (approximately 1.9 percent), Episcopalians (1.6 percent), Lutherans (1.3 percent), and the Church of Christ (1.1 percent). By 1980 only 54.7 percent of all Texans were church adherents, and except for the Churches of Christ all the major denominations had dwindled. Southern Baptists slipped to 18.7 percent; Catholics, 16.4 percent; and United Methodists, 6.6 percent. If the trend continues, church adherents probably will be a minority by the year 2000. Indeed, this has already become a reality in the state's most populous county. Between 1971 and 1980 the number of Harris County residents affiliated with a church dipped from 58 to 49 percent.

While admittedly stronger, Texas churches today face a situation somewhat comparable to that of the 1830s and 1840s. Now as then, Texas is a beguiling land of opportunity. Geographically tied to the prospering Sun Belt, yet set apart by a popular western mystique, Texas has attracted in recent years streams of people searching for a better life. Church membership thus far has failed to keep pace with the population surge. And now as then, this migration will challenge not only the evangelistic zeal and social responsibility of Protestants and Catholics but also the strength of pluralism. Just as Texas Protestants in the late nineteenth century had to make room for Catholics, Protestants and Catholics will have to make similar adjustments in the late twentieth century. The range is becoming more diversified. Substantial numbers of the new migrants are Jews, Moslems, Hindus, and Buddhists. To be sure, Protestants and Catholics will continue for years to dominate the religious life of Texas, but in the future the battle against evil will likely follow a more varied course.

# 20

## The Greatest Challenge: Education in Texas

*James Smallwood*

Education in Texas is an exciting topic. From the early Spanish era down to the 1980s, the story of education, allowing for occasional setbacks, has been one of great strides forward, great progress.

Spaniards first brought education to Texas as early as 1690-93. Spain established missions in the Nacogdoches area to stop French penetration into the East Texas region. Later, Spaniards also established missions on the site of present-day San Antonio (1718) and elsewhere. Although the primary purposes of these missions were religious and political, they also had rudimentary educational goals —to teach the Indians rules of "civilized conduct" and to accustom them to Spanish ways. Friars also taught certain basic skills. For example, some Indian men and boys learned such crafts as brick-making, masonry, and the making of wine. Some women and girls learned such skills as weaving and sewing.

When Spaniards began to colonize Texas, attention was paid to the education of Spanish youth. As early as 1746, a school was founded in San Antonio de Bexar, and eventually, in 1813, the Spaniards erected a sturdy building there to provide for seventy pupils. As settlement increased, so did the number of schools, although only rudimentary education was available. To these early educational efforts was added that of the government of Mexico when the Spanish yoke was overthrown in 1821. Texas was joined to Coahuila, and the new province's constitution made generous provisions for education — stating that primary schools were to be organized in all towns and that, among other subjects, reading, writing, and arithmetic were to be taught in addition to religious instruction.

When — with the planting of Stephen F. Austin's colony — Anglos began entering Texas, a decree required every empresario to provide for schools, and it is known that one Isaac M. Pennington taught an English school somewhere in Austin's colony as early as 1823. Two years later Nacogdoches got its first English school, as did Matagorda in 1828. Later, other schools were established in yet other areas where, in addition to the three "R's," young scholars learned history, rhetoric, composition, a smattering of philosophy, and perhaps one or more languages — usually Latin, Greek, and Spanish. However, despite the fact that a few schools existed prior to 1836, several Anglo leaders frequently charged that the Mexican government neglected education in Texas.

The Texas Revolution of 1836 and the subsequent development of the Republic wrought change regarding education. Many statesmen, including Austin and such men as Anson Jones, wished to establish a strong school system. Consequently, the Constitution of the Republic gave Congress a mandate to provide for a general system of education. Nevertheless, Congress delayed action until 1839. That year legislation provided that three leagues of land (13,284 acres) be set aside in every Texas county to establish a primary school or academy. The allotted acreage could be leased to bring in school revenue but could not be sold. Provision was also made for a grant of fifty leagues for an endowment of two colleges. Another law in 1840 awarded each county a fourth league which could be sold to raise money to begin the primary schools.

Despite lofty goals voiced by Congress in its educational legislation, efforts to establish schools by means of land grants generally failed. Land, for instance, was abundant and therefore cheap. Consequently, counties could secure only small amounts of money from the sale or lease of school grants. Further, there was much public indifference to the founding of county schools. Thus, few primary schools or academies were established during the period of the Republic. Most Texans continued to educate their children at home, with the youngsters instructed by an older family member or by a tutor. In addition to this development, it is also true that private "old field" or "cornfield" schools sprang into existence in many Texas communities when itinerant teachers (or perhaps someone else who was unemployed) started classes and made their salary by charging tuition. However, the number of cornfield schools is impossible to calculate, given the paucity of sources about them.

If common-school education developed only slowly, more attention was paid to higher education, with a number of institutions established, all privately controlled. Rutersville College opened on February 1, 1840, and thus became the first college in Texas. A Methodist missionary who came to the Republic with the goal of establishing a Methodist college, Martin Ruter was the moving force behind the organization of the first college. He died before the institution opened, but his friends got the college chartered and named it in Ruter's honor. In addition to the establishment of Rutersville College, Baylor University (established in 1845), a Baptist institution, was also founded during the period of the Republic at Independence, Texas. Later moved to Waco, Baylor claims to be the oldest continuously operated college in Texas. Other colleges were founded during the era of the Republic such as the University of San Augustine, the University of Nacogdoches, and Galveston University. With the exception of Baylor, however, most private institutions soon faded and did not survive into the twentieth century. Moreover, during the era of the Republic, no public institutions of higher learning were established. Thus the condition of higher education remained woefully inadequate.

When Texas came into the Union in 1845, its Constitution promised change in the field of education. The governing document charged the legislature with making provisions for the maintenance of public common schools to be supported by property taxes. Further, the legislature was to set aside 10 percent of annual state revenues for support of schools. Although the legislature was slow to act, the number of publicly supported common schools began to increase in the late 1840s and 1850s, as did the number of private schools. By the time of the Civil War, a true system of public education was developing.

Just as there was expansion in the number of common schools after 1845, there were many colleges founded in the new state before the Civil War. At least fifty-two colleges were created during this era — the surge explained, to some extent, by boosterism or local community spirit. Since having a college was seen as a mark of distinction, many communities, even those on the cutting edge of the frontier, were determined to have their own institution of higher learning. However, many such institutions lasted only a few years before folding. Nevertheless, on the eve of the Civil War, Texas had forty academies, thirty colleges, twenty-seven institutes, seven "universities," five other schools, three high schools, two seminaries, one collegiate institute, and one medical college.

The Civil War wrought havoc for both common schools and institutions of higher learning. The state system of public education, such as it was, ceased to function after 1862, and many private schools closed as teachers and older students were called away to war and younger children were kept at home to assist their elders. Statistics reveal that colleges also suffered — in 1860 there were twenty-five colleges with a combined enrollment of 2,416 students, but by 1870 the number had dropped to thirteen with a total enrollment of only 800 pupils.

When Radical Republicans under E. J. Davis came to power in Reconstruction Texas, the fate of education was profoundly affected. Radicals favored many beneficial reforms, one of which was the establishment of a strong, truly free, system of public education in Texas. The Radical Constitution of 1869 called for a new, highly centralized system, to be directed by a state superintendent of public instruction who had wide powers. School laws of 1870 and 1871 put the constitutional directive into operation. Jacob C. DeGress, a young Union army veteran, was named superintendent, and he rapidly put the new public system into effect. In September 1871 public free schools opened at a time when Texas had 229,568 youngsters in its scholastic population. By the end of the year, 1,324 schools had opened, and 63,504 students had enrolled. The next academic term (1872-73) saw enrollment explode, with 129,542 children attending. And it might be added that Radicals gave attention to black education, something sorely needed by many ex-slaves. Black schools, many originally organized by the Freedmen's Bureau, were incorporated into the state system and received funding. On the issue of biracial education, however, leading Radicals refused to confront the prevailing racial prejudices of most white Texans — schools remained segregated by race. Still, Radical school reforms represented a quantum leap forward for both whites and blacks.

Despite the beneficial results of the Radicals' educational reforms, many white Texans were antagonistic toward the new system. Black education was, of course, bitterly resented by some whites who argued that blacks should be kept in their place (i.e., semislavery) and that if the ex-slaves *were* educated, such education should be in practical skills only. Further, many white Texans leveled charges that the Radical system was too centralized, giving the state superintendent too much authority, and that the system was too expensive and riddled with corruption (a charge totally lacking supportive evidence). In truth, however, special taxes were levied to support the public system, and these taxes were bitterly resented by some Texans who argued that it was an injustice to use forced taxation to compel one person to educate the children of someone

*This school house in Taylor County near Abilene is typical of the educational facilities in rural Texas from around the turn of the century through the 1930s.*

else. Further, the Radical laws required compulsory attendance, a feature also detested by many Texans who argued that, on one hand, six-year-old children were too young to be sent to school and that, on the other hand, older children were needed for work in the homes, on farms, and in urban areas.

Given the public disfavor of the Radical system, it was little wonder that when Democrats overthrew the Davis Radicals in 1873, a new school law was framed, a law which destroyed the Radical reforms. Under the Democrats, the direction of schools was taken out of the hands of the state superintendent and lodged with local county boards. The people paid lax attention to schools in general. Consequently, attendance fell, and many parents reverted to private schools and tutors.

The new state Constitution of 1875, written by the triumphant Democrats, finished wrecking the old Radical system by turning the matter of education completely over to county authorities and parents. Further, so little tax money was allotted schools that construction of new buildings and of other basic improvements was rendered impossible. Slowly, however, the white public and their politicos realized that in their zeal to abolish the Radical system, they might have gone too far because their loosely constructed, locally controlled system proved chaotic. Thus, to change what was an unworkable system, the legislature framed a new school law in 1884. Its most important features included the following provisions: (1) an elected state superintendent was to supervise all units in the common school system; (2) higher district or local taxation was provided to raise revenue. Thus, the Democrats had, at least partially, returned to the Radical system. Steadily after 1884 the public system grew and thrived, every year counting new teachers and enrolling more students. Moreover, on an ever-increasing basis, high schools were established to offer education beyond the primary grades. As the dawn of a new century approached, Texas appeared to have made great strides in public school education.

The state's minority of black students were, of course, less fortunate, given prevailing Anglo attitudes of racism. Forced into segregated schools, Afro-American students found that their facilities, their supplies, and even the training of their teachers were not on par with that of white schools. Nevertheless, from approximately 1876 to 1900, black education in Texas compared favorably with that of other Southern states. During that period, illiteracy among blacks in Texas declined from approximately 75 percent to just under 40 percent. By 1900, however, statistics revealed that Texas ranked only fifth among Southern states in enrollment of Afro-

American students and in daily attendance and only third in the number of black teachers.

If common education made advances as Texas marched toward the year 1900, so, too, did higher education. In 1876 public higher education finally came to the state. That year the Agricultural and Mechanical College of Texas (now Texas A&M University) was created as a land-grant institution under the Morrill Act passed by Congress in 1862 to promote agricultural education. Texas received 180,000 acres under the Morrill Act to establish this school. In 1883, seven years after Texas A&M opened its doors, the state's premier liberal-arts school, the University of Texas at Austin, opened for classes. Joined by such private institutions as Baylor, these universities would grow as the new century neared.

Some attention was also paid to black higher education during this era. A school for black youths was established in 1876 and was reorganized three years later as Prairie View Normal School, an institution that was destined to survive until the present day. Other black colleges, most of them private, supplemented the efforts of Prairie View.

As the new century dawned, a curious paradox was seen regarding common-school education in the state. In the towns and cities, Texas schools ranked with the best in the nation, but "country" or rural schools ranked among the poorest. Unfortunately, a majority of students were adversely affected, for 571,536 children still attended rural schools, while only 157,681 went to classes in urban centers. The problem, of course, related to quality of facilities and enrichment programs, but money was the greatest factor, with urban districts averaging an expenditure of $8.35 per child, while rural districts spent only $4.97. Further, the average school year was 162 days in towns and cities as compared to 98 days for rural schools. In addition, the value of school property in urban centers was $5,046,461 as compared to $2,648,180 in the country, and "town" teachers were better trained and made almost twice the salary of "country" teachers. And of the 11,460 rural schools, only 930 were graded. The rest were one-teacher, ungraded schools.

Given the overwhelming problems of the rural schools, the movement toward the consolidation of small rural districts began. With consolidation, slender resources could be more effectively used to help the maximum of students. In 1907, for example, 351 small units consolidated into 165 new districts. Or, again, from 1910 to 1914, there were 148 consolidations in 123 counties, and 155 small units were abandoned. By 1922, a total of 757 consolidations had taken place, and by 1930, 1,530. This above trend would continue for decades. Still, as population increased, the total number of districts continued to grow. Altogether, statistics revealed that in 1901-02 there were 5,946 common school districts, 2,500 community schools, and 288 independent districts. By 1922, there were 7,369 districts and 858 independent districts. Nevertheless, consolidation remained the "wave" of the future and would continue unabated down to the 1980s.

While the consolidation movement was underway, other significant events occurred. In 1915, as a result of growing public awareness of the importance of education, the legislature passed a compulsory attendance law. It required children from age eight to fourteen to attend school (in 1916-17) for sixty days a year, unless the children were properly excused. By graduation, the law raised the minimum attendance to eighty days for the 1917-18 term and 100 days for 1918-19. Subsequent revisions by the legislature in the coming years required children from six to sixteen to attend and to attend for most of an approximate 180-day academic year.

Other events also occurred apace. In 1915, the legislature—finally recognizing the handicap facing rural schools—tried to equalize educational opportunities between urban and rural areas. J. M. Wagstaff and others framed a law which appropriated $1,000,000 for the special benefit of country schools. One important development was a constitutional amendment in 1918 which provided for the adoption of free textbooks and for a state tax to purchase the needed books. Another significant amendment, passed in 1920, abolished the limit of taxation which school districts could levy against property.

Regarding the state's largest minority, it was unfortunate that segregation in schools was as rigid as ever. Black schools, as compared to those for whites, were woefully underfunded, and this was reflected in poor facilities and inadequate equipment and supplies. Between 1905 and 1930, salaries for white instructors in rural areas rose by $8.98 per student, but salaries for black teachers increased only $0.16 per pupil. By 1930 black teachers in both urban and rural areas made approximately one-third per scholastic as their Anglo counterparts. Further, although blacks constituted approximately one-third of the school-aged population in East Texas, more than 97 percent of the area's high schools were for whites only.

During these years, the junior college movement expanded. As early as 1897, the Baptist State Convention established Howard Payne College, Rusk College, and Decatur Baptist College as junior colleges to join its senior schools, which included Baylor University and Mary Hardin-Baylor College. Other religious denominations, including the Methodists, also established two-year colleges. By the 1920s, the state had created more new junior colleges—for example, two-year institutions opened their doors at Stephenville and Arlington. Texas cities also entered the field with El Paso taking the lead by founding El Paso Junior College in 1920. By 1940, there were thirty-nine junior colleges (state, local, and church) in Texas with an enrollment of more than 10,000 students.

Four-year colleges and universities also grew in number and size. The state organized a college for women at Denton (now Texas Woman's University) and acquired or founded normal schools at such locations as Commerce, Canyon, Kingsville, and Alpine. In 1923 all the normals became teachers' colleges. That same year, Texas Technological College was established at Lubbock, thus meeting the demands of West Texas for a university in that part of the state.

Although the decade of the 1920s represented years of progress, the Great Depression which started in 1929 disastrously affected the schools. Some sources of school funds dried up as property valuations declined. Also, frequently many people could not pay their taxes in full. Sometimes it was difficult for school districts to pay their teachers. Worse, children often went hungry, finding that they sometimes received their best meal of the day at school when sympathetic teachers—using state, federal, and local aid—started hot lunch programs. The coming of the New Deal under President Franklin D. Roosevelt provided some aid for Texas schools, particularly for such improvements as construction of new buildings, including classrooms, teacherages, gymnasiums, and auditoriums. Slowly, during the 1930s, Texas schools began to recover from the worst aspects of the depression.

One pronounced educational trend of the 1930s was the movement to add a twelfth year to the public schools. Desire to conform to the prevailing practice in other states and the difficulty many of Texas' high school graduates (going through only eleven grades) found in gaining employment during the depression combined to fuel the push for a twelfth year. Consequently, by 1941 about 50 percent of all Texas schools had added the extra year. Soon almost all would follow suit. Another trend was the broadening of the curriculum. By 1940 many schools had, for example, introduced instruction in such vocational subjects as manual training, home economics, agriculture, business, and the like.

In the 1940s schools continued to grow as did the state's school expenditures. Still, Texas lagged behind many progressive states in the quality of its system. Moreover, rural aid had become a subject

*The University of Texas tower and main building are familiar landmarks visible throughout the city of Austin. The twenty-seven-story tower is a symbol of the growth of higher education facilities in Texas.*

of controversy. It was limited to county schools only, and spokesmen for city schools woefully cried that such aid was discriminating and therefore unjust. It was clear that a new comprehensive plan was needed to reorganize the entire school system. That desire led to the Gilmer-Aiken laws of 1949.

Representative Claude Gilmer and State Senator A. M. Aiken led a series of bills through the legislature that drastically improved the development of education in the state. First came reorganization of school administration. The legislature created an elective state board of education consisting of one member chosen from each of the state's twenty-one congressional districts. It was stipulated that the board would appoint the commissioner of education and that the board of commissioners would head the Texas Education Agency and thus assume general control of the public school system. Another law established a "minimum foundations" program; that is, the state would see to it that all children of school age would receive a minimum of nine months schooling per year under teachers who met stipulated minimum training requirements. Further, school facilities — the children's educational environment — had to conform to certain standards.

The Gilmer-Aiken programs quickly showed positive results. The new system eliminated many unoperative school districts, improved school attendance, placed a premium on academic excellence, and encouraged thousands of the state's teachers to go back to their university studies for more schooling. Moreover, the new Texas Education Agency worked to improve schools by emphasizing good citizenship and the productive application of education. Schools improved even more after 1957 when Russia placed satellites in orbit. Fresh emphasis was placed on education, with the sciences benefitting the most, but all fields benefitted when government officials and the general public pushed to make schooling a more serious business.

Public schools had new impetus for growth—and growing excellence—in the 1960s. On assuming the presidency, John F. Kennedy asked for massive federal aid to education but did not receive from Congress the full amount he wanted. President Lyndon Johnson had more success. As part of his "Great Society" programs (1964-69), there were record congressional appropriations for education, and many Texas schools (common schools and institutions of higher learning) received much needed aid. President Richard Nixon, though more conservative than Johnson, continued to seek some monies for education as did the later presidents, Gerald Ford and Jimmy Carter. Only with the coming of Ronald Reagan to the presidency was the above trend reversed as Reagan moved to trim the federal budget.

If public schools made great strides after 1940, so, too, did higher education. The United States involvement in World War II led to a drop in college enrollments from 35 pecent to 50 percent, but in 1944 the federal "GI Bill of Rights" offered returning veterans rich opportunities to continue their education — opportunities in the form of stipends and payments for tuition, fees, and book costs. The same benefits later accrued to veterans of the Korean War. Thus, veterans by the thousands flocked to Texas schools and an enrollment boom hit almost all colleges and universities in the state. And the boom became even larger in 1958 when Congress passed the National Defense Education Act (NDEA), which provided students with either low-interest loans or outright grants. Tremendous growth for colleges in the state continued to be the trend as the 1950s gave way to the 1960s, and the 1960s to the 1970s. The 1960s, for example, saw more sweeping federal aid—and more state appropriations—to higher education in Texas as first President Kennedy and then President Johnson sought and received appropriations for higher institutions as well as for common education. In the late 1960s and 1970s, Presidents Nixon, Ford, and Carter continued to seek some monies for higher education, a trend broken only in 1981 when President Reagan argued for massive federal cutbacks in aid to education. Moreover, the "baby boom" of the post World War II era had passed by the 1980s, and the number of college-age students was declining. Thus, although the future appears uncertain, the 1960s and 1970s were decades of unparalleled growth for Texas' institutions of higher learning. Between 1960 and 1980, thirty new public senior colleges, systems, or branch campuses were created in Texas. And, of course, public common schools also benefitted from the federal government's (and the state's) largesse, as even more dollars found their way to common schools.

During the modern era, Texas also developed several upper-level colleges which accepted only junior, senior, and graduate students. Such a development seemed only logical since, by the 1960s, the state had a highly developed junior college network. Thus, as planned, the community colleges served as feeder institutions for the upper levels, which were located strategically around the state. Texas had ten upper-level institutions by 1980.

Private and/or church-related institutions of higher learning also thrived after World War II that affected public institutions — the baby boom, federal aid to students (not to the colleges), and increasing public support for education. But the early 1980s became years of uncertainty for private colleges because declining enrollments and reductions of federal student aid forced many private schools to "tighten their belts."

Despite some belt tightening and a slight overall dip in enrollments, higher education in the state still thrives. Donald Whisenhunt in his essay, *The Development of Higher Education in Texas* (Boston: American Press, 1983), concluded that, even in the face of problems, Texas institutions would adapt to new conditions and remain viable. Another researcher, Mary Anne Norman, in *The Texas Economy Since World War II* (Boston: American Press, 1983), boldly labeled higher education as a continuing "growth industry" (even in the 1980s).

It is also notable that by the 1980s integration of the state's schools (at all levels) was continuing apace. The historic Supreme Court decision in *Brown* v. *Topeka* (1954) was not rapidly implemented in Texas. It met determined opposition in some quarters. As late as the mid-1960s, the state lagged behind some other states in this regard. Nevertheless, statistics released near the decade's end revealed that Texas had integrated more schools and students than any other state in the historic South. The 1970s saw continuing progress. The state's leaders could by the mid-1980s point with pride to the fact that most schools in the state's system (common and higher) had integrated or had filed compliance plans to do so. Only one area of the school integration question worried concerned observers: What would be the fate of the historic all-black colleges such as little Wiley College in Marshall? Would these institutions survive? To survive, what changes would they have to make? Nevertheless, with the possible exception of some black colleges, the condition of higher education in Texas appears solid and well directed toward the future.

Overall, it is clear that Texas has by the 1980s come far since Spanish missionaries of the seventeenth century began giving rudimentary instruction and training to the Indians they encountered. What would such missionaries think if they could tour the best elementary, junior high, and high schools in Houston? What would they think if they could tour Dallas' junior college network? What would they think if they could walk over the campus of the University of Texas at Austin on a day when classes were in full swing? Texans of the 1980s know the answers. The Spaniards would have marveled to see one of the best educational networks — from primary grades to graduate schools — in the United States.

## SUGGESTED READINGS

This section is included as a guide to the person who wishes to find more information on a particular topic. These suggestions are not meant to be comprehensive; instead, they are designed to provide the standard works on a subject and to provide guidance for the interested reader. The suggestions were made by each of the authors. In some instances, the suggestions are rather short either because little has been written about the subject or because not much is readily available to the general reader.

### CHAPTER 1


Atkinson, Mary Jourdan. *The Texas Indians.* San Antonio: The Naylor Co., 1935, 1953.

Berlaindier, Jean Louis. *The Indians of Texas in 1830.* Edited by John C. Ewers. Washington: Smithsonian Institution Press, 1969.

Bolton, Herbert E. *Athanase de Mezieres and the Louisiana-Texas Frontier, 1768-1780.* 2 vols. Cleveland: The Arthur H. Clark Co., 1914.

____., ed. *Spanish Exploration in the Southwest.* Original Narratives of the Early American History. New York: Charles Scribner's Sons, 1930.

____. *Texas in the Middle Eighteenth Century.* Berkeley: University of California Press, 1915.

Gatschet, Albert S. *The Karankawa Indians: The Coast People of Texas.* Cambridge, Mass.: Harvard University Press, 1891.

Hackett, Charles W., ed. *Pichardo's Treatise on the Limits of Louisiana and Texas.* 4 vols. Austin: University of Texas Press, 1931.

Hodge, Frederick Webb, ed. *Handbook of American Indians North of Mexico.* 2 vols. Washington: Bureau of American Ethnology, 1907-10.

Hyde, George E. *Indians of the High Plains: From the Prehistoric Period to the Coming of Europeans.* Norman: University of Oklahoma Press, 1959.

Jackson, A. T. *Picture-writing of Texas Indians.* Austin: University of Texas Press, 1938.

John, Elizabeth A. H. *Storms Brewed in Other Men's Worlds: The Confrontation of Indians, Spanish, and French in the Southwest, 1540-1795.* College Station: Texas A&M University Press, 1975.

Morfi, Fray Juan Agustin. *Excerpts from the Memorias for the History of the Province of Texas.* Prolog, Appendix, and Notes by Frederick C. Chabot. San Antonio: The Naylor Co., 1932.

Newcomb, W. W., Jr. *The Indians of Texas: From Prehistoric to Modern Times.* Austin: University of Texas Press, 1961.

Opler, Morris Edward. *Myths and Legends of the Lipan Apache Indians.* New York: American Folk-lore Society, 1940; New York: Kraus Reprint Co., 1969.

Reading, Robert S. *Arrows Over Texas.* San Antonio: The Naylor Co., 1960.
Swanton, John R. *The Indian Tribes of North America.* Washington: Bureau of American Ethnology, 1952.
____. *Source Material on the History and Ethnology of the Caddo Indians.* Washington: Bureau of American Ethnology, 1942.
Suhm, Dee Ann, *et al. An Introductory Handbook of Texas Archaeology.* Bulletin of the Texas Archeological Society, Austin, 1954.
Terrell, John Upton. *The Plains Apache.* New York: Thomas Y. Crowell Co., 1975.
Wallace, Ernest and Hoebel, E. Adamson. *The Comanches: Lords of the South Plains.* Norman: University of Oklahoma Press, 1952.
Wendorf, Fred, *et al. The Midland Discovery: A Report of the Pleistocene Human Remains from Midland, Texas.* Austin: University of Texas Press, 1955.

CHAPTER 2

Almaraz, Felix D., Jr. *Crossroads of Empire: The Church and State on the Rio Grande Frontier of Coahuila and Texas, 1700-1821.* San Antonio: Center for Archaeological Research, University of Texas at San Antonio, 1979.
Barker, Eugene C. *The Life of Stephen F. Austin: Founder of Texas, 1793-1836.* Austin: University of Texas Press, 1969 (reprint of 1926).
Bolton, Herbert E. *Texas in the Middle Eighteenth Century: Studies in Spanish Colonial History and Administration.* Austin: University of Texas Press, 1970 (reprint of 1915).
Castenada, Carlos E. *Our Catholic Heritage, 1519-1936.* 7 vols. Austin: Von Boeckmann-Jones, 1936-50.
Henson, Margaret Swett. *Juan Davis Bradburn: A Reappraisal of the Mexican Commander at Anahuac.* College Station: Texas A&M University Press, 1982.
____. *Samuel May Williams: Early Texas Entrepreneur.* College Station: Texas A&M University Press, 1976.
John, Elizabeth A. H. *Storms Brewed in Other Men's Worlds: The Confrontation of Indians, Spanish, and French in the Southwest, 1540-1795.* College Station: Texas A&M University Press, 1975.
Warren, Harris Gaylord. *The Sword Was Their Passport.* Baton Rouge: Louisiana State University Press, 1943.
Weddle, Robert S. *San Juan Bautista: Gateway to Spanish Texas.* Austin: University of Texas Press, 1968.
____. *Wilderness Manhunt: The Spanish Search for La Salle.* Austin: University of Texas Press, 1973.

CHAPTER 3

Barker, Eugene C. *The Life of Stephen F. Austin: Founder of Texas, 1793-1836.* Austin and London: University of Texas Press, 1926, 1969.
Binkley, William C. *Official Correspondence of the Texas Revolution, 1835-1836.* 2 vols. New York: D. Appleton Century, 1936.

Friend, Llerena B. *Sam Houston, The Great Designer.* Austin: University of Texas Press, 1954.
Hogan, William Ransom. *The Texas Republic, A Social and Economic History.* Austin and London: University of Texas Press, 1946, 1969.
Jenkins, John H., gen. ed. *Papers of the Texas Revolution, 1835-1836.* 10 vols. Austin: Presidial Press, 1973.
Lord, Walter. *A Time to Stand.* New York: Harper & Row, 1976.
McDonald, Archie P. *Texas All Hail the Mighty State.* Austin: Eakin Press, 1983.
____. *Travis.* Austin: Jenkins Publishing Company, 1976.
Procter, Ben and McDonald, Archie P. *The Texas Heritage.* St. Louis: Forum Press, 1980.
Siegel, Stanley. *The Poet President of Texas.* Austin: Jenkins Publishing Co., 1977.

## CHAPTER 4

Ashcraft, Allan C. *Texas in the Civil War: A Resume History.* Austin: Texas Civil War Centennial Commission, 1962.
Barr, Alwyn. *Black Texans: A History of Negroes in Texas, 1528-1971.* Austin: Jenkins Publishing Co., 1973.
Campbell, Randolph B. and Lowe, Richard G. *Wealth and Power in Antebellum Texas.* College Station: Texas A&M University Press, 1977.
Casdorph, Paul D. *A History of the Republican Party in Texas, 1865-1965.* Austin: Pemberton Press, 1965.
Clarke, Mary Whatley. *Thomas J. Rusk: Soldier, Statesman, Jurist.* Austin: Jenkins Publishing Co., 1970.
Connor, Seymour V. *Adventure in Glory, 1836-1849.* Austin: Steck-Vaughn, 1965.
Curlee, Abigail. "A Glimpse of Life on Antebellum Slave Plantations." *Southwestern Historical Quarterly,* LXXVI (April, 1973), 361-383.
Elliott, Claude. *Leathercoat: The Life History of a Texas Patriot, James W. Throckmorton.* San Antonio: Standard Printing Company, 1938.
Friend, Llerena B. *Sam Houston, The Great Designer.* Austin: University of Texas Press, 1954.
____. "The Texan of 1860." *Southwestern Historical Quarterly,* LXII (July, 1958), 1-17.
Galloway, B. F., ed. *The Dark Corner of the Confederacy.* Dubuque, Iowa: William C. Brown Book Co., 1972.
Henderson, Harry M. *Texas in the Confederacy.* San Antonio: The Naylor Co., 1955.
Moneyhon, Carl H. *Republicanism in Reconstruction Texas.* Austin: University of Texas Press, 1980.
Nunn, W. C. *Texas Under the Carpetbaggers.* Austin: University of Texas Press, 1962.
Oates, Stephen B. "Texas Under the Secessionists." *Southwestern Historical Quarterly,* LXVII (October, 1963), 167-212.
Procter, Ben H. *Not Without Honor: The Life of John H. Reagan.* Austin: University of Texas Press, 1962.

Ramsdell, Charles W. *Reconstruction in Texas.* New York: Columbia University Press, 1910.

Rose, Victor M. *Ross' Texas Brigade.* Louisville, Kentucky, Courier-Journal and Job Rooms, 1881; reprint, Kennesaw, Georgia: Continental Book Co., 1960.

Silverthorne, Elizabeth. *Ashbel Smith of Texas: Pioneer, Patriot, Statesman, 1805-1886.* College Station: Texas A&M University Press, 1982.

Simpson, Harold B., ed. *Texas in the Civil War.* Hillsboro: Hill Junior College Press, 1965.

Smyrl, Frank H. "Unionism in Texas, 1856-1861." *Southwestern Historical Quarterly,* LXVIII (October, 1964), 172-195.

Wallace, Ernest. *The Howling of the Coyotes: Reconstruction Efforts to Divide Texas.* College Station: Texas A&M University Press, 1979.

____. *Texas in Turmoil.* Austin: Steck-Vaughn, 1965.

Wooster, Ralph A. and Wooster, Robert. " 'Rarin' for a Fight': Texans in the Confederate Army." *Southwestern Historical Quarterly,* LXXXIV (April, 1981), 387-426.

## CHAPTER 5

Adams, Andy. *The Log of a Cowboy.* Boston: Houghton Mifflin Co., 1903, 1931.

Carlson, Paul H. *Texas Woolybacks, the Range Sheep and Goat Industry.* College Station: Texas A&M University Press, 1982.

Dale, E. E. *The Range Cattle Industry.* Norman: University of Oklahoma Press, 1930.

Faulk, Odie B. *The U.S. Camel Corps, An Army Experiment.* New York: Oxford University Press, 1976.

Fowler, Arlan L. *The Black Infantry in the West, 1869-1891.* Westport, Conn.: Greenwood Publishing Corp., 1971.

Gard, Wayne. *The Great Buffalo Hunt.* New York: Alfred A. Knopf, 1959.

Haley, James Evetts. *Fort Concho and the Texas Frontier.* San Angelo: San Angelo Standard Times, 1952.

____. *The XIT Ranch of Texas.* Chicago: Lakeside, 1929; revised, Norman: University of Oklahoma Press, 1953.

Holden, William Curry. *Alkali Trails, or, Social and Economic Movements of the Texas Frontier, 1846-1900.* Dallas: Southwest Press, 1930.

Jordan, Terry G. *Trails to Texas: Southern Roots of Western Cattle Ranching.* Lincoln: University of Nebraska Press, 1981.

Lea, Tom. *The King Ranch.* 2 vols. Boston: Little, Brown, 1957.

Leckie, William. *The Buffalo Soldiers.* Norman: University of Oklahoma Press, 1967.

McCallum, Henry D. and Frances T. McCallum. *Barbed Wire.* Norman: University of Oklahoma Press, 1965.

Matthews, Sallie Reynolds. *Interwoven: A Pioneer Chronicle.* Houston: Anson Jones, 1936; reprinted, El Paso: Carl Hertzog, 1958.

Murrah, David J. *C. C. Slaughter, Rancher, Banker, Baptist.* Austin: University of Texas Press, 1981.

Neighbors, Kenneth. *Indian Exodus: Texas Indian Affairs.* Quanah, Texas: Nortex Press, 1973.
Pearce, William M. *The Matador Land and Cattle Company.* Norman: University of Oklahoma Press, 1964.
Rathjen, Frederick W. *The Texas Panhandle Frontier.* Austin: University of Texas Press, 1973.
Richardson, Rupert N. *The Comanche Barrier to South Plains Settlement.* Glendale, California: Arthur H. Clark, 1933.
____. *The Frontier of Northwest Texas, 1846-1876.* Glendale, California: Arthur H. Clark, 1963.
Scarborough, Dorothy. *The Wind.* New York: Harper Bros., 1925; reprinted, Austin: University of Texas Press, 1979.
Skaggs, Jimmy M. *The Cattle Trailing Industry: Between Supply and Demand, 1866-1890.* Lawrence: University of Kansas Press, 1973.
Utley, Robert M. *Frontier Regulars, the United States Army and the Indian, 1866-1890.* New York: Macmillan Publishing Co., 1973.
Wallace, Ernest. *Ranald S. Mackenzie on the Texas Frontier.* Lubbock: West Texas Museum, 1964.
Webb, Walter Prescott. *The Great Plains.* New York: Grosset & Dunlap, 1931.
Wentworth, Edward N. *America's Sheep Trails.* Ames, Iowa: Iowa State College Press, 1948.
Williams, J. W. *The Big Ranch Country.* Wichita Falls: Terry Bros., 1954.

## CHAPTER 6

Barr, Alwyn. *Reconstruction to Reform: Texas Politics, 1876-1906.* Austin: University of Texas Press, 1971.
Casdorph, Paul. *A History of the Republican Party in Texas, 1865-1965.* Austin: Pemberton Press, 1965.
Cotner, Robert. *James Stephen Hogg.* Austin: University of Texas Press, 1951.
Everett, Donald E. *San Antonio: The Flavor of Its Past.* San Antonio: Trinity University Press, 1975.
Goodwyn, Lawrence. *Democratic Promise: The Populist Movement in America.* New York: Oxford University Press, 1976.
Green, James R. *Grass Roots Socialism: Radical Movements in the Southwest, 1865-1943.* 1978.
Greene, A. C. *A Place Called Dallas: The Pioneering Years of a Continuing Metropolis.* Dallas: Dallas County Heritage Society, 1976.
Horton, Louise. *Samuel Bell Maxey.* Austin: University of Texas Press, 1974.
Jones, Billy M. *The Search for Maturity.* Austin: Steck-Vaughn, 1965.
Martin, Roscoe C. *The People's Party in Texas.* Austin: University of Texas Press, 1933.
McComb, David G. *Houston: The Bayou City.* Austin: University of Texas Press, 1969.
McMartin, Robert C., Jr. *Populist Vanguard: A History of the Southern Farmers' Alliance,* Austin, University of Texas Press, 1975.

Procter, Ben H. *Not Without Honor: The Life of John H. Reagan.* Austin: University of Texas Press, 1962.

Rice, Lawrence D. *The Negro in Texas, 1874-1900.* Baton Rouge: Louisiana State University Press, 1971.

Sibley, Marilyn. *The Port of Houston: A History.* Austin: University of Texas Press, 1968.

Spratt, John S. *The Road to Spindletop: Economic Changes in Texas, 1875-1901.* Austin: University of Texas Press, 1955.

## CHAPTER 7

Acheson, Sam Hanna. *Joe Bailey: The Last Democrat.* New York: The Macmillan Co., 1932.

Alexander, Charles C. *The Ku Klux Klan in the Southwest.* Lexington: University of Kentucky Press, 1965.

____. *Crusade for Conformity: the Ku Klux Klan in Texas, 1920-1930.* Houston: Texas Gulf Coast Historical Association, 1962.

Gould, Lewis L. *Progressives and Prohibitionists: Texas Democrats in the Wilson Era.* Austin: University of Texas Press, 1973.

Mason, Herbert M., Jr. *Death from the Sea: Our Greatest Natural Disaster, the Galveston Hurricane of 1900.* New York: Dial Press, 1972.

Maxwell, Robert S. and Baker, Robert D. *Sawdust Empire: The Texas Lumber Industry, 1830-1940.* College Station: Texas A&M University Press, 1983.

McComb, David G. *Houston, The Bayou City.* Austin: University of Texas Press, 1969.

Richardson, Rupert N. *Colonel Edward M. House, The Texas Years.* Abilene: Hardin-Simmons University Press, 1964.

Sibley, Marilyn M. *The Port of Houston: A History.* Austin: University of Texas Press, 1968.

Steen, Ralph W. "The Ferguson War on the University of Texas," *Southwestern Social Science Quarterly,* XXXV (March, 1955), 356-362.

____. "Governor Miriam A. Ferguson." *East Texas Historical Journal,* XVII (Fall, 1979), 3-17.

Stephens, William E. "The 'Open Door' Policy of Texas: The Penal Policies of Miriam Amanda Ferguson," M.A. thesis, Stephen F. Austin State University, 1957.

Taylor, A. Elizabeth. "The Woman Suffrage Movement in Texas." *The Journal of Southern History,* XVII (May, 1951), 2:194-215.

## CHAPTER 8

Banks, Jimmy. *Money, Marbles and Chalk: The Wondrous World of Texas Politics.* Austin: Shoal Creek, 1971.

Bartley, Ernest R. *The Tidelands Oil Controversy.* Austin: University of Texas Press, 1953.

Green, George N. *The Establishment in Texas Politics, The Primitive Years, 1938-1957.* Westport, Conn.: Greenwood Press, 1979.

Kinch, Sam, Jr. and Procter, Ben. *Texas Under a Cloud.* Austin: Jenkins Publishing Co., 1972.
McKay, S. S. and Faulk, Odie B. *Texas After Spindletop.* Austin: Steck-Vaughn, 1965.
Soukup, James R., McCleskey, Clifton, and Holloway, Harry. *Party and Factional Division in Texas.* Austin: University of Texas Press, 1964.
Whisenhunt, Donald W. *The Depression in Texas: The Hoover Years.* New York: Garland Publishing Co., 1983.
____., ed. *The Depression in the Southwest.* Port Washington, New York: Kennikat Press, 1980.

CHAPTER 9

Atkins, Irvin Milburn. *A History of Small Grain Crops in Texas: Wheat, Oats, Barley, Rye, 1582-1976.* College Station: Texas Agricultural Experiment Station Bulletin 1301, 1980.
Bizzell, William Bennett. *Rural Texas.* New York: The Macmillan Co., 1924.
Bonnifield, Paul. *The Dust Bowl: Men, Dirt, and Depression.* Albuquerque: University of New Mexico Press, 1979.
Carlson, Paul H. *Texas Woolybacks: The Range Sheep and Goat Industry.* College Station: Texas A&M University Press, 1982.
Dale, Edward Everett. *The Range Cattle Industry.* Norman: University of Oklahoma Press, 1960.
Dethloff, Henry C. and May, Irvin M., Jr., eds. *Southwestern Agriculture: Pre-Columbian to Modern.* College Station: Texas A&M University Press, 1982.
Fite, Gilbert C. *The Farmer's Frontier, 1865-1900.* New York: Holt, Rinehart and Winston, 1966.
Green, Donald E. *Land of the Underground Rain: Irrigation on the Texas High Plains, 1910-1970.* Austin: University of Texas Press, 1971.
Jordan, Terry G. *Trails to Texas: Southern Roots of Western Cattle Raising.* Lincoln: University of Nebraska Press, 1981.
Miller, Thomas Lloyd. *The Public Lands of Texas, 1519-1970.* Norman: University of Oklahoma Press, 1972.
Murrah, David J. *C. C. Slaughter: Rancher, Banker, Baptist.* Austin: University of Texas Press, 1981.
Myres, Sandra L. *The Ranch in Spanish Texas, 1691-1800.* Social Science Series Number Two. El Paso: Texas Western Press, 1969.
Sitterson, J. Carlyle. *Sugar Country: The Cane Sugar Industry in the South, 1753-1950.* Lexington: University of Kentucky Press, 1953.
Spratt, John S. *The Road to Spindletop: Economic Change in Texas, 1875-1901.* Austin: University of Texas Press, 1955.
Webb, Walter Prescott. *The Great Plains.* New York: Ginn and Company, 1931.
Whisenhunt, Donald W., ed. *The Depression in the Southwest.* Port Washington, New York: Kennikat Press, 1980.
Worster, Donald. *Dust Bowl: The Southern Plains in the 1930s.* New York: Oxford University Press, 1979.

## CHAPTER 10

*General Studies:*

Allhands, James L. *Railroads to the Rio.* Salado, Texas: Anson Jones Press, 1960.

____. *Looking Back Over 98 Years: The Autobiography of James L. Allhands.* Malibu, California: Pepperdine University, 1978.

Clark, Ira G. *Then Came the Railroads: The Century from Steam to Diesel in the Southwest.* Norman: University of Oklahoma Press, 1958.

Potts, Charles L. "Railroad Transportation in Texas." *Bulletin of the University of Texas,* 1909.

Reed, S. G. *A History of Texas Railroads and of Transportation Conditions Under Spain and Mexico and the Republic and the State.* Houston: St. Clair Publishing Co., 1941.

Riegel, Robert E. *The Story of the Western Railroads.* New York: The Macmillan Co., 1926.

Stanley, F. *Story of the Texas Panhandle Railroads.* Privately published by the author, 1976.

Stover, John F. *American Railroads.* Chicago: University of Chicago Press, 1970.

Zlatkovick, Charles P. *Texas Railroads: A Record of Construction and Abandonment.* Austin: Bureau of Business Research, University of Texas, 1981.

*Corporate histories:*

Allhands, James L. *Boll Weevil—Recollections of the Trinity & Brazos Valley Railway.* Houston: Anson Jones Press, 1946.

Bryant, Keith L., Jr. *History of the Atchison, Topeka & Santa Fe Railway.* New York: The Macmillan Co., 1974.

Hayes, William E. *Iron Road to Empire: The History of the Rock Island Lines.* New York: Simmons-Boardman, 1953.

Hedge, John W. and Dawson, Geoffrey S. *The San Antonio & Aransas Pass Railway: The Story of the Famous "SAP" Railway of Texas.* Privately printed by the authors, 1983.

Kerr, John Leeds and Donovan, Frank P. *Destination Topolobampo.* San Marino, California: Golden West Books, 1969.

Masterson, V. V. *The Katy Railroad and the Last Frontier.* Norman: University of Oklahoma Press, 1952.

Maxwell, Robert S. *Whistle in the Piney Woods: Paul Bremond and the Houston, East & West Texas Railway.* Houston: Texas Gulf Historical Association, 1963.

Miner, H. Craig. *The Rebirth of the Missouri Pacific, 1956-1983.* College Station: Texas A&M University Press, 1983.

Overton, Richard C. *Gulf-to-Rockies: The Heritage of the Fort Worth & Denver—Colorado & Southern Railways, 1861-1898.* Austin: University of Texas Press, 1953.

Waters, L. L. *Steel Rails to Santa Fe.* Lawrence: University of Kansas Press, 1950.

Wilson, Neill C. and Taylor, Frank J. *Southern Pacific: The Roaring Story of a Fighting Railroad.* New York: McGraw-Hill, 1952.

*Electric railroads:*

Grant, H. Roger. " 'Interurbans are the Wave of the Future': Electric Railway Promotion in Texas." *Southwestern Historical Quarterly,* LXXXIV (July, 1980), 29-48.

Hilton, George F. and Due, John F. *The Electric Interurban Railways in America.* Stanford: Stanford University Press, 1960.

Middleton, William D. *The Interurban Era.* Milwaukee: Kalmbach Publishing Co., 1961.

Myers, Johnnie J. *Texas Electric Railway.* Chicago: Central Electric Railfans Assn., 1976.

Woods, Herb. *Galveston-Houston Electric Railway.* Glendale, California: Interurban Press, 1982.

*Passenger trains:*

Beebe, Lucius M. and Clegg, Charles. *The Trains We Rode.* 2 vols. Berkeley: Howell-North, 1965-1966.

Dubin, Arthur D. *Some Classic Trains.* Milwaukee: Kalmbach Publishing Co., 1964.

____. *More Classic Trains.* Milwaukee: Kalmbach Publishing Co., 1974.

Kratville, William W. *Steam, Steel and Limited.* Omaha: Kratville Publications, 1962.

*Railroad stations:*

Alexander, Edwin P. *Down at the Depot: American Railroad Stations from 1831 to 1920.* New York: C. N. Potter, 1970.

Bryant, Keith L., Jr. "Railway Stations of Texas: A Disappearing Architectural Heritage." *Southwestern Historical Quarterly,* LXXIX (April, 1976), 417-440.

Droege, John Albert. *Passenger Terminals and Trains.* New York: McGraw-Hill, 1916.

Grant, H. Roger and Bohi, Charles W. *The Country Railroad Station in America.* Boulder, Colorado: Pruett Publishing Co., 1978.

Meeks, Carroll L. V. *The Railroad Station: An Architectural History.* New Haven: Yale University Press, 1956.

*Townsite and land development:*

Gaines, John S. "The Saga of a Railroad Town: Calvert, Texas (1868-1918)." *Southwestern Historical Quarterly,* LXXXV (October, 1981), 139-160.

Hofsommer, Donovan L. "Town Building on a Texas Short Line: The Quanah, Acme & Pacific Railway, 1909-1929." *Arizona and the West,* XXI (Winter, 1979), 355-368.

____. "Townsite Development on the Wichita Falls & Northwestern Railway." *Great Plains Journal,* XVI (Spring, 1977), 107-122.

Taylor, Virginia H. *The Franco-Texas Land Company.* Austin: University of Texas Press, 1969.

*Other:*

Allhands, J. L. *Uriah Lott: The Southwest's Great Railroad Builder.* Privately published by the author, 1949.

Bryant, Keith L., Jr. *Arthur E. Stilwell: Promoter With a Hunch.* Nashville: Vanderbilt University Press, 1971.

Fornell, Earl W. *The Galveston Era.* Austin: University of Texas Press, 1961.

Hofsommer, Donovan L. *Katy Northwest: The Story of a Branch Line Railroad.* Boulder, Colorado: Pruett Printing Co., 1976.

Spence, Vernon Gladden. *Colonel Morgan Jones: Grand Old Man of Texas Railroading.* Norman: University of Oklahoma Press, 1971.

## CHAPTER 11

Very little work has been done in the area of Texas highway development. The state's newspapers, *The Dallas Morning News, Houston Post-Dispatch, Austin American,* and *San Antonio Express* are good sources on road-related, political activity. Contemporary journals such as *Texas Monthly, Texas Highways, County Progress,* and *Parade Magazine* report regularly on Texas highway development. For the period before 1917, the University of Texas and the Texas Agricultural and Mechanical College bulletins are invaluable as good road promotional literature.

## CHAPTER 12

Boatright, Mody C. and Owens, William W. *Tales From the Derrick Floor: A Peoples History of the Oil Industry.* Lincoln: University of Nebraska Press, 1982 (reprint of 1970 edition).

Olien, Roger M. and Olien, Diana Davids. *Oil Booms: Social Change in Five Texas Towns.* Lincoln: University of Nebraska Press, 1982.

Rister, Carl Coke. *Oil! Titan of the Southwest.* Norman: University of Oklahoma Press, 1949.

Rundell, Walter, Jr. *Early Texas Oil.* College Station: Texas A&M University Press, 1977.

## CHAPTER 13

Antone, Evan Haywood. *William Farah: Industrialist.* S. D. Myres, ed. El Paso: Farah Company, 1969.

Barr, Shirley. "The Texas Apparel Industry: Weaving a Pattern of Profits." *Texas Business,* I (August, 1976), 29-68.

Bennett, Carol T. F. "An Economic Profile of the Texas Apparel Industry." *Texas Business Review,* LII (January, 1978), 1-7.

Berman, Phyllis, and Mack, Toni. "Renaissance on the Rio Grande." *Forbes,* September 1, 1980, pp. 38-40.

Ennis, Michael. "Rags to Riches." *Texas Monthly,* X (September, 1982), 96-166.

——. "The Empress's New Clothes." *Texas Monthly* X (September, 1982), 156-231.

Green, George N. "ILGWU in Texas, 1930-1970." *The Journal of Mexican-American History,* I (Spring, 1971), 144-169.

Hardesty, Rex. "Farah: The Union Struggle in the 70s." *AFL-CIO American Federationist,* June 1973, pp. 1-13.

Rich-McCoy, Lois. *Millionairess: Self-Made Women of America.* New York: Harper and Row, 1978.

Rust, Joe Carrol. "The Texas Apparel Industry." *Texas Business Review,* XXXIV (January, 1960), 1-47.

Spiegel, Joy G. *That Haggar Man: A Biographical Portrait.* New York: Random House, 1978.

## CHAPTER 14

Doughty, Robin W. *Wildlife and Man in Texas: Environmental Change and Conservation.* College Station: Texas A&M University Press, 1983.

Green, Donald E. *Land of the Underground Rain: Irrigation on the Texas High Plains, 1910-1970.* Austin: University of Texas Press, 1973.

Head, Stephen Chalmus. "A History of Conservation in Texas, 1860-1963." Ph.D. dissertation, Texas Tech University, 1982.

League of Women Voters. "A Study of Land Management in Texas." Bulletin No. 101, July, 1973.

____. "Fresh Water for Texas Bays and Estuaries." 1981.

Texas. Office of the Governor, Division of Planning Coordination, *Natural Resources and Environmental Agencies in Texas: a Report of the 64th Legislature.* Austin, 1974.

Texas Research League, Report, *State Government Organizations in Texas, Part II, General Administration,* February, 1975.

*Texas Observer,* selected issues.

North Texas State University Oral History interviews
Bob Armstrong, former land commissioner
Fred Agnich, state senator from Dallas
Ned Fritz, Texas Committee on Natural Resources
Reverend James White, former chair Citizens for a Sound Trinity
John Henry Faulk, chair, Citizens Against Water Taxes
Stuart Henry, lobbyist for the Sierra Club

## CHAPTER 15

Abernethy, Francis Edward. *Legendary Ladies of Texas.* Publications of the Texas Folklore Society, Number XLIII. Dallas: E-Heart Press, 1981.

Caro, Robert A. "Sad Irons," *The Years of Lyndon Johnson: The Path to Power.* New York: Alfred A. Knopf, 1982, pp. 502-511.

Carrington, Evelyn M. ed. *Women in Early Texas.* Austin: Jenkins Publishing Co., 1970.

Crawford, Ann Fears and Ragsdale, Crystal Sasse. *Women in Texas: Their Lives, Their Experiences, Their Accomplishments.* Burnet, Texas: Eakin Press, 1982.

Day, James, *et al. Women of Texas.* Waco: Texian Press, 1972.

Degler, Carl M. *At Odds: Women and the Family in America From the Revolution to the Present.* New York: Oxford University Press, 1980.

Henson, Margaret S. *Anglo-American Women in Texas, 1820-1850.* Boston: American Press, 1982.

Jenson, Joan M. and Miller, Darlis A. "The Gentle Tamers Revisited: New Approaches to the History of Women in the American West." *Pacific Historical Review,* 1980, pp. 173-213.

Kessler-Harris, Alice. *Out to Work: A History of Wage--Earning Women in the United States.* New York: Oxford University Press, 1982.

Lasher, Patricia and Bentley, Beverly. *Texas Women: Interviews and Images.* Austin: Shoal Creek, 1980.

Malone, Ann Patton. *Women on the Texas Frontier: A Cross-Cultural Perspective.* Southwestern Studies, Monograph No. 70. El Paso: Texas Western Press, 1983.

McAdams, Ina May Ogletree. *Texas Women of Distinction: A Biographical History.* Austin: McAdams Publishing, 1962.

Myers, Sandra L. *Westering Women and the Frontier Experience, 1800-1915.* Histories of the American Frontier. Albuquerque: University of New Mexico Press, 1982.

Pickrell, Annie Doom. *Pioneer Women in Texas.* Austin: Jenkins Publishing Co., 1970.

Ramsey, Glen V., *et al. Women View Their Working World.* Austin: Hogg Foundation for Mental Health, University of Texas, 1963.

*Report of the Governor's Commission on the Status of Women.* Austin: State of Texas, 1967.

Rodenberger, Lou Halsell, ed. *Her Work: Stories by Texas Women.* Bryan, Texas: Shearer Publishing Co., 1982.

Rogers, Mary Beth. *Texas Women: A Celebration of History.* Austin: Foundation for Women's Resources, 1981.

____. *We Can Fly: Stories of Katherine Stinson and Other Gutsy Texas Women.* Austin: Ellen C. Temple, Publisher, in cooperation with Texas Foundation for Women's Resources, 1983.

Texas Employment Commission. *Women in the Labor Force.* Austin, 1978.

Tjarks, Alicia V. "Cooperative Demographic Analysis of Texas, 1777-1793." *Southwestern Historical Quarterly,* LXXVII, January 1974, pp. 291-338.

Winegarten, Ruthe, ed. *Texas Women's History Project Bibliography.* Austin: Texas Foundation for Women's Resources, 1980.

## CHAPTER 16

Baenziger, Ann Patton. "The Texas State Police During Reconstruction: A Reexamination." *Southwestern Historical Quarterly,* LXXII (April, 1969), 470-491.

Barr, Alwyn. *Black Texans: A History of Negroes in Texas, 1528-1971.* Austin: Jenkins Publishing Co., 1973.

____ and Calvert, Robert A. *Black Leaders: Texans for Their Times.* Austin: Texas State Historical Association, 1981.

Crouch, Barry A. and Schultz, L. J. "Crisis in Color: Racial Separation in Texas During Reconstruction." *Civil War History,* XVI (March, 1970), 37-49.

Elliott, Claude. "The Freedmen's Bureau in Texas." *Southwestern Historical Quarterly,* LVI (July, 1952).

Gillette, Michael L. "The Rise of The NAACP in Texas." *Southwestern Historical Quarterly,* LXXXI (April, 1978), 393-416.

Haynes, Robert V. *A Night of Violence: The Houston Riot of 1917.* Baton Rouge: Louisiana State University Press, 1976.

Hine, Darlene Clark. "The Elusive Ballot: The Black Struggle Against the Texas Democratic White Primary, 1932-1945." *Southwestern Historical Quarterly,* LXXXI (April, 1978), 371-392.

Krammer, Arnold P. "When the Africa Korps Came to Texas." *Southwestern Historical Quarterly,* LXXXI (April, 1978).

Leckie, William H. *The Buffalo Soldiers: A Narrative of the Negro Cavalry in the West.* Norman: University of Oklahoma Press, 1967.

Moneyhon, Carl H. "George T. Ruby and the Politics of Expediency," in Howard Rabinowitz, ed. *Southern Black Leaders in the Reconstruction.* Urbana: University of Illinois Press, 1982, pp. 363-392.

Rice, Lawrence. *The Negro in Texas, 1874-1900.* Baton Rouge: Louisiana State University Press, 1971.

Scott, Alan. "Twenty-five Years of Opinion on Integration in Texas." *Southwestern Social Science Quarterly,* XLVIII (September, 1967), 155-163.

Smallwood, James. *Time of Hope, Time of Despair: Black Texans During Reconstruction.* Port Washington, New York: Kennikat Press, 1981.

## CHAPTER 17

Anders, Evan. *Boss Rule in South Texas: The Progressive Era.* Austin: University of Texas Press, 1982.

*Aztlan: Chicano Journal of the Social Sciences and Arts.*

De Leon, Arnoldo. *The Tejano Community, 1836-1900.* Albuquerque: University of New Mexico Press, 1982.

Thompson, Jerry D. *Vaqueros in Blue and Gray.* Austin: Presidial Press, 1976.

## CHAPTER 18

Bartholomew, Ed. *Cullen Baker: Premier Texas Gunfighter.* Houston: Frontier Press of Texas, 1954.

____. *Wild Bill Longley: A Texas Hard-Case.* Houston: Frontier Press of Texas, 1953.

DeShields, James T. *Border Wars of Texas.* Waco: Texian Press, 1976 [1912].

Fehrenbach, T. R. *Comanches: The Destruction of a People.* New York: Alfred A. Knopf, 1974.

____. *Lone Star: A History of Texas and the Texans.* New York: Macmillan Publishing Co., 1968.

Ford, John Salmon. *Rip Ford's Texas.* Austin: University of Texas Press, 1963.

Greer, James Kimmins. *Colonel Jack Hays.* New York: E. P. Dutton & Co., 1976.

Haley, James L. *The Buffalo War.* Garden City, New York: Doubleday & Co., 1976.

Hardin, John Wesley. *The Life of John Wesley Hardin.* Norman: University of Oklahoma Press, 1961 [1896].

Martin, Jack. *Border Boss.* San Antonio, The Naylor Co., 1942.

Metz, Leon C. *Dallas Stoudenmire: El Paso Marshal.* Austin: Pemberton Press, 1969.

____. *John Selman: Texas Gunfighter.* New York: Hastings House, 1966.

O'Neal, Bill. *Encyclopedia of Western Gunfighters.* Norman: University of Oklahoma Press, 1979.

Paine, Lauran. *Texas Ben Thompson.* Los Angeles: Westernlore Press, 1966.

Shirley, Glenn. *Shotgun for Hire.* Norman: University of Oklahoma Press, 1970.

Sonnichsen, C. L. *I'll Die Before I'll Run.* New York: The Devin-Adair Co., 1962.

____. *Ten Texas Feuds.* Albuquerque: University of New Mexico Press, 1957.

Wallace, Ernest. *Ranald S. Mackenzie on the Texas Frontier.* Lubbock: West Texas Museum Association, 1964.

Webb, Walter P. *The Texas Rangers.* Austin: University of Texas Press, 1935.

Wilbarger, J. W. *Indian Depredations in Texas.* Austin: The Pemberton Press, 1967 [1889].

## CHAPTER 19

Baker, Robert A. *The Blossoming Desert, A Concise History of Texas Baptists.* Waco: Word Books, 1970.

Brackenridge, Douglas. *Voice in the Wilderness, A History of the Cumberland Presbyterian Church in Texas.* San Antonio: Trinity University Press, 1968.

Bronder, Saul E. *Social Justice and Church Authority: Public Life of Archbishop Robert E. Lucey.* Philadelphia: Temple University Press, 1982.

Carroll, James M. *A History of Texas Baptists.* Dallas: Baptist Standard Publishing Co., 1923.

Castaneda, Carlos E. *Our Catholic Heritage in Texas, 1519-1936.* Austin: Von Boeckman-Jones, 1936-1958.

Halvorson, Peter L. and Newman, William M. *Atlas of Religious Change in America, 1952-1971.* Washington, D.C.: Glenmary Research Center, 1978.

Hogan, William Ransom. *The Texas Republic: A Social and Economic History.* Austin: University of Texas Press, 1969.

Johnson, Douglas W. *Churches and Church Membership in the United States, 1971.* Washington, D.C.: Glenmary Research Center, 1974.

Phelan, Macum. *A History of Early Methodism in Texas, 1817-1936.* Nashville, Tenn.: Cokesbury Press, 1924.

Quinn, Bernard. *Churches and Church Membership in the United States, 1980.* Washington, D.C.: Glenmary Research Center, 1982.

Red, William Stuart. *The Texas Colonists and Religion, 1821-1836.* Austin: E. L. Shettles, 1924.

## CHAPTER 20

Eby, Frederick. *The Development of Education in Texas.* New York: Columbia University Press, 1925.

Evans, C. E. *The Story of Texas Schools.* Austin: Texas Education Agency, 1955.

*Handbook of Texas.* 3 vols. Austin: Texas State Historical Association, 1952, 1976.

Texas Education Agency. Biennal reports.

Whisenhunt, Donald W. *The Development of Higher Education in Texas.* Boston: American Press, 1983.

# CONTRIBUTORS

**EARL H. ELAM** is professor of history and vice president for academic affairs at Sul Ross State University at Alpine, Texas. An authority on Caddoan and Wichitan Indian history, he has conducted research on several occasions for the United States Department of Justice as a part of Indian claims against the government. He attended Midwestern State University for his undergraduate degree and earned the Ph.D. in history at Texas Tech University in 1971. In addition to his work for the Justice Department, he has also published in such journals as the West Texas Historical Association *Yearbook* and the *Kansas Quarterly*.

**MARGARET SWETT HENSON** received three degrees from the University of Houston, including the Ph.D. in history in 1974. She has taught in the Houston Public Schools, South Texas Junior College, Houston Community College, and is now at the University of Houston Clear Lake City. In addition, she has been associated with the Southwest Center for Urban Research and the Houston Metropolitan Research Center. Dr. Henson is a specialist on early Texas history. Two significant publications are *Samuel May Williams: Early Texas Entrepreneur,* winner of the Summerfield G. Roberts Award in 1976, and *Juan Davis Bradburn: A Reappraisal of the Mexican Commander at Anahuac* (1982). Both were published by Texas A&M University Press.

**ARCHIE P. McDONALD** is a noted Texas historian. He is the author and/or editor of fourteen books and numerous scholarly articles and reviews. Included are such books as *Travis* (1977) and *The Texas Heritage.* Since 1972 he has been editor of the *East Texas Historical Journal.* He is also a member of the Texas Committee for the Humanities; he has served in various capacities, including the Executive Council, of the Texas State Historical Association. In addition, he has served as a consultant and manuscript reader for many projects. A native of Port Neches, Texas, he attended Lamar University and Rice University before moving on to Louisiana State University, where he received the Ph.D. in history in 1965. He is currently professor of history at Stephen F. Austin State University at Nacogdoches, Texas.

**RALPH A. WOOSTER**, a native of Baytown, Texas, attended the University of Houston for the B.A. and M.A. degrees and earned the Ph.D. in history at the University of Texas at Austin. He joined the faculty at Lamar University in 1955 and presently serves as Dean of Faculties and Assistant to the Vice President for Academic Affairs in addition to being a professor of history. He is a widely recognized authority on the history of Texas and the South. He is the author or co-author of five books, including *Secession Conventions of the South* (1962) and *The People in Power* (1969) and some fifty scholarly articles. He is a Fellow of the Texas State Historical Association and has been a Minnie Stevens Piper Professor and Regents Professor of History.

**PAUL H. CARLSON** is associate professor and chairman of the Department of History at Texas Lutheran College, where he has taught since 1973. He is a graduate of Dakota Wesleyan University, Mankato State University, and Texas Tech University, where he received the Ph.D. in history in 1973. He is the author of over thirty articles on Texas and frontier history and numerous book reviews. The most recent of his three books was *Texas Woolybacks, the Range Sheep and Goat Industry.* Married and the father of three children, he is also active in local, state, and national historical associations.

**ROBERT A. CALVERT**, a native of Stephenville, Texas, holds the Ph.D. in history from the University of Texas at Austin. He is currently associate professor of history at Texas A&M University. He has been very active in the Texas State Historical Association, having been on the Editorial Board and Book Review Editor of the *Southwestern Historical Quarterly* and on the Executive Council and the Nominating Committee of the Association. He is active in numerous other historical associations, has been a consultant on the teaching of history, and has received numerous grants and awards. He is the author or co-author of five books, including *Black Leaders: Texans for Their Times* (1981) and *Chicano: The Evolution of a People* (1983).

**ROBERT S. MAXWELL** is currently Regents' Professor of History Emeritus at Stephen F. Austin State University. A native of Kentucky, he took the B.A. at Kentucky Wesleyan College, the M.A. at the University of Cincinnati, and the Ph.D. at the University of Wisconsin. He has taught at the University of Kentucky as well as at Stephen F. Austin State University. He has been a Fulbright Professor in England and a Guest Lecturer in the German Summer Seminar. He is active in several historical organizations and has served in various offices in several of them. He has written many scholarly articles and several books, including *Whistle in the Piney Woods: Paul Bremond and the Houston, East and West Texas Railway* (1963) and *La Follette* (1969).

**DONALD W. WHISENHUNT** is currently professor of history and vice president at Wayne State College in Nebraska. At the time this book was started he was professor of history at the University of Texas at Tyler. A native of Meadow, Texas, he attended McMurry College for his undergraduate education and Texas Tech University, where he earned the Ph.D. in history in 1966. He has also served in teaching or administrative positions at colleges in Kentucky, Pennsylvania, and New Mexico. He is the author of over fifty articles and several books including *Fort Richardson: Outpost on the Texas Frontier* (1968), *Texas in the Depression: The Hoover Years* (1983), and *The Depression in the Southwest* (1980).

**GARRY L. NALL** is professor of history at West Texas State University at Canyon, where he has been on the faculty since 1963. He attended the University of Texas at Austin for the B.A. and M.A. degrees and received the Ph.D. in history from the University of Oklahoma in 1972. A specialist in agricultural history, he has published articles in the *Panhandle-Plains Historical Review* and has contributed chapters to several books including *The Depression in the Southwest* and *Rural Oklahoma.* He is active in several local, regional, and national historical organizations.

**DONOVAN L. HOFSOMMER** is a specialist in the history of railroads. He is the author or editor of five books on railroad history including *Katy Northwest: The Story of a Branch Line Railroad* (1976) and *Railroads in the West* (1978). He took the Ph.D. in history from Oklahoma State University in 1973 and has taught at several colleges and universities including Lea College in Minnesota and Wayland College at Plainview, Texas. He is currently employed by the Southern Pacific Transportation Company as a special representative-historical writer.

**JOHN DAVID HUDDLESTON** is assistant professor of history at Schreiner College at Kerrville, Texas. He has also taught at Blinn Junior College and Pan American University. He attended Wharton County Junior College and the University of Texas at Austin, where he took the B.A. and M.A. degrees. He was awarded in 1981 the Ph.D. in history at Texas A&M University, where his dissertation was a history of the Texas Highway Department from 1917 to 1947. He has been active in Phi Alpha Theta, the international history honorary, and has read several papers to scholarly meetings.

**BOBBY DEARL WEAVER** has published extensively on the history of the Panhandle Plains area of Texas. A native of Gatesville, Texas, he has been the Curator of Ethnology at the Panhandle-Plains Historical Museum in Canyon, Texas, since 1979. He has also been a Field Representative and Archivist at the Southwest Collection at Texas Tech University. He received the B.A. degree from Texas Tech University and the M.A. degree from Texas A&I University. His doctoral work was done at Texas Tech, where his dissertation was "Castro's Colony: Alsatian Immigration to Texas, 1842-1860." He completed the Ph.D. in 1983.

**DOROTHY DELL DeMOSS** is the authority on the history of the apparel industry in Texas. She earned the Ph.D. in history at Texas Christian University in 1981. Earlier she attended Rice University for the B.A. and the University of Texas at Austin for the M.A. Her M.A. thesis was published in condensed form in *Texas Cities and the Great Depression,* edited by Robert C. Cotner and published by the Texas Memorial Museum in 1973. She is currently assistant professor of history at Texas Woman's University at Denton.

**J. B. SMALLWOOD, JR.**, has been involved in research in conservation and environmental history for several years. He has published articles and delivered several papers on the subject. Currently, an associate professor of history at North Texas State university at Denton, he has also taught at the University of North Carolina, the University of Maryland, and the University of Florida. He earned the B.A. and M.A. degrees from North Texas State University and the Ph.D. in history from the University of North Carolina in 1963.

**FANE DOWNS** holds three degrees from Texas Tech University, including the Ph.D. in history which she earned in 1970. She moved from professional Girl Scout work to the teaching of history. She has been at McMurry College at Abilene since 1970 where she currently holds the rank of associate professor. She has published widely and has been especially active in providing historical research in the activities surrounding the centennial of the city of Abilene and Taylor County. She is currently Book Review Editor of the West Texas Historical Association *Yearbook.* She is also active in several other historical organizations.

**ROLAND CALVIN HAYES** is the Dean of Instruction, Ridgeview Campus, Austin Community College, where he has been a faculty member or administrator since 1973. He previously taught in high school and at Tarrant County Junior College. He attended Langston University in Oklahoma for his undergraduate education, and he earned the M.A. in Afro-American history at Michigan State University in 1971. He has also done additional graduate work at the University of Texas at Austin.

**RODOLFO ROCHA** is assistant professor of history and curator of the Rio Grande Valley Historical Collection at Pan American University at Edinburg, Texas. A native of Brownsville, Texas, he attended Pan American University, where he earned the B.A. and M.A. degrees. He then moved on to Texas Tech University, where the Ph.D. in history was conferred in 1981. He has presented several papers to scholarly meetings and has published articles in *Studies in History* and *The Journal of the Texas Association for Bilingual Education.*

**BILL O'NEAL** is a native of Corsicana. His grandmother came to Texas in a covered wagon in 1881, and a great-grandfather was a cowboy in Lampasas County and fought in the Horrell-Higgins range feud during the 1870s. Mr. O'Neal is married and the father of four daughters, and since 1970 he has taught history at Panola Junior College at Carthage, Texas. He is the author of numerous articles and book reviews. His first book, *Encyclopedia of Western Gunfighters,* was published in 1979 by the University of Oklahoma Press. In 1981 the Creative Publishing Company of College Station released *Henry Brown, The Outlaw Marshal,* and the University of Oklahoma Press has accepted *Encyclopedia of Western Indian Fighters* for future publication.

**JOHN W. STOREY** has researched widely and has published several articles on Baptist history in Texas. He currently has a book length manuscript on Baptists in Texas under consideration for publication. He has also published in several other journals and has been an editor of *America's Heritage in the 20th Century.* He holds degrees from Lamar University, Baylor University, and the University of Kentucky, where he earned the Ph.D. in history in 1968. He has taught at Baylor, the University of Kentucky, and Lamar University, where he has been since 1968.

**JAMES SMALLWOOD** holds two degrees from East Texas State University at Commerce. He earned the Ph.D. in history from Texas Tech University in 1974. He is presently associate professor of history at Oklahoma State University, where he has taught since 1975. The author of numerous books on Texas and the Southwest, he won the Coral P. Tullis Award from the Texas State Historical Association for the best book on Texas history during 1981-1982 for *Time of Hope, Time of Despair: Black Texans During Reconstruction.* He has published numerous scholarly articles and reviews.

# INDEX

T

EP